FOOTBALL
in America:

GAME
OF THE
CENTURY

Also by Bob Oates

Rams: The Inside Story
Roman Gabriel: Player of the Year
Sixty Years of Winners

FOOTBALL
in America:

GAME

OF THE
CENTURY

By Bob Oates

Quality Sports Publications

For information write or FAX:
Quality Sports Publications
24 Buysse Drive, Coal Valley, IL 61240
(800) 464-1116 • (309) 234-5016 • (309) 234-5019 FAX
www.qualitysportsbooks.com

Duane Brown, Project Director
Melinda Brown, Designer
Susan Smith, Editor

Printed in the U.S.A.

Publisher's Cataloging-in-Publication Data
(Provided by Quality Books, Inc.)

Oates, Bob.
    Football in America : game of the century / by
Bob Oates. -- 1st ed.
    p. cm.
    Includes index.
    ISBN: 1-885758-16-2

    1. Football--United States--History.
I. Title.

GV950.O28 1999   796.332'0973
                        QBI99-1419

For
ROJR and STEVE

Table of Contents

FOREWORD: *The Supreme Spectator Sport*   11

PART ONE

I. Rockne: *Superstar of the Golden Age*   17

1. Football's First Major Leaguer – 2. The Invention of Pass Offense –
3. George Gipp: As Good as His Legend – 4. The Four Horsemen – Postscript.

II. Creation: *Football Emerges from the Mists*   35

1. In the Beginning – 2. Oldest Game in the World? –
3. Walter Camp, Seminal Innovator – 4. Why Camp? Why HERE?

III. Culmination: *The Rise of Pass Offense*   47

1. The Great Rules Debate – 2. Fab Five of Football's First Century –
3. Mayhem and Beyond – 4. The Single Wing – 5. Clark Shaughnessy and the
T Formation – 6. Vince Lombardi, Counterrevolutionary –
7. Bill Walsh: The Apotheosis of the Pass

IV. Campus: *America's Place for Books and Games*   63

1. Football and Academics in Europe – 2. Georgia: Cheers for Two Flags –
3. Texas versus Oklahoma: Don't Forget to Duck – 4. Wisconsin: The Badger Band
Always Wins – 5. Football at Dartmouth: The Bonfire and Beyond –
6. University of Chicago: Hail Copernicus – 7. Stanford: Pursuit of Preeminence –
8. USC: Football Builds a University

PART TWO

V. Champions: *All Pros of All Kinds*   99

1. Red Grange, Galloping Ghost – 2. Bronko Nagurski,
Football's First Big Winner – 3. Dick Daugherty: Watching the Game
Change – 4. Raymond Berry, Self-Made Player – 5. Hugh McElhenny:
Born into the Hall of Fame – 6. Tom Mack: Is Money the Motivator? –
7. Merlin Olsen: Concentration Is What Counts – 8. O.J. Simpson: Rise and
Fall of an Idol – 9. Fred Dryer: Life in the NFL's Fantasy World –
10. Ronnie Lott, Football Student – 11. Paul Hornung: The Century's Most
Decorated Player – 12. Marcus Allen: The Play That Changed Everything –
13. Gene Upshaw: All-Pro to All-Labor –
14. Terrell Davis: Most Efficient of the Running Backs.

VI. Quarterbacks: *Throwing and Thinking*   163

1. Sammy Baugh on Calling the Plays – 2. John Unitas: Confidence Man –
3. Frank Ryan: Ph.D. Passer – 4. Joe Namath Invents a National Holiday –
5. George Blanda: How to Win Football Games at Forty-Seven –
6. Jim Plunkett: The Sensitive Quarterback – 7. Jim Kelly: How to Lose Four
Super Bowls With a Team That Wasn't That Good –
8. Steve Young and the Passers of the Century.

VII. Control: *It's a Coach's Game Now*   205

1. Amos Alonzo Stagg: The Old One – 2. George Halas: Founder of the NFL –
3. Paul Brown Systematizes Football – 4. Clark Shaughnessy: Spiking
the Shotgun – 5. Vince Lombardi: Champion of the Century –
6. Woody Hayes: Top Seven Tyrant – 7. Bear Bryant: Football's Biggest Winner –
8. Bobby Bowden: Best Active College Coach – 9. John Madden: Football's
Best Talker – 10. Dan Reeves: Born to Win (in Georgia) –
11. Mike Shanahan: The New Heavyweight Champion –
12. O.A. (Bum) Phillips: Life Goes On.

VIII. Exemplar: *Team of the Century*   275

1. San Francisco 49ers: A Record Eighteen Years on Top –
2. Joe Montana: Four-Time Champion – 3. Eddie DeBartolo: Model Club Owner –
4. Bill Walsh on West Coast Football.

APPENDIX   303

AFTERWORD: *A Writer's Life*   313

INDEX   343

*Like painted kites
the days and nights
went flying by.*

– Johnny Mercer

Foreword The Supreme Spectator Sport

Amerian football is a phenomenon of the American century. Nothing in 1899 was like 1999 football. In the last hundred years, as the United States has moved from second-rate power to world dominance, U.S. college and pro football leaders have built on a distant soccer-rugby foundation to invent the nation's favorite sport.

Reflecting precise attention to American tastes, style and preferences, the inventors, most of them gifted football players or coaches, have carefully created the game of the century.

This book, without being a history, is the story of how and why that happened, and who did it.

From the first, the game's builders have acted boldly. They have turned over hundreds of rules and customs. But at any one time, as the sports public in any era has known, they have acted with deliberation, proceeding so gradually that many football fans are unaware that the game has been invented incrementally – during the evolutionary moves of a full century.

My run as a football writer has taken me to the big games of most of that century. Representing Los Angeles newspapers, I have covered each of the thirty-three Super Bowls. More than sixty years ago, as a college student doubling as a South Dakota newspaper reporter, I covered the old Chicago All-Star Game for the first of many times. That was in 1936.

It seemed to me then, as it has ever since, that the sport I watched that first night – football as created and constantly recreated by and for Americans – is the world's supreme spectator sport.

In its first century, football has evolved into America's most widely accepted major league pastime: first in the polls, first in the ratings. To viewers and participants alike, it is the most intriguing of the team games.

For this, there are contradictory reasons. Football is, to begin with, a celebration of big-hit violence, of daunting physical collisions. Yet at the same time, it is the most intellectual of the team games, the most intricate, comprehensive and demanding, the most absorbing to play or see and contemplate. No other game so profoundly challenges body and intellect alike.

It is football's combination of physical and mental competition that gets the attention of so many millions of Americans. And although the violence ensures that only the strong and courageous may participate, it is the game's computer complexity that redeems it for a civilized nation.

This is a sport for those who love a spectacle of courage and drama that you have to think about to fully enjoy. Football was made for the thinking person.

And it *was* made.

During the final years of the nineteenth century, the indispensable first moves were made by groups of Ivy League soccer and rugby players who, searching for something more cerebral and also rougher, ultimately abandoned both Old-World pastimes.

During the twentieth century, the new game was shaped into what it is today by groups of inventive football players and coaches: by Yale's Walter Camp, author of football's first rulebook, and by many others, from Knute Rockne of Notre Dame, to Clark Shaughnessy of Stanford, to Bill Walsh of San Francisco. Just in the last quarter century, football people have been learning that, as Walsh first demonstrated, the game can be played more successfully with fast-tempo passing than with ball-control runs – a sacrilegious finding to those who favor brawn over brains but a culmination of the long evolution of football both as a game to play and a spectacle to watch.

Elsewhere, in overwhelming numbers, the world is still playing soccer, the game that was ours once upon a time. Until well after the U.S. Civil War (1861-65), every American who in the fall months played any game played soccer. We gave it up voluntarily. And, consciously, we have chosen another course. As anthropologist William Arens noted: "In contrast to our language and many of our values, football was not forced upon us. We chose it."

Soccer has been called the best of the kids' games, but among U.S. adults the demand has been constant throughout the century for something more imaginative, more stimulating; and football's innovators, aware of the demand, have kept supplying it. Plainly, most of us appreciate having something to look forward to on a crisp fall weekend. This is a book for the many who choose football.

I can identify with them all. Scrolling back through the years of an active newspaper career, I note that I have spent more time on football than all other sports combined. This has been consistently true in Los Angeles, where, after starting on the old *Examiner* and then the *Herald-Examiner*, I had the luck to join the *Times* in time to participate in the most remarkable newspaper adventure of the century, the Otis Chandler renaissance.

During Chandler's twenty years as publisher (1960-80), the *Times* rose from mediocrity to become one of the world's two or three best and most profitable newspapers. In part this happened, analysts have said, because Chandler and his editor, Bill Thomas, stressed in-depth articles at luxurious length with datelines from everywhere – an agenda that brought me assignments of unprecedented scope for a sports reporter. After a summer assignment in Europe one year, I went from beat writer covering the local pro football club to a position that then existed on no other paper: national pro and college football writer. And in these pages you will meet some of the coaches and players I have known, many of them artists or artisans whose vision and actions changed and enriched football in its big century.

From the beginning, I have held to a single course: I track winners. Over all the years, I have never voluntarily entered a losers' locker room. Even though some of the nation's best writers insist that losers are the best story, an inference that leads them to specialize in heartbreak, turmoil, gossip or scandal – the fruit of human frailty – my interest is in the game itself and in whatever brings game-time success. The will to achieve doesn't, I'm sure, lead automatically to achievement. Winning doesn't just happen, and for me the most compelling question is always the same: "What did you do to win?"

Not that I'm touting my way to anyone else, and not that I have anything against losers. Some of my best friends are losers. But I have spent most of the American century as a witness to the sport that was built in America to challenge the human body and mind. And every year without exception, the most appealing contestants have been, to me, the individuals who could meet the challenge.

Marina del Rey, Calif.   BOB OATES
October 1, 1999

PART ONE

I. Rockne: Superstar of the Golden Age – 17

II. Creation: Football Emerges from the Mists – 35

III. Culmination: The Rise of Pass Offense – 47

IV. Campus: America's Place for Books and Games – 63

ROCKNE:
Superstar of the Golden Age

1. Football's First Major Leaguer
2. The Invention of Pass Offense
3. George Gipp: As Good as His Legend
4. The Four Horsemen
Postscript

Knute Rockne, the large-minded 1920s coach of Notre Dame, remains, after all these years, the pivotal figure in the history of football. He didn't invent the game – he was just one of the hundreds who have helped invent it in the last hundred years – but it was Rockne who made football a major league sport. His teams played, and won, everywhere from South Bend to West Point to Chicago to California.

Twenty years into the twentieth century, the game in Rockne's day wasn't much like today's. Still, it was recognizable as American football, and it had become a sectional hit here and there. With a scientist's mind and the heart of a showman, plus a tenacious commitment to this distinctive, newly minted game, Rockne made it big time.

Of the Americans who most obviously influenced other Americans in the twentieth century, four were U.S. presidents, Theodore Roosevelt, Franklin Roosevelt, Dwight Eisenhower and John Kennedy. And Rockne made five. As farseeing as he was unique, as shrewd as he was influential, Rockne enriched and enlivened what has been called the Golden Age of Sports. He was the first superstar; and without him, sports in the American century would have been quite different. This, in a package with five parts, is his story:

1. Football's First Major Leaguer

A HIGH SCHOOL dropout was the earliest in a
long line of eminent American football coaches.

For most people, big news stories have the power to freeze an event in memory. Thus old-timers who have forgotten everything else that happened in two portentous years, 1941 and 1963, can readily recall where they were and what they were up to when they heard about Pearl Harbor and the assassination of John Kennedy.

For football fans a bit older, the shock they couldn't get over came on March 31, 1931, when an airplane crashed in Kansas to end it all for the greatest football coach of his time, perhaps of any time, Knute Rockne of Notre Dame.

Very early in the age of commercial air travel, it all ended so very soon for Rockne, who was forty-three years old that spring. At the summit of an unparalleled career, he died just weeks after completing his fifth undefeated and untied season in thirteen years at Notre Dame with a 27-0 upset victory over USC. Playing some of the nation's strongest schedules, his teams had lost only twelve games in those thirteen seasons and won 105, with five ties. And after all these years, his winning percentage, .897, is still football's all-time record, college or pro, among those coaching ten years or more.

Yet in a fast-moving century, even the most celebrated names tend to fade. To most sports fans today, Kenneth Knute Rockne is a legend if that. America today is farther removed from the living Rockne than his generation was from the American Civil War. Not long ago when a reporter asked three Californians in their forties if they knew about a man named Rockne, each answered tentatively. "He gave great halftime speeches," said one. "There was a movie about him," another recalled. The third asked: "Isn't he the hunchback of Notre Dame?"

Rockne wasn't handsome, but he wasn't a hunchback, and he was a lot more than a legend who made speeches and inspired movies. Those who remember him and his era, or those who have studied the early twentieth century in America, rank Rockne with the leaders of the 1920s in any field. Though a high school dropout, he was a brilliant chemist who graduated magna cum laude from Notre Dame.

At age thirty, after beginning as the track coach there, he took over the football team in 1918 just as the curtain was going up on the Golden Age of Sports, so-called – a time that coincided with what also was known as the Flapper Era, and, as well, the Era of Wonderful Nonsense. It could have been any of that and more. World War I was just over, and for prosperous America in 1918, looking into a gleaming future, anything at all seemed possible.

Thirteen years later, at the dawn of a disastrously different American experience, the Great Depression, the tragic end for Rockne brought down the last curtain on the golden age of Babe Ruth, Jack Dempsey, Red Grange and the other sports personalities of the Roaring Twenties, not to forget the historians: Will Rogers, Grantland Rice and, among others, F. Scott Fitzgerald. The day after the crash in Kansas, in his *Los Angeles Times* column, Rogers wrote: "It takes a mighty big calamity to shake this country all at once, but you did it, Knute. You did it."

ii

Rockne was the first American celebrity to perish in a commercial airline disaster; and in his time, few celebrities were more widely known. Born in Norway, an immigrant obliged to learn a new language in the public schools of Chicago, he had become, in the years before Winston Churchill and Franklin Roosevelt and Adlai Stevenson, one of the world's most effective communicators in English. It was the heyday of newsreels and radio broadcasts (the new technological marvels of that age, comparable to television and computers at a later date) and by 1931 Rockne's was an instantly recognized face and voice in most American communities.

The voice in particular was at least as familiar as those of the other prominent personalities of that day, including actor-philosopher-writer Rogers, tenor Enrico Caruso, and crooner Rudy Vallee. A contemporary writer, Jerry Brondfield, remembering Rockne, observed: "Nobody used the human voice with more startling and unforgettable emphasis. It was flat, nasal, metallic. Each word emerged as though coated with brass."

A football fan who never knew him said recently: "One thing about Rockne is that he looked like a coach and sounded like a coach. Even his name sounded like a coach's name." To historian Brondfield, "Rockne proved that not all Vikings are blond, tall and lithe. He was only five feet eight and weighed 160 dumpy, irregular pounds. His pumpkin-shaped head was balding, and he was deeply furrowed above the eyes. His nose, broken at least three times, was the wayward feature of a preliminary boy who never made the main event. But then there was that famous Rockne smile – a broad, rippling, lopsided smile soaked in warmth and charm. And there was that voice. . ." To sportswriter Grantland Rice, who knew everybody, "Rockne was a man of great force, deep charm and an amazing personality. I have never known anyone quite his equal in this respect."

Sartorially, Rockne was a bum, coaching in baggy pants and torn sweatshirts. Even when dressed for a night out, he usually resembled, in a cliche of his time, an unmade bed. Yet in 1951, a half century after football was first played, and twenty years after he died, Rockne was the runaway winner of an Associated Press poll for all-time coach. He had 526 votes to 127 for Pop Warner and 89 for Amos Alonzo Stagg.

Rockne's influence on the America of then and today has been if anything underestimated. His is now the country's most popular sport, and, though foreign-born, he did more to make this distinctively American game nationally important than anyone (or anything else) except television.

Before Rockne, football was a provincial pastime. It developed fierce rivalries, but only within the Ivy League and selected other precincts. The so-called National Football League was then a parochial eastern league, and college football was a sport with one bowl game. So rarely did teams venture out of their local territories that they had a word for those games: intersectionals. Into this void, Rockne moved with surprising self-confidence in the 1920s. He was the first to aggressively schedule intersectionals – from New York to Los Angeles – and, annually, he went after the best teams that would play him in any part of the country.

This was something brand new. No other U.S. team, in any sport, had ever set out to compete regularly on a national stage, certainly no other major league baseball or basketball or pro football team. And no one else did until long after, when, somewhat reluctantly, the mid-century NFL moved West.

Also undervalued is Rockne's role in promoting his university. His teams had the country talking. Most Americans, reacting intensely, seemed to be either for or against the small Catholic boys school in rural Indiana. A contemporary newspaper observer, Paul Gallico, wrote years later: "With the skyrocketing of Notre Dame out of the West (sic), hundreds of thousands of people who had never been to college or near any campus identified themselves with the school with the wonderful sobriquet, 'Fighting Irish.'"

And hundreds of thousands didn't, rooting hard against the Irish.

Gallico on the Notre Dame-Army series: "New York was never before or since so sweetly gay as it was when Rock brought his boys to town and the city was electric with excitement." Or as Chicago writer Bill Gleason summed up: "In the '20s and '30s, before TV, most sports fans could only read about the stars. They never came to *their* town. Rockne was the first national hero to get around – almost everywhere – close enough to touch."

iii

Those who knew about Rockne during the century's teen years and early 1920s were aware that he didn't burst out of nothingness. As a Notre Dame undergraduate, he was possibly the school's most energetic student ever. He did all this:

- Played the flute in the Notre Dame symphony orchestra, playing in every concert, and almost every rehearsal.
- Took a major role in every school play of his four years.
- Wrote regularly for the student newspaper and yearbook.
- Fought semiprofessionally (at 145 pounds) in club smokers in downtown South Bend and in Elkhart. His second was quarterback Gus Dorais.
- Worked his way through school, first as a janitor and then as a chemistry assistant to Professor Julius A. Nieuwland, whose discoveries led to synthetic rubber. From time to time, Rockne himself made some of the minor tests for these discoveries.
- Went out for the varsity sports in season, setting a school record for the indoor pole vault (12-4) and making Walter Camp's All-American football team as a third-string end.
- Reached the finals of the Notre Dame marbles tournament in his junior year.
- Considered himself primarily a student, and graduated with grades averaging 90.52 (on a scale of 100). In some of the tougher subjects, he was well over 90. As a freshman he had a 99 in bacteriology and 97 in chemistry, as a junior 98 in English, and as a senior 94 in philosophy and 98 in human anatomy.

What all this indicated, of course, was a high degree of energy and intelligence, the two things all supremely successful people seem to have in common. "Rock could have been anything," the school's veteran athletic director, Edward W. (Moose) Krause, once said. "He had the brains, energy and personality to do anything he chose to do."

He chose football, then demonstrated that the work required to create five undefeated football teams in thirteen years wasn't enough for a restless genius. As head coach of the Fighting Irish, these were some of the other things he did simultaneously:

- During his first four years in charge, including the year of his first national championship, Rockne worked without assistants and at the same time served as Notre Dame's athletic director, trainer, doctor, equipment manager, track coach, intramural sports director, business manager, ticket director and chemistry instructor.

- Drawing on his medical and anatomical knowledge, he designed all the equipment his players wore from their shoulder pads down. He also designed the Notre Dame uniform and was the first to put his players in sleek, streamlined, satin-and-silk pants (before streamline was in the dictionary). He wanted a smaller target for opposing tacklers, and, as a scientist, he wanted to cut down wind resistance, increasing speed.

- Seemingly inexhaustible, Rockne toured the Midwest making public speeches both in season and out, many of them sales speeches for a car manufacturer, Studebaker, which paid him more than he got from Notre Dame, a lot more.

- As another sideline, in the midst of his last season, he opened a stock brokerage firm in South Bend.

- He wrote a nationally syndicated newspaper column three times a week.

- He wrote several books, one a volume of juvenile fiction. (To speculation that some of this might have been ghosted, there are a couple of rejoinders: he was accustomed to working on three or four things at once, and the prose isn't that good.)

- He was a dedicated family man and gardener who for years raised much of the family's food, "and who otherwise spent hours with his four children," one friend said.

- In one November week in 1929 he coached two football teams simultaneously, preparing Notre Dame for Northwestern Saturday, and the Notre Dame all-stars for a benefit game Sunday.

- To the delight of later football generations, Rockne was also the principal designer of Notre Dame Stadium, where his final team played the 1930 season, and which for a half century subsequently remained a nearly ideal stadium for its size (49,000 seats, all Notre Dame could at first afford). Although Rockne was a track expert with track roots before he became interested in football, he knew better than to clutter up a stadium with a running track – the bane of most stadiums built about then, and later. Said one historian: "It's inconceivable that a less than perfect sports stadium could ever have been built here in Rockne's time."

- On the practice field, Rockne was a teaching coach who, after perfecting each blocking technique personally, got down in the dirt and instructed his players himself. Said one of them, Rip Miller: "Because Rock only weighed about 155, he had to make a study of blocking angles and leverages. And he got right in there, without pads, smacking into us, hitting us with a shoulder, hip, upper arms, everything that was legal. He'd yell: 'Come on, now, I won't hurt you!'"

iv

The energy and intelligence that drove Rockne were possibly in his genes. His grandfather and great grandfather, both of them blacksmiths, were for years prominent civic leaders in Voss, Norway, a picture-postcard resort town on a lake near the North Sea. Knute was born there on March 4, 1888. His given name is pronounced 'Ca-nute' in Norway but usually 'Nute' here. His father Lars was a machinist who created and also built horse-drawn carriages.

When he sold several to Kaiser Wilhelm of Germany, Lars Rockne was encouraged to enter one in the 1891 World Fair in Chicago, where he won the grand prize. This encouraged him to send for his family, an idea that detoured Knute to the Rose Bowl from a probable trip to the World Cup.

The gainer, in addition to Notre Dame, was American football, in which, in his lifetime, Rockne was best known to the strategists of the game for two innovations: shock troops and the Notre Dame shift. In using a full team of second-stringers at the start of most games (he called them shock troops) he was giving bunches of players game experience and sweater letters, improving morale. At the same time he was anticipating two-platoon football – a refinement that was still decades away.

A 1990s two-platoon approach was impossible in Rockne's day because 1920s rules prohibited free substitution; but the shock-troop scheme showed that football improves when played by alternating groups of players (some of whom might be passers and receivers with not many other skills). And so football was a better game in the late 1920s than it had been a decade earlier.

The Notre Dame shift, in which all four backs were in motion at the snap, was a tactic of such precision and grace that it was compared to a

New York chorus line. In truth, Rockne, a stage fan, was rumored to have got the inspiration watching Broadway's long-legged, closely-synchronized female dancers. When his opponents couldn't handle his version of the chorus line, they persuaded the College Rules Committee to legislate against it. Hence the present rule requiring all backs except one to come to a one-second halt before the snap of the ball.

The rule change didn't slow Rockne down. For, philosophically, defying most other practitioners in a power era, he preferred light, fast, smart players, even on the line of scrimmage. Using a pony-size backfield, a gang known as the Four Horsemen, he sprinted past Stanford in the 1925 Rose Bowl.

Throughout his coaching career, Rockne also preferred to deceive rather than run over opposing players. His goal at all times was to misguide opponents as to the real strength of the Notre Dame team. He loved to talk about the time when, as a Notre Dame receiver, after first limping around the field to fool the other team's defensive backs, he raced away to catch a big touchdown pass. Later he was to fool, and rout, USC with a speedy fullback wearing the uniform number of a slow fullback.

In short, antedating Clark Shaughnessy, Al Davis, George Allen and other winners who have coached that way, Rockne was football's original first Great Deceiver.

Rockne was, moreover, one of football's original pass-offense designers (see next page), although he insisted that winners win physically first. You must beat them running the ball, he said.

At heart, however, as those who knew him invariably say, he was first and last a cheerleader – as were Vince Lombardi and other big winners later. Football is that kind of game. And so the legends properly accent Rockne's halftime speeches as the explanation for his achievements. In the 1990s he couldn't have moved football players with 1920s oratory, perhaps, but since they still have to be moved, he would have found a way.

v

Rockne was a winner, a delight, and a vibrant part of America's collective consciousness as well as a widely appreciated public speaker. To have his trumpet voice suddenly stilled in a great airplane accident, at the very peak of the man's extraordinary and heavily publicized career, and at such a comparatively young age, threw a pall over the country in that long-ago spring of 1931.

The first thought of many was for Rockne's means of transportation. What, they asked, was he doing in an airplane? Though he was an enthusiastic flyer, commercial air travel was then so unusual that Rockne had to take a train from Chicago to Kansas City to catch the Los Angeles plane that last morning. A frequent Los Angeles visitor, he had contracted to make a football demonstration movie in Hollywood.

On 3/31/31, at 0930, Transcontinental-Western's Flight 599 was scheduled to depart Kansas City rain or shine. A year-old, eight-passenger, tri-motor Fokker, it left on time with two pilots and six passengers. All those years ago on 599, there were already two no-shows. The primitive airliner flew immediately into a storm, picked up a load of ice, and lost momentum, falling into a wheat field. There were no explosions, no fires, no survivors. Rockne's body was retrieved by a Kansas farmer. The nearest village: Bazaar.

"It is out of the question to consider the airplane itself defective," designer Anthony Fokker said at the inquest. "I inspected it personally, two days (earlier), and found it in perfect condition."

The national impact of Rockne's spectacular life and violent death made his funeral week one of America's most emotional between Lincoln's in 1865 and Roosevelt's in 1945. More than sixteen hundred of the nation's seventeen hundred daily papers carried Rockne editorials that week. The funeral procession from his modest South Bend home to Notre Dame's stately Sacred Heart church – a replica of a medieval French Gothic cathedral – was witnessed by an estimated hundred thousand persons lining the streets of a city of about eighty-five thousand. Some two hundred Rockne players who had moved along to careers as college and high school coaches returned for the funeral.

Rockne was gone. "But he still lives," the Reverend Edmund P. Joyce, Notre Dame's executive vice president, said on March 31, 1956, a quarter century later. "Knute Rockne is still a vibrant living force at this university because of the powerful personal influence he exerted over so many Notre Dame men." Among others. So many others.

2. The Invention of Pass Offense

FOOTBALL'S FIRST FAMOUS passing combination, Dorais to Rockne, started something big.

The event that first showed what football could be – the first game bearing a similarity to today's game – was a November happening in 1913 at West Point, New York, where Notre Dame defeated Army the first time they met, 35-13. Quarterback Gus Dorais completed fourteen of seventeen passes that afternoon, most of them to Notre Dame's captain and left end, Knute Rockne, for 243 incredible yards, a total that shocked college football people as much as it disquieted them.

Previously, football had as a contest been more like tug of war. Now, in the exhilarating early years of airplane flight, it could be seen as an up-to-date air show.

Passing had been legalized earlier, as early as 1905, but at first it was severely restricted with bundles of quaint rules. Hamstrung legally, few teams passed. Even after many of the restrictions had been lifted, one or two at a time, in the years between then and 1912, there wasn't much passing.

No one had ever seen a passing attack. No one seemed to know how to take advantage of the new rules.

Then in 1913, Dorais and Rockne gave it some thought. They had accepted off-season jobs waiting on tables for meals and spending money at a Lake Erie resort, and there, in the long afternoons that summer, they invented pass offense. That was the summer before their senior season at Notre Dame, in an era when players often did more coaching than coaches.

It was no easy thing, though, to create the rudimentary first tactics and strategy of passing. Dorais had to learn how to throw a spiral with what was then a fat, awkwardly shaped ball. And Rockne had to learn how to catch it with extended hands while in stride. There was nobody to teach any of this. In every former year, if the football were thrown at all, it was pushed or sometimes flung with two hands and caught in the stomach or chest like a medicine ball.

The 1913 Fighting Irish had a new coach, Jesse Harper, who, doubtless at the instigation of the devious Captain Rockne, used the new pass offense sparingly through their first three games, walloping teams like South Dakota without it. Not until November did they open up at West Point to rout Army, too, in the game that brought two new phenomena to national attention, Notre Dame and pass offense. *The New York Times* got the point immediately, carrying this headline the next morning: "Notre Dame Open Play Amazes Army." Said the *Times* writer: "The Westerners (sic) flashed the most sensational football ever seen in the East."

Army also got the point immediately. The Cadet coach, one Charley

Daley, put in an embryonic pass offense to win the *big* game a week later, beating Navy's good ball-running team to end Army's season with only one defeat.

Most other coaches, alas, never did get the point – it would be nearly thirty years before passers first came to prominence nationally – but Dorais and Rockne had shown them how.

3. George Gipp: As Good as His Legend

TRIPLE-THREAT FOOTBALL reached an all-time peak,
most likely, with Rockne's most unusual player.

Was anyone at Notre Dame more important than Knute Rockne – in Rockne's time? It's hard to believe, but one guy apparently was. The established star in 1920, when Rockne, thirty-two, had been a head coach for only two years, was a senior running back named George Gipp, who pronounced his last name with a hard g, as in gosh.

Ending a brilliant four-year college football career, the 1920 Gipp averaged 8.1 yards carrying the ball, still the Notre Dame record, on the way to what would have been almost certain Heisman Trophy recognition if the trophy had been awarded that early in the century. Instead, there was then something of an official All-American team – as selected by Walter Camp, a Far Easterner who chose mostly Far Easterners – and Camp, who thought of Gipp as a Westerner, made him his 1920 fullback, the first Notre Dame All-American. Before the year was out, Rockne was to say, "Football will never again see Gipp's equal, as a player or a person."

Was he all that? Where does the legend leave off and the man begin? Nobody really knows. Despite Gipp's prominence in South Bend, he was never interviewed by any newspaper reporter. He was never even quoted in a locker-room story. That was a very different media era, and hence every fact about 1920 football can be challenged.

It is with inferences that Gipp has to be reconstructed, and to use that method is to envision a classic triple-threat football player – an athlete who, from at least the twenty-five or thirty-yard line, was a constant threat to score with a run, pass or drop kick.

One inference is that Gipp was a superior kicker. He handled all the kicking for Rockne as both punter and drop-kicker at a time when field goals could be scored with either drop kicks or place kicks. And the legend has Gipp drop-kicking the ball sixty-two yards in one game. Take twenty yards off the legend and it's still pretty good. In 1920, Gipp drop-kicked nine field goals, the Notre Dame record for fifty-seven years until 1973, when Bob Thomas, later an NFL place kicker, matched him.

A second inference is that Gipp was a good passer. As the running back who took most of the direct passes from the 1920 center in Rockne's Single-Wing backfield – the famous Notre Dame box – Gipp was also the team's primary forward passer. The legend says that on his longest touchdown completion, the ball was in the air fifty-five yards. Take a few yards off the legend and it's still pretty remarkable with the pumpkin they threw in those days. For three years, Gipp led Notre Dame in passing. And as a senior, heaving the pumpkin at will, he completed thirty of sixty-two, not great, but better than most passers of his day.

The final inference is that Gipp was most valuable when carrying the ball. To have averaged 8.1 yards as a running back – in football's push-and-pull era – the 1920 Gipp must have been a terror, setting up his passes and drop kicks with a lot of big runs. It was an assignment for which he had the size. At six feet even and 180 pounds, he was one of the four biggest men on the team, heavier than most linemen, and the biggest back Rockne ever had except for Marty Brill (190) in the 1930 season, Rockne's last.

In historical terms, Gipp, who was recreated by actor (later President) Ronald Reagan in a mid-century movie, lived and died an elusive figure. Son of a Congregational minister in Laurium, Michigan, Gipp drove a taxi after high school, and, like Rockne, was already an old man in his twenties when he first saw Notre Dame. Coincidentally, both laid out four years before college, Rockne as a Chicago postal clerk. In the last tragic coincidence, both died young, each at the peak of his career.

Four years older than his classmates, Gipp preferred to live off-campus, and the legends have him gambling at cards and in pool halls weekdays, and nights, until Thursday, when you could usually count on him at football practice.

It's in the record that unlike Rockne, he was no scholar. Academic problems in the spring of 1920 cost Gipp the captaincy that had been awarded by his teammates.

The evidence suggests that coaching a player as big, gifted and honored as Gipp permanently changed Rockne. Never again did a single person star for this coach. The prominence of the 1924 backfield known as the Four Horsemen – whose four principals shared the headlines with one another and therefore with Rockne – does not seem entirely accidental.

Gipp's shocking death in the December of his twenty-fifth year – the greatest year of his life – wrenched the campus like no other until March 31, 1931, when Rockne went at forty-three. Before costing him his life, a strep throat ending in pneumonia cost Gipp a chance (in Notre Dame's last two games) to become a 1,000-yard gainer in 1920, when he had 827 yards in his first seven games. Not for another fifty-six years did any Notre Dame man reach 1,000.

Whether on his death bed Gipp actually asked his coach to tell a Notre Dame team someday to win one for the Gipper is a secret that Rockne, a dedicated psychologist, took to the grave. The clippings tell us that Gipp played his best games against Army – he never lost to Army – and when Rockne used the Gipper story, it was to win an Army game that doubtless couldn't have been won any other way in Rockne's worst-ever season.

Legends are one thing, the record another, and Gipp's place in the hearts of the Notre Dame men of his time can be reconstructed from a poem that appeared anonymously in the issue of the campus paper that carried his obituary:

> *O Lady, you have taken of our best*
> *To make a playmate for the Seraphim;*
> *There on the wide, sweet campus of the blest*
> *Be good to him.*

4. The Four Horsemen

THE MOST STORIED backfield in football
history gave Rockne three big seasons.

Even amongst the richness of Rockne lore, one group of four backs stands out. As "outlined against a blue-gray October sky," it was the Four Horsemen who, in the Roaring Twenties, made Knute Rockne and Notre Dame internationally storied, climaxing three big years with an undefeated senior season and a national championship as well as Rockne's only Rose Bowl appearance. They won that game, too.

In the most famous backfield ever, Jim Crowley combined with three other Horsemen, Elmer Layden, Don Miller and Harry Stuhldreher, on the most celebrated of Notre Dame teams. And their place as number one has been assured for the ages by the tactical changes in football that have made four-man backfields obsolete.

As sophomores, the Four Horsemen came together during the 1922 season when Layden was reassigned to fullback. At the time, he weighed but 160 pounds. The halfbacks, Miller and Crowley, weighed 150 and 158. The five-foot-seven quarterback, Stuhldreher, packed only 148.

Even in the 1920s, in an era of smaller Americans, there had never been so much football talent in such a small package. To this day, they're unmatched as a backfield, pound for pound, anywhere in this century. Their nickname came from a sportswriter, Grantland Rice, but their success came from their individual and collective skills, tightly practiced.

In all, the Fighting Irish played thirty games with Layden, Crowley, Miller and Stuhldreher, and lost only to one team, Nebraska, losing twice (by a touchdown each time in 1922 and 1923) before turning on the Huskers in 1924, 34-6.

The 1924 team was the first that Rockne took from coast to coast meeting all comers – from Army to Nebraska to Stanford – but it wasn't an easy road act to manage. Because the backs had the Horsemen sobriquet and national hero-worship, the linemen, feeling unloved, took the name Seven Mules. Rockne worked hard to keep matters in perspective. One day, he asked the players to vote secretly on who was more important to Notre Dame, the backs or the mules, and later he called a press conference to announce: "The mules won, 7 to 4."

Rockne also separated the players on Notre Dame's special trains, assigning linemen to the cushy lower berths and backs to uppers. That wasn't warmly appreciated by the backs, particularly Stuhldreher, the feisty little quarterback. Interviewed one day in Chicago, he was asked: "What makes the Four Horsemen so agile?" Said Stuhldreher: "Getting in and out of upper berths."

Since agile athletes pleased Rockne the most, the Horsemen were ideal Rockne backs, light enough and gifted enough to play the game his way, swirling around each other in the backfield while handing and passing the ball back and forth. "Our timing was spiritual as well as physical," halfback Miller, later a lawyer, once remarked. "Lord, how we meshed."

As football players, the Four Horsemen were each a little different, unified only by their size. The fastest was Layden, whom Rockne called the most unusual fullback in football. "He pierced a line with sheer speed," his coach said. The right half, Miller, was the breakaway threat, shiftier than Layden. At quarterback, Stuhldreher was cocky, self-assured, ambitious, a wise signal caller and good enough passer. In short, said Rockne, he was "a typical Notre Dame quarterback." The left half, Crowley, was the most modern runner of the four, a clever cutback runner who, as he often said, liked to "break back against the grain." As a group, they couldn't play with today's football players, but in 1924 they couldn't lose.

ii

Their final game, the 1925 Rose Bowl win over Stanford, 27-10, appears from the score a wipeout. And in a sense, it was. Stanford, except on the scoreboard, wiped out Notre Dame. As fullback Ernie Nevers outran the Four Horsemen combined, Stanford outgained Notre Dame, 298 yards to 179. The Irish made only seven first downs (to seventeen for Stanford) and completed only three passes (to eleven for Stanford). The longest sustained drive by the Horsemen measured thirty-two yards.

As an offensive performer, Nevers, at the time, was thought of as the best player in the country with the exception of an Illinois junior named Red Grange. But the 1925 Rose Bowl was a defensive game. The decisive clutch plays were defensive plays, and there were many of them, and the Irish made them all.

"The Four Horsemen were better defensive than offensive players," Rockne once said, and they proved him right in Pasadena.

A principal explanation for their success that day was that Layden rose up with possibly the greatest all-around game ever played in the old bowl. Of his three touchdowns, two were scored on defense. Intercepting two passes, he twice displayed his rare fullback speed on two long sprints, going sixty-five yards for one touchdown and then seventy. A faulty twenty-two-yard Stanford punt set Layden up for his other touchdown, which he scored on a short fullback run. Providing still a fourth touchdown for the winning team, Stanford obligingly fumbled.

The game's turning point came in the second half after a long, scoreless Stanford drive ended at the Notre Dame one-foot line. On Stanford's last play of that series, Nevers scored, they said in the press box, but the officials said he didn't. A moment later, standing inches in from the end line, Layden made the greatest clutch punt in Rose Bowl history, booming the ball back nearly ninety yards – eighty-two from the line of scrimmage – to the Stanford eighteen-yard line, where it bounced out of bounds.

"That was the ballgame," Stuhldreher said afterward.

iii

Speaking strictly of comparative skill, it's possible to argue that the Four Horsemen were not even the best backfield Rockne had as a college coach. The best may have been his last: Schwartz, Carideo, Mullins and Brill. The most influential backfield ever on any team anywhere was the one that converted football into the present T-Formation era. The four in that 1940 Stanford backfield were Kmetovic, Standlee, Gallarneau and Albert. A few years later, Army Coach Red Blaik had one of the great ones: Davis, Blanchard, McWilliams and Tucker. The best some of us have seen was a mid-century pro backfield in San Francisco: McElhenny, Perry, Johnson and Tittle.

Some Notre Dame fans argue for the 1929 backfield immortalized by an anonymous poet:

> *Is it the ghost of the Four Horsemen that ranges the field*
> *Advancing the pigskin to scoring position?*
> *But no! Those mad shadows that mass for the kill*
> *Are Elder, Carideo, Mullins and Brill.*

But for romance, the Four Horsemen will always be first. There has never been another team like theirs. From the ranks of those who played for Rockne in the Four Horsemen era came head coaches for ten major college teams (Alabama, North Carolina, South Carolina, Fordham, Purdue, Navy, Notre Dame, Wisconsin, Villanova, Duquesne) and other college teams as well as four pro teams (Cleveland, Pittsburgh, the Los Angeles Rams and the old Chicago Rockets). Stuhldreher, along with most of the others, won for awhile but ran out of luck at Wisconsin in 1948, inspiring the first of college football's famously insulting signs, a huge "Goodbye, Harry" banner that was draped in front of the Wisconsin rooting section one otherwise brilliant fall afternoon.

Crowley, who coached both college and pro clubs, remained a close student of football to the end of his life. In his final interview, he described USC's O. J. Simpson as "the best running back I ever saw." He named Army's Glenn Davis next and then the big, powerful Stanford fullback he met in the Rose Bowl, Ernie Nevers.

As for the Four Horsemen, Crowley thought, they were typically American. "If we'd lost a game in 1924," he said, "I don't think we'd be remembered."

But they finished 10-0. And so the memory of what they did has merged neatly with the apocalyptic imagery of sportswriter Rice.

Postscript

It was perhaps the most widely talked-about sports story ever written. Grantland Rice, who could mix metaphors with anybody, began a 1924 football report with these words:

"Outlined against a blue-gray October sky, the Four Horsemen rode again. In dramatic lore they are known as Famine, Pestilence, Destruction and Death. These are only aliases. Their real names are Stuhldreher, Miller, Crowley and Layden. They formed the crest of the South Bend cyclone before which another fighting Army football team was swept over the precipice at the Polo Grounds yesterday afternoon, as 55,000 spectators peered down on the bewildering panorama spread on the green plain below.

"A cyclone can't be snared," Rice continued confidently. "It may be surrounded, but somewhere it breaks through to keep going. When the cyclone starts from South Bend, where the candle lights still gleam through the Indiana sycamores, those in the way must take to storm cellars at top speed. Yesterday the cyclone struck again, as Notre Dame beat Army, 13 to 7, with a set of backfield stars that ripped and crashed through a strong Army defense with more speed and power than the warring cadets could meet."

This rhetoric in the old *New York Tribune* was to make five people famous, including Rice, who, his associates said, had the bent if not the talent of a poet. The "dramatic lore" of his second sentence alludes to a World War I novel, *The Four Horsemen of the Apocalypse*, by Spanish writer Vicente Blasco Ibanez. It was made into a movie starring a popular 1920s actor, Rudolph Valentino.

In the fifteenth century, German painter Albrecht Durer's conception of "The Four Horsemen of the Apocalypse" had illustrated the Book of Revelation (or Apocalypse) in a famous edition of the Bible, of which it is the last book. Although Rice, a religious man, may have seen that, too, he followed Ibanez in naming the horsemen Famine, Pestilence, Destruction and Death. In the Bible they are Conquest, Slaughter,

Famine and Death. All typify war, to which football is often compared.

The fact that there are four riders in Revelation was a break for Rice, who lived and worked in the four-back era before the time of two or three backs and three or four receivers. Four is a poetic word, like seven or eleven. The Apocalypse, as ascribed to the apostle John, is full of such words.

Even so, to pump air into the myth of football's Four Horsemen, Rice needed some help from Notre Dame's publicity people, who (most likely at Rockne's suggestion) hired four horses to immortalize their riders in a widely reprinted photo made the day after Rice came up with the most lasting of the contrived surnames of sports, doubtless the most recognizable, possibly even the most fitting. To this day in football, when you have the talent, you have the horses.

The image immortalized Rice, too, but no one rode the Four Horsemen farther than Knute Rockne.

CREATION:
Football Emerges from the Mists

1. In the Beginning
2. Oldest Game in the World?
3. Walter Camp, Seminal Innovator
4. Why Camp? Why HERE?

S ome inventions are acts of the instant: products of blinding, instantaneous flashes of intuition. Some take longer. Some inventions take years of burnishing and refinement between conception and fulfillment – between the first surge of insight and the day it can be said truly, "We've got this thing made."

Football took a hundred years. A uniquely American creation, football was invented in a stretch of time that memorably included the Knute Rockne innovations but began before Rockne and continues to this day.

It is likely, in fact, that no other U.S. product has had more inventors than the game you see on fall weekends now in company with thousands of stadium-goers or millions of television viewers.

It could only happen in America. It *has* happened only in America.

1. In the Beginning

*AMERICA'S FIRST student-athletes changed
the recreational habits of the New World.*

With considerable media attention, the hundredth anniversary of inter-collegiate football was observed prematurely, erroneously, one afternoon in 1969 when Princeton kicked off to Rutgers. For it wasn't football that

U.S. athletes had been playing at Princeton and elsewhere a century earlier in the decade of the American Civil War. It was soccer.

Lining up twenty-five players to a side, they used a round soccer ball in the 1869 Princeton-Rutgers series, and the ball couldn't be carried or thrown, just kicked. The rules were insistent.

That 1869 series was a two-day event, with games on successive afternoons, which is typical of many sports but not football. And there was no way to score a touchdown. Accruing one point at a time, the players could only score by kicking the ball under a cross-bar. As old Princeton/Rutgers files and newspapers make clear, they called it inter-collegiate football because these were, indisputably, the first intercollegiate games and they were, unarguably, played with the feet.

Yet the players weren't having all that much fun. It was sport, but not, for Americans, great sport. And presently at Princeton and other Ivy League schools, at Yale particularly, they began talking about changing a few of the game's rules. These were some of America's earliest student-athletes, and as such they were accountable only to themselves. There was no NCAA to hold their feet to the fire. There were no imperious lords or nobles in the castle. There were no *castles,* no authority figures, no coaches, no athletic directors – no athletic departments. The game that Americans know as football today wasn't then even a dream. As free Americans, those student-athletes were free to do as they pleased.

And in the 1870s, after talking about it for several years, it pleased them to change some of soccer's venerable rules. In the 1880s, they changed a few more. Then they discarded soccer outright and changed over to rugby, adopting most of the rugby rulebook. Next, they began changing *those* rules. And by the 1890s, soccer was unrecognizable and rugby barely recognizable in their drastically reconstructed intercollegiate game. It wasn't football yet; but they were getting there.

You learn about that – about their unhappiness with soccer, about their troublesome experiments with rugby, about their revolutionary, restless searching and striving for a different and better game – in the minutes of the meetings of the late-nineteenth century College Football Rules Committee, as mostly chaired by Walter Camp of Yale.

When elected to the committee, Camp was a Yale student, a halfback on the school team, a sophomore halfback at that, which tells you most of what you need to know about that committee. The members weren't "faculty athletic advisers" or college deans, they were just a bunch of bright, energetic kids from Yale, Harvard and other Eastern colleges.

Given a choice, they would spend their mornings and evenings in college classes or libraries and their afternoons on athletic fields playing games, preferably rough games.

They were all of European (mostly English) descent; and over there, their fathers (or grandfathers) had played the British games, soccer and rugby. Both games apparently stirred their ancestors in the old country, but somehow both seemed different in a big new country, in the land of opportunity and rich possibilities. Neither sport stirred America's college athletes, then or thereafter.

It was to find something that *would* stir them that Camp and his committeemen kept writing and rewriting the rules in the 1880s and '90s; and, finally, they got it. By the time Camp finished his long committee tour in 1910, they had come up with a new game.

Football was conceived by committee.

In other countries, the game that Americans think of as soccer is also called football – has always been called football (or fussball or futbol). Throughout the sports world, the same word identifies two distinct and extraordinarily different games.

And the explanation for this is also to be found in the records that Camp's committeemen kept:

When they began carving football out of soccer and rugby (when, that is, they were recreating the game they had always called football) they went on calling it football, every year and every day, as football players still do.

They kept making improvements each year, but not too many in any one year, in what was otherwise the same game they had played *last* year.

So there was never any compelling reason to change the name of the game.

As there still isn't.

American football is the first great sport ever created with rule changes in other sports. The nineteenth-century soccer players of America, and the players and coaches who succeeded them, built football with, in all, more than seven hundred new rules. By far the largest number of these improvements have been made in the twentieth century. An 1899 American sports fan, if transported overnight to a 1999 football field, would fancy himself on another planet.

Of all the changes, however, two of the very earliest seem most significant – at least to such scholars as rugby historian A. Jon Prusmack, whom I looked up one day at his New York office.

"Everything else in football followed naturally from two of the first big rule changes," Prusmack said, commenting on the game's origins. "One new rule reduced the number of players to eleven on each side. Previous teams had usually had twenty, twenty-five players, sometimes more – but eleven made their game more manageable. The second change was more drastic. That was the scrimmage concept guaranteeing possession of the ball to one side or the other for a set number of plays. This was a really sharp break with the rules of both rugby and soccer. There is nothing like it in either sport. Nobody is guaranteed the ball in either."

In other words, the decision to muster opposing players face to face along a line of scrimmage and consign the ball to one side or the other – a process so familiar to football fans now that they ignore it while focusing on the players – made the cardinal difference that made the American game possible. Think back to any player-strewn soccer field you ever saw, and think of yourself as a Football Rules Committee member a century ago. How would you bring some discipline out of all that confusion? Who would even *think* of a controlled war along an orderly line of scrimmage?

Apparently, one man did.

According to Camp's 1926 biographer, Harford Powel, who identifies the onetime Yale halfback as "the father of American football," it was the Rules Committee chairman himself who proposed and wrote most of the critical early legislation, including the ball-possession and eleven-man rules.

"Some of his friends regard the scrimmage as the greatest single invention in any game in the memory of man," Powel wrote. "The distance to be gained in three or four downs is a detail. Blocking is a detail. The scrimmage is the essential feature of American football."

As for the distance to be gained in three or four downs, Camp apparently figured that out, too, as Powel and other historians have testified. In any case, the Rules Committee first allowed the offensive team three plays to make five yards – meaning in most instances (in an era before passing was authorized) only a couple of running plays before the offense had to give up the ball. That didn't work. So Camp let the offense have four downs to make ten yards, and that did work. That rule has lasted through the century.

To trigger the plays in their new ball-possession game, the Camp committeemen invented centers first. Centers were essential, Camp wrote in 1910 in *The Book of Foot-Ball*, because, "The first thing we had to do was get the ball out of scrimmage."

Soccer doesn't have to worry about that.

Camp empowered the center to deliver the ball to a teammate *"without hindrance from members of the opposing team,"* and much of the American difference was to result from that imaginative concept.

U.S. players could then develop football into "a game of sophisticated plays and play-calling and warlike strategy – the aspects that differentiate it from the other sports" – as Princeton historian Parke H. Davis wrote in his 1911 book, *Football.*

As a Princeton man confounded by a Yale person, Davis, to the end of his life, continued to rank Camp's mandatory ball-possession proposition as one of the great academic discoveries of the age. "This," he once wrote, "is the device which introduced the principle of an orderly retention of the ball by one side at a time, thereby making possible the use of prearranged strategy, the most distinctive and fascinating characteristic of the American game."

Soccer players, by contrast, to gain possession in their sport, must scramble for the ball. And for the most part, the continuous flow of action in soccer deprives their coaches of the "leisure to plot strategy," in Davis' words, once the match is under way.

In football, plotting strategy is the American way, and not just for coaches and players. Part of the game's hold on the U.S. public rests on the fact that most football fans are strategists, too. Trying to outguess the quarterback and his coach on what they might do next is one of the great parlor pastimes of America. Soccer fans, as Parke Davis noted, don't have that leisure. Neither do basketball fans, unless someone calls time out. Baseball fans, who *do* have the leisure, even have time to go to the bathroom before the next pitch, and that, many have concluded, is going too far.

Football alone seems to have it right. Said Prusmack, the rugby writer: "When people come up with a game that lasts a century, they've done something."

2. Oldest Game in the World?

*FLASHBACK: IN THE long history of football, three
landmark events helped take it from 28 B.C. to 1999 A.D.*

The startling changes by Camp and his colleagues and successors can best be understood against the comparatively static history of a sport that stretches back to antiquity. Although *American* football is a relatively new game, football in earlier versions pre-dates the Christian era. In fact, it is a candidate for world's oldest game. Since at least 28 B.C., men and boys have been playing various forms of football, sometimes kicking around the skull of an old enemy instead of a ball. The barroom toast, "Skoal," lingers as a reminder of those heady days.

Until 1640, however, all forms of football shared one fate: They were repeatedly banned by the authorities. The game was too disruptive for the kings and queens of England and other lands, or it was too brutal, or not military enough, or not serious enough for Sabbath afternoons.

Similar complaints were in time to be heard in America, and some are still being heard, although genius has usually appreciated football. A female character asks in Shakespeare's "Comedy of Errors":

> *Am I so round with you as you with me*
> *That like a football you do spurn me thus?*

If, as a sport, the game that everyone on every continent now calls football led an uncertain life before 1640, it has been consistently played, somewhere, ever since – most frequently in its British versions. Looking back, historians see three landmarks:

- After soccer football had been alternately played and prohibited from 28 B.C. or earlier to 1640 A.D., it took hold in the latter year, at last, with a number of indoor games in a London church that's still there, Westminster Abbey, where it was called cloister football. The 1640 turning point was made during the reign of a different kind of leader, young Charles I, who dissented from the sports views of the monarchs who had preceded him. In allowing the games to go on, Charles set a precedent that has bound his descendants down to Elizabeth II.

- One day in 1823, at a time when the various soccer-playing private schools of England were also developing their own games, a Rugby School student-athlete named William Webb Ellis picked a soccer ball up and ran with it, scandalizing his peers. But after they'd thought about it awhile (somewhat uncharacteristically for English athletes), they began carrying the ball around themselves, birthing rugby. A school plaque still commemorates Ellis' big run, which gave the Rugby School kids two pastimes, rugby and soccer, and which, many years later, may have encouraged U.S. student-athletes to make even more changes.

- Somebody somewhere kicked the first ball over a cross-bar (for a field goal) instead of under (for a soccer goal), establishing a scoring method that has become integral to American football. But the time and place of this inspired innovation and the name of the kicker have disappeared into the mists of time.

As for the precedent-setting king who first tolerated athletes, his was a short, tumultuous life that was shortened unceremoniously even though, for his support of sports, he deserved a better fate. In 1649 when Charles I was hanged by his enemies outside his London banqueting hall, a place that still stands, the soccer football players of Westminster Abbey went on playing their game as usual. It's a hardy game. About that time, it even reached America, where, failing to last out the nineteenth century in its British form, it has prospered ever since in more progressive forms.

To be sure, in a largely soccer-playing world, American football players seem out of step. But the usual explanation – that they grew up with football and don't know soccer – is inaccurate. They used to play it. They tossed it.

3. Walter Camp, Seminal Innovator

A YALE MAN was more influential than but never as famous as John Heisman or Abner Doubleday.

The monumental changes in soccer, and the first steps toward American football, began with Walter Camp. Insufficiently recognized by later generations, Camp was until 1910 the most important figure on the College Football Rules Committee, where he served for thirty-three years. At the time he joined on, 1870s student-athletes ran the athletic programs everywhere. And though amateurs, the young athletes remained in charge until football began paying off at the gate. Then, as any later sports fan would understand, college administrators took over and put the students in their place, where they can be found to this day, overworked and underpaid.

Happily for football, Camp, a genius type, could as a Yale sophomore do absolutely anything he wanted to do to reform and revise football, with one proviso: He needed the approval of his associates on the Rules Committee. That turned out to be effortless because they all regarded him (as one said) "as a one-in-a-million type: precocious, patient, persistent, persuasive."

Continuously involved in the game through the first quarter of the twentieth century, Camp recapitulated the history of football in his own career. To begin with, as a college freshman, he had been a soccer player because soccer was then the only fall sport Yale had. In his sophomore season, he and his pals at Yale and elsewhere switched to rugby, but that didn't satisfy them either.

So Camp went to work. And before the end of his sixth season as a Yale athlete (in an age when graduate students were eligible for varsity sports as long as they kept going to class), he had accomplished his breakthrough. If it sounds easy now to substitute systematic scrimmaging for soccer's impromptu, harum-scarum ways, it was profoundly revolutionary then. Indeed, the whole Camp package constitutes one of the great accomplishments in sports history.

Inexplicably, he has received hardly any credit for the achievement. In baseball, ironically, Abner Doubleday has been extensively honored for inventing a game he may never have seen. In football, John Heisman (of the trophy Heismans) is considerably more celebrated than Camp although he was neither the athlete, the coach nor the man that Camp was. It is sadly true that Heisman was the greatest pour-it-on coach ever. One of his efforts (222-0) is still an American football record.

By contrast, Camp was a civic-spirited statesman sort who in the 1920s, after a lifetime reforming football, reformed golf as well. After discovering that the annual dues for golf in England were less than the cost of one round at an American country club, he led the campaign for municipal golf courses in this country.

Compassion was also the quality that helped Camp get his innovations through the Rules Committee. With one decision, he won the gratitude and support of Harvard (then and now Yale's great rival) by establishing the official width of a football field at the odd distance of fifty-three and one-third yards. Under pressure to reduce injuries by opening up the game with a larger field, Camp settled for fifty-three and a third because that was the largest that would fit in Harvard's new stadium, now Harvard's old stadium.

Of English descent, Camp, everyone said, was soft-spoken and mild of manner. Lean, he made it a point to stay physically fit. In appearance he could have been an English country gentleman. Son of two New Haven schoolteachers, he married the daughter of Yale's most respected professor.

He is still warmly remembered in his hometown. "Camp's spirit still lives here," New Haven newspaper editor Bruce Reynolds said.

Often defined as a winner, Camp also knew how to lose with grace and purpose. He once said, "When you lose to a man in your own class, shake hands with him, do not excuse your defeat, do not forget it, and do not let it happen again."

Acting on his own advice during the years when he was the football coach at Yale and then Stanford, he became the biggest winner of his time, the 1890s, when, granted, the game was embryonic, a combination of rugby and football. But it was thought of as football; and among the intercollegiate coaches who have lasted eight or more years, Camp, with a won-lost record of 79-5-3 (.940), bests even Rockne's ten-year percentage.

Even so, his careers as football legislator and coach were only two of five in a lifetime of urgent versatility.

Primarily a businessman, Camp put in forty years with the New Haven Clock Company, rising to sales manager, treasurer, president and chairman. He wrote twenty books (fiction, history and sports) and became probably the highest paid nonfiction magazine writer in the country.

His *Colliers* file each year included the Walter Camp All-American team – the world's first All-American or all-anything – and in the first twenty-four years of this century, his was the only All-American team. *Everybody* accepted it in a very different time predating football's present era of uncertainty and controversy, as provoked by a multitude of wire-service and other competitors.

In 1914, a world war launched Camp on his fifth career as the nation's most prominent physical fitness expert. Inventing the exercise program known as the Daily Dozen, he promoted it nationwide. In his advanced years, continuing to excel in tennis and golf, he also composed passable poetry, and played cards with great skill, writing one of the early bridge manuals.

In 1925, at sixty-five, he died in his sleep. "It can truly be said of him," an associate wrote, "that even death, last enemy of us all, came to him like a friend."

Harvard's Dean Briggs, summing up an era, said: "I knew Walter Camp as the great master of football whose advice – if the Yale captain would listen to it – meant inevitable defeat for the college I loved best."

4. Why Camp? Why HERE?

THE AMERICAN SPIRIT leads to free
thinking, which led to this American game.

What accounts for Walter Camp? More generally, why did the athletes of this country transmute the games so loved elsewhere? In the rest of the world, the two big international pastimes, soccer and rugby, have remained substantially unchanged throughout the same century in which American football has constantly evolved. What prompts such differences? Why, for example, did American rugby players suddenly start blocking their opponents (illegally by British standards)? Why did they decide to line up and run set plays (instead of flinging the ball into a crowd from the sideline in the immemorial mode)?

There are parallels in other fields. To take a major instance, not long after the twentieth century got under way, Americans were mass-producing automobiles at a time when a horse was still good enough for an Englishman. In truth, a comparison can be made between America's early first steps in the creation of a lively new game and Henry Ford's early first steps in the creation of the flivver. The two things were going on at precisely the same time: the birth and development of football and the birth and development of automobiles.

And to this day, Americans enthusiastically accept both: There is nothing they'd rather have than an automobile and nothing they'd rather watch than football.

Ironically, the people of Great Britain could have had the first automobiles. English inventors were the first to test drive a horseless carriage on a public road. But that event, a big one, was predictably greeted negatively in their Parliament, which, a hundred years earlier, had lost the American colonies with obtuse and unimaginative policies. This time, Members of Parliament ruled obtusely and unimaginatively against horseless carriages, which, strange as it seems now, were banned from all British roads.

That left the game to Henry Ford.

Britons opted to put up with horses because they always had. Similarly, they have put up with, for example, rugby's rules against blocking because the rules are in the book. One day when American football father Walter Camp was counseling courage and enterprise to members of the Football Rules Committee, he put the British attitude in two sentences:

"What has been done can be done. What has not been done must be illegal."

The American attitude is, for better or worse, the hell with the book. After early U.S. athletes had widely ignored the no-blocking rule (as, in the same spirit, other Americans soon ignored alcohol Prohibition), they presently got a legalized-blocking rule they could live with.

Here, in short, free thinking is simply taken for granted.

The fundamental difference is that the United States was founded on the principles of the 1776 Declaration of Independence: freedom and independence. By comparison, the soccer-playing nations were founded on restrictive principles by an upper crust of nobles and aristocrats ministering to a populace of yes men.

The world's first democracy, America was populated by volunteers who had fled the authoritarian countries of their soccer-playing ancestors *precisely* to make their own decisions and live their own lives. And, here, democracy has always been the preferred political way, inspiring one generation after another to defy authority and tradition while demonstrating individual ingenuity and creativity.

There are, of course, nobles here, too. In America, a noble is any person in any field who plays by the rules and wins.

CULMINATION:
The Rise of Pass Offense

1. The Great Rules Debate
2. Fab Five of Football's First Century
3. Mayhem and Beyond
4. The Single Wing
5. Clark Shaughnessy and the T Formation
6. Vince Lombardi, Counterrevolutionary
7. Bill Walsh: The Apotheosis of the Pass

Across the American century, the evolution of football has mirrored the eons-longer evolution of life itself: Brutish physicality has been joined, and often outpaced, by refined skill and bright intellect. In football, most simply, the evolution has involved the transition from a game based on running the ball to one based on the forward pass. It is the pass, the ball soaring overhead, that transcends the hard-nosed tangle at the line of scrimmage and develops long gains and high point totals with often instant ease.

Always in the context of physicality and courage, with big hits often delivered on both passer and receiver, passing showcases spectacular feats of eye-hand coordination and in-depth strategizing by coaches and players alike.

For the better part of my sixty years as a football writer, it has seemed to me that most coaches have resisted this natural evolution, have illogically feared and undervalued forward passes. Through most of this century, it was not the science and artistry of passing but the violence of the running game that most obviously appealed to most of the most prominent coaches: "Hurry Up" Yost, Red Blaik, Bernie Bierman, Jock Sutherland, Buddy Parker, Bud Wilkinson, Vince Lombardi, Woody Hayes, John McKay, George Allen, Chuck Noll. Reflecting a mainly physical orientation toward football and life, and basing their offensive systems invariably on power-running plays, these coaches, along with most of their opponents and most of their successors, have all apparently regretted the 1905 legalization of the forward pass.

And I have regretted their regretting. Instructed in the 1940s and early '50s by the early airmen of the Los Angeles Rams (Bob Waterfield and Norm Van Brocklin throwing to Tom Fears and Elroy Hirsch), I learned that in most games, more and better passing would have made winning easier for the winner and losing less likely for the loser. For a half century, I have remained confident that:

- The way to play football is with a passing team that isn't afraid to pass on first down and that, secondly, can run the ball when it must.
- Most coaches in their standard philosophy, with their insistence on running first to set up passes, have all this time had it just backward.
- It has been fear – an unreasoning fear of turnovers and a widespread "fear of the perfected forward pass," in Walter Camp's phrase – that has unnecessarily delayed the evolution of pass offense.

Historically, progress toward the perfected pass has not been smooth and incremental. In fact, through much of my career I might have basked in the glow of burnished passing games had it not been for the great Vince Lombardi counterrevolution in the Green Bay of the 1960s. Until then, the evolution of the sport from running to passing had seemed as inexorable as the rise of life out of the primordial ooze.

1. The Great Rules Debate

IN A LAND where one goal is always improvement, the rule changers, though often opposed, have improved football steadily.

The problems with passing surfaced early on. Of all the people who have coached football since the first decade of the twentieth century, the few who favor throwing the ball have continuously struggled with the many who'd rather not.

This has meant, in addition to the long debate, much work for the most progressive of the rule changers, particularly since 1900. Virtually all of the changes that make the game recognizable as football to 1999 sports fans were proposed and implemented in the years after 1900.

The ball, for one thing, was entirely different in Walter Camp's coaching heyday in the 1890s. Bulbous and unwieldly, it was more rugby ball than football, and nearly impossible to throw (had passing been legal, which, then, it wasn't). The gear and uniforms of the 1890s were also rudimentary; the athletes valued physical bulk over quickness (though they had little bulk by today's standards); the leadership was radically younger, and even the scoring system was out of another world: On the eve of the twentieth century, a field goal in an American football game was worth *more* than a touchdown.

Indeed, gyrating changes in the scoring system show the almost desperate creativity of the early football people. At first, a touchdown was only worth two points. That was a time when the goal-after touchdown was valued at four points. Field goals in the early years earned five points. Subsequently, the value of a touchdown was doubled to four points. Next, when touchdowns were raised to five points, the conversion finally became the point after.

Not until long into the twentieth century – when the game finally began to shake down as an activity that might be perceived today as football, more or less – did field goals (1909) and touchdowns (1912) achieve their present values, three and six points. And even those numbers aren't sacred. Since the day they found their way into the rulebook, somebody has proposed to change one or the other every year.

For most of the century, though, as argument followed argument, passing has provoked the wildest struggles between proponents and opponents of change. When in 1905 the progressive camp got passing legalized, sort of, for the first time, the conservatives made sure it was impeded by an astonishing number of eccentric restrictions. In the early years of the air age, for example, passes could be legally completed only if caught fewer than twenty yards downfield, and only if the ball crossed the line of scrimmage within five yards to the left or right of center. To help the officials in their calculations, the field was chalk-lined vertically as well as horizontally into a maze of five-yard squares. And such is the nature of man and sports that even though the grids disappeared nine decades ago, the field has been called a gridiron ever since.

The grids were plainly as silly as they were quaint. And so were many of the other passing restrictions that prevailed at times during the years between 1905 and 1912. Thus:

An incomplete pass, like a fumble, could be recovered by the defense (unless an offensive man had touched it).

A completed pass into the end zone didn't count. It was ruled a touchback, not a touchdown, and the other team was awarded the ball.

The innate conservatism of most football coaches was responsible for such nonsense. To many of them, passing was a moral transgression, an aerial escape from the earth- and muscle-bound confrontations which, in their view, formed the essence of a "man's game." And, unhappily, from the day that non-playing coaches wrested control of football from the more adventurous student-athletes, they have been a powerful component on the Rules Committee. Accordingly, even as passing was eased in during the great rules debates of 1905-12, the coaches insisted – throughout every lengthy confrontation – on two critical and extremely conservative principles that lasted for decades:

- The first was a rule requiring the passer to position himself at least five yards back of center when throwing the ball. Precluding any kind of sophisticated offense, that rule lasted into the 1930s.
- The second requirement, which effectively kept skilled passers and receivers off the field, was the ban on free substitution. One-platoon (or ironman) football, as everywhere played throughout most of the first half of the century, meant two things: (a) When the ball changed hands, the same eleven players stayed on the field, playing offense and defense both, and (b) when the coaches chose the members of those teams, they chose defensive instead of offensive experts on the theory that, as most coaches said, "If they can't score on you, they can't beat you."

Hence one-platoon football was regularly a battle of defensive teams trying to play a little offense. From one season to the next, passing hardly figured.

2. Fab Five of Football's First Century

FIVE TIMES IN a hundred years, adventurous, game-changing leaders have shown up to bend football in new directions.

Given the long twilight struggle to keep football grounded, the initial change from running to passing, when it came, was flabbergastingly swift and decisive. Football's Clark Shaughnessy era, which is still alive, began in the 1940 holiday season with two smashing T-Formation wins. And within a decade, the end had come to the most famous of the power-running formations that dominated football from one world war to the next – the Single Wing – and all it stood for.

Through the 1940s, the entire football world edged away from the Single Wing and moved inflexibly to the Shaughnessy T, a system accenting not muscle but speed, mobility, deception and the constant search for big-play passes.

To the football public, the change was more revolution than evolution. And in an ultimate tribute to Shaughnessy, who is today barely remembered, modern sports fans rarely call the game T-Formation football. They just say football. They don't think of Dan Marino and Steve Young as T-Formation quarterbacks. They just say quarterbacks. Watching and relishing today's big pass plays, few young fans realize that football was ever played any other way.

Even though this is a game invented by many, it seems obvious, therefore, that Shaughnessy ranks, in the progressive development of football, as one of the century's most important and inspiring figures, as, perhaps, one of the principal five.

As influential leaders, these five have come on stage – every twenty years, almost exactly – in this order:

- *Walter Camp,* the turn-of-the-century Yale coach who headed the Rules Committee until 1910, had by 1900 scripted the changes that ended the reign of soccer as the national pastime.
- *Knute Rockne,* the 1920s coach of Notre Dame, anticipated three modern refinements (passing, deliberate deception, and two-platoon football) while making the game a national spectacle.
- *Clark Shaughnessy,* the 1940s coach of Stanford's turn-around team, reinvented offensive football with a creative, new T-Formation approach to three compelling strategic elements: motion, illusion, and big-play passing.
- *Vince Lombardi,* the 1960s Green Bay coach who won five NFL championships, led a conspicuous but temporary counterrevolution, influencing a generation of coaches to again rely on running plays rather than passes.
- *Bill Walsh,* the 1980s San Francisco coach who built another five-time champion, reversed Lombardi and transformed passing from a quest for big plays and instant points into a quick-throw system of carefully timed passes – into what any previous coach would have considered an oxymoron: ball-control passing.

Perhaps no other coaches in any sport have done so much for so many. And, granting to Camp the first two decades of the century, it probably isn't a coincidence that leaders of their stature have come along every twenty years.

Quite possibly, it takes about that long for changes as profound as theirs to take root before a new philosophy can be effectively advanced. If so, it is also possible that a sixth leader of their stature, potentially, is even now altering football in important ways. Twenty years after Walsh overturned Lombardi, it is conceivable that Mike Shanahan is now modifying Walsh.

As coach of the Denver Broncos, Shanahan won the 1998 and 1999 Super Bowls with a team that got there by throwing long passes to set up long runs. Thus, he could be modifying *both* Shaughnessy and Walsh – proving that long passes are not only more efficient, as Shaughnessy asserted, but as safe as Walsh's short passes. (For more on Walsh, see Chapter VIII; on Shanahan and Shaughnessy, VII; on Camp, II and on Rockne, I.)

3. Mayhem and Beyond

ONE OLD PLAY, the flying wedge, illustrates the role
and power of tradition in football and on men.

The road to Walsh's pass-first game has been long and winding. For all the promise of Camp's ball-possession and line-of-scrimmage rules, American football in its early manifestations said little for the brains or skill of the species. There was instead at the turn of the twentieth century one dominating offensive play – a dramatic, all-embracing play. They named it the flying wedge, and it was to hold football hostage long into the century.

Sometimes called the most infamous tactic in U.S. sports history, the flying wedge, as developed in the late nineteenth century, was an outgrowth of football's changing rules. And though it hardly testified to humanity's evolutionary gains, it was still awesome to witness.

Commenting many years later, football historian Parke Davis said: "No play has ever been devised so spectacular and sensational as this one."

And so *enduring*. It lasted through years of Rules Committee efforts to root it out.

The flying wedge was a mass-momentum play (or, more exactly, formation) in which big men lined up far behind the line of scrimmage, then charged full-speed forward before the play began. As first used, by Harvard against Yale, the flying wedge had been a kickoff play. But later, most teams developed ways to use it also as a scrimmage play (with nine- or ten-man backfields) based on the original flying-wedge machinery, which had these six components in an era when it was legal for the kickoff team to retain possession:

First, the Harvard quarterback (who doubled as the kickoff man) stood with the ball on his 40-yard line. Second, the other Harvard players, who had been divided into two five-man sections, were deployed twenty yards behind the quarterback near each sideline. Third, at a signal, the two sections sprinted toward the quarterback, gathering momentum as they advanced. Fourth, when they reached him, the quarterback put the ball in play (that is, conforming to the rules of the day, he touched the ball with his foot and handed it to a sprinting teammate). Fifth, at that moment, one of the five-man sections executed a quarter turn and fell in behind the other to attack the Yale team with a daunting instance of the mass-times-momentum equation. Sixth, the ballcarrier proceeded untouched behind the flying wedge until he could be found and tackled, which was usually far down the field.

Running with the football in such a system required little in the way of agility or skill, and, on every team, linemen doubled as ballcarriers. The most celebrated of football's All-American guards, W. W. (Pudge) Heffelfinger of Yale, gained much of his fame carrying the ball in the flying wedge. He was Yale's leading ground gainer one year.

Not surprisingly, flying-wedge football was lethal. It maimed and even killed so many players that an appalled U.S. president, Theodore Roosevelt (1901-09), stepped in. Having watched the carnage at first hand, Roosevelt warned the colleges to abolish either football or the flying wedge.

They chose the latter. And, repeatedly, they tried in and after 1905 to obsolete the wedge with rule changes such as the legalization of the forward pass. That was a radical remedy – mankind's first attempt ever to get athletes to do something to a football or soccer ball besides kick it or run it. But as we have seen, the early passing rules were too restrictive. Moreover, the game's coaches had by then crowded out the players to take control of most football teams, and as devout conservatives, the coaches didn't get the hint. They simply continued to refine, embellish and rely on flying-wedge running plays as usual.

Not until 1910 did the Rules Committee finally knock the wedge out (if not the thinking that nurtured it) with some drastic new rules that are still in the book — the last and among the most significant changes ever ordered up by Walter Camp, who was then in his final months on the committee. The most revolutionary of the new rules:

First, only four players were permitted to line up in the backfield (behind a mandatory seven on the line).

Next, offensive linemen were barred from using their hands to grab or hold onto opponents.

And, finally, the kickoff man, instead of merely touching his foot with the ball, was required to kick it at least ten yards.

Even then, the revisions were only partially successful. The flying wedge was to have another incarnation in a new formation.

4. The Single Wing

WHEN FOOTBALL'S COACHES want to run the ball, they're going to run the ball: If they can help it, they're not going to throw it.

Early-century football people called their new formation the Single Wing. A formation massing moving blockers in front of the runner as effectively as possible (given the new rules), the Single Wing proved to be a textbook example of the unintended consequences of legislation: It dominated the game for thirty years.

For, in 1912, the Rules Committee was merely trying to open football up – once more – when it adopted a provision known as the second-man rule, the provision that brought the Single Wing in. The second-man rule, whose intent was plainly sound, authorized any back to carry or pass the ball. Until that year, the first two offensive men handling it, the center and quarterback, had been ineligible to run or throw it – meaning that every team was until then operating in a rudimentary form of the T Formation, with a quarterback taking the ball from center before distributing it to those eligible to carry it.

Specifically, the new rules:
- Tightened restrictions on the center, forbidding him to personally run, kick or pass the ball forward. (To this day, he must deliver it to a teammate.)
- Authorized him to snap the ball directly to any player in the backfield (much as today's centers do in the Shotgun Formation).
- Empowered the second man touching the ball (any of the four backs) to advance it by ground or air.

The new rules had been designed to make the quarterback a more useful player. Displaying a stunning lack of imagination, the coaches simply turned him into a pulling guard, jumping at the chance to preserve intensively blocked, flying-wedge-type running plays in a Single-Wing format.

The mass of the new formation was obvious to all. On Single-Wing plays, seven players (four linemen and three backs) lined up to the right (or left) of center, with a running specialist tailback several yards directly back of center. Only two lineman were left on the other or "weak side" of this one-winged formation. And with three backs often leading the way for the fourth, and pulling guards thrown in for good measure, the Single-Wing approach in fact resembled a cut-rate flying wedge.

Lip service was paid by some coaches to a search for the largely apocryphal "triple-threat" halfback – the talented ballcarrier who could also pass and kick – but in the doing, most Single-Wing coaches simply settled for specialist runners who could, for play after play, plunge or scamper forward behind pulling masses of blockers.

For the next three decades (until the World War II years) the over-whelming majority of all coaches warmly embraced Single-Wing football.

It was an era in which different kinds of systems based on direct snaps to deeply set backs also appeared – including the deception-oriented Notre Dame Box and a sometimes pass-oriented *Double* Wing (Sammy Baugh began as a tailback in the Washington Redskins' Double Wing). But on most teams, the featured plays were simple Single-Wing stampedes off tackle.

In spite of all that, football's early inventors had by now accomplished greatly. Though the task was huge and though they were still feeling their way, the basics of their game were now in place, the basics that were shortly to make football the most popular sport in the United States.

Counteracting the Old-World thinking that had made soccer the national pastime in 1870s America, a line-of-scrimmage game had been established, ball-possession belonged exclusively to one team at a time, prearranged plays were the norm, and every week brought a systematic war over territory – the field-position struggle that is still vital to winning and losing. Most propitious of all, passing had been made possible – and sometimes, some passes were being thrown.

Even in the conservative days of the Single Wing, American football had become a game of structure and intelligence — a game like nobody had seen before.

But the best was yet to come.

5. Clark Shaughnessy and the T Formation

IN THE EVOLUTION of American football, this one man achieved more for offense and also defense than any other man.

During the seemingly endless Single-Wing era between the big wars, there were, among the nation's major football powers, but two significant holdouts. Into the 1920s and through the 1930s, only the University of Chicago, coached by Clark Shaughnessy, and the NFL's Chicago Bears, owned and coached by George Halas, resisted the rush to the Single Wing. Both teams continued to use variations of what football people like to call the original T Formation, meaning the only offensive system there was before the rule changes of 1905-12.

The Bears under Halas were, however, essentially a power-running team lining up in the full-house T – with three backs abreast – a formation in which they threw passes principally for change of pace. At the University of Chicago, on the other hand, Shaughnessy was inventing a whole new T.

Destined eventually to take over the world, the Shaughnessy T had these among other creative characteristics:

- The quarterback was no longer a drone whose great responsibility was to hand the ball to power runners. He was first a passer. Second, denoting that Shaughnessy was influenced by Rockne's interest in deception and illusion, the quarterback was coached to be a sorcerer whose tricky ball-handling could disguise plays and transfix defenses.
- Running plays, most of them quick hitters or cross-bucks, were based not on the mass-blocking principles that were universal else-where – as a legacy of the flying wedge – but on quickness and guile. On typical runs, the quarterback faked to one back going one way and handed the ball to another back headed another way. Or handed to the first man and *faked* to the second. Many plays developed so quickly and ingeniously that the ballcarrier frequently sped untouched through the line and into the secondary.
- Introducing mobility to football, Shaughnessy broke the full-house backfield mold with a daring new plan: the use of one of his two halfbacks as a man-in-motion. After heading laterally just before the snap, the man-in-motion became a downfield pass receiver – leaving only two runners in the backfield, still the standard disposition in 1999.
- For the first time, football was played by specialists. Shaughnessy's

quarterback was there to pass and direct the show. Two backs remained as ballcarriers. The other back was now a specialist receiver – in effect bringing to three the number of ends or wide receivers on the team. On the Bears, previously, the most successful passer had been a full-back, Bronko Nagurski, who threw for two NFL titles. But in the backfield now, Shaughnessy's best passer played quarterback; the best two running backs lined up to run; the best receiver was the man-in-motion.

• Shaughnessy's teams called many more passes than had formerly been customary on a Halas team. And not only that: Their passes were integrated into the offense. On a characteristic Shaughnessy pass play, the quarterback first faked handing off to one or two backs, then threw to one of his three receivers.

During the fall and winter of 1940-41, the harvest of all that was imaginative offense of a kind never seen before. In Chicago, Shaughnessy had persuaded Halas to try the new offense. In California, Shaughnessy had taken over as head coach of a losing Single-Wing team at Stanford and converted it into a T-Formation team. Installing his matured brainchild in two places at once, the inventor of the new modern T traveled back and forth from Chicago to Stanford.

The results of two championship games that December and January staggered pro and college people everywhere and unveiled the future of football. First, in the 1940 NFL championship game, the Bears used Shaughnessy's concepts, formations, and plays to defeat Sammy Baugh's Washington Redskins by an unimaginable score, 73-0. Two weeks later in the 1941 Rose Bowl, Shaughnessy's unbeaten Stanford team toppled Nebraska, 21-13, as quarterback Frankie Albert first demonstrated the plucky legerdemain of the model Shaughnessy quarterback.

And immediately, a new rush was on – the rush, almost everywhere, to play the game the Shaughnessy way. There were, as usual, a few dissenters, but by the 1950s they were gone, too. The T Formation was no longer the T. It was – and is – just football.

It's no coincidence that, in just this period, football transitioned from one platoon to two with new rules authorizing freer, and eventually free, substitution.

For the Shaughnessy T *demanded* a game of specialists on both sides of the ball.

During the sport's younger years, substitutions had been forbidden altogether, then harshly restricted as in baseball, rendering football's modern game inconceivable. Not until mid-century – the Shaughnessy years – did the coaches, under heavy pressure, relent and permit substitutes (that is, specialists, and especially passing and receiving specialists) to come and go between quarters, then between possessions and, eventually, between plays.

The two-platoon revolution, which disrupted the defense-dominant mindset that still hobbles soccer and other sports, revised football into a series of contests between offensive and defensive experts, between, for example, fast and talented contingents of wide receivers and defensive backs – the kinds of athletes who had rarely had the size to fit in anywhere on a one-platoon football team.

The approval of free substitution has been the most influential single rule change of the last fifty years – in any sport. It has transformed football within the memory of many living fans into a sophisticated two-platoon game, bringing in more science and a great deal more offense.

No one man had more to do with that mid-century transformation than Clark Shaughnessy. And his influence was no accident. A genius-type as well as a classic introvert, Shaughnessy was a lifelong scholar who immersed himself everlastingly in the tactics and strategy of football.

As one result, he had trouble remembering, for example, the names of close friends. During the first of his two years in Los Angeles as coach of the Rams (1948-49), he could call only two players by name. He knew the team's All-Pro quarterback, Bob Waterfield, of course, and he identified tight end Red Hickey by the color of his hair.

Then, as now, a famously confused franchise, the Rams loved Shaughnessy through his first unexceptional season (6-5-1) and fired him after his second (8-2-2), when he led the team to its first Western Division championship and on to the NFL title game. He had rebuilt so comprehensively that the Rams, with him and without him, breezed to that game (the Super Bowl of its time) in three consecutive winters (1949-51), winning it all once. They haven't won since.

As a person, Shaughnessy in his coaching days cut a slim, professorial figure on the practice field and at football meetings. A six-footer prematurely gray in his forties, he had been a 200-pound fullback at the University of Minnesota, where, as he liked to say, he was the biggest man on the team. His was an age of swift physical change in which, moving here and there as an NFL coach, he lived to be one of the smallest men on the team.

And all the way, Shaughnessy was as continuously absent-minded and forgetful as he was shrewd and effective. His problem was football. Through his adult lifetime, he thought about it almost every waking hour, usually every minute.

He couldn't keep his mind off X's and O's and middle guards even while driving a car, and, therefore, accumulated traffic citations with alarming regularity. One day when he was forced to idle away an hour in a courthouse line while waiting to pay off on a spread of seven traffic tickets, an idea occurred to him. Hopefully, Shaughnessy addressed the sergeant: "Couldn't I just leave $500 here on deposit?"

His passion for football was unique. Above all the coaches I have known, Shaughnessy was driven to excel in every aspect of the game. Two decades after the Shaughnessy T changed offensive football for all time, he was back in Chicago as defensive coach of the Bears to do for defense what he had done for offense: introduce movement, deception, and a new aggressive approach.

In the 1990s, Shaughnessy's defensive legacy, along with his T Formation, lives on, increasingly dominating *fin de siecle* football. Today's blitzing defensive backs, coming from all sides and odd angles, illustrate the continuing evolution of defensive movement. The rapidly spreading zone blitz, with defensive linemen occasionally backing out to cover pass receivers, illustrates modern defensive deception.

Before Shaughnessy, football had been a fundamentally static game in which, after each play, the players simply stood or crouched on the line of scrimmage until the ball was snapped for the next play, when they jumped up and crashed into one another. Since Shaughnessy, the art of deluding one's opponents, as once practiced convincingly but almost alone by Rockne, has come to rank in game planning with beating people up. As one of the NFL's high draft choices said last year, "When I was in college, I used to wonder if I could block a pro. But that's the easy part. The hard part is finding the right one."

A half century ago, playing defense against Shaughnessy's long-pass offenses was even harder. After the 73-0 shocker and then Albert's ball-handling magic in the Rose Bowl, it was the new offense that had football people worrying – and doing.

And in the late 1940s and '50s, standing on the shoulders of such pass-offense geniuses as Shaughnessy and Sid Gillman, some of the game's greatest T-Formation quarterbacks came along to win one championship after another with superior downfield passing:

Waterfield in Cleveland and Los Angeles.

Otto Graham in Cleveland.

Johnny Unitas in Baltimore.

Norm Van Brocklin in Los Angeles and Philadelphia.

And, among others, a rising college quarterback named Joe Namath of Alabama.

For awhile, during my first fifteen years as a newspaper reporter, it looked as though the great passers and receivers would completely take charge, elbowing everyone else out of football.

But not yet.

6. Vince Lombardi, Counterrevolutionary

AS SMART FOOTBALL took a long holiday, this man won big with a philosophy that was the antithesis of Shaughnessy's.

The heights that football could reach with the elaborate downfield pass offenses of the 1950s were just coming into view when, abruptly, the views, and the road, were blocked. A coach with totally different preferences and priorities, a native New Yorker named Vince Lombardi, walked into a little Wisconsin town and fired the first shots of a great counterrevolution.

A nearly invincible head coach, Lombardi, in his Green Bay incarnation, proved in a strategic sense to be a throwback to the game's early years. On his team, indeed, as he told me one day, he was really playing the Single Wing in a T-Formation setting. And nobody has ever played *either* the Single Wing or the T with more success. During nine short years in Green Bay (1959-67), Lombardi coached the Packers to five NFL championships and the first two Super Bowl championships.

He won the seven titles within a span of seven years.

Conceivably, Lombardi was the best coach of all time – conceivably in any sport considering the complexities and competitiveness of *his* sport, and factoring in, as well, his accomplishments during a career so brief. A lawyer and scholar who obviously could have excelled in the intricate Shaughnessy game, Lombardi simply believed in the virtues he talked about: character, determination, will power and what little else it takes to win when football is simplified and distilled to muscle versus muscle. Working with typical NFL material, he made ordinary athletes into great blockers and tacklers first and then into a proud team that executed simple schemes with step-for-step precision.

Privately, in his inner being, Lombardi surely knew that the simple football he symbolized wouldn't beat skilled, well-organized passing teams. If he were coaching in the 1990s, he wouldn't attempt to play 1960s football – surely. But as it happened in his decade, the ablest pass offenses were in the other league, the upstart American Football League.

In Lombardi's league, there was at the time only one great passing team, the Dallas Cowboys, then coached by Tom Landry. And instructively, on the only occasion they met in good football weather in a big game, Lombardi converted the Packers into a remarkable passing team, doing it only because he had to or lose to Landry. On that sunny December day in Dallas, with the NFL's 1966 title on the line, Lombardi won a 34-27 shootout in what I still believe was the greatest football game ever played. It was Lombardi's greatest game, beyond doubt, though he is more famous for ordering a quarterback sneak to win the dispiriting Ice Bowl a year later, in Green Bay, against the same opponent.

The man's results with a throwback running team had the predictable effect, nationally, on most other coaches, college and pro. They would rather have been running the ball in any case; and with Lombardi as their model and inspiration, they quickly gave up on the passball nonsense they'd had to put up with in the age of Van Brocklin and Unitas, and, gladly, resumed off-tackle football. Dulling up most of the first fifteen Super Bowls, they had a new model passer, Bob Griese of the Miami Dolphins, the quarterback who could win a Super Bowl while throwing only seven times.

7. Bill Walsh: The Apotheosis of the Pass

AS THE GAME changed again, passing returned to football in the century's final years, when there was a new way to do it.

Through the 1970s, as pro and college coaches alike worked hard to imitate Lombardi, most football fans disapproved. There was a lot of talk about dull games and thrill-less Super Bowls. The plodding, ground-oriented game that cluttered up the post-Lombardi years was put up with because it was football. It was better than anything else. But it wasn't loved.

In historical terms, though, the Green Bay counterrevolution of the

1960s and '70s merely delayed the progress of the game. Evolution isn't to be denied. And, happily, an even twenty years after Lombardi won his first title in 1961, a different sort of coach, Bill Walsh of San Francisco, took the 49ers to the NFL championship with a new kind of passing team.

Gone was mass blocking. But gone also was the bombs-away drama that had made champions of Waterfield and Van Brocklin before the Lombardi takeover, when, on Van Brocklin's career day, in Lombardi's first championship game, he even beat the great man himself.

The Walsh focus was instead on perfectly executed, quickly thrown, short-to-medium-length passes – many of them on first down, the game's traditional running down.

What Lombardi had shown was that winning teams must control the ball, preferably on long, clock-moving drives. What Walsh showed, shockingly, was that ball control can be produced most reliably not with runs but with quick, well-designed passes. With that approach, Walsh built a dependable winner in San Francisco, coaching the first three of five 49er Super Bowl champions himself.

And at last, the forward pass was an integral part of safe and sane football.

It took a decade for Walsh's cerebral, meticulously detailed way to penetrate the league, mostly through the travels of former San Francisco assistants such as Mike Holmgren (to Green Bay of all places) and Mike Shanahan (to Denver). Since 1992, however, it has been impossible to win the Super Bowl with any other approach.

Earlier in the century, the blockers and ballcarriers had had their way, first in the era of the flying wedge, then during the Single-Wing era, and finally in the age of Lombardi. But the destiny of football, I have always believed, had to be something more skill-filled and creative. From its earliest years, from at least the big day of passer Dorais and receiver Rockne in 1913, football was meant to be a game in which good passers and receivers would be as important and productive as good ballcarriers and blockers – on first down or any other down – and by 1999, that goal had been reached.

By now, in fact, the notion of perpetual passing has penetrated back into the colleges, back to the birthplace of the game. As the new millennium approaches, you can watch Deep South undergraduates play all day in the Shotgun, throwing on every down.

Walter Camp would have trouble recognizing his game.

But he would enjoy it. And he'd be proud.

CAMPUS:
America's Place For Books and Games

1. Football and Academics in Europe
2. Georgia: Cheers for Two Flags
3. Texas versus Oklahoma: Don't Forget to Duck
4. Wisconsin: The Badger Band Always Wins
5. Football at Dartmouth: The Bonfire and Beyond
6. Chicago: Hail Copernicus
7. Stanford: Pursuit of Preeminence
8. USC: Football Builds a University

Football could only have been invented by American college kids, by New World youngsters who were obviously as intelligent and iconoclastic as they were energetic. But there has been an unintended consequence of the years of imaginative work by Walter Camp and his peers and heirs. Their successful quest for the best of all games has left America's universities living a well-publicized paradox.

Beginning in the earliest years of the century, when college coaches and administrators wrested control of football from the student-athletes who had made it a game that was fun both to play and to watch, the university campuses of America have evolved into what they are today, an incongruous academic home, jointly and severally, to the biggest of big-time sports.

At the nation's major educational institutions, football has become big business even though, to its critics and many others, it is an activity that seems plainly incompatible with the purpose and mission of any serious university. Scholars have for decades asked: How could that happen to us?

There is a simple explanation.

The game the kids made – and at first played just to amuse themselves

– simply became *too* popular and profitable, much too profitable, for the schools to throw out. At a point quite early in the century, as football flourished on the vacant campus spaces that were to become stadium sites and parking lots in the automobile age, the scholars awoke to an uncompromising reality. Football was already ingrained in the campus fabric, already an important factor in the annual budget as well as in campus life.

Today as the American century closes down, the game is as integral to most campuses as the library or classrooms. Moreover, college football weekends have evolved into festive pageants, into two- and three-day parties – into central functions of the collegiate lifestyle – with distinctive and mostly delightful variations from section to section and school to school.

The cognitive dissonance produced by the game's warlike combat sited amidst the staid halls of academia has led to decades of discussion about football's "proper place." It has also afforded me, personally, repeated opportunities to cover the college scene – and I never saw a campus I didn't like.

It's an intrinsically American image – the three-hundred-pound offensive tackle sweating it out in Sociology 108 – impossible in, for example, Europe, where athletes must opt for sporting careers and against higher education as early as age ten. But the incongruities on American campuses, I have come to feel, are not incompatibilities. The following essays, based on campus visits of mine over many years, look at this fruitful paradox from many angles and amount to an extended meditation on what I now consider to be the mostly healthful symbiosis of big-time football and quality education. Football may be the best game; but for U.S. universities, it is far more than a game.

1. Football and Academics in Europe

AS VIENNA first showed me on a European tour, the U.S.-style nexus of sports and academics is nearly nonexistent in the Old World.

Major league football in both Europe and America begins with what happens on the playgrounds of the elementary schools. The best of those who star in pickup games rise eventually to the majors. But the way they get there is radically different on the two continents.

In America, the pro football player is almost always a high school graduate who goes on to three or four years in a good college, spending most of his life, if incongruously, as a celebrity in the academic world.

In Vienna – which is typical of Europe, where football is what Americans call soccer – the professional player is a career athlete who makes a choice at age ten to end his years of formal education four years later, in the eighth grade. After age fourteen he seldom sets foot in a classroom. Indeed, the high school graduate on a European soccer team today is about as rare as the high school dropout who makes good in American football.

Thus, the ancient Greek ideal of the well-rounded man has, in modern Europe, shattered into extremes of specialization. Twenty-three hundred years ago in polytheistic Greece, whose citizens competed in everything from poetry to the sprints, the goal for all was a sound mind in a sound body. But over the centuries, religious differences splintered Western civilization. And in that process, academic learning and sports competition in Europe divided to become completely separate activities – carried on in widely different subcultures to the detriment of athletes and scholars alike. The U.S. marriage of football and academe is therefore both an innovation and a classical throwback – and by comparison with European athletic apartheid, may even seem civilized.

"Our athletes are all undereducated," Ferdinand Wimmer, an Austrian editor, told me one day in Vienna. "Austria's leading skiers and soccer players all lack higher education. And these are the nation's favorite athletes. Most of them finished school at fourteen. It's the system."

For youngsters with average intelligence, he said, there isn't time in an Austrian high school for both homework and sports. So instead of high school, which Austrians and other Europeans call gymnasium, athletes attend Hauptschule, a vocational school.

Wimmer, a veteran of more than twenty years on Vienna news desks, added, "Among the boys and girls of high school age in Austria, about half go to Hauptschule and half gymnasium. The exceptions are the athletes. Virtually every (would-be athlete) takes the vocational way."

During my summer week in Austria, this is what I observed or what Wimmer and other Austrians told me about a country which, they said, is in these respects like others in Europe:

In all, eight grades of education are compulsory. The first four are called Volkschule. Then after competitive examinations, Viennese students diverge to spend either eight years in gymnasium or four years in Hauptschule.

If they qualify for gymnasium, they can still choose Hauptschule, instead, and learn typing, perhaps, or printing, as well as football.

In either case, while still in fourth grade, they make an all but irrevocable life-determining decision.

"On school days," Wimmer said, defining the Old-World system, "classes end at 1 or 2 p.m. A gymnasium boy must go home and study. He has much more homework than any Hauptschuler, or any American. A Hauptschule boy can play soccer all afternoon, if he wishes, and if good at it he probably does."

Thus by the fifth grade at the latest, when he is ten or twelve years old, an Austrian with either a talent for or an interest in athletics is already spending his time learning to be a pro athlete – or at least aiming for a career as a pro athlete – with no real understanding of what that means, or what's ahead.

ii

Though they may have been heedless of their environment, Vienna's boy athletes, when I was there, were working out in one of Europe's most beautiful cities. One-time capital of the Austro-Hungarian empire, Vienna is a city of clocks, castles, music, and streetcars, of tree-lined boulevards and winding streets.

The beauty of the inner city is in the graceful trees and the many large baroque stone buildings of the former empire, including the palace and opera house, which are linked to Vienna's suburbs by one of the most efficient streetcar systems in the world.

It is the fleet of streetcars – narrow-gauge, electric, red, fast and numerous – that brings the young athletes together. Within thirty minutes after school is out, regardless of how far they have to come, they're on the city's soccer-football grounds. And to those watching them in action, it was evident that soccer was already a way of life for many Vienna Hauptschulers aged ten – or younger.

No organized sports were visible in or near the gymnasiums or Hauptschulen themselves – and this is another striking difference between Austria and America.

The pomp and circumstance of high school athletics in the United States, involving a high percentage of non-athletes, are entirely absent in Vienna. There are no marching bands or manly yell kings or short-skirted song girls or attractive cheerleaders and majorettes or big, noisy teen-age crowds. To a European man or woman, sports and school plainly go together like sausage and candy. It never occurs to a citizen of Vienna to connect the two.

The Viennese sportsmen of this century have developed, instead of high school football, a multiple-division web of soccer teams that may either be amateur or pro but are unrelated to any school systems. Some aspects of their way:

- Fifty football (soccer) clubs lie within the city limits of Vienna.
- There are also swimming clubs as well as handball clubs, ski clubs and others for athletes age ten to sixty.
- Most clubs are amateur, but all, including those competing in professional as well as amateur soccer, enter teams in all soccer leagues at every age level from ten to over-thirty.
- Scouts for Vienna's best pro team (Rapid/Wien) and for all other pro clubs recruit aggressively on Austrian playgrounds, signing players ten years old and up. Thenceforth, as regular members of the club, these youngsters practice under professional coaches four times a week.

  This means, among other things, that a European soccer scout has one of the worst jobs in sports. Picture an NFL coach, Bill Cowher, say, or Jimmy Johnson, evaluating ten-year-old guards and tackles.

Or think of the Los Angeles Dodgers drafting their 2012 catcher this summer out of grade school.

At an age when American boys are just going out for fullback or defensive end in high school, Viennese youths are skilled veterans who, besides, keep improving faster than Americans. An Austrian lad has year-round coaching and training that appear to be more intensive and extensive than that offered in America by most Pop Warner and other youth programs.

In one recent year, the captains of three first-division European soccer teams – one of them based in Austria – were eighteen, the age at which American athletes are just beginning four years of college football.

If, for qualified athletes, sports are overemphasized in Austria – and in Europe generally – it isn't the same for the unqualified. When I was there, life appeared to be much different for Viennese high school students whose athletic ability is no more than average. Although they take some exercise in their versions of gym class, prep students play few games in Vienna schools, and compete in few sports.

And this may account for a nationwide sedentary tendency among those not actively involved in any sport club. In Austria, it often seems, the national pastime is sitting, talking, eating, and downing beer. As a way of life, that has its attractions – but not if accompanied, among overweight people, by a lack of respect for those who appreciate physical fitness.

A century or so ago, the truth was discovered by Austria's Empress Elizabeth, an accomplished horsewoman who was roundly criticized in Vienna for two eccentricities: her rigid, low-calorie diet and exercising.

In her dressing room in the Hapsburg family's massive Vienna palace, her exercise bars and rings are still in place. They helped the beautiful Elizabeth to be for a time the best woman athlete in her realm – and doubtless always the slimmest. When assassinated at age sixty-one, she was wearing a dress which, as laid out in her bedroom today, appears to be about a size six or eight.

Much of the Viennese population now needs at least twice that much dress, and, in fact, the Ministry of Education has lately isolated the country's two major problems: the athletes are undereducated and the nonathletes are out of shape. "We know what's wrong," Dr. Robert Mader of the ministry, a former professor, said. His office is across the street from that of another former Vienna University professor, Sigmund Freud. "The dichotomies aren't good," Mader continued. "We're trying to find the best possible combination of school education and physical education."

One experimental response is a Sportsschule, in which students get the regular Austrian gymnasium (high school) education plus intensive instruction in one sport, usually skiing.

As for the football players, most of them "are bright enough for Vienna University," one Austrian pro said. "They would go to college if they could go to high school first. It's too bad they must leave school in the eighth grade to have a pro career." To the Viennese citizenry and to Europeans in general, that, for years, has been the challenge.

2. Georgia: Cheers for Two Flags

COLLEGE FOOTBALL IN America could hardly be more unlike Viennese soccer, not least in the air and flair of the Saturday afternoon game as presented in, for example, the deep South.

As established throughout the United States by the final decades of the twentieth century, college football had become more than a high-quality team game. It had become and still is the most characteristic American ritual event. Sports competition in an academic setting, so unlikely in Europe, seems the most natural thing in the world to the millions of Americans who love a football weekend for two reasons: There's both a campus tribal celebration and a chance to see another game.

For Americans with any kind of attachment to any good school, college football is a habit that regularly attracts national, sectional and local attention. And from coast to coast, from state to state, from village to village, the pageantry, the game, and the ritual each week are similar if not quite the same.

On autumn Saturday mornings all over America, numberless old grads get up early and pack a lunch, mix cocktails in a mason jar, load up on ice, throw in a few blankets and sometimes the kids and take off for the football stadium. There they pull into a parking lot, greet the friends of their youth, lunch together, imbibe beer or tea or vodka together, cheer together, boo together, and, joining the traffic jam afterward, often get together again for dinner somewhere down the road.

From Hanover to Ann Arbor to Athens to Austin and on West, the attraction is the same game played by the same rules and arousing the same passions, thrills, joy, tears. Only the details differ. Thus at the tailgate picnics in New Haven, the tablecloths are mostly white. In Texas, they are checkered red and black. At USC, the song girls are more attractive but at Purdue there are more of them, many more. At Oklahoma in the years when, for example, a coach named Barry Switzer was winning big, the variation was Wishbone football, which gave way to the Veer in Georgia, the I Formation at Nebraska, and quarterback-in-motion plays at Harvard.

From the twang of New England to the drawl of the South, it is the accent that changes in college football.

But though the game and its milieu differ significantly in various sections of the country, a focus on any single regional variation helps bring out the underlying unity of the whole.

Thus at the Georgia-Auburn game one Saturday a few years ago – a game played at the University of Georgia football field in Athens, Sanford Stadium – both the unity and the variety were plain. The largest flag on view was the American, but the largest number of flags were Confederate.

By the dozens, moreover, recently manufactured CSA flags were waving in almost every row.

One strength and also one weakness of college football is that, embracing change unwillingly, it is everywhere a traditional happening. And not every tradition is culturally sensitive. Hence Confederate flags still wave in Georgia, offending thousands. At the same time, thousands of Southerners are still aggressively and ambivalently loyal to their two favorite countries.

As the Stars and Stripes went up the Sanford pole at the Auburn game that November afternoon, the Georgia crowd sang the Star-Spangled Banner with more gusto and, on the whole, more affection than Northern crowds normally muster. Nevertheless, eleven decades after the surrender of Robert E. Lee, Georgia fans hailed every Georgia touchdown by waving the CSA Stars and Bars.

Over the public address system before the game, the invocation was delivered from the playing field by a Georgia divinity student. Invocation? That's another staple in Southern football.

ii

The details can be quaintly different. At the University of Georgia, instead of a galloping white horse, the mascot is a dog. Georgia teams are called Bulldogs.

Had it originated the other day, this nickname could not have stuck. By the 1990s, the worst thing you could call a man, almost, was a dog – except at Georgia and Yale.

Indeed, Georgians have customarily taken pride in their canine relationship. In the years when Georgia was a big winner, in the brief stillness following the final words of the invocation one day as the Georgia team remained bareheaded in silent prayer, a gravel-voiced alumnus across the field shouted: "Go, Dogs!"

At the top of his voice, he had the same message a week later and, presumably, years later.

One of Georgia's largest athletic symbols in those days, which on game day was frequently drawn across the football field like a chariot by four red-striped cheerleaders, was a massive red fire hydrant. It was an imitation hydrant, to be sure. It was so big, looming into the Georgia sky, that the dog didn't know what it was.

The dog's name was UGA V. Two of his predecessors, UGA II and UGA III, lay buried at Sanford Stadium in a little cemetery behind the goal posts in the eastern end zone. One marble headstone read: "UGA

III, 1966-1972, 2 SEC Championships, 5 Bowl Teams: Not Bad for a Dog."

Georgia alumni used to say it was strictly a coincidence that the president of their university at that time, Dr. Fred Davison, was a veterinarian.

iii

Comparing football North and South, Pepper Rodgers, who coached in both regions at, among other institutions, UCLA and Georgia Tech, said:

"Football is exciting in the South because it's such a masculine-oriented country. What's that word? It's machismo country. Kids are brought up to consider it an honor and a privilege to play football. In a Southern high school, you have to play football to be accepted as a man. It's like fighting for your country."

Reminded that such views are sometimes now considered sexist, Rodgers nodded and continued: "It's just the style here. They love the hard work of football. They love the contact. Do you know what it's like to shake hands with a Southern-born man? He looks you straight in the eye, and likes to break your fist."

Quite possibly this explains, at least in part, why Southern football men were at first slow to join up with Florida State Coach Bobby Bowden in the fun of throwing the ball. Instead, the South remained for years a stronghold of Wishbone and Veer-T football, in which the emphasis was on running the ball like a man instead of throwing it like a bunch of kids.

Both Auburn and Georgia were Veer teams when I first saw them in championship games in the 1970s, and both played lively football, blocking recklessly and running at will up and down the field until they fumbled the ball. The fumble always was one of the basic Veer plays.

iv

It doesn't much look like it now but the Bulldogs' playing field was a dense forest when the University of Georgia was chartered in 1785. The oldest chartered state university in the nation, it was set down in a wilderness area by men who feared and distrusted cities.

In time when a village grew up around their campus, the ambitious but undereducated old Georgians named the place Athens because their community centers on seven hills. The name persisted even after they learned it was Rome, not Athens, that had the seven hills.

In general, these are like the gentle, red-clay hills that Scarlett O'Hara might have worked at Tara. But Athens is not really that wonderful. Its main street, Clayton Street, one block over from the university, is a three-block jumble of architecturally indifferent two- and three-story buildings, all but indistinguishable from those in any other Southern or Midwestern hamlet.

The university, however, being a university, is a picturesque assortment of white-trimmed, red brick buildings.

And Sanford Stadium is one of the best viewing stadiums in America, built as it was in two facing sections, each seating nearly thirty thousand. The east and west ends are open because the stadium was placed in a ravine over a river that still runs through culverts under the playing field.

A bridge crosses the stream as it emerges from one end of the field, and at gametime, every time I've been there, the bridge has been crowded with football fans. Enjoying one of the best free viewing sites in America, they gather the night before, bringing folding chairs, blankets, breakfast, beer, flags, and police dogs. Crime in America, like football, is boundless.

Hundreds of nonpaying fans also have good views of the football from the other open end of the stadium. There, standing on a railway embankment on Saturday afternoons, they occupy the ground from which some of their forebears shot at the Federal Army's left wing during Sherman's march through Georgia to the sea in 1864.

More than a century later when I first saw the place, the Confederate flags waving from the embankment made time stand still.

3. Texas versus Oklahoma: Don't Forget to Duck

IT MAY BE one of the less edifying arguments in favor of
the mix of athletics and education, but football in the
Southwest is sometimes an excuse for a three-day holiday.

As the Texas-Oklahoma game ended at Dallas in 1947, the players were arguing over a touchdown. And when the argument spread to the stands, Oklahoma alumni and students began throwing whiskey bottles at the referee. That was too much for the Dallas police, who, driving a patrol car onto the field in a bold rescue operation, picked up the officials.

"As they drove off," an eyewitness remembered, "the Oklahoma guys threw everything they could get their hands on at that police car. This was before cans replaced bottles, you know, and Dallas set the record that day for most beer bottles in the air at the same time."

Shuddering at the memory, the witness recalled: "Beer bottles and whiskey bottles were spattering off the patrol-car windshield like rain."

Although that was a half century ago, many in Dallas still warmly remember the day. For one thing, Texas won. For another, the Texas-Oklahoma football game was the biggest thing in town that year, as it frequently is. With usual understatement, Texans call it, simply, "The Biggest Game in Football."

In its heyday, when I was last there and when football's national championship was sometimes on the line, the "Biggest Game" needed a two-day running start. The Dallas Police Department and the fans of both teams began gearing up simultaneously on the Thursday before the kickoff, when thousands of college students set out from their dormitories, sorority houses and fraternities at Norman, Oklahoma, and Austin, Texas. The event was like a home game for both schools. The campuses are each two hundred miles distant from Dallas, close enough to make the students possessive, and far enough to help them slip easily and smoothly into a party mood.

By Friday noon on those big weekends, following ancient custom, the kids were exultantly installed in Dallas and taking over the town. And by Friday evening, following another custom, they were drunk. At least most looked it.

And sounded it. The hotels and motels and the streets outside were full of old grads and undergraduates from both schools sipping bourbon and beer and shouting at one another.

The eye of the storm was in downtown Dallas, where a narrow street named Akard knifes into one named Commerce and makes an end run around the historic Baker Hotel, which is catty-corner from the historic Adolphus Hotel. In this small, intimate, famous intersection in the early years of the century, during the white-flannel era before students had cars, the Texas-Oklahoma game began every year – on the night before – and there, I'm confident, it still begins. In recent years, there has been one refinement. Warily watching the noisy, shoulder-to-shoulder marches and noisier bumper-to-bumper parades, the police have begun confining pedestrians to the sidewalk, and cars to the street. Unhappily, you can't walk up and down the streets anymore, or drive up and down the sidewalks.

ii

In the timeless pattern each year in Dallas, for everyone in Oklahoma red, the objective is to insult everybody in Texas orange. And vice versa. The hostilities are fueled by alcohol. Every hour of every day, there's a drink in almost every hand. The managers of the Baker and the Adolphus issue identification cards to their guests, say their prayers, and lock their doors. And day or night, helmeted Dallas police, before opening those hotel doors to anybody, demand identification.

What's more, on a sidewalk near the Baker, there's a mobile police station, with, to keep things moving, a municipal judge in residence. Armed guards sit right behind in two police vans, climbing out only to book drunks under the trees, which they continue to do throughout the hot night. Hour after hour, the troublesome are separated into two clusters – not red and orange, as you might imagine, but plain drunk and aggressive drunk. The quieter types are held at the mobile station until they sober up. The fighting drunks are hauled off to proper Dallas jails in paddy wagons that leave the Baker at intervals of ten or fifteen minutes, like airport buses. They make the return trip with sirens screaming, for no useful purpose, apparently, except to raise the holiday noise level.

It is at the jail houses that Texas and Oklahoma alumni, students and fans – and/or their wives, girlfriends, or boyfriends – are carefully segregated. There are Texas drunk tanks and Oklahoma drunk tanks. "If we threw them in together," a police sergeant said, "they'd fight all night. They'd be too tired to make the kickoff, and that would be a shame. We haven't declared war here. We just want them sober enough to see the game."

An alcoholic sports event is not, of course, unique to Dallas. College football traditionally attracts hard drinkers from the Ivy League to the Big Ten to UCLA alumni invasions of the Bay Area. And everywhere, there's a police presence. In Dallas, a police lieutenant, asked if the department favored the removal of the Texas game to Oklahoma or, better, Nova Scotia, said: "Hell, no. It's a lot of fun, and it's good for business."

iii

Quaint as it doubtless seems to most other Americans, the average Texan thinks he's more sophisticated than any Oklahoman. Whereas Austin (home of UT) is often referred to as the most civilized city in the Southwest, Norman (home of OU) is a small, inward-looking college town. All this brings more tensions. Said Dallas sportswriter Blackie Sherrod, "They have a bunch of free-thinkers in Austin. On the day of a football game there, all the tennis courts are full."

Texas' enrollment, however, is forty-two thousand. For the Oklahoma game, it can fill every tennis court and library and still turn out as many football fans as the Sooners can – about thirty-five thousand each.

In any Texas-Oklahoma crowd, the schools' two big marching bands sit impatiently and blare intermittently to amuse rooters from every county in both states. Hundreds of former students commute to the event by private plane. For, on Texas and Oklahoma ranches, there are still two kings, oil and football, and alumni wealth and interest in the game are such that scalpers can get their hands on few tickets.

There have been years when you couldn't find a scalper in the Cotton Bowl area to let you into the Texas-Oklahoma game at any price. This is the only sports event I've attended anywhere (including Super Bowls and World Series games) where on game day, scalped tickets have been unavailable on the sidewalks outside.

The natives know this and proceed accordingly. A Texas alumnus who had to be out of town one year placed a classified ad in the morning paper offering to trade his pair for either "a citizens band radio, a fishing boat, or a cement mixer." Hours later, reportedly, he took the cement mixer. The next day, a Fort Worth citizen advertising for a pair offered to trade "my color television set" or "a date with my wife." By failing to submit the lady's picture, he no doubt cut his chances significantly.

If he did get into the game, he never had the fun his Texas forebears used to in the days of bottled beer. It's much harder to hit a referee with a paper cup.

4. Wisconsin: The Badger Band Always Wins

THE AMERICAN GAME is different everywhere. At Wisconsin,
the difference is that the focus is on marching musicians.

At the University of Wisconsin football games I've seen at Madison, the crowds have always neared capacity win or lose. Secondly, win or lose, Badger fans have always been entertained in the second half by troupes of high-kicking college women in short red dresses and high heels.

Dancing around the edges of the field, the young women are regularly accompanied by at least twenty rock drummers from the university's massive marching band.

Each time, however, a token four drummers stay in their seats, along with the hundreds of other Badger musicians, "in case of an emergency," as the band director, Mike Lekrone, told me one day.

What emergency?

"We might score a touchdown," he said.

Not to worry. This is a century in which Wisconsin's football players have won less than half the time. As a game there, the game can be a little slow.

Of course, no big-university football team loses forever. Twice in the 1990s, Wisconsin has emerged to play in the Rose Bowl, and has won twice, beating UCLA both times. Still, for the century as a whole, the best that can be said for Wisconsin is that it's been up and down. As of one game I covered at Madison early in the fall of 1987 – a game enticing alumni from every county in the state – it had been twenty-five years since the Badgers last represented the Big Ten in the Rose Bowl. In their most recent seventeen years, they'd only had five winning seasons.

That was a truly daunting record for futility, but nobody in Wisconsin seemed to mind. Elsewhere when the football teams fall on hard times, attendance typically dwindles. At Wisconsin, it holds steady at more than seventy thousand, as a rule, in a stadium seating seventy-six thousand. Everybody who's anybody in Wisconsin turns out for Badger football.

And the reason is the Badger band. Wisconsin people live on the music and color of college football. "It's the band that brings us together," Badger fan Peder Culver II said after one losing game in which the marching musicians were largely responsible for the unique holiday ambiance. The trombone, tuba, and trumpet blowers were the big players on the afternoon of another Badger defeat, and as usual they were the high scorers. This is a place where the band is bigger than the game.

Purdue graduate Mary Jane Hunt, alluding to Wisconsin's musically creative post-game programs, said: "At Madison, they always win the fifth quarter."

That's when the world's largest rock band, two hundred strong, plays for thirty or forty minutes after the game while the musicians gyrate madly about the field.

Marching musicians are, to be sure, part of the college game every-where; but only at Madison do they seem to be *the* game. A Wisconsin football Saturday is more than a game, more than an event. Win or lose, it's a colorful, musical way of life.

And when the team does get better, the fans are revved up and ready. On New Year's Day 1999, for example, when Badger fans seemed to outnumber Bruin fans at the Rose Bowl, they broke the all-time record for enthusiastic behavior and turned UCLA into the visiting team on its own field. Everyone in Los Angeles said it was the unbounded enthusiasm of Wisconsin fans that unhinged and ultimately upset the heavily favored Bruins.

That came as no surprise to anyone who ever saw Wisconsin *lose* at home.

ii

During a Minnesota game some years ago at Camp Randall Stadium, site of a Civil War training camp and now home to the Badgers, a grade-school basketball player, age about seven, tore a football program apart and bunched the pages into paper balls. Then as the Badger band marched by, the youngster completed one jump shot after another into the tubas.

One day, reportedly, he slam-dunked a tuba carried by a bandsman standing six feet six. And that was to have picturesque consequences.

First, the university, foiling the grade-school shooter and his many imitators, bought a light-weight, bright-red, form-fitting cover for each tuba.

Next, the band's twenty or thirty tuba players, proud of their musicianship and their improved appearance, took off occasionally on game-day marches of their own, leaving the rest of the band behind. They paraded along the edges of the field and into the crowd – single-file – to create a series of musical diversions. For, as they paraded, they played the old marching songs in soft, deep, mellifluous tones.

As they do to this day.

At all home games, periodically getting up from their seats in the band, the tuba players transform themselves into uniformed visions in red and white – carrying big red and brass tubas – as they snake about the field, marching in step, playing beautiful close harmony.

Thanks to a nameless, long-forgotten kid basketball player, there's nothing like it anywhere.

iii

But the real show is after the game. As the band begins the fifth quarter, nobody sits, and nobody leaves. The bandsmen and -women play on the run or while lying down – some standing on their heads – or while dancing on the football field, the trombone section perhaps dancing with the tuba section, the trumpet section with the cheerleaders, the drummers with the pom pon girls. "We're a very physical band," a student musician said. "At preseason rehearsals, we spend seventy-five percent of our time on physical conditioning."

The massed students and alumni at Camp Randall are very physical, too. Rocking the upper decks as they sing along with the band, they dance with dates or with neighbors – or by themselves – dancing in the aisles, or on their seats. The music is "On, Wisconsin" or "Beer Barrel Polka" and the other drinking songs, and everyone is singing or shouting the familiar lyrics.

Commenting on the phenomenon of a big rock band with seventy thousand lead singers, University of Wisconsin sociologist Dan Parks said: "It's a nonsensical outlet of a kind that appeals to most people. What so many of us want is something to do in common with other people."

Band director Lekrone, who sees it as all of that and more, said: "I've always doubted that people take winning and losing as seriously as we're sometimes led to believe. I think we're showing at Wisconsin that a good time can be had by all as an alternative to winning or losing."

As a point of view, that is doubtless taking the Badger phenomenon too far. On the other hand, maybe, the problem elsewhere is that few people have the Badger alternative.

5. Football at Dartmouth: The Bonfire and Beyond

THE IVY LEAGUE twist is that there can be an agreeable coexistence involving academics, athletics and fun times.

Of the eight Ivy League schools, Dartmouth, which graces Hanover, New Hampshire, is farthest north. It often snows there in October. Accordingly, there was no objection some years ago when members of the Dartmouth senior class decided to build a giant bonfire at a football rally the night before the Harvard game. As college seniors have done before and will do again, they left the details up to the freshman class. The kids were told only to tear down an abandoned barn at the edge of town and bring it in as firewood.

On a dark night in rural New Hampshire, however, one barn looks very much like any other. The freshmen ripped up a new one by mistake; and although it made a hell of a fire, the university had trouble balancing the budget that year after paying off the angry farmer.

Despite such setbacks, it is a measure of Dartmouth's interest in freshmen, bonfires, rallies and football that all are still flourishing on a campus that for twenty decades or more has pleased generations of students and visitors. In the years after World War II, when General Eisenhower was president of Columbia, he once made a speech at Dartmouth, where everybody remembers only the remark he made on a campus tour, "This is just what I've always thought a college should look like."

Ike had it right.

The college is built like a small New England town around three sides of a town green. The dominant structure, Baker Library, whose front lawn is the enormous green, is a stately brick building topped by an unusually tall, slim, white clock tower. The rest of the campus is a park rolling through the wooded acres of Hanover, a village on the Connecticut River across from Vermont. Before the American Revolution, Dartmouth was carved out of a forest. And, during football weekends, this idyllic tract becomes the setting for some of college football's most enthusiastic pageantry.

On a night before a typical late-twentieth century Dartmouth-Harvard game, for example, the Big Green band, blaring "Dartmouth's In Town Again," paraded smartly through the park and straight into the library – clearly the place to find students at any Ivy League school. Gathering, as they marched, a train of more than a thousand students, the musicians burst down the main hall of the library – rattling walls covered incongruously with the angry Marxist murals of Mexican painter Jose Clemente Orozco — and spun through the revolving front door onto the green, launching a pep rally.

For awhile, there were two main events, the band and the bonfire, and then the fire took over, the flames leaping seventy feet above the green and attracting a crowd estimated by the fire department at four thousand.

An annual tradition, Dartmouth's big-game bonfire is one of the last remaining such spectacles in college football. Over the years, Big Green freshmen, called Pea Green, have found and trucked in marvelously combustible hen coops, shanties, barns, trees, and telegraph poles, but the best fires are still laid with railroad ties.

The disappearance of American railroads may soon end this sport, and even now, in Avis trucks, freshman scouting parties must forage into Maine and Canada. But by working at it, they're still collecting enough abandoned railroad ties to keep the fire going all night.

The last time I was there, the ties were stacked as high as a two-story building before the blaze was lit by four Dartmouth seniors holding red highway flares. When the top half of the flaming structure collapsed into the middle, it looked like a settler's log cabin fired by the Indians.

It's hard to say what effect a thing like this has on football players – the Big Green team was introduced at the pep rally, and a few hours later played well against a better team – but the effect on others was profound. The pyromaniacal urges of hundreds were surely assuaged for another year. Half the crowd was still there at midnight, four hours after the fire began. And at 1:30 a.m., a Hanover father instructed his three children, the oldest about twelve, "One more walk around the fire, and then we go."

At dawn, as the Hanover Fire Department was hosing down the embers, the Ivy League's reputation for rapscallion ferment was also upheld.

The big Harvard marching band, with barely enough light to see, tip-toed out to the Dartmouth residential area, formed up in full regalia, and started blowing. On a parade past dormitories, fraternity houses, and, unfortunately, the downtown Hanover Inn, the band woke up every Big Greenie (and every visitor) playing "Fair Harvard" fortissimo.

The morning, cold, clear, and enchanting, climaxed with, among other things, punch parties at the fraternity houses, where the entertainment was the sing-along at the house piano: "And if I had a son, sir, I'll tell you what he'd do. / "He'd yell 'TO HELL WITH HARVARD' like his daddy used to do."

The punch was the perennial, effective screwdriver, served out of a cafeteria garbage pail. A clean garbage pail, I hope. The game was almost an anticlimax.

ii

The bonfires and dawn parades are not the only difference in Hanover, or in the Ivy League in general. On a fall weekend at Dartmouth, student-athletes and other students, as Ivies, do it their way. Thus, a recent Harvard-Dartmouth freshman game was delayed two hours while thirty-one members of the Harvard team took an economics test in a

Dartmouth classroom. The examination had been scheduled for 1 p.m. by the Cambridge profs, who made only one concession, moving it to Hanover so the game needn't be canceled altogether.

While many American universities aim for academic distinction while also trying to field near-professional level football teams, the Ivy solution to the ancient academic-athletic puzzle is to put books first – without trivializing football – and without abandoning the tribal lifestyle of a football weekend. The football isn't big league, though it isn't bad, and there's almost always something more important to do.

One year, for example, Harvard's best defensive back, Mike Page, accompanied the team as usual to New York for the Columbia game but didn't play. He was excused to take the state law-board examinations.

Other Ivy League students appear to be equally ambivalent. On the morning of the big game against Harvard – three hours before the kickoff – scores of Dartmouth underclassmen were still hitting the books in Baker Library. Yet of those questioned, most said they intended to make the opening kickoff, or at least much of the game. And this may define intercollegiate football Ivy-style. It isn't the biggest thing on campus, certainly not as big as the bonfire, but like math classes and rock concerts it has a place. It belongs.

Deemphasis indeed seems to be the wrong word for what's happened to Ivy League sports in recent years. Football hasn't been deemphasized there, just decommercialized. Items:

- There are no athletic scholarships. Athletes pay their own way unless they qualify for aid on a basis of need.
- Pro football scouts in this neighborhood are as rare as the great-tailed grackle. In the NFL's intercollegiate farm system, the Ivy League is Class D.
- The pressure to win has been relieved somewhat by a decision to exempt football and other Ivy sports from gate-receipts funding. The athletic department, along with the history department, biology department and the others, is financed out of general university funds.

As a Dartmouth athletic director, Seaver Peters, told me on one visit: "If intercollegiate athletics are worth having, they're worth being supported like any other university program."

So this is what's really different about Ivy League people. They like football so much they're willing to pay for it.

How good is their game? It can be colorful, well-coached, pretty well-played and competitive. Thus, the score was 17-15 the day that Harvard's Crimson ended a five-year domination by Dartmouth's Big Green.

Of the eight seventeenth-century schools in the Ivy League – Brown, Columbia, Cornell, Dartmouth, Harvard, Penn, Princeton and Yale – Harvard had the most modern football team in the years when Joe Restic coached there. One day against Dartmouth, as the Crimson took command with a number of smart, subtle plays, the game's decisive run, measuring thirty-three yards, was made by Harvard's left-handed Hawaiian quarterback, Milt Holt, from a strange-looking formation that seemed to be a variant of the Power I.

Harvard used more formations in the Restic era than possibly any other team in football, college or pro. The Dartmouth offense, less flamboyant, embraced a sophisticated mix of modern option plays, spread formations, and clever passes. For years, the other Ivies have also played imaginatively. In terms of intrinsic football interest, it could be said that Ivy teams put on the best show in the country. Yale's Carmen Cozza, the senior Ivy coach when he retired, once said: "Our teams are exciting because none of the offenses is stereotyped."

The academic bent of the players apparently dictates the Ivy League's more wide-open style. "Our athletes are a special type," Harvard's Restic said. "They're inquisitive, well-rounded, highly motivated. They have to be challenged, so we put in a lot of motion plays, a lot of different formations and changeups, a bunch of defenses." This approach tends to enliven Ivy football at the expense of smoothness. "But," the Crimson coach said, "what you lose in polish, you more than make up for in surprise value."

Admitting to some unique problems, he continued: "The difference at a school like this is that we practice around the players' lab schedules. Sometimes we're out there early in the afternoon, sometimes we don't start until 5 p.m. Football takes more time than many of them can really afford. They're in class or studying every day before I get them, and after practice they go right back to their labs and libraries. What you need to play football here is the ability to turn it off and on. You turn it on going out of your last class, and you've got to turn it off in the shower, and that isn't easy." But they do it.

The official Ivy attitude toward intercollegiate sports is expressed in the charter of the league that calls itself the Ivy Group. In one of the strongest endorsements ever given college football, the eight Ivy presidents announced in 1954: "The Group affirm their conviction that under proper conditions, intercollegiate competition in organized athletics offers desirable development and recreation for players and a healthy focus of collegiate loyalty."

Yet the intellectual bent of the student body gives rooting and playing for the Ivies a unique air. At New Haven, a Yale student from Los Angeles, Frank Jones, said his roommate told him how to behave at football games the first time they went to the Yale Bowl: "Pretend you're not interested unless we get ahead. Then yell like hell." And at Cambridge, Coach Restic, a big winner, always maintained that losing can be more instructive than winning. "Winning doesn't put you to a test," he said. "You might know in your heart you played a lousy game, but it's overlooked because the team won. If you're a player on a losing team, what are you going to do about that? You must measure up in spite of losing."

At Dartmouth, in either case, what they're mostly after is a good time. Before the Harvard kickoff, the entire Dartmouth freshman class was on the field. And as the Big Green team entered the stadium, it jogged through two long files of jumping, cheering, Pea Green rooters. By the fourth quarter, much of the capacity crowd was on the field, too, thronging both sidelines in a scene resembling pictures of turn-of-the-century football before the stadiums were built.

For Big Green football, there are ticket-sellers, but no ushers. Those vending hot dogs and soft drinks are Hanover children aged eight to twelve. The waterboy is a girl. The cheerleaders have also changed: They're still energetic – the men in long green pants, the women in short green skirts – but not quite with it. In the last thirty seconds, with Harvard on the march, Dartmouth's yell kings called for a round of "Hold that line" instead of "Get that ball." Not that it mattered.

What really mattered was the bonfire, the books, and a brand of football that engaged the mind.

6. University of Chicago: Hail Copernicus

WHEN I FEEL the urge to exercise, I lie down until the feeling passes.
— Robert M. Hutchins

The inconsistencies and ironies of football in academia have in this century been judged insufferable at only one major American university, Chicago. Though the Ivy League has long demonstrated that football can mix with first-rate education, Chicago was not persuaded. There, several generations back, the anti-football argument was taken to its extreme with a destructive blow that simultaneously terminated the on-campus values of the big-time college game, if any, and the joys of a football weekend. Two landmark dates:

- Seventy-five years ago, on November 21, 1924, the University of Chicago won a precedent-setting sixth Big Ten football championship under Coach Amos Alonzo Stagg.
- Sixty years ago, on December 27, 1939, the University of Chicago, by order of Robert Maynard Hutchins, president, abolished football.

Not many events in the history of college affairs have caused more commotion than these. In 1924, Chicago stood alone as the only Big Ten university with six undisputed conference football championships — a record which, all these years later, few others in the Big Ten have exceeded, or even matched.

Yet, in 1939, within fifteen years of Stagg's finest hour, intercollegiate football perished at his university. "Unbelievable," Chicago fans said that winter when Hutchins liquidated their most popular sport. "Incomprehensible," the alumni said. "A sellout," students said, noting the time frame of the Hutchins' announcement: Christmas Week. Nobody was around to protest, or even dissent.

Then and ever since, the questions have been the same. By giving up football, what did Chicago prove? Was it a good idea? Did it portend the eventual end of big-time college football everywhere?

To those spending their days on the university's Old-World, graystone-Gothic campus, the answers are still elusive. Their school, some students know, had been a pioneer in two extraordinary if disparate U.S. achievements: the evolution of football and the evolution of atomic energy. Indeed, World War II was won at the University of Chicago — at its football stadium — where in 1942, three years after the football team left, a physics team found the key to nuclear power, creating the weaponry that shortly killed Imperial Japan. The nuclear workshop was under the stands of Stagg Field.

Years earlier, Stagg and his players had built that stadium with their own hands, devoting their summers and weekends to the project.

Simultaneously, they had helped build football into a modern game on the foundation laid by their nineteenth-century forebears.

Stagg's teams eventually introduced, among other things, quarterback keepers, draw plays, reverses, lateral passes, knee pads, tackling dummies, huddles, place kicks, linebackers, cross-blocking and many of the other tools and techniques of twentieth-century football.

Then suddenly at Chicago it was all gone. And that shook college people everywhere, for, if one of the game's most successful and innovative powerhouses could give up football, could the rest of the country be far behind?

In the year that the blow fell, that was plainly the hope of UofC administrators. But today, it is just as plain that at least until now, they have failed. The number of college teams in the big time has increased substantially since 1939. And nationally interest in football is much higher.

The game's critics have, of course, also multiplied in recent years, warning ever more loudly against overemphasis. But in the country at large, those who disapprove of college football seem still to be in the minority. Said the president of a Chicago-based corporation, Robert Feltes, "What it all comes down to, I suppose, is this: College football doesn't belong, but it's here."

> *They say football builds character. But is it the business of the university to mold the character of a few football players? Character building is a function of church, family or state.*
> — Hutchins

As the "boy president" who in 1939 led Chicago off the football stage, Hutchins condemned the game as an "object of irrelevance" that was not only alien to an academic community but injurious. He believed this when inaugurated UofC president at age twenty-nine, he believed it at fifty, and at seventy-five-plus he still believed it in the years when, at my request, we talked about it several times.

That was in Santa Barbara, California, where, for many years before he died, Hutchins administered the Center for the Study of Democratic

Institutions. Speaking of his part in terminating football at the University of Chicago, he insisted: "It was one of the few totally successful things we did. At Chicago, and also in the Midwest generally, the emphasis on winning football games tended to preoccupy the constituency – alumni, trustees and students – in a non-educational enterprise that prevented us from getting on with the business of an educational institution. And at the universities where the game is still valued, this is still true. Everything that has happened in college football since 1939 has confirmed the wisdom of our course."

As a view, that still gets both support and criticism on Hutchins' old campus. Among those in the support group is Mary Ann Lynch, who as a psychology major from Lockport, Illinois, said one year: "In high school I was incredibly into football, but in college there are different focal points: classes, music, movies, conversation, and many other things. It is vital to be involved in something – but in the first year or two I was here, I never heard football mentioned. And I haven't missed it."

A college racing stable makes as much sense as college football.
Jockeys could carry the college colors, the students could cheer, the
alumni could bet, and the horses wouldn't have to pass a history test.
                                                            – Hutchins

Even though the Hutchins logic seems irrefutable, his performance as a salesman has disappointed his best friends. In the city of Chicago and its suburbs as well as on campus, those favoring football are still as earnest as ever. And among the anti-Hutchinses, there is one pervasive point of view: In discontinuing intercollegiate football, the university took the fun out of campus life.

More than one visitor has reported that UofC students today lack the fire that seems to radiate out from the football team at other universities. Chicago's students move from class to class and home again in a distinctively solemn style. By comparison with universities like USC or Michigan – or even Harvard, where the Yale football team is still an object of conversation and obloquy – Chicago seems, quite simply, dull.

This is conceded by many Chicago scholars, professors and alumni. When I was there several years ago, a med student from Norwich, Connecticut, Jeff Trantalis, told me that he only has one complaint against Chicago: "There's no school spirit here." Leslie Mason, a U of C administration employee, said: "I was a cheerleader at Ripon. Football was a diversion, and everyone needs a diversion." Business major Howard Bimson: "Football encourages mingling. If you don't mingle, you aren't human."

James Vice, who for years was Chicago's assistant dean of students, conceded: "I think we can agree that the average Big Ten campus is livelier. Or at least the gusto is more evident. Life is more adult here. The fun is not so structured. Instead of a Big Ten game against Purdue, a student may be thinking of a chess club meeting, or a pizza trip with a few friends."

Hutchins, unmoved by any of the heresies, continued to take an uncompromising view. "To the serious student, the curriculum is what's exciting," he said. "The one thing most clearly established when football was discontinued at Chicago was that this is a serious educational institution. There was no thought that anyone was deprived of the joys of football. You can always watch the pros."

To Willie Davis, an old pro, this argument begs the question. A Los Angeles businessman now, Davis earned his master's degree at Chicago after a long career as a Hall of Fame defensive end for Vince Lombardi in Green Bay. "For either an undergraduate or graduate student, going to school at Chicago is like going to work on a real job," said Davis, who at graduation sifted sixty-seven business offers with the help of the business school dean, George Schultz, later secretary of the treasury. "This is the only college in the country where the library is the busiest place on campus."

It's also the only college that ever tore down a football stadium to build a library. Chicago's Joseph Regenstein Library was erected in 1969 on the site of Stagg Field – smack in the middle of campus. Regenstein has been called the nation's finest.

Still, the suspicion lingers that there were more laughs in the days when the place was a football field.

American higher education is unique. In no other nation does the university tangle up academic and athletic programs to the confusion of both. In England, the difference is that winning a boat race doesn't establish the merits of one university over another.
                                                                  – Hutchins

It should not be supposed that when Hutchins left, the University of Chicago gave up athletics entirely. On intramural and minor league levels, the games went on as usual – even football games, of a sort. Once the scourge of the Big Ten, Chicago's football team tied the Wheaton Junior Varsity one year, 6-6, then dropped six in a row – failing to score in five games against Class D opponents.

The new product has been emphatically amateur. There are no locker room speeches at new Stagg Field – it seats a thousand – principally because there are no locker rooms. After home games, the players of both teams walk three blocks to the showers.

But except to the players, on-campus interest in the new football has been minimal. A graduate student from New York, Pete Keers, had the characteristic comment one day: "I can't take the time to watch Chicago play Lake Forest."

On the major league level, however, the argument continues unabated. Dean of Students Vice, who saw both sides, said: "The academic strength of the university at present is shown in many ways. No class is taught by a student teaching assistant. We don't even have student assistants, except in some of the labs. Full professors teach freshmen. The average class has seventeen or eighteen students. Three-quarters of the faculty live within walking distance of campus.

"But there is one negative aspect without football," he said. "We suffer in national publicity. Some of it may be the wrong kind of publicity, but a football game does provide an occasion for people to hear about your school and come to your campus."

Chicago isn't a very good university. It's just the best there is.
– Hutchins

Post-Hutchins, what did Chicago do for fun? What *can* you do?

This is a thought that occurred one year to D.J.R. Bruckner, who at the time was Chicago's vice president for public affairs. So one year on February 19, Bruckner threw a birthday party for Nicolaus Copernicus. The occasion was the five hundredth anniversary of the astronomer's birth. More than seven hundred students showed up to share a gigantic eight-layer cake on which each layer had been labeled, in Latin, with Copernicus' descriptions of the sun and its satellites.

Instead of a marching band and drum majorettes, there was medieval music by an ensemble of specialists in the oldies but goodies of 1473. Instead of a traditional pep talk, there was a toast by Astronomy Professor Subrahamanyan Chandrasekhar.

Said Bruckner: "At Chicago, it's hard to shake the students out of the library. The party was a response to the feeling that there should be more mirth on this campus."

Thus today's Chicago. Although they no longer fear Purdue on that campus, and although they can no longer beat Ohio State, this is the one place with the wit to appreciate – and the lassitude to need – a big-time party for a Polish genius who never saw any football either.

7. Stanford: Pursuit of Preeminence

SPEAKING OF BOOKS and games, there is one
university that aims for excellence in each.

Then there is Stanford's way. Unlike the book havens in the Ivy League (where they play football but aren't really passionate about it) and at Chicago (which threw in the towel), Stanford tries to do it all and do it right. Good students and good athletes alike regularly head for the campus that has made Palo Alto the most famous college town in California.

Though Stanford football teams have in recent years infrequently reached the Rose Bowl, the Stanford way has, despite many changes in athletic and academic leaders, remained much as it was before and during the times I used to visit with the university's former athletic director, Joseph H. Ruetz, at Pacific-10 Conference games. The goal at Palo Alto then and ever since: number-one recognition nationally in both scholarship and sports.

Academically, Stanford continues to rank among the country's three or four leading universities as surveyed by the American Council of Education and other eminent organizations. And athletically – in more than one sport – Stanford is still contending for national championships and, more often than you might think, getting there.

A generation ago there were two Stanford Rose Bowl winners, and in every year since then, every athletic director, asked if there will be another Rose Bowl visit soon, has said the same thing: "We're shooting for this year."

Or as Ruetz said: "At Stanford, football is still in there with geology, pharmacology, and tennis."

ii

Although in the last half century, Harvard, Yale, the University of Chicago and other great institutions have deemphasized or abandoned football, Stanford doesn't see the point in retreat. "Variety," Ruetz said, "is what a university is all about – variety of learning and experience. Isn't diversity what you face in life? The athletic field provides another place for excellence to show itself."

His university is nothing if not diverse. In this century alone, Stanford has produced a remarkable balance of thirty-nine Rhodes Scholars and thirty-six All-American football players. Some of Stanford's best have become NFL All-Pros, quarterbacks John Brodie, Jim Plunkett and football's most recent Super Bowl winner, John Elway, among them.

But for a half century, more Stanford football players have gone into graduate school than pro football.

Fred E. Hargadon, dean of admissions when Ruetz was there, suggested that pursuit of excellence in many forms is a result of deliberate choice at a university where only 1,450 of 9,400 applicants can be accepted in a typical year "although 90 percent have been qualified." The emphasis, Hargadon said, "remains on a diverse student body representing many kinds of geographic areas, backgrounds, and talents."

Thus, good biologists, musicians, and athletes are consciously recruited each year.

But the athletes must also be able to make it in political science or perhaps economics, Hargadon added, because there is no physical education major at Stanford. And though at most universities, contrary to popular belief, a higher percentage of athletes than non-athletes graduate with their class, at Stanford it's ridiculous. Of those completing their Stanford athletic eligibility one recent year, 100 percent of the basketball team graduated and 91.8 percent of the football team.

So Stanford is different. Of course, it has always been different. One of its athletes, Hank Luisetti, revolutionized basketball, discarding the two-hand set shot of the game's early years for today's ubiquitous one-hander. And one of its coaches, Clark Shaughnessy, revolutionized football, bringing in the modern T Formation in 1940. Over the years, Luisetti, Shaughnessy, and four kinds of champion quarterbacks – left-hander Frankie Albert, precise passer Brodie, strongman Plunkett, and bomb-thrower Elway – have done a lot to characterize this most diverse of universities.

As Sociology Professor Sanford Dornbusch put it, there is no typical Stanford man. Instead, he said, "There is an enormous variety of persons all of whom think they're in the majority."

Even with the stipulation that variety is a virtue, doesn't the sweeping attention football gets detract from the educational purpose of a university such as Stanford?

That is a popular assessment – but don't number the school's athletic directors among those who agree with it.

"When you think it through, I don't see how you can conclude that college football is detracting," Ruetz said one Saturday afternoon at Stanford Stadium. "On Saturdays if there were no games, some students would adjourn to a pub, some would go to the beach, and some, naturally, would study. They do now. To assume that without football, the whole student body would focus on studies is unrealistic."

Nonetheless, big-time football as an entertainment item does seem to do more for the public and alumni than for college students. What's wrong with that statement?

"At Stanford, the athletic program is well supported by all three of those groups," Ruetz said. "With a student body of 11,500, including 6,500 undergraduates, we sell about 8,000 student season tickets – on a voluntary basis. On some campuses, football tickets are tied into a mandatory package, but not here, and our student support is excellent."

What do Stanford's professors have to say about that?

"With 1,110 faculty members, we sell 3,500 faculty and staff season tickets to football games. Most of the faculty are warmly in favor. An esoteric science club reunion, for instance, can only get a quorum on a football weekend."

Isn't Harvard superior today in the minds of some academicians precisely because it doesn't fool around with big-time football? Stanford's jock image must at times be harmful.

"On balance, a sports image is more helpful than harmful – that is, it gives you a better-rounded image – if you keep your academic and athletic programs sound and consistent with the university's goals and demands. In short, we think an intercollegiate athletic program is a good thing provided the coach maintains athletic integrity and the school maintains academic integrity. We make a point of both."

Your student-athletes are obviously serious about their classwork. Why shouldn't Stanford trim down to Ivy League-type football and quit trying to keep up in a conference as difficult as the Pac-10?

"First, we really don't have a choice. There aren't enough schools in our geographical area willing and able to compete in an Ivy-type conference. We can either accept the challenge of major intercollegiate competition or get out, and we think there are more than enough values in the challenge to meet it. Second, from a financial point of view, it would be disastrous for us to deemphasize football. Receipts from football support 70 percent of the Stanford athletic program in all sports at all levels – intercollegiate, club, and intramural."

If that's the case, shouldn't college players get paid? They're the lowest salaried workers in the country considering the revenue they generate.

"That's one way of looking at it. Another way is to realize that players don't generate all that football money. The crowds come to see the teams – the Stanford team or Notre Dame. If Notre Dame's players all quit school and played as the South Bend Tigers, they wouldn't draw five thousand against the Palo Alto Reds."

iv

Insofar as football players and other athletes are concerned, Stanford measures academic integrity in four ways. It keeps track of grade-point averages, academic majors, athletes graduating, and athletes going on to graduate study.

In one characteristic year, Ruetz said, "Our athletes maintained grade-point averages of 3.3 to 3.94 on a scale where 3.0 is a B and 4.0 an A. Thirty-five of our athletes majored in political science, thirty in economics, twenty-three psychology, nineteen English, nineteen history, eighteen engineering, and sixteen biology. Some 86.3 percent graduated with their class compared to the university-wide average of 85 and the national average of 50. And 83 per cent of our student-athletes went on to graduate school."

Doesn't that mean that, finally, at Stanford, books are more important than football? Ruetz, like most at Stanford, then and now, would not agree.

"No," he said. "What I'm saying is that the Stanford emphasis is on excellence in everything. That's what makes this university what it is."

8. USC: Football Builds a University

THE FINAL ARGUMENT in favor of football on campus is that it strengthens, rather than weakens, excellence in academics. It's a case that can be made at many universities, none more so than USC.

During the last three quarters of the twentieth century, the University of Southern California has reversed the usual college football pattern in America. In other regions, high-quality schools have made it a point to create high-profile football programs. At USC, high-profile football has helped create a high-quality university.

USC's major academic improvements have mostly come during the decades of three late-century presidencies, those of Norman Topping, John Hubbard and Steven Sample, all of whom, focusing first on classroom excellence, have intensified administration efforts in three disparate areas: to recruit eminent scholars, enrich the libraries, and build delightful buildings.

All this has made USC steadily more important. Its carefully landscaped campus today is as attractive as any in America – and conspicuously more pleasing than most – although the school's focus remains elsewhere, notably on education. And near the end of Hubbard's presidency (just before he rejoined the faculty for another long tour as a history professor), I visited with him several times about the view from the top, whence two things appeared to be self-evident.

- A long, successful run in intercollegiate football had, in Hubbard's view, largely made this university what it is. "Frankly, I have no idea what SC would be without football," he said. "It might now be an ordinary small college at best."

- Nonetheless, nearly a century of athletic success has left USC's athletic teams as "no more than a handsome auxiliary" to one of the nation's fine academic institutions. "The greatest thing we have going for us now is our increasing academic reputation," Hubbard said. "We have become in recent years one of the major research institutions of the United States. And this progress has been accompanied by steadily increasing quality in the three ingredients that make a university: faculty, students, and library."

The changes have been nationally recognized. "Any impartial observer looking at SC's total academic picture would have to say we've made a very significant improvement," the university's eighth president added. "I'd use the word dramatic, but that would be immodest."

ii

On his feet, moving around, Hubbard always looked a great deal more like a football coach than a college president. His were the rugged features and expansive bearing of an old grad who went to college on an athletic scholarship. In fact, though, growing up as the son of a college president, he was to spend most of his life studying British history or teaching it.

A World War II naval aviator, father of three daughters, he was also, as president of USC, an ex-officio assistant football coach who routinely rode the bench on Saturday afternoons wherever the Trojans played. The team during his presidency went to seven bowl games.

"And of the seven, we lost only one," Hubbard said one day, beaming.

How did that happen?

"It was Woody's best team," he said, identifying a famous Ohio State winner, Woody Hayes.

In the beginning, what got you interested in football?

"I have always been interested in all sports," Hubbard said, thinking of his boyhood in Texas and his school days there at the state university. "As far back as I can remember, sports have been part of my daily affairs."

What was your game as a boy?

"I tried to play every game there was. And I made one important discovery. I found that team sports are more enjoyable than anything individual – at least for me. I have felt since then that nothing people do is more beautiful than some kind of disciplined activity in unison."

In or out of athletics?

"Either. I love to see teamwork of any kind. I find soloists less appealing than symphonies or big bands. The old Benny Goodman and Tommy Dorsey (jazz) bands were examples of brilliant teamwork. In education, too, it's the cooperative aspect that is the most exciting. The way I look at this university, we have a lot of great academic stars – some magnificent individual performers – but what attracts me is the collegial atmosphere: the group sense of purpose, the team effort, if that's not too corny a term."

What's your idea of collegial?

"I'm speaking of the interaction between and among students, faculty and library. The academic word is synergism."

iii

Where, Hubbard was asked, does football fit into all that?

"A good athletic program is indispensable as a kind of adhesive that holds the university and community together," he said, "It keeps the alumni and our other friends interested in the university – actively interested."

But does big-time football really belong in an academic setting? When

Robert M. Hutchins was at the University of Chicago, he threw the football players out. What's your view of that?

"I understand it. But I can't say Chicago has been a greater university without football. It was already a great university when he took that step. Secondly, the fiscal picture on the college administration level is so much different now. Just ten years ago, my first SC budget was seventy million dollars. The next one will be three hundred million. For whatever reason, football is the activity that does the best job of attracting those who can help us. And the task of the administration is to channel interest in sports into other areas of the university."

How much exactly does football mean to USC in dollars and cents?

"There's no way to quantify it. Nobody knows how many friends we would have been able to make – or even what would have happened to SC – without sports. But we are sure that it's football that gets their interest now – ergo their generosity. And they are generous."

How can a mere game play such an energizing role in the affairs of a group of scholars?

"To a college administration, football is more than a game, it's an event. It comes under the rubric of tradition: the pre-game parties, the band marching across Exposition Park to the Coliseum, the song girls, the card stunts, the galloping Trojan horse. On a Saturday morning at SC during the football season, as many as ten different support (fund-raising) groups will gather on campus for brunch. The fiscal well-being of the university is tied up with these people. And their appearance on campus is tied up with the spectacle that is a Saturday-afternoon football game. The catalyst is the game."

How do you measure the importance of winning in football?

"By and large, I'd say athletic success leads to a meaningful increase in the resources of a university. I get a far better reception after we've beaten Notre Dame or won a game that's put us in the Rose Bowl. People know what I'm after, but almost invariably their opening gambit is, 'Great game.' After a defeat, those who represent a college feel like apologizing. Winning puts everyone in a better mood. People become proud of their institution. It makes for a more congenial atmosphere."

Coaches have a lot to do with winning. When John McKay left several years ago, why did you choose John Robinson as his successor?

"What I liked about Robinson was his broad and curious intellect. During a fund drive for KUSC – our classical music station – the most effective speaker I heard on the subject of what good music means in his personal and family life was John Robinson."

As to your personal future, you decided to resign the presidency after one decade. Why is ten years about the limit now for almost everybody in what used to be a lifetime vocation?

"The explanation is in the complexities today. A college president used to be an academic statesman, essentially. Today, the fiscal pressures make him a jack of all trades. It requires an energy level that is unbelievable. In an academic department, the energy teaching takes is bearable."

What are you going to do when you leave the university once for all?

"I decided that a long time ago. In my next incarnation, I'm going to come back as a sportswriter."

PART TWO

V. Champions: All Pros of All Kinds – 99

VI. Quaterbacks: Throwing and Thinking – 163

VII. Control: It's a Coach's Game Now – 205

VIII. Exemplar: Team of the Century – 275

CHAMPIONS:
All Pros of All Kinds

1. Red Grange, Galloping Ghost
2 Bronko Nagurski, Football's First Big Winner
3. Dick Daugherty: Watching the Game Change
4. Raymond Berry, Self-Made Player
5. Hugh McElhenny: Born into the Hall of Fame
6. Tom Mack: Is Money the Motivator?
7. Merlin Olsen: Concentration Is What Counts
8. O.J. Simpson: Rise and Fall of an Idol
9. Fred Dryer: Life in the NFL's Fantasy World
10. Ronnie Lott: Football Student
11. Paul Hornung: The Century's Most Decorated Player
12. Marcus Allen: The Play That Changed Everything
13. Gene Upshaw: All-Pro to All-Labor
14. Terrell Davis: Most Efficient of the Running Backs

Football was almost exclusively a college sport for a quarter century, but beginning in 1925 – beginning, to be precise, with the day Red Grange turned pro – its excellence and evolution have been embodied increasingly in the National (professional) Football League.

Organized by George Halas and others in 1919 as a jumped-up semi-pro league, the NFL floundered for awhile, then gained instant legitimacy and renown when Grange, its first bright star, joined Halas' Chicago Bears a few days after his last college game for a wintertime coast-to-coast barnstorming tour. For the first time, fans across the nation knew that pro football existed. For the first time, talented college players knew they had a future in cleats after graduation.

Since Grange, annual infusions of new talent plus the NFL's marked willingness to experiment, to improve and to evolve have meant that, across most of the century, the pros have not only had the best players but also the best game.

And since Grange, the growth and development of that game have been generated in large part by successive All-Pro athletes gifted with far-reaching individual brilliance. The exploits and significance of many of these transcendent athletes are in this chapter set down variously: as essays, personality profiles or interviews.

1. Red Grange, Galloping Ghost

*IN THE Roaring Twenties, Red Grange changed
the future of spectator sports in America.*

The most celebrated football player of the twentieth century, the most influential, the most popular in his own time, and perhaps the most controversial, was Harold (Red) Grange, a 1920s University of Illinois All-American halfback.

As a college junior in 1924, Grange caught the public's attention with the most dramatic game-day accomplishment of the century: Against powerful Michigan, he scored four touchdowns in the first twelve minutes on four long runs. Awed sportswriters could only estimate the distances: ninety-five, sixty-seven, forty-five and fifty-six yards. As a coup, it still seems impossible. (More on that on Page 106.)

A year later, Grange, known as the Galloping Ghost, parlayed the drama of his college life into his most historic achievement: putting the National Football League on the map.

Before Grange turned pro, the NFL was a back-page item in the newspapers, literally, and a financial failure at the gate. With its unique new star, the league became an overnight success.

There has never been an American sports idol like Grange, and it is sobering to reflect on what pro football was without him in an era when big games attracted three or four thousand spectators. Sometimes in those years before Grange, in places like Green Bay and other NFL franchise cities in Wisconsin and Ohio, the entire crowd, at gametime, stood along the sidelines. For several years, George Halas wrote all the game stories that appeared in any Chicago newspaper the day after the Chicago Bears won or lost.

Regularly, Halas, who doubled as club owner and All-Pro end, changed clothes hurriedly when the games were over and made the rounds of all the city's newspapers, of which there were once seven. On the morning before a Bear game, Halas considered himself a lucky man if the *Chicago Tribune* kept a paragraph or two of the Sunday-advance story he had left with the editors. Some Chicago editors cut him more than that.

It was similar or worse in New York until suddenly, on December 6, 1925, Grange was there. Astonishing every newspaper in the city and alarming every college in the country, Grange, playing left halfback for the Bears against the New York Giants, was the magnet for an over-capacity crowd of sixty-five thousand New Yorkers who overflowed the Polo Grounds. He was then twenty-two years old. Playing another game that first week with the Bears, Grange drew another sixty-five thousand in Philadelphia; and eventually he topped that in Los Angeles, where Coliseum capacity was then 65,270. He sold every seat. His share of the Los Angeles gate receipts came to $49,000. He made about $1 million in his first three years with the Bears, when, for the first time, they also sold out their own stadium, the venerable Wrigley Field, then and now the summer home of the Cubs.

The NFL was suddenly respectable – although, to his surprise, Grange wasn't. He had dishonored himself in the eyes of millions of Americans. In particular, two groups of his countrymen complained that Grange had let them down: the nation's church-minded, who said he had desecrated the Sabbath, and the amateur-minded, who said he had desecrated college football.

One week before Grange's debut with the Chicago Bears, he had played his last college game against Ohio State, at tailback in the old Single Wing, dazzling the folks that day not with runs but passes. He had completed nine of twelve – which, this year, wouldn't have been a bad day's work for some NFL quarterbacks, let alone running backs. But this year, no young football player could have turned pro immediately after his final college game. Modern-day rules prohibit that.

The world was different in the fall of 1925, when, as Grange pondered whether to leave Illinois to take a pro offer, there was a national debate over whether he should. Insane as it might seem to today's Americans, the controversy disrupted the country. Everybody appeared to be taking sides. To many citizens, turning pro was an act of immorality. To many others – to those who, for example, worked six days a week in the era of the ten-hour day – it was a chance to see Red Grange on Sunday.

But Sunday was for church and reflection, the devoutly religious said. Grange was denounced from pulpit to pulpit. He was also denounced by his own coach, the Illinois veteran, Bob Zuppke, for putting on a pro's uniform. It wasn't only church people who called turning pro immoral. It was the college people who said it loudest.

As of the mid-1920s, they and many of their countrymen had been influenced – some said brainwashed – by the amateur movement's Olympic and college sports leaders, Avery Brundage prominently among them, who thought of pro football as faintly but definitely wicked, even un-American. In that faraway interval of the twentieth century, college football was revered, the pros detested and dreaded.

"Nobody today realizes how hard the colleges fought pro ball," Grange said in one of his last interviews after retiring to Florida in 1983. "The colleges were afraid that pro football would ruin college football. I'd have been more popular with some people if I'd joined Al Capone's mob in Chicago instead of the Bears."

In Los Angeles, there were those who much preferred Capone. Leaders of the two Los Angeles universities, USC and UCLA, combined forces to enlist the newspapers and lobby the City Council in a campaign to keep the pros out of the publicly owned Coliseum for even exhibition games. The colleges had been negligent once: Underestimating pro football, they had shortsightedly allowed Grange to draw his sixty-five thousand to the only Los Angeles stadium that could hold that many.

So now, they vowed never to repeat that mistake. And with the help of the press of that day, USC and UCLA were wildly successful. After Grange's one Los Angeles appearance, the college campaign, renewed annually, kept the pros out of California for twenty years. Thus in 1927, when the NFL placed a franchise in Los Angeles for the first time, the team was denied access to the Coliseum by a consortium including, among others, USC, UCLA, the *Los Angeles Times*, the Los Angeles City Council and the Los Angeles County Board of Supervisors. Forced to play its entire schedule on the road that season, Los Angeles' first NFL team gave up a year later and moved away.

Not until 1946, when Cleveland Rams owner Dan Reeves orchestrated a successful Coliseum campaign of his own, did the pros regain the right that Grange had – the right to play in the city's stadium on the afternoons when the colleges were absent.

The history of America in the twentieth century often appears to be a serial story of one controversy after another, although, in retrospect, most of the fussing seems quaint or irrelevant or both. The national controversy over Grange in 1925 was characteristic. He was himself swept up in it, wavering at times before deciding to accept a professional offer. What convinced him was a guaranteed $100,000 in a day when $100,000 was worth a million or more in end-of-the century dollars.

He never regretted it, he said, even though he never graduated from college (antedating a practice that is unhappily widespread today) and even though in his sophomore year with the Bears he injured a knee so severely that thereafter he could only make All-Pro three times.

His speed, impaired by the injury, had been his longest suit, as it was to be later for Jim Brown, O.J. Simpson, Eric Dickerson and other All-Pros. In truth, Grange had preferred track over football both in high school and for awhile at college, where he went out for football only at the insistence of Illinois fraternity fellows.

"The boys at Zeta Psi changed my mind," Grange, who wore uniform number 77, said in Florida the day he turned seventy-seven, adding that they changed it by thumping him harder with paddles than necessary during freshman hazing.

He was still hale and hearty in his seventies, unlike many broken-down old pros, and he was enjoying his time in a Florida community at Indian Lake with his wife, Margaret, who had been a twenty-four-year-old flight attendant the year he became a married man at thirty-eight. Theirs was a small house with a white picket fence in front but no football trophies inside. "I sent all my trophies and pictures to Illinois or the Hall of Fame," he said.

The first football player to earn enough money to retire on, Grange said he never joined the joggers who ran along the Florida beach near his home. He apparently belonged to Exercisers Anonymous. "If you have a car," he asked, "why run?"

Born in 1903, Grange had been more ambitious in his boyhood at Wheaton, Illinois, where he was raised by a single father, a lumberman. In four high school years, the Galloping Ghost earned sixteen letters in football, basketball, baseball and track.

He grew up to be a 166-pound six-footer in a day when that didn't seem abnormal for football players. His high school goal, however, was to be a big league baseball player, so he strengthened and added to his slight frame with a summer job hauling ice in Wheaton neighborhoods. From the back end of a horse-drawn wagon in the years before electrical refrigeration, Grange tuned up by lifting two-hundred-pound blocks of ice, previewing, if unwittingly, the era of weight-lifting. Before he was the Galloping Ghost, he was known to the Big Ten as the Wheaton Iceman.

Like all of football's great running backs, the Wheaton Iceman could never explain exactly what he did on a crowded, broken field while playing keep-away with eleven opponents. But there was one clue. As a high school athlete, he said, he had owned a hound dog named Jack who "loved to run and play like all dogs."

One day, Grange said, "I got Jack in a corner, boxed him in, and moved this way and that to keep him off me. As long as I kept jumping from side to side, Jack couldn't touch me."

That gave Grange an idea. Thereafter, whenever he had the time, he worked out with Jack.

"Whether that helped me on the football field," he said, "I don't know."

The great backs never know.

iii

The morning of the Michigan-Illinois game of 1924, when Grange was a college junior, dawned bright and clear and hot. The temperature rose to eighty as the crowds on the special trains began rolling in from everywhere to see not just a redheaded Illinois All-American but an event that had been billed as the game of the century.

It might have been the most spotlighted football game ever. For it matched the Big Ten's two great teams in an age when the great Midwest was the hotbed of college football. It was a matchup of undefeated teams. In 1923, Illinois and Michigan had tied for the conference title with identical 8-0 records. The Illini had not lost in, altogether, ten games. The Wolverines had not lost in twenty. Their coaches were (and are still remembered as) two of the better ones of football's first hundred years, Zuppke versus Michigan's Fielding H. (Hurry Up) Yost. There was also a matchup of feared triple-threaters, Grange versus the Michigan captain, Herb Steger. Adding to the fun, Illinois was dedicating the new stadium it has played in ever since. And though tickets were expensive ($2.50 per seat), all 66,609 seats had been sold for eleven months.

For such an event today, football fans would flock in by automobile and airplane. In 1924, when automobiles were few and planes fewer, they came by special train. Forty special trains in all moved into Urbana, Illinois, site of the game, from Chicago alone. Other trains from Detroit carried twelve thousand Michigan students and alumni. Until gametime, the partying Michigan people had had the most fun. They'd come on overnight trains – overnight each way.

Sleeping cars and dining cars were parked all over Urbana, where one reporter counted what was then called the rolling stock of six railroads: Santa Fe, Northwestern, Erie, Soo Line, Burlington, and Illinois Central.

Five years before the disruptive 1929 stockmarket crash that led to the Great Depression, Urbana's big-spending visitors bought up most of what they could find that day in the way of groceries, bottled refreshments, restaurant fare and suchlike goods in a small college town and waited for a big game that wasn't quite what they'd bargained for. In an era of low-scoring, bitterly fought football, they had expected to see the nation's top two teams in an even contest.

And whenever Grange could be kept away from the ball, the game *was* reasonably close. In fact, in the non-Grange minutes, and there were many of them, Michigan had the better of what action there was, winning, 14-0. With Grange's work added in, Illinois coasted, 39-14.

After ending the suspense instantly with his four first-quarter touchdowns, Grange sat out the second quarter but returned in the second half to score his fifth touchdown and throw a touchdown pass as the architect of all six Illinois scores. Playing both ways for forty-five minutes, he also intercepted a pass.

Amos Alonzo Stagg, one of football's great early-century coaches, was asked later what happened. "In the first twelve minutes," Stagg said, "Red Grange scored four touchdowns against the mighty Michigan machine, the most spectacular single-handed performance ever made in a major game."

A Michigan writer, E.A. Batchelor, who covered the 1924 Illinois game for the *Detroit News*, agreed. "What made it special," he wrote, "is that Grange ran wild against a championship contender in a game that was expected to settle the championship."

He did this, moreover, in circumstances that were less than ideal in two respects. First, graduation had taken away most of the Illini linemen who the year before had made possible their perfect season. Second, the best two remaining Illinois blockers were ill or injured or both.

Grange nonetheless burst across the goal line five times, zigging, zagging, stiff-arming and sprinting ghost-like for immense distances whose exact length has been in dispute ever since. The sportswriters of the 1920s were less interested in facts than in writing football poetry or making up nicknames like Four Horsemen, Galloping Ghost and Wheaton Iceman. What's more, they worked for newspapers with multiple deadlines that came and went every hour or so. For a reporter, covering football in those days was a matter of glancing up from his typewriter only occasionally; and in a time when 6-0, 7-6 and 12-7 games were common, he didn't miss too much.

Thus instead of making precise notes, all reporters got in the habit of relying on college publicists for pertinent yardage details. But the Michigan-Illinois game that year was a home game for Illinois, and the members of the Illinois public relations department, all Grange fans, spent so much time jumping up and down and cheering that they missed many of the details. For example, there is no reliable information on how many passes the Illinois passer – a man named Red Grange – threw that afternoon. Reporters and publicists alike agreed afterward only that he completed six and attempted "about ten."

They also agreed that he raced "at least ninety yards" for his touchdown on the opening kickoff. Most put it down at ninety-five. For Grange's other three touchdowns in the first twelve minutes, there is a consensus – but no agreement – that he ran about sixty-seven, forty-five and fifty-six yards. Everybody in the press box got a different number on the forty-five yard touchdown, one writer calling it forty-one yards, another fifty-one, with the rest in between. Most landed near forty-five.

The only fact they all got the same on every touchdown is where Grange finished up, which was in the end zone.

So it was a unique day. After a century of football, Grange's achievement stands alone. No football player since that afternoon has accomplished anything of comparable significance, no football player, that is, save Grange himself when he turned pro – that long ago December in New York. He was a legend who delivered. A 1920s newspaper bard said this about the Galloping Ghost:

There are two shapes now moving, two ghosts that drift and glide,
And which of them to tackle, each rival must decide;
They shift with spectral swiftness across the swarded range,
And one of them's a shadow, and one of them is Grange.

2. Bronko Nagurski, Football's First Big Winner

IN THE DAYS when football was played largely on the ground, everyone was in awe of another Chicago ballcarrier.

Of the All-Pro football players who stirred America in the twentieth century, Bronko Nagurski joined Red Grange and Sammy Baugh in the first wave. And to sports fans, each symbolized something different.

Baugh was a precision passer, Grange a matchless open-field runner, Nagurski the ultimate power symbol.

As a physical specimen, Nagurski, of the three, was the most masterful. In a time when the game wasn't as intellectually demanding as it was to become, Nagurski took charge as a famously feared power runner who seemed to be the essence of what football was all about. Even so, ironically, in his two biggest games, this embodiment of football's brute force helped demonstrate the tactical superiority of the forward pass. In championships won as a passer, Nagurski equaled Baugh: two each.

A 225-pound fullback standing six-two, Nagurski, who in 1933 led the Chicago Bears to victory in the National Football League's first championship game, is identified in his hometown as the greatest football player of all time. The town is International Falls, which is in the far north of Minnesota.

There the leading hotel, a new Holiday Inn, opened a Bronko Nagurski Room one July in the big fullback's final years. A tinted, life-size Nagurski photo was unveiled when the room, a banquet hall, was dedicated, and everybody was there – almost everybody in Kouchiching County, that is – except Nagurski, who refused to come. "That's Bronko," a friend said that summer. "He's a shy one. Always has been."

In his seventies, Nagurski was then residing on the U.S.-Canada border at Rainy Lake, just four miles up the Rainy River from International Falls (population 6,940). With his wife, the former Eileen Kane, with whom Nagurski raised six children, he had moved into the lakeside cottage during the years when he was playing three positions – tackle and linebacker as well as fullback – for the 1930s Bears.

Numerous Kanes and Nagurskis lived in the neighborhood in those years and still do. It's a neighborhood that is alternately a winter wonderland and a domain of brief, joyous summers. And the summer Bronko was seventy-five, his relatives and in-laws held a family reunion, with Bronko and Eileen as guests of honor.

Eileen enjoyed herself as usual, but Bronko, of course, wouldn't come. "He's reclusive," Dave Siegel, a reporter for the *International Falls Daily Journal*, said. "We've been trying to get an updated file picture of Nagurski for ten years, and we hung around the reunion all day, but no luck."

He was easier to shoot in the 1930s, when, at one time or another, almost every Chicago cameraman caught Nagurski ferrying an opponent or two across the goal line on his back. For decades, his name summoned the raw energy of football. And to this day, they point out the brick wall in Chicago that Nagurski cracked when he ran into it carrying a football one fall afternoon in Wrigley Field, home of the Cubs and, then, the Bears. Scoring the winning touchdown in that game – at the south end of a cramped field where the end zone was only nine yards deep – Nagurski stomped on two opponents, leaving one unconscious and the other with a broken shoulder. Next he collided with a goal post and spun into the wall, which stopped him at last. Picking himself up, he told a teammate, "That last guy hit pretty hard."

At an NFL game years later, when former quarterback Fran Tarkenton asked him about that day, Nagurski remembered everything but fracturing the wall.

"But I've seen the crack myself," Tarkenton said.

"Oh, c'mon now," Nagurski said. "No human could crack a brick wall."

No human, maybe. But Nagurski had super-human strength. Everybody who played in that era said so. He was the NFL's first big winner, and he was the one they talked about the most whenever old-timers got together, as they did one summer in Canton, Ohio, home of the Pro Football Hall of Fame. "I saw Nagurski for the first time when I was an NFL rookie," remembered Don Hutson, who has ranked as one of football's top two or three receivers, all-time, since his All-Pro days at Green Bay. "At Alabama, I'd been known as a good defensive end, so I played Nagurski the way I'd play a Georgia fullback. On first down they gave him the ball, and he ran straight over me. I mean he ran me down and kept going without breaking stride."

Arch-rival Green Bay fullback-linebacker Clark Hinkle recalled: "He was the most bruising runner ever. The first time I tackled Nagurski, I had to have five stitches in my face. My biggest thrill in football was the day he announced his retirement."

At their Canton reunion that summer, Hutson and Hinkle were joined eventually by no fewer than four other all-timers: center Mel Hein, halfback Johnny Blood (McNally), guard Danny Fortmann, and, of all people, Bronko Nagurski himself. Hutson and Blood lured Bronko out of International Falls, Hein said, by putting pressure on Eileen Nagurski, somehow persuading her to fly in with the Recluse of Rainy Lake.

It isn't true that he hadn't left his lakeside cottage for twenty years, but he hadn't left it often, and his appearance at Canton made the show for old-time fans.

Hein, the old New York Giants' Hall of Fame center, was asked how the Hutson-Blood connection could get Nagurski all the way to Canton when the International Falls people couldn't get him downtown. "In the last few years, Hutson and the rest of us have called on Bronko at the lake," Hein said. "He knows what we look like, and we know what he looks like now. So he doesn't mind being around us. But I think he's embarrassed to show himself in public at International Falls. He'd rather they remember him as he used to be, as he used to look, when he had his strength – when he was tough and trim, and awesomely vigorous."

ii

In his last years, he had lost a lot of the vigor, no doubt about that, but Nagurski was still spunky, still aggressive, still forthright. Braced by a visiting reporter one day, he was asked if he sometimes wore his Hall of Fame ring. Pointing one massive but arthritically gnarled hand at the other, he said: "I can't get it on any more, but I still carry it around with me." And, reaching deep into a front pants pocket, he brought it out and showed it happily as a bride – a size nineteen and a half ring. It was the largest player's ring ever made until well into the Super Bowl era, when the 300-pounders arrived to dismantle all the records.

Fact is, to the end, much of Nagurski was still a match for many of the game's biggest NFL people. He still had those massive arms and wrists. His collar size was nineteen. He had ballooned to 300 himself until, reluctantly but firmly, taking some of it off. During the 1930s, in an era of 175-pound linemen and 165-pound backs, he had been two or three sizes bigger than the other players. And he was rock hard. "Running into Bronko was like getting an electric shock," Red Grange said.

Post-NFL, as introverted as ever, Nagurski seemed genuinely distressed by personal questions. When a reporter asked him how fast he was in 1933, he grinned and said, "Fast enough." Asked about his dimensions, he said, "I was big enough." Later, he also said he was strong enough. He would talk some about football, but not much about himself. His preference was to let the old Nagurski records do the talking.

They have plenty to say. As a 1930-37 running back, Nagurski gained more than three thousand yards against NFL teams and averaged 4.4 – an excellent number for a fullback in a day that was long before the big-play era. Simultaneously, as a sixty-minute regular, he was also excelling as an offensive tackle, defensive tackle, and linebacker. "Most versatile football player ever," his college coach, Doc Spears, once said of Nagurski, who came to fame at the University of Minnesota in the years when some of us first saw him in 1927-29. "He could be All-American at any position."

At Minnesota he was, in fact, a consensus All-American at two positions, tackle and fullback – the only football player of the century with that distinction.

Still, in a depressed time, his income never reflected his skills. Looking back, he said: "The first contract I signed with (Bear owner-coach George Halas) was for $5,000. Even though I had a good year, my salary was cut to $4,500 my second year. The Depression was on, and the club was losing money. I got $3,700 my third year with the Bears, and that's where my salary stayed. They finally upped it to $5,000 again in 1937 when I talked about retiring. But when I asked for $6,000 in 1938, they turned me down. I went home figuring they'd call me, but they never did."

So in 1938, in the prime of his career, age twenty-nine, Nagurski slipped away to the obscurity of Rainy Lake, emerging only to wrestle occasionally at county fairs – a lucrative pastime he hated – and to play one wartime season with the Bears in 1943. He was then thirty-five. Significantly, they won the NFL championship again that season – their third in Nagurski's years. It may also be significant that in all the years since 1943, the Bears – minus Nagurski – have won but two more championships.

iii

In the picturesque Canadian border community of International Falls, there is now a liquor store on an historic site at Third Avenue and Third Street. Until age fifty-five, when he retired from the business world, Bronko Nagurski pumped gas on that corner. In the whole of America today, there probably isn't another old pro working in a service station – certainly not another old All-Pro – but Nagurski lived in a different time.

Needing work, he bought the International Falls Pure Oil station after leaving the Bears, and, in a long-gone American era when service stations actually offered service, he worked the place alone, coming out to fill your tank himself whether it was ninety above or ninety below.

In the chilly attic of America, it was more often the latter. But the people of greater International Falls don't seem to mind the weather as, celebrating winters, they barge around on the coldest days of the year. They love the town's designation – Ice Box of the Nation – and they take great pride in hearing that theirs is the coldest weather in the U.S.

Among those admiring the place have been four generations of Nagurskis, beginning with Bronko's parents, who for years ran a mom-and-pop grocery store at Ninth Avenue and Eighth Street. They had migrated from the Ukraine to the village of Rainy River, Canada, where Bronko was born into a family that was to include two boys and two girls. He was four when they moved across the river to America, where, early on, he acquired what has been termed the most intimidating name in sports. When playmates couldn't pronounce his given name, Bronislau, they started calling him Bronko. A violinist might prefer Bronislau, but in football, as an opponent said, the very name of the man, Bronko Nagurski, struck a note of terror.

Four and a half miles out of International Falls, going north in Nagurski's time, the scent was of pine trees and wood-burning fireplaces as you came first to the old fullback's extensive vegetable garden. It stretched a half block along the lakeshore road. And behind the garden, snug in a wooded acre or two, stood the little Nagurski cottage with its wide green front lawn that swept some thirty-five yards down to the lake. The lone sound emerged from a Boise Cascade lumber train whistling in the distance.

The conversation piece in the little cottage when the massive fullback lived there was another life-size color photo of Nagurski running the ball.

He hadn't seen the inside of a football stadium in years, he said, although he always kept up on television, watching the Bears and other teams regularly. He said the Bears had developed a tendency to rely too heavily on their best running back. "They overworked Gale Sayers," he said, "and they overworked Walter Payton. The Bears would be better with more balance." The implication was that they were better balanced in their championship seasons in the 1930s, so Nagurski was asked how often he carried the ball in a typical pro game. "Ten or twelve times," he said after thinking about it for a moment. "Of course, in those days, we had to play defense, too. We had to save something for that. But I think fifteen carries is about right for a running back."

Though it's hard to believe Nagurski built his workhorse reputation carrying the ball only ten or twelve times a game, he was a reliable source, obviously. His knees weren't what they once were but his mind was. And he'd had a lot of time at Rainy Lake to remember.

iv

If anyone had thought of it, Super Bowl would have been a good name for the NFL's first championship game. It was pro football's event of the year in 1933, when the fourteen-year-old league was first split into Eastern and Western divisions. A Christmas-Week attraction in Chicago's Wrigley Field, the '33 title game set the Eastern-Champion New York Giants against the Bears, best of the West. And it showcased Bronko Nagurski, the first of the MVPs in the league's long title series.

To get the two decisive touchdowns of a 23-21 spectacular, rarely matched in the later, less exciting, more prominent Super Bowl era, Nagurski reared up and threw the ball. He only faked the plunges that worried 1930s defensive teams the most. Both times, as he thundered toward the line of scrimmage, the powerful fullback straightened up, jumped like a basketball player, and passed the ball with enough touch and accuracy to get touchdowns on eight- and thirty-three-yard plays. Before he delivered the longer of these passes in the fourth quarter, the Giants had moved into a 21-16 lead. They never led again.

The massive fullback didn't realize it that day – and neither did his coach, George Halas – but Nagurski had won the game with an early example of football's play-action pass. In today's game, the running back fakes the run and the quarterback does the throwing, but Nagurski was man enough to handle both responsibilities himself.

Asked about his winning throws, however, Nagurski said, simply, "I wasn't much passer."

Maybe not but, the year before, he'd thrown a pass to Grange that won a specially arranged one-game playoff for the 1932 league championship against the old Portsmouth Spartans. That throw changed the game. Until then, the ball could only be lawfully launched from a point at least five yards behind the line, and Portsmouth protested, unsuccessfully, that Nagurski's pass was illegal. The 1932 controversy persuaded the NFL to legalize passes from any point in the backfield beginning in 1933, when Nagurski got off his title-game touchdown passes against the Giants. Because few other football rule changes have ever been comparably influential, the removal of the five-yard restriction put Nagurski in the history books if he had never, before or later, touched the ball.

The New York center-linebacker, Hein, who lost the championship game to Nagurski's touchdown passes, could remember years later only the big man's runs. "Bronko was the toughest running back I ever met," Hein said. "If you hit him low, he'd run over you. When you hit him high, he'd knock you down, and then run over you."

Thus the irony of Nagurski remains: Though his passing is responsible for his place in history as a winner, people have always talked only about the other Bronko, the crushing ballcarrier. There are countless stories about him. At Midwest sports banquets into the mid-century years, they liked to talk about the day that the Pittsburgh Steelers' special car derailed with a sickening jolt on their train trip home from a defeat in Chicago. As the Steelers scrambled away from the train, their coach, Forrest (Jap) Douds, shouted after them, "Run for your lives, men, Nagurski is still after you!"

A quarter century following his retirement, when Nagurski was guest of honor at the annual New York dinner meeting of the Baseball Writers Association of America, an applause meter would have given him the unanimous decision for the night, people said. For the century, maybe.

3. Dick Daugherty: Watching the Game Change

AS FOOTBALL EVOLVED toward an ever more sophisticated sport, it also evolved into a much longer workday for the players.

From its power base in the 1920s and '30s, football began to move in the 1940s into a game that was both a mental and physical challenge. The T Formation was taking over, and the forward pass was getting to be a familiar play, but the daily intensity and focus of the modern football lifestyle was not yet. As of the mid-1950s, the laid-back day-to-day routine of the average NFL player was basically unchanged from Red Grange's time.

But change was coming. In Los Angeles, the landmark year was 1955, when scholarly Sid Gillman took charge of the Rams and won the division as a rookie NFL coach. Under Gillman, who in his coaching outlook was a scientist like fellow Ohioan Paul Brown, the game became a different way of life for Los Angeles' players, as I learned by visiting with them.

The most articulate of these players was All-Pro linebacker Dick Daugherty, who also had been my most reliable source on the 1949-51 team, when in three consecutive years the Rams played in the NFL championship game, the Super Bowl of that distant age. By 1959, Gillman's last year in Los Angeles, Daugherty alone of that team's active personnel wore the black-and-gold 1951 watch, the only trophy of the only world championship the Rams won in forty-nine years in Los Angeles. The attrition of but eight years had wiped out all thirty-four of Daugherty's teammates.

Looking back one day, he said, "It would have been amusing to bring in the 1951 team for one week at the end of the '50s. They'd have thought somebody invented a new game."

Making a comment that could have been made by any NFL predecessor in the 1920s or '30s, Daugherty said, "When I first came up (in 1950), a football career was fun seven days a week. There were two hours of practice a day and parties every night, except Saturday."

By 1960, "It was only fun on Sunday afternoons," he said. "The rest of the time, football players were businessmen – on the job at 9 o'clock, home at 5:30 or 6."

How did the Rams get ready to win the NFL championship in 1951 with only two hours of practice a day?

"We didn't spend much time on movies," Daugherty said. "Instead of exchanging movies with the other teams, we sent scouts to every game, and all we had to do was look over the scouting report. It didn't take long. Suppose I was going up against (guard) Ray Bray of the Bears. The report on Bray would give me this information: 'Been in the league seven years, one of the toughest guys in the league, will knock your hat off and step on your face.' I could digest a report like that by noon on Tuesday and take the rest of the week off."

What kind of scouting reports did Gillman ask for?

"We got the reports on a movie screen. If we were playing the Bears, for instance, we had the movies of three different Bear games, and we ran them back and forth, over and over. The Bears still had guys who would step on your face, but now we could see exactly how they went about it."

Why did it take a week to get through a horror movie?

"Everything took longer by then. The whole bit was more complicated than in the old days, when a football practice was a lark. In my rookie year, it required practically no mental effort. In a typical week in 1951, we spent half our time running through every offensive play we had. We spent the rest of the time polishing up the only two defenses we had. We could have done that in our sleep. In fact, I often did."

114

How would you describe the difference in the years after you began exchanging movies?

"We began making an original approach to each new game. We concentrated on just a small percentage of the plays we were capable of operating, and we varied them specifically to fit the other team's weaknesses. Preparing for a football game became a full-time thinking job, and the biggest change was on defense. We had more than two hundred defenses under Gillman, compared to the two we had in 1951."

Quarterback Bob Waterfield won two championships for the Rams (one in Cleveland in 1945 before the team moved to Los Angeles, the second in 1951). How do you suppose he would have done against two hundred defenses?

"Bob was a quarterback who would have thought of something. I remember the day in Chicago when one of their best players, George Connor, was giving us some trouble. We had some great players on our team, too, including Tom Fears at one end and Dan Towler at fullback, but we couldn't move the Bears with the plays we'd been practicing every blasted morning for five months. So Waterfield improvised in the huddle. He turned to Fears and said, 'Listen, Fears, if Connor goes out wide with you this time, I'll send Towler through the hole he leaves. If Connor stays in the line, I'll throw you a quick one. Be ready for anything.' Connor went with Fears, and Towler went for a touchdown. Now, that's exactly the way we did things after Gillman came in – except we didn't improvise in the huddle. We prepared special plays like that all week."

What else was different in your early years?

"The year I came up, the coaches' idea of mental preparation was a memory test. Before every game in 1951, when we won the NFL title, we had to memorize the names and numbers of all the players on the other side. If you missed one number, it was an automatic fine."

That was Jumbo Joe Stydahar's first year as the Rams' head coach, and I remember there were a lot of fines.

"I think Tom Fears still holds the club's all-time practice-field record. Tom had one argument with Stydahar that went on for fifteen minutes. And every time Tom shouted something at him, Jumbo raised the price. Jumbo won the argument by rounding out the fine at an even one thousand dollars."

What was the original crime?

"Tom had been one minute late for practice."

4. Raymond Berry, Self-Made Player

*MOST ALL-PROS are gifted athletes. A few, though, have
been self-made players whom practice made almost perfect.*

Raymond Berry was a skinny, near-sighted, crooked-legged, bum-backed
Texan who, in the decade after 1955, as a receiver for the old Baltimore
Colts, played his way into the Hall of Fame by practicing football
thoughtfully, meticulously, scientifically. As the NFL's coaches became
more systematic and organized in the 1950s and '60s, players like Berry
and his quarterback – another Hall of Famer named John Unitas – refined
their skills with hard work and dedication.

Berry and Unitas shared three things in common: They formed the
greatest passing combination of their age, they led the Colts to two NFL
championships, and they did it as, fundamentally, self-made football
players. Neither was born to win championships or, indeed, even play in
the NFL. But they helped set a standard for effort and dedication that has
since been followed by such All-Pros as Emmitt Smith, Jerry Rice and
others who began with much greater natural talent.

Berry in particular made more out of less than any other pro I've
known – probably any other twentieth-century football player. In addition
to his uneven legs and pain-wracked back, the fingers on one of his hands
were permanently out of joint, and his eyes were a joke. He was the first
big-time athlete to wear contact lenses, and, whenever the sun was bright
behind Unitas, Berry put on specially designed bug-eyed dark glasses.

For all his physical flaws, he compensated with a shrewd and unique
practice program. And the first year Berry made All-Pro, I tracked him
down during the week before a Baltimore game and asked him what he
worked on in practice.

"As a pass receiver, the payoff for me," he said, "is getting my hands
on the ball, and holding it. So I have a daily hand drill that's the most
important thing I do in practice. Although I've been playing this game for
quite a few years, I've found that I can't do such a simple thing as catch
a football unless I work at it regularly."

During your hand drills, I asked him, what are you specifically trying
to achieve?

"My objective," Berry said, "is one hundred percent concentration on
the two parts of the job: watching the ball into my hands, and getting it
under my arm fast."

When you're working on this, what is Unitas doing?

"I don't rightly know, because I never use the regular passer in practice. Our practice goals are so different that it would get Unitas into bad habits if he worked with me. In a practice situation, his goal is to throw good passes, and mine is to catch bad ones. I ask the fellow who works with me – it's usually Billy Pricer, the (backup) fullback – to throw the ball over my head, on my shoes, behind me, and everywhere else. What I'm doing with Pricer is simulating the tail end of a pattern when I might have to move away from where Unitas expects me to be. Or Unitas might be rushed into less than a perfect throw."

Is Pricer any threat to Unitas?

"Billy has a good arm. He stands twenty-five yards away and slams it in. We work with a backstop to block overthrows because part of the time, I turn my back to him. He fires at one of my ears, and hollers, 'Ball.' "

For what period of time do you actually work with Unitas at practice each day?

"It's a matter of seconds, not minutes. We're lucky if we get in twenty minutes a week. A pro team is trained and polished not during the week but at training camp. It doesn't matter how tired you get in July when you're not playing games. But when the season starts, overwork is the worst thing you can do. The trouble with even one day of overwork during the week is that you can't recover by the weekend. At least seventy-five percent of the job of catching passes is done by the legs."

Getting under the ball?

"Footwork, yes, but also the spring. It takes a good spring to get a lot of balls, and when your legs are tired, you don't have the pep for it. You drop more balls when you're tired."

"You dropped one the other day. What did Unitas say?

"He said, 'Pricer can play quarterback for this club, Berry, but what's he going to use for receivers?' "

5. Hugh McElhenny: Born into the Hall of Fame

STAR RUNNERS, UNLIKE other stars, are born great. But few have ever matched this ballcarrier's greatness.

They called him Hustlin' Hugh. Or simply the King. And there are those who still think of Hugh McElhenny as the greatest running back of the century. For he was born to play football the way every daydreamer loves to do it: with flash and dash and the open-field grace to leave a trail of empty-handed tacklers lying behind him.

McElhenny came up in 1952 when for the first time most NFL coaches were experimenting with creative offenses that gave high-skill players like him the opportunity to play elegantly. And elegant he was. On his first play from scrimmage, starting a Hall of Fame career as a San Francisco 49ers rookie, McElhenny ran for a forty-yard touchdown.

Thereafter he was to show that although running backs aren't renowned for durability, he had that, too. The year he turned pro after an All-American career at the University of Washington, there were forty-six other halfbacks in the National Football League. By 1960, McElhenny and Frank Gifford were the sole survivors of their halfback generation.

"It's sort of a Last Man's Club," McElhenny told me in San Francisco one day. "They say that (Ram defensive tackle) Big Daddy Lipscomb is surprised there are any of us left."

As a halfback or tailback – the primary or featured running back on every team he played on – McElhenny was to have thirteen NFL seasons in all, most of them big seasons, for the 49ers, Minnesota Vikings, New York Giants and Detroit Lions. And during his last year with the 49ers, I looked him up because I agreed with him that as an NFL running back, he was nowhere near the end – a view the 49ers disputed. They were to regret it.

I asked him the obvious question that day: What accounts for the rapid turnover of running backs in pro football?

"Halfbacks are always moving full steam when they get hit," McElhenny said. "Linemen take a beating, too, but it's a quieter beating – like taking six-inch punches in the ring all night. Halfbacks take haymakers. They're knocked out of football in about three years on the average."

How have you managed to last three times as long?

"Some people say I've been plain lucky. Another guy, (San Francisco fullback) Joe Perry, says it's because I never threw a block in eight years with the 49ers. Take your choice."

The ability to move fast is one of your strengths. What's the importance of speed to a running back?

"I'd say balance is more important. By balance, I mean a feel for running. The ability to bounce around and keep going. I'll give you an example. In our game one year in Los Angeles, one of our toughest defensive players hit (Ram Hall of Fame halfback) Ollie Matson squarely on the five-yard line. Matson shivered and shook there for a second, looked the guy in the eye, and walked into the end zone."

How does your style differ from that?

"I don't know what kind of a style I've got. I've never thought about it."

What is it that you do think about when you have the ball?

"Nothing. With the ball in his hands, no experienced pro back ever thinks about anything. Once through the line of scrimmage, he has no idea whatsoever where he's going. In my case, I just feel my way along. My mind is a complete blank. Except I do know the destination."

Suppose a tackler shows up. Don't you give some thought to the best way to get around him?

"No, sir, none whatever. It's just like someone shining a bright light in my face. Naturally, I jump. I jump away. I'm not going to stand there and stare at the light."

6. Tom Mack: Is Money the Motivator?

THIS HALL OF FAMER, a blocking guard for the Rams, made a business of football while setting himself up in business.

Few NFL players supported themselves playing football in the earlier decades of the twentieth century. Most held other jobs as salesmen, teachers, meat packers, steel workers and the like. Even in the 1950s, with the Rams installed in Los Angeles and finally drawing big crowds after their financially disappointing birth years in Cleveland, Ram wages were so low – $5,000 or less annually for most players – that most held day jobs.

In the 1960s, when the sudden stunning success of televised football made salaries go up, slightly, all NFL players still faced a bleak post-NFL future. In those days, there was no pension to cushion the trauma of the end, no league-organized nest-egg arrangement of any kind. The million-dollar NFL salaries and the cozy lifestyles of the 1990s weren't even a dream in the 1960s, or even the 1970s. Thus the wiser pros, capitalizing on the NFL's new popularity, began connecting with automobile dealers or beer distributors or other employers who might help keep them going during their playing careers and then make places for them in their post-NFL lives.

And so it was that a 1966 Michigan graduate named Tom Mack, in his first year out of the university, landed two jobs. An All-American football player who in school had majored in engineering, Mack, to begin with, joined the Rams, launching a thirteen-year career as a Hall of Fame guard, then he joined the Bechtel Corporation, launching a career as a business executive that continues to this day.

On a July day in 1971, in his NFL prime after five big Ram seasons, Mack drove a hard bargain with the club, getting his salary up to $25,000. On top of his Bechtel income, he didn't really need the money; but as an annual Pro Bowl performer, as the great blocking guard of his time, he went for, and signed, a contract that almost any quarterback would have been proud of only a few years earlier.

He signed on the day before the first day of training camp, and when I met him that day, and asked for a comment on his negotiations with the club, Mack said: "Offensive guards are finally getting what they're worth."

I asked him, How much?

"I'm sorry," he said, "but my attorney won't let me tell you."

Some say money is a major motivator in the way a pro performs. How true is that notion?

"Few things mean more," Mack said. "If two guys have about the same ability, the best-paid player tends to play better."

Doesn't a real pro put out regardless?

"Sure, a real pro will give you a hundred percent in every game, regardless of whether he's underpaid. But that's not what I'm saying. My point is that salary is the most important ingredient in a man's self-confidence."

How do you explain that?

"A player puts the same value on his ability that the club has. Let's say you have a veteran who, by comparison with others in his position around the league, is worth $25,000. And let's say he has a penny-pinching general manager who gets him to sign for $18,000. In that case, you can look for him to play more like a $18,000 man than a $25,000 man."

Why?

"If your club doesn't respect you enough to pay you what you're worth, there's no way to keep your confidence up. Subconsciously, you believe the club may be right, and that you're not as good as you think you are. Your performance inevitably suffers."

What does an individual football player use for a yardstick in evaluating his own ability?

"Well, in the case of offensive guards, the first thing is the new respect that offensive guards as a class have these days in the league. We aren't as famous yet as defensive linemen, but we're getting there – thanks to instant replay. Before TV had instant replay, the only players anybody ever saw in a football game were the quarterbacks, running backs, and receivers. The rest of us were just spear-carriers – just part of the background."

The coaches must have known who was valuable and who wasn't.

"Yes, but why pay big money to an offensive guard if he's just part of the background? Suddenly, with instant replay, everybody in the world can see that there really are eleven men on a football team, and that offensive guards are as essential as quarterbacks. People still look at the man with the ball the first time around, but on instant replay they are forced to see the rest of us."

What do you think when you watch yourself in one of those isolated TV scenes?

"Invariably I'm messing up. I mean, I'm always blocking the wrong guy, or doing something else wrong. But that doesn't matter. What does matter is that I'm wiping somebody out – showing the world that an offensive guard has a big job to do. Who knows or cares if I'm mistakenly wiping out the safetyman instead of the cornerman? The only reason I'm on instant replay is that I've blocked somebody, anybody, and so brought great distinction to every offensive guard in the league."

And more money?

"Ah, yes, that, too."

Lately, you've been getting more and more publicity personally. Does this help an athlete's game or hurt it?

"It's a problem in one way. Your opponents get up for a game against a man who plays in Pro Bowls and makes All-Pro teams. But it works for you because it provides a challenge. You feel you've got to live up to the label, so you play harder. On balance, I'd rather have the challenge."

How important is experience to your success – in football or business?

"That's a big reason I went with Bechtel early on. I wasn't after the money, I wanted to be ready. Let me tell you how important experience is. A lot of people think Vince Lombardi was the best coach of all time – but back in 1960, he lost the first championship game he was ever in. He hadn't had enough big-game experience to beat an experienced old quarterback, Norm Van Brocklin."

Van Brocklin was protected by what two guards?

"Who knows? That was before instant replay."

7. Merlin Olsen: Concentration Is What Counts

CONSISTENCY IS THE key to winning in football,
and concentration is the key to consistency.

Merlin Olsen, from his first day as a Los Angeles Rams rookie to his last as a manifest Hall of Famer in the mid-1970s, was about one thing:

Playing smart. By the time he arrived in the NFL, the game's complexity had so evolved that even physically commanding defensive tackles (like Olsen) had to play bright football. As a consequence, Olsen's one personal goal – unique among the massive linemen of his time – was to master the game mentally. I've never known an athlete in any sport who more thoroughly understood the intellectual aspects of his game.

A giant for his time at six feet five and 270 pounds, Olsen was a physically ideal football player who, the day he arrived, seemed to know instinctively that the physical demands of the game were the lesser part of the challenge. And there was an instant payoff. Almost overnight, he became known around the country as the NFL's most consistently effective athlete.

When he retired fourteen years later after making the Pro Bowl fourteen times – an NFL record for consistency – Olsen was widely recognized as the most constant contributor in the game's history. All told, he played for five different head coaches in Los Angeles – a new one about every three years from the early 1960s on – and each said the same thing about him: He never had a bad season or a bad game and hardly ever a bad play.

It was a prized fringe benefit of my career on Los Angeles newspapers that I got to watch Olsen week in and out. And one day when it was all over, I met with him and asked him how he did it.

"The key to consistency of performance is concentration," he said. "I probably held my ability to concentrate over a longer period of time than some athletes."

What, I asked, did you concentrate on?

"Each game at the beginning of each new play, I thought of it as the most important play of the year," he said. "I went into every play as if the game depended on it."

In a lopsided game, how did you convince yourself that a fourth-quarter play was important?

"I didn't think about the next play or the preceding play or anything else. I approached every play as if it were an individual, distinct incident – a complete little game of its own. I considered a new play to be not only a separate situation but a new challenge. This doesn't mean I played perfect football on every play – but I tried."

That's a daunting challenge.

"The first thing I learned as a rookie is that if you don't completely involve yourself in every play, you suddenly find you've lost it. If you take it easy for ten minutes, it takes a long time to get it back, sometimes a week or two. Like everything else, concentrating is a habit."

How does one get into that kind of habit?

"After each play, I would start thinking about the next play, using a simple little system. First, I'd tell myself the down and distance, then our position on the field, then I mentally reviewed the tempo of the game. After those three things, I recalled what I knew – or what I'd learned during the week – about what the other team liked to do in that particular situation. Then I cleared all of those things out of my mind, and prepared myself for the play."

Why tell yourself the down and distance and then forget it?

"It's like putting material into a computer. The significant difference between the human mind and a computer is that a computer can't be distracted. And that's what I was trying to achieve. I wanted to eliminate everything that could be distracting. When the play starts, computers don't guess, and I didn't want to guess, either. I was just reacting. I knew the two or three things the other team liked to do in every situation, and as the play developed I was cued by what they did to react correctly."

When talking to yourself, what sort of thing did you say?

"Just the most obvious things. If it was third and twelve, I was thinking, 'Off on the ball. Get to the quarterback.' If it was fourth and one on our five-yard line, my thought was, "Off on the ball, hold them.' You should always begin by reminding yourself to go with the snap. The only thing that comes ahead of that is the correct stance."

As a veteran of so many years in football, how much would you say that concentration has to do with longevity?

"Longevity starts with love of the game. Second, you have to develop concentration until it's a habit. Athletes differ, of course, but those who can sustain their concentration last longer than others. And third, good coaching helps."

What football player in your time was able to concentrate most effectively?

"John Unitas. The thing that gave Unitas his concentration was his courage. He's the bravest man I've known in football. Out of the corner of his eye, when Unitas could see you rushing him, I swear he'd hold that ball a split second longer than he really needed to – just to let you know he isn't afraid of any man. Then he threw it on the button."

(Ram defensive end) Deacon Jones played at 255. He was six feet five. Unitas was 196 and six feet one – and thirty-four years old the last time he saw the Deacon, who was then about twenty-eight. How could Unitas even think of getting involved in such an uneven match?

"He was a quarterback. No position in football requires more ability.

No position in any sport is even remotely as hard to play. NFL quarterbacks are the greatest athletes in America today."

8. O.J. Simpson: Rise and Fall of an Idol

HE WAS the best of all the football players, though that's not how he will be remembered.

The tragedy that took two young lives in O. J. Simpson's California neighborhood in 1994 left him a murderer in the minds of most Americans. In one night of terrible trauma, Simpson descended about as far as a man can from the unique pedestal he had reached.

The shock to those who knew him as an indescribably gifted running back – as an artist who played football with unmatched distinction – is that in his playing years he displayed, in addition to physical brilliance, a generous and solicitous character rare among sports superstars. He was not only the best player on his teams but the best-liked.

That happens to Hall of Fame running backs about once in a hundred years. Thus Simpson's teammates, most of them journeymen, played hard to make him look good, stretching themselves to the limit and beyond.

Although it is obvious now that there are at least two O. J. Simpsons, that wasn't so obvious in the 1960s and '70s, when the one we knew seemed to be the most civilized of the great athletes, and when, one year, he became the first to gain two thousand yards in a single NFL season. During the years he carried the ball for USC and for a pro club with otherwise ordinary personnel, the Buffalo Bills, Simpson was so much better than the other players that, every chance I got, I watched him run and visited with him about it.

Long before the Brentwood tragedy, I was to rank him best of century – not just best running back, but best football player, given both his skills and the character he showed in relations with coaches, teammates and others in football. For that reason I called on Simpson and his first wife Marguerite and their two children at their home in Buffalo, New York, one September week in the early 1970s – an even twenty years before the most widely publicized double homicide of the century.

To keep from seeing yesterday's Simpson through today's eyes, the following is the way I wrote it in 1974. He is now the protagonist in an ongoing tragedy, and it is chastening to remember the heights from which he fell.

ii

The scene is the O.J. Simpson residence, a stately new ten-room, two-story English Tudor mini-mansion, beautifully crafted, set down on a large lot in a small new Buffalo suburb full of trees, streams, big green lawns and other big new houses.

 Last night's football game has left O.J. aching in every muscle; and at breakfast, moving very slowly, he serves orange juice and Sanka, and watches a leaf drop.

"Who wouldn't enjoy the woods and open spaces around here?" he asks. "In the West, everybody has a fence that tells you this is my property, this is your property. The East is friendlier. You don't see any fences here. And better than that, in thirty seconds you can be alone in wooded country. Just looking at these woods makes you feel like Huckleberry Finn."

A big man in a brown bathrobe, Simpson smiles. It's a pleasant smile that seems to say, "I like everybody."

The 1968 Heisman Trophy winner mentions his four-year-old son and continues: "Last week I took Jason snake hunting. He came in one day with his eyes big, talking about a boa constrictor he saw on television, and I asked him, 'Want to go catch a snake?' We got a Baggie out of the kitchen and a big stick, and went on a safari across the street. Came back empty-handed, but we saw frogs that can jump a six-foot stream, and we sat right next to the biggest toad I've ever seen. Big as a football."

Elsewhere in this county, 1970s people spend less time watching frogs and toads than discussing O.J., but that's O.K. with O. J., who in Buffalo, whether running a football or hunting snakes, is no longer Orange Juice. He is merely the Juice, as in electricity. His offensive line is called the Electric Company because, in the words of All-Conference guard Reggie McKenzie, "We turn on the Juice."

Last night, in the first home game of the year, they turned him on for a 6.5-yard average and seventy-eight yards in less than a half, when Simpson left with a minor injury. After Buffalo won, upsetting Oakland, 21-20, everybody figured Simpson was a prophet. For he's been saying that the 1974 Bills are a Super Bowl team. From a pulpit as the NFL's best running back – as well as most popular Bill and the most visible individual in the city – he has been trying to talk his team into the title. And it could be that by sheer force of personality, he has already built the Bills into a contender. Some fans are beginning to say so. There are even some Bills who say so.

GAME OF THE CENTURY   125

Twelve noon. That's the doorbell. It penetrates every room of the Simpson house, a full-blown Westminster chime that sounds like a grandfather clock. The 1974 car pool has come to pick O. J. up for football practice, Reggie McKenzie driving, Ahmad Rashad riding shotgun. Tomorrow, it's Simpson's turn at the wheel. A passenger today, he has turned himself out in an orange outfit – with jeans to match – and when he hits the car, everybody, remembering Oakland, is smiling. "You're up early," says Rashad, who a few hours ago caught two touchdowns in two minutes to beat the Raiders. Says O. J.: "I haven't been to sleep yet."

After the excitement of a night game, Marguerite had confided earlier, O.J. never can sleep.

The car pool hears the latest about the Simpson daughter, Arnella, five, as O. J. says: "When we got home at 3:30, Marguerite said, 'There's no way I can get up to get Arnella off to school this morning.' I said, 'Don't worry, baby, I'll be up.' I got her some breakfast while she got ready, and she looked like a million when the school bus came."

In McKenzie's bus, a black Mercedes, Simpson slumps in the back seat for the half-hour ride to work as the talk turns to tonight's team party. As part of his role as the club's self-installed cheerleader, Simpson rounds up the Bills one or two nights a week for beer, cards, music and small talk. Togetherness. Let's beat (fill in name of opponent). Attendance isn't compulsory, but the crowd usually equals the club roster count.

"Whist tonight at the team trip," O.J. says happily. He is an excellent card player.

"Where's it at?" McKenzie asks.

"Mulligan's," O.J. replies, naming a Buffalo night club. "Bring money."

As McKenzie turns onto another throughway, rain suddenly lashes the windshield. "I know it's September already, but I hope the snow holds off a little while," Simpson says. "Once the snow is on the ground, a football team can't get in that hard work."

A visiting passenger asks: How tough is Buffalo weather on a Californian? Says Simpson: "I think of cold weather as a good thing, a very good thing. It gives our football club the advantage. I don't know if you've noticed, but the top two teams in our division play in extreme climates, Miami hot, Buffalo cold. And physically, Miami's players are better off. It's harder for us to get rid of aches and pains. But psychologically, Buffalo is the place to play. Our weather worries the other teams. And it toughens up our team. The Bills always play better late in the season. Remember that."

iv

Movietime. The Bills are in a team meeting, dissecting the filmed version of the Oakland game. And while the players are sequestered, there is a moment to reflect on what Simpson has become as a football player – in his seventh season in the pros – and on how he compares against the many others who have played his game. And to put it abruptly, it seems possible at this time to conclude that this is the most accomplished running back the game has known, better than Jim Brown, better than Gale Sayers.

More than that, he is the most accomplished football player some of us have seen yet at any position, although, to be sure, such comparisons are as difficult as they are subjective.

Three things set Simpson apart.

One: He is the only football player ever acknowledged to be, first, the best running back in college football and, then, the NFL's best running back. Since the origin of sports, he's the only Heisman Trophy winner who has also won the Hickock belt as America's number-one pro athlete.

Two: As a stylist, Simpson is something of a combination of Brown and Sayers, who until the other day ranked one-two in the minds of most critics. Carrying the ball, Simpson, like Sayers, can make full-speed right-angle cuts. And he can do it faster – at 9.4 speed – with almost Brown's breakaway power. Simpson at USC was on the 440-yard relay team that *still* holds the world record.

Three: By disposition, Simpson is the most dedicated and determined team player of all the great running backs. None of the great runners before him – surely not Bronko Nagurski nor Hugh McElhenny nor Jim Brown – ever attempted to psychologically recreate a football team. At Buffalo, drafted number one by the worst football team in the league, Simpson discovered early on that, in an eleven-man sport, he needed ten other dedicated souls to help him do what he knew he could do as a matchless running back. And to do it – to build a showcase for his talent – he has, among other things, shamelessly advertised the Bills as a good football team, clearly expecting them to live up to his billing.

He has, they say, willed a little sophomore quarterback, Joe Ferguson, into a winner – by continuously identifying him as a winner – and he has willed the offensive line into a power by calling it powerful. Moreover, when questioned by an old acquaintance from Los Angeles, Simpson makes no attempt to hide this strategy. "There's a close ratio between recognition and production in football or anything else," he says. "The more recognition you get, the more you want to put out."

So this is Simpson's mission for the 1970s: to lift Buffalo into Super Bowl company with his talent, his fidelity, and an uncommon personality. The Bills are starting from a long way back, particularly on defense, but Simpson has already achieved uniquely in one respect. Whereas, before him, a single athlete has occasionally made a good team great – as Joe Namath did, and as Kareem Abdul-Jabbar did – O.J. is the first to make a lousy team good.

v

Late afternoon. The Bills have finished for the day. Simpson now has time to talk, and he's willing to take the time. Newspaper people have ranked him as the most considerate of news sources since his first game at USC. Standing in the locker room after a game in which he has played either well or passably, or worse, he answers routine questions from any accredited reporter patiently, politely, forthrightly, and almost interminably.

"I want them to get the story right," he says. "A long time ago, I learned from (basketball star) Kareem Abdul-Jabbar to say exactly what you mean. Don't leave anything to an individual's interpretation."

How does one learn that from Kareem?

"I saw him interviewed once," Simpson says, "and I knew what he meant when he said there are a lot of insincere, superficial people in Los Angeles. I feel that way myself. But when it came out in the media, Kareem was quoted as saying that Los Angeles is a phony town. It isn't, and he didn't say it, but it came out that way. Since then, I've tried to be precise."

Speaking precisely, why do you think it's necessary to seek applause for highly paid major league athletes?

"If the quote star is a regular guy who takes an interest, the sky's the limit in this business. Pro football is like a forty-seven man relay race. No other sport needs half that many guys pulling together. One sure way to get such a big group going is for an O.J. or Joe Namath to make sure guys like McKenzie aren't overlooked. Sports fans think I know something about football – and as a matter of fact, I do."

Calling on that expertise, what would you say first if you were invited to speak on the mechanics of running a football?

"I'd say that in football today, there are two kinds of great running backs, the sidesteppers and the challengers. I'm a sidestepper. I never challenge a great defensive player. I never let him hit me square, and if I can avoid him altogether, I do. I study the films during the week, and on the field I always look for the baddest dude on the other team. I get it in my mind he's never going to hit me. My favorite tacklers are the little cornerbacks and safetymen. I run at those guys, and sidestep the linemen."

Your challengers, so-called, must live in a different world. What runner would deliberately run into a lineman?

"The thing that makes (Washington's) Larry Brown great is his courage, his desire. Larry will challenge anybody, and he isn't as big as I am. One year he took such a beating he couldn't play the last two games. That's the only way I won the league running championship that time."

What if it's third and one and Dick Butkus is standing in the hole?

"Larry will take Butkus on if necessary and I won't. Larry is always going head-over-heels. How often do you see O. J. on his head? My game is to juke the tough guys. I put the okey-doke on them, bounce around, and look for daylight. If I can't find a hole, I won't just slam in there. I'll run out of bounds before I'll run into a wall. All great running backs are insane, but I'm not that crazy."

Insane?

"A great ballcarrier is the most unpredictable guy in sports. The great backs don't know what they're doing. There's no way to explain what they do when they have the ball – there's no rhyme or reason to what they do – and no way to teach it. You can teach a running back to block or catch, but running with the ball is completely instinctive. You hear passers, receivers, blockers, pitchers, hitters, shortstops, pole vaulters and everybody else say they've been out working on their thing, but you never hear a great running back say, 'I'm going out to work on my cutting,' or whatever. All he says is, 'I'm going out to work out,' or, 'I've been working out.'"

What three or four qualities have the great running backs, in your opinion, all had?

"They've had blockers, coaching, speed and power – and one more thing: running knowledge, or what some people call instinct. You either have it or you don't."

Who had the most of it? Do you put any one running back at the top?

"Jim Brown is much the biggest guy who had everything a great running back has to have, including blockers, so you've got to put Jim on top. He could run over them or around them, but like me he went around them when he could. He lasted nine years without injury. The one I used to identify with was Gale Sayers. I'm the faking type, and so was Gale."

Comparing yourself to Sayers in his prime, what's your edge?

"He didn't get to play for the Buffalo Bills."

vi

Night. The trip. And O.J. is having more fun than anybody, getting a lot of mileage out of two beers. The ribbing is merciless. In one weekend, Simpson has been struck by two disasters – USC was upset and Buffalo won big without him – and there are forty-six other football players in Buffalo who won't let him forget it.

Buffalo linebacker John Skorupan has a new nickname for Simpson, "22 to 7," the score of Arkansas' win over USC, where Simpson won his Heisman. "Hey, 22 to 7, how about another beer?" Skorupan shouts. Skorupan is from Penn State.

"Is Vassar still on your schedule?" Simpson fires back. "Think you can beat Hofstra this year?"

The dialogue, when athletes get together, would never make Broadway, though much of it is obscene enough. But the thing they seem to like best about life on a winning football team is just the "messin' around with the guys," the ribs and pranks, the horseplay. This they miss the most when their careers are spent. They all say so. And Simpson fits right in, continuing his old USC role.

The similarities between Simpson in college and as a pro are his talent – the ability to make a ninety-degree cut at 9.4 speed – and his endless campaigning to make All-Americans and All-Pros out of the people around him, from Ron Yary to Reggie McKenzie.

As president of the Electric Company, O.J. roasts them in the locker room and toasts them in the press. He turns *them* on.

9. Fred Dryer: Life in the NFL's Fantasy World

TO MOST SPORTS fans, absolutely nobody has it better
than a professional athlete. Here's confirmation.

For nutritional and other reasons, football players kept getting bigger throughout the twentieth century. The most famous Hall of Fame guard, Danny Fortmann of the 1930s Chicago Bears, weighed 210 pounds. By the 1990s, most NFL guards weighed a hundred pounds more, and some were up to 350 or better. Even so, from time to time, dedicated NFL lightweights have managed to excel in various positions, including defensive end, which was Fred Dryer's position when he weighed in at 228 for the New York Giants and Los Angeles Rams in the 1970s.

In all, four things about Fred Dryer illuminated him. He was, first, a great football player, probably the best defensive lineman in the game, pound for pound. Second, he was the smallest NFL lineman of his time. Third, of the athletes I've known, he had the most aptitude for acting roles on television and in Hollywood. And fourth, he has always enjoyed a lively lifestyle. In Dryer, the good-old-boy culture of pro football encountered the counter-culture lifestyle of late-'60s California. No one ever lived the pro game the way Dryer did, and in the hot summer nights of training camp, nobody had a better time.

Like many other athletes, Dryer moved into an acting career as soon as he left sports; and like most of them, he closed the door on his first career with regret. The difference with Dryer is that as a football player, he knew what he had while he had it. Thus from one year to the next, he lived every second to the full. Indeed, of his days in the NFL, in which he played 174 consecutive games, he once told me: "I lived a fantasy for thirteen years."

During his first tour as an actor, I ran into Dryer again one day when he came into the Baldwin Hills area of Los Angeles, my neighborhood, on location. A 1990s Hollywood film company, instead of building a fake house on an old set, often films in a real house leased temporarily on a Southern California street, and the house that was leased on this occasion is a city block from mine.

During a break, I asked Dryer, a former San Diego State athlete, to tell me more about his fantasy time as a defensive star in pro football.

"In the back of my mind," he said, "I knew from the first that as great as it was – and it was so great, so exciting, so rewarding – it was all slipping away. The lucky part for me was to be successful within the fantasy, starting the first day."

How did it start?

"It all began in New York City," Dryer said. "Walking around the big city in a New York Giants windbreaker, tasting the excitement, smelling it, living it. To be twenty-one years old, a first draft choice, and introduced at Yankee Stadium as the starter for an NFL team – that was every football player's dream. I loved those days."

Was it as enjoyable playing for Los Angeles later on?

"Hell, yes, this is home. I grew up with the Rams. Going out into the world, making it, coming back to play for my home town team, that's like writing down the things you want, and they all come true."

What's it like, being a pro football player?

"It's a continuously self-gratifying feeling. For awhile, you think everyone on earth is interested in what you're doing. When you grow out of that, you still keep asking yourself, Why am I so lucky? For thirteen years I lived a fantasy that was chock full of life and dreams come true – emotionally, physically, spiritually. You know, of course, that it isn't going to last. There's a part of you, way down deep inside, that is always uneasy about that. And it does end so fast. It all went by in a heartbeat."

What's the best thing about an NFL career?

"It keeps you young. You're getting old, but you feel as young as ever. You're stockpiling memories – and later, your memories do a great deal to keep you young within yourself. Pro football is a mysterious, monstrous subculture, a self-contained fragment of society. Yet it *is* the society when you're living it. The NFL is like a gigantic bus station. You feel like a character in a book, and all the people you meet and know are the other characters."

Who was the most interesting character you met?

"Well, Tommy Prothro was one of them. When I came back to Los Angeles, Prothro was coaching the Rams, so I got to spend one training camp without a curfew."

How did you spend it?

"We tested it right along, (receiver) Lance Rentzel and I. At times I was so tired, I could hardly go out again the next night. I remember once just before midnight when Lance banged on my door and said: 'Let's go.' I said: 'Not tonight, man, Hollywood can wait. I'm asleep.' He said: 'You can sleep tomorrow at practice.' So I got dressed, and we walked right out the front door, and there was Prothro, having a cigarette with an assistant coach. I cringed, but Lance kept us marching along to his car. And as he pulled out from the curb, I looked back. There was Prothro on the sidewalk, following us. I couldn't think of anything to say to him, so I waved – and he waved back."

Most of those who played for Prothro say he was the most unusual coach they ever knew.

"I respect him a lot for daring to be so unconventional in such an inbred society as pro football. The best time we had during two-a-day practices one July started at lunch one noon when Prothro got up to make a speech. He said: 'We've been working pretty hard, men' – we hadn't, but nobody argued with him – 'so why don't we all go to the beach today?' For a good fifteen or twenty seconds, there wasn't a sound. Everybody was stunned. Then everybody got up at once and stamped for the door. I thought I had it made, but didn't quite get there, and got knocked down and trampled in the rush. It was the only time I was injured all year. The funny thing was, when I finally did get outside, my car wouldn't start. The battery or something was dead. I was under the car, cursing, and everyone else had driven away, when Prothro strolled by. He leaned over, put his hands on his knees, looked down at me, and said: 'Dryah, you're losin' the bettah paht of the day.' "

Calling your attention now to some other NFL characters: Who's the best player you saw in your thirteen years, excluding the Rams?

"That would have to be (Chicago Bears middle linebacker) Dick Butkus. Nobody ever beat up on a running back like Dick Butkus. When Larry Smith was a halfback with the Rams, I remember we warned him one year not to run upright in the Chicago game. He didn't listen to us – and for a week after we played the Bears, Larry couldn't wear a helmet. His forehead swelled out so much after Butkus worked him over that he couldn't get a helmet on."

Who else do you think of?

"Gale Sayers was the best running back of my time. I never saw Jim Brown, but Sayers has to be right there with him. He's the most electrifying runner I ever tried to tackle. The best quarterback was Terry Bradshaw. I don't want to take away from Joe Namath and others, but Bradshaw and (New Orleans quarterback) Archie Manning affected my life adversely more than anybody."

Of all the characters in your life, Rams and non-Rams, who do you think of first when you're asked to name the one greatest football player.

"I think of (Ram defensive tackle) Merlin Olsen first."

Who would you say best epitomized pro football in your day?

"That was (Ram defensive end) Jack Youngblood. It takes a special kind of person to play pro football – after the first game, everyone plays hurt for six months – and that requires a rare kind of devotion. But Jack Youngblood is the only player I ever knew who would, and did, play a football game on a broken leg."

How did you get along with (Ram coach) Chuck Knox?

"The only thing I didn't like about Knox was that he kept telling me, over and over, You'll have to prove yourself this week. Although my playing weight was 228 – I was the lightest lineman in the league – I thought I should be judged on performance, not size. Performance and consistency. Starting my rookie year, I played every game until they wouldn't pay me any longer."

I looked it up the other day. Of the 11,700 people who have played pro football since the NFL was organized in 1920, you stand twenty-eighth in consecutive games. How did you do that at your size?

"I gained a lot of strength from my fantasy. For thirteen years I saw myself playing brilliant football. I saw myself as a great 228-pound defensive end. You'll probably never know another lineman that small. I was the last of an era."

10. Ronnie Lott: Football Student

*COLLEGE KIDS WHO play big-time football
and also graduate have done something.*

Football began on the campuses of higher-education institutions, and it is still played there enthusiastically, but their game has an additional role today. The major college football conferences serve de facto as pro football's minor leagues. High school stars move first up to a new life in America's great universities, then a few of them move on to the big money in the NFL. It's a process that offers thousands of American youngsters an opportunity to get an education – but sometimes, opportunity doesn't knock.

Of the All-Pros who have spoken out persuasively on that subject over the years, as football evolved from an Ivy League hobby to a billion-dollar national enterprise that both benefits and harms so many individuals, one was the great defensive back of his decade, the 1980s, Ronnie Lott of USC and the San Francisco 49ers.

When the 49ers drafted Lott on the first round in the spring of 1981, his life was about to change rather drastically in two ways that immediately set him apart from other athletes. In chronological order:

• Lott graduated from college. Four years after entering USC, he graduated with his class. That made him something of an educational oddity. Of the many students – athletes and nonathletes – who enroll annually as freshmen in America's four-year colleges, fewer than half work hard enough to get their degrees on time. Increasingly, if they finish at all, they spend five or more years in college. Of the football players who graduate today, fewer than ten percent finish in four years. "You can only do it in four," Lott said at the time, "if you make it your first priority."

- On the field, he changed positions. An All-American strong safety at USC, Lott became San Francisco's left cornerback, playing the most difficult position in a National Football League secondary.

During the months and years that followed, Lott's life kept changing. On the San Francisco team, he became recognized, first, as one of the league's great cornerbacks, and then, at the height of his career, as the league's most valuable free safety. Next, after leaving the playing field, he stayed in football as a knowledgeable network football analyst.

Looking back one day, he said the study habits he got into at USC, where he won a B.A. degree in business administration, laid the pattern for his life. "More football players would graduate if they could see how vital it is," he said. "But that's surprisingly hard for an athlete to grasp. He knows he's in college because he's a good athlete. He has a scholarship to prove it. So he thinks football is what's important."

In Lott's opinion, any youngster with enough on the ball to be admitted to a college can get an education if he goes to every one of his classes and reads every assigned book. "It isn't that difficult to pick up a book and read it," he said. "You just have to want to. I keep hearing that a lot of kids can't read today, and maybe that's true, but the ones I knew at SC could read and read well. To play football, you have to be able to read a playbook, and playbooks aren't all X's and O's. The terminology you need to play and compete is in there. It's pretty sophisticated stuff, and if you can read a playbook, you can read a history book."

One problem, Lott discovered long ago, is having to concentrate on football one minute and biology the next. "Take your average businessman," he said. "I wonder if he could focus his whole body and mind on something as dazzling and demanding as football for three hours and then turn around and focus on the stock market. I think there's an insufficient realization of what college football players have to go through to be college students. The critics think they're just a bunch of lucky kids, but the truth is, they're under more stress than most people."

The stress takes many forms. "Suppose you're in college on an athletic scholarship and you're not playing," Lott said, remembering some of his schoolboy friends. "You were a high school star, but now nobody notices you. You keep going out for practice, and going through those same hard three hours the starters go through, but the coaches aren't using you in games. That's a big worry. It's very stressful. But as worried as you are, you're supposed to go back to your room and study. You're nineteen or twenty years old, and you're supposed to handle a crushing disappointment as if you were a sophisticated adult. Your big dream of a pro career is disappearing, and you're supposed to carry on bravely in the classroom. That's just unrealistic."

For Lott, the big dream came to life. He's one of the lucky ones. Well-adjusted, self-disciplined, self-motivated, and greatly talented, he moved from the USC classroom into a big career. But for the overwhelming majority of America's prep and college athletes, the future, as Lott knows, is past. And his compassion is for them. "The least we can do is understand," he said. "People who knock lazy athletes for 'not taking advantage of college' don't make allowances for all the stressful things that can happen to young guys under twenty-one."

11. Paul Hornung: The Century's Most Decorated Player

THE GOLDEN BOY, an athlete for the ages, still
holds the NFL's all-time scoring championship.

Shortly, the twentieth century will be naught but a memory, a virtual figment in time, a lost rite of passage. So in a football context, who was Player of the Century? My choice is O.J. Simpson, but on the basis of statistics and honors, and all-around ability, many would argue that the principal candidate was 1960s All-Pro Paul Hornung. Without doubt, the one-time Golden Boy of Notre Dame and the Green Bay Packers was a unique football man.

To begin with, Hornung, the most inspirational member of the Green Bay team that won five 1960s NFL titles, scored more points in a single season than anyone else ever has. In a league that now has sixteen-game schedules, no other player has yet come close to Hornung's 176 points in 1960, when the league had a twelve-game schedule. He scored fifteen touchdowns that season, kicked fifteen field goals, and added forty-one extra points.

Even more impressively, in three seasons at Notre Dame and nine with Green Bay, the Golden Boy became the most decorated football player of all time, the only one who ever earned all this: the Heisman Trophy (as a member of a 2-8 Notre Dame team in 1956); top pick in the NFL draft (1957); NFL MVP twice (1960 and 1961); NFL championship game

MVP (1961); consensus All-American membership; consensus All-Pro and Pro Bowl membership; college football Hall of Fame, and pro football Hall of Fame.

Hornung was the only player from a losing team to get the Heisman since it first went to Jay Berwanger of Chicago in 1935.

Though Simpson and others were plainly more skillful carrying the ball, Hornung remains the leading candidate for recognition as the best all-around football player yet. Consider: At both Notre Dame and Green Bay, he successfully played all three backfield positions, quarterback, halfback and fullback, excelling as runner, passer, receiver, and blocker. He was the blocker for a Hall of Fame fullback, Jim Taylor. Moreover, Hornung punted, kicked off and kicked field goals, and at Notre Dame he returned punts and kickoffs. As a pro, his skill as both passer and runner allowed his coach, Vince Lombardi, to emphasize the run-pass option as a basic Packer play – uniquely. It has never in the age of the T Formation been a basic play for any other coach.

A sixty-minute man in college ball, Hornung doubled on defense as a safety at Notre Dame, where, one season, he was second in total tackles.

"Second in tackles," the old quarterback mused one time when I looked him up at his home in Louisville, Kentucky. "I'm kind of proud of that one."

ii

The Golden Boy was born in Louisville. And on a February morning in 1986 when we renewed an old relationship, one that had begun in his Notre Dame days, he allowed that he'd seen bigger places than Louisville. Then he confessed to a lifelong love affair with his native city. As a football player and later as a Louisville businessman, he had seized every opportunity to get around the country, of course, but he always came home. "Who wouldn't?" he asked. "Like the man said, I've never met a Kentuckian who wasn't on his way home."

Until he was thirty years old, nearing football retirement, he lived in his mother's house in Louisville except for the months when he was away playing games. While he was an All-American quarterback at Notre Dame, Hornung returned every month or two to spend a day or two with his mother. "I always hitch-hiked back and forth to South Bend," he recalled. "I must have made thirty or forty round trips to Notre Dame in those days, and it was my thumb that did it. Never went any other way."

Later, when Hornung was an All-Pro halfback with the Green Bay

Packers, he cruised back to his old Kentucky home each winter in newly-purchased convertibles – a new one every spring. "Been tooling new Cadillacs for twenty-eight years," he said in that 1986 interview, adding that he'd just made an exception, tooling home from Hawaii on a jet. He had ventured to Honolulu at the request of a committee from the Pro Football Hall of Fame in Canton, Ohio, a group that proudly introduced him there as a new member. It was a long time coming. Nine other 1960s Packers had preceded him to Canton despite Hornung's status as the champions' big gun.

The delay was due to a habit he'd picked up in his hometown. For nearly two centuries, betting on the ponies has been fashionable in the land of horsemen and cardplayers — a tradition that was already ancient while horseman-cardplayer-statesman Henry Clay represented Kentucky as a United States senator for a third of the nineteenth century. At the height of Hornung's NFL career, the Golden Boy was banned from football for a year for betting – for, in this case, betting on himself as a football player – and that troubled some members of the Pro Football Hall of Fame selection committee. Emphasizing what they called Hornung's immorality, they kept him out of the hall, year after year.

Hornung's bitterness, if any, isn't evident. "The thing I'm proudest of," he said, "is that I made the College Hall of Fame as a quarterback and the Pro Hall of Fame as a running back."

He was that versatile. He was that good.

iii

Later when Hornung showed me his new office, a high-floor corner office in downtown Louisville, he dropped into a big leather chair behind a big modern desk and cheerfully took the winter sun that was flickering uncertainly in from the Southeast. It was obvious that he favored bright colors and mixes of modern and antique furniture. The dominant decoration was an oil portrait of his old leader, Lombardi, as painted by a Hall of Fame receiver, Tommy McDonald. The distant view was of Muhammad Ali Boulevard, a thoroughfare named for another Louisville champion. It is a measure of Ali's clout that nothing in Louisville is yet known as Golden Boy Boulevard.

In his sixties, the Golden Boy wasn't quite as golden as he used to be. He'd turned into a gray-toned blond who had come to work in old jeans and a pullover yellow sweater. The sweater fit snugly. He admitted to 255 pounds, but it was more. The familiar 215-pound athlete had disappeared when he quit smoking some years ago but kept eating. "Paul is always on time for dinner," Angela Hornung, his second wife, said.

Between meals, he toured the country extensively as football announcer and business developer. The distinctive Hornung trait, most noticeable in airports, was his gait, which was fast-forward. A bundle of nervous energy, he always seemed to be in motion. He said he can get in and out of any restaurant in America in twenty-eight minutes. Though his reach reportedly wasn't that fast when the check came, Hornung remained essentially good-hearted, open, unreserved, trusting. Particularly loyal to old friends, he had asked one of them, Max McGee, to make his Pro Football Hall of Fame presentation in 1986.

On the Hornung teams at Green Bay, McGee doubled as a wide receiver and fellow fun-loving curfew-buster, but he, too, settled down soon, married, and grew rich. A bit sadly, he said: "You can't party all your life."

Hornung remembered when they tried. "Max was my roommate on the Packers, and one year at training camp, he was out every single night," the Golden Boy said. "I know, because once or twice I had to get him up and make him come along."

iv

During Hornung's days as a businessman, an automobile tour of Louisville was also always a trip into the past for the Golden Boy, who in the course of many years had traveled from the blue-collar west end of the city, where he was born, to the more affluent east side, where he was to live later. "See that house across the street?" he said, driving with one hand and pointing with the other to a tiny, one-story, white-frame cottage. "Mom and I used to live there. We could only afford to rent one room, that front room there. We had two cots, and not much else."

His grandparents, who once ran a mom-and-pop grocery store in Louisville, were deceased. During the Golden One's early boyhood, his mother was just getting started in Kentucky's civil service. After her first promotion, she and Paul rented the second floor of a slightly larger, two-story, white-frame house nearby.

"There it is," he said, indicating a house in a low-income Portland Street area once filled with an immigrant group known as the Portland Irish. That was his home through high school, and it was to that house that he returned so often from Notre Dame, hitch-hiking as far as possible, then riding up in a Portland Street bus. "That's the Marine Hospital across the street," he said. "As you can see, their front yard is as big as a football field. That's where I learned to play football. Played every day."

His mother, Loretta Horning, vouched for that when I saw her later. Speaking as a Hornung fan who saw most of his games at Notre Dame and Green Bay, she said, "No boy was ever crazier about football."

During his first year in high school, she recalled, there was a September Friday when the coach ended practice early. He was saving the legs of his athletes for a big Saturday game, so Paul dressed and, as usual, made the five-mile trip home on his bicycle. When he got to Portland Street, he noticed that a pickup game was still in progress on the Marine Hospital grounds. Rushing into the house, he changed clothes again, and played sandlot football until dark. "That gave him an idea," his mother said. "After that, he always hurried home when high school practice ended early. He loved playing football twice a day. The day of the game was always kind of a letdown."

Her boy confirmed that high school in Louisville was the best time of his life despite his penniless circumstance and despite the fame, fun and financial security he was to get eventually. "High school is the only time when you can play every day," he said. "I looked forward to basketball so much that I couldn't wait for the football season to end. Then in the late winter, I couldn't wait for baseball. How could you have a better life? Studies came easy. Mom made sure I studied enough to get to Notre Dame."

On the day of Hornung's guided tour through Louisville, it ended in the Windy Hill district, where he and Angela shared a three-bedroom condominium on a pleasant, carefully landscaped little street in a lush residential area. Two prominent bars, one upstairs and one down, were stocked with the best in gin and Scotch, but the bottles looked like rarely touched museum pieces. They were apparently token reminders of a bygone era in the life of a reformed playboy.

In his playroom, the many framed pictures on what he called the Wall of Fame were dominated by three *Sports Illustrated* covers featuring Hornung in his Golden Boy decade, the earliest in 1956, one in 1963, another in 1966. The conversation piece in the master bedroom was an attractive oil painting of Angela Hornung, who was wearing, all told, long blonde hair. A bathroom statue and most of the other portraits in the house were also discreet nudes. No Windy Hill resident could ask for more.

V

In his Windy Hill den, Hornung glanced at a book on the coffee table and started talking about football. "As a passer, Marcus Allen was as good as I was," he said, bringing up a subject that still interests him. "And Marcus was a better runner." The others who have attempted to throw halfback passes, including Walter Payton, didn't fake the run properly, Hornung said, adding: "Most guys slow down too soon and retreat too fast. Marcus did it just right. He's the best halfback passer since the Single Wing."

Hornung was talking about his own best play, the one that made him famous. "It's the most neglected play in football today," he said. "Teams like the Raiders should use it all the time. They think it's a surprise gimmick play, but it isn't. It's a game-plan play. In one series at Philadelphia (in the early 1960s), we ran it on every down. It was a regular-season game, but Coach Lombardi thought we needed work on the halfback option. So we ran it for about sixty-five yards. I mean, I was out there throwing or running on six or seven consecutive plays until we scored."

It is the view of Hornung's old teammates, including Jerry Kramer, that as always, the Golden Boy that time scored spectacularly. As Lombardi used to say, speaking of what is now called the red zone, or the distance from the goal line out to the opponent's 20-yard line, Hornung was the most dangerous running back he ever saw in there – in part because a halfback pass was usually a threat. Summing up Hornung's career in his book, *Distant Replay*, Kramer put it this way: "Paul was, really, the only player we had in Green Bay who came in a superstar and left a superstar."

He also came and left a playboy. Former Bear linebacker Bill George, who drew Hornung as a roommate one week in the era when the Pro Bowl was a Los Angeles institution, was asked after the game what it was like rooming with a legend. "I never saw him," George said. "Haven't seen anything but Hornung's luggage. I roomed with his luggage all week."

12. Marcus Allen: The Play That Changed Everything

*FOR YEAR AFTER year, the Raiders were a pivotal team
in the evolution of the NFL until one play ended it all.*

Of the twists and turns in the hundred-year course of American football, few have been sharper than the abrupt collapse of the Los Angeles/Oakland Raiders toward the end of the century.

At the time they foundered, that was Marcus Allen's team. It was a team for which he once gained 191 yards in the Super Bowl. But long before the Allen decade, 1982-92, Al Davis had built the Raiders into a power.

As their managing genius for more than a third of the century, Davis kept them on top, or close to it, through the 1960s and '70s and into the '80s, three decades in which the Raiders reached the Super Bowl four times, at least once in each decade, and won three.

In that pre-collapse era, in each of three roles, Davis had helped mold modern football as few others ever have. As a coach, he pioneered bump-and-run pass coverage – which is now integral to every NFL defense – as well as a bombs-away passing attack that for years terrorized the league. As AFL commissioner, he equally terrorized his opponents with aggressive raids on NFL quarterbacks, a policy that forced the older league to prematurely accept the historic 1960s merger. And as Raider CEO, he has, despite the adversity of recent seasons, given his club a higher lifetime winning percentage (currently .628) than that of any other NFL franchise since Davis first saw Oakland in 1963.

His high point was his fourth and last Super Bowl appearance on January 22, 1984. When the Raiders smashed the Washington Redskins that afternoon, 38-9, their second-year running back, Allen, emerged as Most Valuable Player. His 191 yards set a Super Bowl record.

In that game that year, the Raiders, two years after departing Oakland, were representing Los Angeles. And they'd still be in Los Angeles, and still winning almost certainly, but for a single cataclysmic play on their home field two years thereafter, followed by two dreadful Davis decisions that flowed therefrom.

One bad play. Two bad calls. In the NFL, that can start a landslide.

ii

Implausibly, the central character in the landslide that knocked the Raiders down was their finest player, Marcus Allen. An incomparable all-around offensive back, Allen was the NFL's best-ever goal-line runner (save, perhaps, for Green Bay's Hornung). And otherwise, he had nonesuch versatility. Allen in his time or probably any other time could have made any team in the land as a running back, passer, blocking back or receiver.

The great Allen play was the run-pass option. As Hornung implied, incorporating the Allen option as a game-plan play would have been a recipe for any coach's instant success. If Al Davis, a proven champion, had built his offense around two plays instead of one – if he had featured the vertical long ball along with Allen's run-pass option – the Raiders might have dominated the league indefinitely.

As it was, they were still in business as a 1986 title contender when, only two years removed from his MVP Super Bowl performance, Allen continued to produce big winning plays. At San Diego in a late-November overtime game that year, for example, Allen's slashing twenty-eight yard touchdown run brought Davis' team to the peak moment of its second season after its fourth Super Bowl.

It was one of his greatest runs. It might have been a candidate for pro football's hundred best runs, or even the fifty best, considering that Allen was moving that day on a bad ankle, and considering also what the play meant. For it put the struggling Raiders snugly on the heels of the division-leading Denver Broncos, who lost that same afternoon.

After toppling San Diego, the Raiders were 8-4 to Denver's 9-3 and seemingly playoff-bound, with four games left, three at home, against teams they could beat. But they never won another game. They were upset four straight times by Philadelphia, Seattle, Kansas City and Indianapolis.

What went wrong?

iii

The explanation is that, ten days after his brilliant overtime run had beaten San Diego, Allen let slip a calamitous fumble in overtime to hand a game to Philadelphia. That was a gut-wrenching play, twisting certain victory into certain defeat, and putting Denver beyond reach all but mathematically.

Before that fumble, the Raiders had overcome an 0-3 start on the season. They had overcome the injuries that kept bothering their best offensive player, Allen, and their best defensive player, Howie Long. Against a Philadelphia team with hot young quarterback Randall Cunningham playing his hottest game of the season, the Raiders, with the overtime clock running down, had just overcome third and twenty with a big play at midfield. On a scramble, it was their veteran quarterback, Jim Plunkett, a two-time Super Bowl champion, who made that play, a typical Plunkett play, throwing what seemed to be the turning-point pass twenty-seven yards down the sideline. He threw it to his most reliable clutch receiver. That was Allen, who made a sure-handed catch, advancing the Raiders to a first down at the Philadelphia 20, well within field-goal range.

As the Raiders lined up for the game's last few plays, they had put their season back together. Spurred on by their high-scoring halfback and their persevering thirty-nine-year-old quarterback, they had gained the momentum for a final run at the fading Denver team.

It wasn't to be.

On second and six at the Philadelphia 16 – within sight of an easy game-winning field goal – Allen fought for extra yardage and dropped the ball. The Eagles, picking it up, ran it back stripe after stripe, eighty-one long yards to the Raider four-yard line, then scored easily themselves, using a rare, last-minute, tide-changing, long-distance fumble return to astonishingly win from a team that thought it had them nailed.

After that play, the Raiders in that strange 1986 season, with Denver now out of sight, could never find the emotion to get themselves going again. They couldn't rush a passer, they couldn't pass-block, they couldn't run the ball, they couldn't hold it, they couldn't beat anyone. The bright future they had glimpsed when they lined up on the Philadelphia 16-yard line that afternoon – in the enchantment of overtime – was replaced by total darkness. One fatal play had torn their hearts out.

iv

Although I reported it that night as a season-changing play, it turned out to be a franchise-changing play. For after a fumble that was indeed unnecessary and inexcusable – as second-effort fumbles always are when a winning field goal is only yards away – Davis never forgave Allen. He'd had enough of a halfback who like most halfbacks had sometimes fumbled in other games. So he benched him. Making the first of two awful 1980s blunders, Davis benched Allen not for a game or two, or a month or two, but for years – before finally trading him away.

When in 1988 Davis brought in a bright young new coach named Mike Shanahan, he denied him Allen. Davis hadn't traded Allen yet, he had simply discarded a valuable player whose multiple skills qualified him as just the right offensive back for the Shanahan offense.

Nor did Davis find or develop a quarterback to replace Plunkett. He never has.

And it gets worse. In mid-season 1989, Davis blundered again, firing Shanahan a year and a half after hiring him. Minus Shanahan, minus Allen, minus a quarterback, and minus their familiar old poise and arrogance, the Raiders went quietly down the drain. Allen, meanwhile, went on to Kansas City, where he continued to star for the Chiefs, setting an all-time NFL record for most running-back touchdowns. Shanahan went on to Denver, where he led the Broncos to consecutive Super Bowl victories as the NFL's first $2 million coach.

The Raiders went back to Oakland, where that old silver and black magic was missing, as it still is. A single play had led a mighty franchise into the sharpest downturn of the NFL century.

It was the closest thing to Greek tragedy in the history of the sport.

13. Gene Upshaw: All-Pro to All-Labor

FOOTBALL PEOPLE DON'T have to stay in football
to make an impression on the country.

To those who remember how it used to be for athletes, NFL labor leader Gene Upshaw is the best thing that ever happened to the sports-labor movement in America. With an assist from the courts in the early 1990s, Upshaw, a Hall of Famer who in his playing days was a Raider All-Pro guard, negotiated a contract with the league's club owners that now pays the average football pro about $1 million a year.

Under terms of the Upshaw-NFL contract, some make many millions more than that. And, of course, most sports fans think the players are overpaid. Fans allege that all professional athletes are overpaid – most of all, perhaps, in baseball, where $5 million a year isn't unheard of for shortstops who in a good season can hit .240.

But there are valid and persuasive reasons why today's pro athletes are generally overpaid – or as they say, getting what they're worth – in the present multi-billion-dollar sports market. The multi-sports explanation is in three parts:

- Until the final years of the twentieth century, all club owners in all sports kept all player salaries unrealistically low, absurdly and injuriously low, with artificial restraints such as the reserve clause.
- The dam holding down baseball salaries finally broke when the club owners fatuously agreed to a system of impartial arbitration for their best players.
- The dam holding down NFL wages finally broke when Upshaw ran a brilliant misdirection campaign, and won in the courts what he had never been able to win while bargaining. The owners had fought hard in a haughty, expensive attempt to hold onto their outdated player restraints, fighting to the end in a mistaken belief that they couldn't lose.

As they had in every other sport, salaries soon explored the stratosphere. But it needn't have happened. Had the club owners and their legal representatives been more civilized, more compassionate, more considerate of their players in the 1970s and '80s – when the sports boom took off – players' salaries would now be smaller and more seemly to angry sports fans.

Today's high salaries for professional athletes are the inevitable consequence of the club owners' century-long policy of hard-nosed containment.

It was Gene Upshaw who saw that the owners' dam was defective, who ran the courageously inventive campaign that in 1993 cracked it, and who won free agency for the NFL's indispensable element, the athletes.

ii

Upshaw had entered pro football as a player, and by the 1970s, when the Raiders were still winning and winning big, he was both captain and player rep of the club. He was, as they said then, a born leader. And recalling those stirring days, his former teammates report that they've never known a more inspirational leader. They say that at the Raider meeting that made the most enduring impression on the other players, Upshaw stood up seven days before one Super Bowl game and told the coaches: "I've heard that you want a curfew starting Friday night, but we're changing that. We're starting the curfew tonight."

Then he glared around the room to see if any player disagreed. Nobody did – not even the club's most famous playboys – and presently, the well-rested Raiders won the game. "Gene knew he could do that because he always knows what football players are thinking," Richard Berthelsen, his chief lawyer, said.

That, in fact, is what Upshaw is all about. During his Hall of Fame career, he made it a point to maintain a close personal relationship with everyone else in pro ball, even rookies. "I think he was the only NFL player who ever knew every other player in the league," an aide, Doug Allen, said.

Upshaw's other priority, Allen noted, is, "Winning."

As a winner, he began as a pulling guard. Employed by the 1967-82 Raiders in two cities, Oakland and Los Angeles, Upshaw played the game with concentrated aggression. "Pulling to lead a sweep was my play," he said in an interview later. "Receivers want catches. Defensive linemen want sacks. I got my satisfaction pulling out of the line to lead a running back sweeping around end. That's a play that comes down, at the end, to just me and one man. If I block him clean, we're going to make a long gain. If I miss him, we don't get a yard. So my goal was to crush him."

Upshaw in his playing days disapproved of any other way to proceed. He remembers with mild disdain the cute blocking schemes used in Miami by the offensive line of the Larry Cszonka-era Dolphins – blockers who tricked defensive players as often as they blocked them head-on. "I couldn't believe the junk blocking that line got away with," Upshaw said. "They called it misdirection. Misdirection, hell. On the Raiders, you blew your man off the ball, or they got someone who could."

But the world looks different to a labor leader – particularly a pro football labor leader. You can't blow a rich bunch of club owners off the ball – they're much too tough for that – and Upshaw showed the patience and flexibility to adjust.

He won with misdirection.

iii

To beat the NFL that pivotal year, Upshaw needed, above all, the continuing support of the players, whose inclination for years has been to see themselves as brilliant, talented individual contractors, not union members. Somehow, in the crunch, Upshaw kept their support and prevailed. "Gene is a born politician. We used to call him Governor," said his former Raider roommate, Art Shell, who rose later to head coach. Said Upshaw assistant Allen: "I remember the day that Gene went down a list of nearly a thousand players and told me exactly how each of them differed (on a controversial matter)."

If reading a thousand minds sounds impossible, consider a little thing that Upshaw did one year when I saw him at his Washington, D.C., headquarters. Returning to his office after lunch, Upshaw picked up forty-seven telephone messages – from his lawyers, his wife, friends, co-workers, newspaper reporters, Commissioner Paul Tagliabue, and one player, Jamal Anderson, as I remember. Stacking the messages on his desk in order of priority, he called Anderson first. "In this shop," Upshaw said, "nobody comes before a player."

Officially, Upshaw's union is the NFL Players Association, and officially he's the executive director. His most valuable associate, general counsel Berthelsen, architect of the NFLPA's most successful campaigns, ranks as the smartest of the sports-labor lawyers. The union's assistant executive director, Allen, deals smoothly with NFL players, but audaciously and sometimes abrasively with NFL executives and the media – whatever works.

With Berthelsen, Allen and other handpicked stars on his team, and with his uncommon commitment to the members of his union, Upshaw has achieved smartly as the ultimate payer rep in three historic ways:

- An AFL-CIO vice president, he has become one of the most powerful labor leaders in America. As a California AFL-CIO executive, Bill Robertson, said several years ago: "Our three bright lights are Richard Trumka of the Mine Workers, Ron Carey of the Teamsters and Upshaw."

- Though Upshaw is but one of hundreds who have fought the NFL over the years, he's the first to bring the rich and mighty old league to its knees. Pro football's club owners, united and unbending, had held off free agency for three-quarters of a century before Upshaw dropped them in 1993 – in the courts and then at the bargaining table – freeing hundreds of players.

- Upshaw has emerged, finally, as one of a small handful of Americans who have found extraordinary success in two prominent, very different fields. Of the thousands who have played pro football since Red Grange, Upshaw is one of a couple of hundred in the Hall of Fame. And of the thousands who have led labor unions since Samuel Gompers, Upshaw is one of the few spectacular winners.

Said Commissioner Tagliabue: "The explanation is that Gene has shown the same level of ability at the NFLPA that he showed on the field."

iv

It was in the late 1980s that Upshaw and his players, after taking one blow after another from the owners of NFL clubs, hit bottom.

With their first blow that time, the owners broke a critical NFLPA strike with what they called replacement players – a dignified term for undignified people – and what the players called scabs, also undignified but more appropriate.

Then, after the NFLPA voted to end that strike in time for the sixth weekend of a torn season, the owners decided to teach the players another lesson, locking them out – without pay – for still another week. "The owners rubbed their noses in it," former Commissioner Pete Rozelle said.

Finally, a few months thereafter, a U.S. Appeals Court ruled that although a 1982 bargaining agreement had lapsed, the players' union was still bound by its provisions. Spectacularly one-sided, this decision meant that there was no reason for the owners to deal with the union again – and many never meant to.

Depressed but unyielding, Upshaw called his staff together in Washington the next morning to consider a new game plan. In his view, he had four options. He could (1) sign with the owners on their terms and resume the NFLPA's age-old bargaining for incidental perks, such as more meal money. He could (2) start another court case in a different district and hope for a better result. He could (3) resign. Or he could (4) run a misdirection play, disbanding the NFLPA. Union commitments to the owners, made in 1982, would no longer be valid if there were no union.

In the end, astounding some associates, he adopted the fourth option.

"If the owners can ignore us for as long as we're a union, then we won't be a union anymore," Upshaw said, making one of the century's most dramatic and far-reaching labor decisions.

That surprise action stirred many doubters – few unions ever willingly decertify – but it is regarded today as one of the century's boldest moves by a union leader. "It was brilliant strategy," Robertson said from his AFL-CIO office.

Rozelle, who wasn't involved in the negotiations, said: "To my knowledge, the owners had never considered a situation where the union would cease to exist. Under labor law, they could have stonewalled Upshaw and his union indefinitely. Decertification changed everything."

What it changed the most was the courtroom status of the players. Left alone to face the owners as individuals, they became, instantaneously, free agents. Since the players no longer had their union, the owners could no longer use the old agreement with that union as a shield against antitrust allegations.

A New York Jets halfback, Freeman McNeil, and several other players whose contracts had expired, immediately shopped themselves around the league but got no offers. Then Upshaw's lawyers used this obvious collusion by the owners as the basis for an antitrust suit.

And in a series of legal proceedings in Judge David Doty's district court in Minneapolis, judge and jury both ruled for the players. Suddenly, it was the owners who faced the hard choices. They could either, one, risk their net worth in antitrust cases; two, accept total free agency with no draft of college players; or three, crawl back to Upshaw and make a deal. In the end, they adopted option three, whereupon he certified the union once again.

Upshaw watchers say, however, that it wasn't all quite as easy as it sounded afterward. His game plan wasn't unanimously popular in the NFLPA, although the lawyer who had the most input, Berthelsen, said it was foolproof. From the start, the hardest part wasn't convincing the courts or influencing the club owners but keeping the NFL's players in line. In U.S. team sports, that is never easy. During the 1998 National Basketball Association strike, for example, the players' union was broken not by the NBA's club owners but by the players themselves. When the power forwards and reserve guards lost their commitment and unity, they fell easy prey to the billionaire ownerships.

In the NFL fight, Upshaw made sure that that wouldn't happen. "Our strategy wouldn't have succeeded without Upshaw," Berthelsen said. "Winning took all the personal leadership and courage that Gene could muster."

The NFL in its long war against Upshaw fought him with everything it had. For one thing, needing an agreement from a union of some kind to justify their annual collusion in the player draft, the owners continuously sought to overthrow him. In three distinct instances, they strongly backed three former players who had set out to organize pliant new unions. Moreover, at a time when Upshaw commanded the loyalty of ninety-three percent of his membership, NFL executives repeatedly said, "The player sentiment I hear most often is, 'Save us from our union.'"

There was no truth to that. The NFL just said it.

Most threatening of all – and most mean-spirited – the league struck hard at Upshaw's revenue base: the NFLPA's licensing arrangements for trading cards and other products. The owners offered large cash sums to players who would abandon the NFLPA and sign exclusive licensing permits with the league.

Even though that made the road grotesquely rocky for Upshaw, NFL people still say that during the most bitter stages of their fight, the public was generally unaware of just how rocky the road was. Upshaw found three potholes to be particularly deep:

- To begin with, as the leader of a football players' union, he was negotiating with uniformly prosperous club owners who could have resisted a settlement indefinitely. Indeed, without some key Upshaw compromises, they would be resisting still.
- The NFL's club owners were, in addition, some of the toughest individuals who have ever owned sports teams. They had invariably

fought every other NFLPA leader — and until Upshaw, they had invariably won.

• A majority of the owners had said publicly, and frequently, that they would oppose player free agency forever. Thus, more than their money was at stake, and more than their will. Repeatedly, they had committed themselves in public – putting their pride on the line.

The effect of all this was to put Upshaw's career on the line. The union had so much at stake that if the owners had won, Upshaw, almost certainly, would have been forced out. "But he didn't waver once," Berthelsen said. "Weaker people would have settled sooner, for less. Gene's leadership was decisive."

V

On Texas' gulf coast, Kingsville, population twenty-five thousand, is the big town between Corpus Christi and Brownsville. And, once, Upshaw knew Kingsville well. More than three decades ago, the oldest of three sons of an oil field roustabout, he hitchhiked the twenty-four miles from his birthplace at Robstown to start a new life at the university there, Texas A&I. "My father gave me $75 and sent me off to get an education," Upshaw said. "He wanted me to play college baseball, and hopefully sign a pro baseball contract sometime."

But on the way to baseball practice one day, Eugene Thurman Upshaw II stopped to watch football practice. And soon the football coach came over to watch *him*. He wondered why a big man was just standing there, and when Upshaw showed some interest, "the coach gave me a uniform, and three days later gave me a scholarship," he recalled.

In college, he began as a six-footer weighing 205 pounds. "I grew to six-five and 260 in one semester," he said. "That's five pounds more than I weigh today."

Upshaw got his first brush with the outside world during the college bowl season of 1966-67, his last year at Texas A&I. "I was an unknown from an unknown school when they invited me to the Senior Bowl," he said. "I played with guys who had never heard of either me or Texas A&I, but it was a thrill to play with the best players of my generation: Bubba Smith, Gene Washington, Bob Griese, Steve Spurrier, Floyd Little, Mel Farr, Nick Eddy, George Webster, Alan Page."

Six months subsequently, Upshaw was invited to a bigger show, the Chicago All-Star game. New venue, same players. And one day Griese and Little called a players-only meeting. By then, the unknown from the unknown school was everybody's friend. He was elected captain, unanimously.

Associates report that in his management style, Upshaw, who in recent years has lived in Great Falls, Virginia, with his wife Gerri and two sons, is unpretending, open-handed and open-minded. "I don't think of myself as a (labor boss)," he said. "My philosophy is that the NFLPA only has one boss: the players."

An employee who noticed Upshaw visiting spiritedly with a letter carrier at the NFLPA building one day said: "Gene is the only one I know who treats everybody the same." That is a result, no doubt, of Upshaw's background. "My earliest memory is picking cotton in the Texas heat," he says. "My brothers and I were out in the fields every day, from dawn to night, well into our teens. You don't feel like pushing people around when you remember the years you spent tearing up your hands picking cotton."

Years later, his back-breaking cotton-field background helped give him the determination not to take his football talent for granted. "Every year when I headed for training camp with the Raiders, I never had a job, the way I figured it," he said. "I always went in fighting for a starting position."

He has run the NFLPA about the same way, fighting for his job every day, striving for labor peace in his time. And when a peaceful player-owner solution was finally reached, Upshaw was applauded by all of his members except the few who had demanded what they called total free agency.

At the time, as usual, he talked back like a statesman. "Total free agency would have been unhealthy for the players as well as the owners," he said, mentioning the need for a draft to maintain competitive balance. "Our union and the league both made major compromises in a win-win situation. The NFLPA wants the NFL to be successful. We're all better off if both sides are making a lot of money."

For a labor leader, that attitude, as conciliatory as it is enlightened, is a match for the creativity and raw courage Upshaw showed during the negotiations. His legacy is that, for better or worse, the league will never be the same.

14. Terrell Davis: Most Efficient of the Running Backs

IT TAKES TWO threats to win today: See Terrell run to set up the pass, which in Denver sets up the run.

To the defensive football players and coaches who have to control him or lose, Terrell Davis of Denver is the running back of his time. And, an increasing number argue, of all time. Along with football itself, the game's best ballcarriers have been improving steadily for a hundred years. Ever-increasing excellence has extended from Pudge Heffelfinger, a converted guard, to Bronko Nagurski, a converted tackle, to Jim Brown to O.J. Simpson to, as many maintain, Terrell Davis.

At the same time, it is true that many of us continue to grade Simpson as the best of all the running backs. Others vote for Brown. Or Gale Sayers, say, or Eric Dickerson or Hustlin' Hugh McElhenny. But if the basic requirements for the position are fundamentally dissimilar – either straight-ahead power and strength or broken-field quickness and elusiveness – Davis seems to be uniquely qualified. Nearly as strong and powerful as Brown, he is nearly as quick and evasive as Simpson.

In short, during his first four years in the NFL, Davis has combined greatness in each of the disparate but primary virtues, plunging and cruising, to mold himself into the most efficient ballcarrier of the century. After but four NFL seasons, Davis is:

- One of only four members of the two-thousand-yard club. The others with two thousand single-season yards are Simpson, Dickerson (whose 2,105 is the record), and Barry Sanders.
- One of only three members of the seven-game club, running backs who gained a thousand yards in the first seven games of any NFL season. The others are Simpson (who did it twice) and Brown.
- One of only three running backs with a per-game NFL career average of more than a hundred yards. Davis is first (105.1), followed by Simpson (105) and Brown (104.3).

It is also clear that as a late-century star, Davis is luckier than any predecessor. He came into pro ball just in time to join up with a successful veteran quarterback, John Elway, now retired, and a winning coach, Mike Shanahan. And the interlocking benefits have been imposing.

For, on the championship level, against defenses that have been improving for a hundred years, football has evolved into a game that can now be effectively played only by a well-coached offensive team that has two eminent forces, one at quarterback, one at running back.

That kind of two-position eminence hasn't until lately been a need. In former decades, Nagurski, Simpson, Jim Brown, Earl Campbell and other running backs often carried the offense. And at times, passers have done it – passers like Norm Van Brocklin and Joe Montana who could win big without the supplemental services of a superior running back.

Against late-century defenses, however, neither Simpson nor Van Brocklin, as they once performed in Buffalo and Philadelphia, respectively, could expect to get far without their alter all-pro.

The problem facing every offensive coach these days, and every offensive player, is that the evolution of defensive football has changed the NFL in historic ways. Today's good defensive teams have the power, agility, and know-how to handle any great running back who has to do it alone – Detroit's Sanders, for example – or any great but unsupported passer, say Miami's Dan Marino.

What the defenses can't stop – what a pro club must have to win now – is a quarterback-running back pair so gifted that when they play off the talents of each other, they disrupt every possible defense. In the course of winning seven consecutive Super Bowls in the 1990s, all NFL champions have had that combination, Dallas with Troy Aikman and Emmitt Smith, San Francisco with Steve Young and Ricky Watters, Green Bay with Brett Favre and Dorsey Levens. And most recently, Denver with Elway and Davis.

In the Super Bowl games of 1998 and '99, good NFL defensive teams were successful against one Bronco threat or the other – either one they chose – but not both, leaving Davis as MVP one year and Elway the next.

In the Davis Super Bowl, Elway passed for only 123 yards and was called by some critics a non-factor in a game Davis dominated with assertive forays through the Green Bay secondary. But the unseen story that day was Elway's arm, and the attention paid to that arm by the Green Bay defense, which prevented a single Elway completion to a wide receiver until deep into the third quarter. With eyes to the sky, the Green Bay defense was run into the ground by Davis.

The next year, the Atlanta Falcons ganged up on Davis, only to watch Elway, his old bones loosened by the Florida sun, have what would have been for a less bionic being a career day.

Addressing defensive players who were about to lose twice to Denver last season, Kansas City Coach Gunther Cunningham put the problem this way: "I told them, 'You guys only have two things to worry about – the run and the pass.'"

A Denver writer who is often critical of hometown teams and players, Woody Paige, made the point another way. "Elway and Davis," he said, "are to the Broncos what Ruth and Gehrig were to the Yankees, Magic and Kareem to the Lakers, Ike and Monty to the Allies."

The two-star impact can be breathtaking. In most Bronco games, for example, Davis starts fast. Setting up Elway's pernicious play-action passes,

Davis one season averaged more than seven yards on first-quarter carries. But Elway set up Davis, too. Though Elway's pass-efficiency rating each year was usually on the NFL's unimpressive side – low to mid-80s – it was often very high on first-quarter throws. His first-quarter rating has hit 120 and more.

Thus if Davis, for instance, sometimes seems to be making the Denver offense go singlehandedly, Elway, just by being there, has been a major contributor nonetheless. That is the view of, among others, Bronco full-back Howard Griffith, who, cornered by Denver writers one day, asked, "Would Terrell be able to do all these things if he were playing for the Carolina Panthers?"

In Detroit last season, a Davis booster had one comment on that. "Defenses know I'm not going to run through them," said running back Sanders, "but Terrell can run over you, and he can run around you."

What's his secret?

ii

In the very early light of a recent October Monday morning, as Denver Coach Shanahan walked by the club's weight room, he was jolted by the sight of a familiar figure hoisting heavy bars with the determination of a marginal rookie at training camp. Weight lifting, Shanahan knows, is beneficial but boring. Thus few Denver players were then in sight as Terrell Davis, who takes body-building more seriously than probably any other Bronco or opponent, lifted away as single-mindedly as he had run away from the Seattle Seahawks just the day before. He had gained 208 yards that afternoon in Seattle. He had carried the ball thirty times.

"If I'd known you were going to be in here this early," Shanahan told him, "I would have given you ten more carries yesterday."

Just kidding.

And anyhow, ten might not have done it.

Davis is a running back whose goal, seemingly, is an iron body. Of all the unusual things about him, the most unusual, possibly, is that in weight rooms and elsewhere in his awesomely physical world, he keeps himself as hard as his helmet. So tacklers tend to bounce off him like bumper cars in an amusement park. And attacking the NFL's toughest defensive players, he can comfortably carry the ball thirty times or more when asked.

Game-time overwork has damaged, in some cases ruined, many other running backs. It has slowed down Emmitt Smith, for one. The physical fitness experts say there are only so many hits in any human body, Ali's or Emmitt's or Terrell's or yours. But so far, Davis has prospered despite what often appears to be overwork. After a loud game-time collision, he is typically the first player up. Everyone in the league talks about his durability.

A few days before Super Bowl XXXIII, he was asked to explain this. "The one thing that scares me the most is failing, especially on this level," Davis said. "That's why I stay in Denver year-around and work out. When I go places, my first priority is working out, trying to condition my body, keep it in shape."

And there's something else.

"The one thing I've always said that I'm blessed with," he added, "is that I'm probably the only running back in this league that didn't really play college football. So I'm still fresh. These are my college years."

In other words, he saved himself a lot of hits at Georgia, where he backed up Garrison Hearst, the running back who has rejuvenated San Francisco.

"At Denver, we don't practice with pads," Davis said. "I don't get hit during the week. And on Sunday, I really don't look at the carries. I don't measure the way I feel by how many carries I get."

Or how many hits.

On the day of the 1998 Super Bowl game at San Diego, where Davis at age twenty-five was the MVP, he weighed just 200 pounds, or a touch under. Though he had added ten pounds for his second Super Bowl appearance and though his height, 5-11, is ideal for Davis' weight and type, he remains one of the smallest of the NFL's first-rate running backs. He *needs* that iron body.

The more so because he is not only small but slow.

In the NFL from the start, his lack of speed "was no secret to me," he said. "I always knew that. Even running around and racing with the kids in the neighborhood, I wasn't the fastest. In high school, they put me at fullback because I didn't have the speed."

As a pro, nonetheless, he often leads the league in plus-fifty yard runs. What he has is what the league calls sneaky speed. Once in the open, Davis is seldom run down by even the fastest defensive backs, some of whom, no doubt, as they trail behind, wonder what has made their shoes so heavy.

Davis can blast through the smallest holes in the scrimmage line. Still, to watch him carefully is to understand that on running plays from scrimmage, power isn't Davis' main weapon. The qualities that drive him are uncanny vision, first, and then instant acceleration.

No other great ballcarrier of my time has matched Davis' full-field vision. During Bronco games, while running laterally behind the line after a handoff, he seems to spot the hole *before* it opens. Then, turning into the line, he accelerates into high gear with his first few steps; and before the linebackers see there *is* a hole, he's through it.

It's his inborn nature that gets this done, of course, and Davis, like any other running back, is the sum of his instincts. "Sometimes I don't even realize I'm doing half the stuff I'm doing," he said.

He is also the sum of everything in his background, much of which no one envies. The product of a harsh and humble San Diego childhood, he used his 1998 autobiography, *TD: Dreams in Motion,* to talk about what it's like growing up in a troubled family.

In that volume, which he wrote with Denver sportswriter Adam Schefter, Davis reviewed the times when his late father, out of jail for awhile and drunk again, beat him and his brothers with an extension cord, or lined them against a wall and fired a gun above their heads. He also reviewed the times when he was arrested for an old, familiar California crime, stealing car rims, and when, more seriously, his brother shot a pregnant woman and killed the baby she was never to know.

"But you can control your life," he said. "If you're in trouble as a child, you can turn your life around. That's one of the messages."

Another message is that the migraine headaches that have bothered Davis for most of his life, ruining much of his 1997 season and benching him temporarily in his first Super Bowl, can be controlled. "I have a preventive medication that I'm taking," he said. "Any time I work out or practice, I take it."

Whenever he is going to need medication, he reminds himself mornings at home, before the day begins. For Davis, who is still a bachelor, home today is a big house in the Denver area where he lives alone.

Of the troubles and handicaps he surmounted on his drive to the top, not the least was his sixth-round place in the draft. He was passed over by all thirty NFL clubs, including Denver, until 195 other players had been drafted. He wasn't even Denver's *first* sixth-round choice that spring. At training camp, on some teams, he would have gotten hardly a look. On Mike Shanahan's team, he got a thorough test, and passed it, and he and Mike have been happy about that ever since.

Along the way, Davis, as he reminds all interviewers, has had a lot of help, starting with one of the best blocking lines – and one of the best line coaches, Alex Gibbs – of recent NFL years. Davis' personal bodyguard, he said, is fullback Griffith, and he's also aware that Denver's wide receivers willingly do more for him than they do for themselves.

Bronco tackle Harry Swayne, giving up few secrets of the Gibbs system, said, "We just come off with the ball, hit people under the chin, stay with our blocks, try to get away with as much as we can."

Center Tom Nalen, talking about blocking for Davis, said, "We'd be blocking the same way for any back. But he makes us look a lot better than another back would."

Davis, asked about that, didn't try to deny it. He said: "It's a game of angles. It's all about setting up your blocks."

So in study hall every day in Denver, Davis spends more time on linebacker tendencies than any other subject. He is an expert on every veteran linebacker in the league. The result according to former Super Bowl MVP Marcus Allen: "Terrell sets up his blocking better than anyone in football."

Accordingly, Dallas running back Emmitt Smith has found the secret to the Broncos' success. "I know there is a reason to be afraid of Elway," he said. "But Davis is the one killing you."

Davis or, some would say, Shanahan. Or Elway.

The correct answer in two big Super Bowl campaigns was all three.

Shanahan and Davis have spent their entire four-year varsity careers together in Denver; and after all that, Shanahan sums up: "Terrell is the only guy I've ever been around who doesn't have a weakness."

iii

Despite the undisputed excellence of Shanahan and Davis and their offensive linemen, they needed Elway, or someone like Elway, to go as far as they've gone in the NFL's late-century years.

Someone like him? There's nobody like Elway.

And their challenge now in a world without Elway is to somehow succeed without him. For it was the bombs-away Elway game that opened the field to running back Davis, spreading the defense from sideline to sideline and, what's rarer, from the scrimmage line to the goal line on most plays.

Bronco wide receiver Ed McCaffrey was generally aware of this when Shanahan brought him in from the 49er team in 1995. But he didn't really believe it until the first day of his first Denver minicamp, when, McCaffrey said, the design of a Bronco play sent him flying sixty yards down the field. Turning, he saw that Elway, studying the defense, was still deciding whether to hit McCaffrey or the other wide receiver, Rod Smith.

"So I started to slow down," McCaffrey said, "thinking there's no possible way that he's going to throw it to me now."

At just that instant, Elway fired.

"He overthrew me about ten yards," McCaffrey said. "I tried to accelerate and get it, but it was too late. From then on, I realized that anytime the ball is still in Elway's hands, you have a chance. He can get it to you anywhere on the field."

Like Elway, McCaffrey went to Stanford, but that was years after Elway's time, too late to join the society of the Elway cross. Old Cardinals still talk about it. The Elway cross was the mark made by the nose of the football on your arms or chest when his passes whooshed through your hands and hit you fast and hard.

"You adjust to his velocity or you go play somewhere else," they've been saying for what seems like most of the century at Denver and Stanford and at California's Granada Hills High School, where Elway pitched and batted the baseball team to the Los Angeles City championship and where the football field has been renamed Elway Field.

Before his spring-time retirement after his second Super Bowl win, Elway played quarterback so long and so well that he holds most of the NFL's quarterback-longevity records, among them:
- Most wins all time.
- Most scrambles all time.
- Most sacks all time.
- Most comeback wins (forty-seven).
- Most Super Bowl starts (five).
- Most disappointments.

Well, maybe he's had competition on the last one. But in Elway's sixteen years in the league, considering his skills, he had too many disappointing years – fourteen in a row, in which he lost three Super Bowls – before hitting the jackpot with Shanahan in the 1998 and '99 Super Bowls.

His problem during his first fourteen NFL years was a coach-player incompatibility. Always the most daring good quarterback in the league – always poised for a long risky pass or a long risky scramble – he played year after year for conservative coaches who hated what they thought of as daredevil football. His head coach through most of those years was Dan Reeves, clearly a gifted leader who has gone to four Super Bowls, but has yet to win one. Always conservative, Reeves in the Super Bowl has turned almost obtuse, once trying to bang for a one-yard touchdown on four straight runs, with the most gifted run-pass quarterback in football handing off, against the brutal New York Giants goal line defense, for a grand total of no points.

On January 31, 1999, when Elway's team, now under a passing coach, Shanahan, beat Reeves' new but still conservative running team, Atlanta, in Super Bowl XXXIII, there were lessons to be learned. The Broncos won by taking chances with Elway that the Falcons repeatedly declined to take with their passer.

Reeves, who had turned his new quarterback loose just the game before, and watched Chris Chandler win the NFC championship, tightened up in the Super Bowl once again. As Elway, after faking to Davis, threw first-down bombs, Chandler handed off until the game was gone.

Among those who couldn't have been happier with the result were Elway's parents, Jan and former coach Jack, who now heads pro scouting for the Broncos, and the rest of John's family: John's wife Janet (who first met him at Stanford) and their four children, Jessica, age thirteen at that Super Bowl; Jordan, eleven; son Jack, eight, and Juliana, seven.

Continuing advice from Jack has benefited John all these years, his mother told *USA Today* writer Jill Lieber at Super Bowl XXXIII.

"John Elway didn't just happen," his mother said that day, recalling his boyhood years. "Jack would tell him to do something, and he would practice and practice."

John grew up throwing things, always throwing something. "Footballs, baseballs, mudballs, rocks," his mother said. "He'd stand in front of the house for hours on end, throwing rocks at a telephone pole."

One day when his mother was at the market, John went next door and uprooted a neighbor's gravel driveway one stone at a time, hitting a distant tree with one stone after another.

Said Jan: "Jack had to pay for a load of gravel to have it resurfaced."

So it was no upset that he could hit McCaffrey in the Super Bowl. Said sister Lee Anne: "John is the best quarterback ever."

Going into Game XXXII, though, Elway's Super Bowl record had been 0-3, the three defeats inspiring three long bursts of tears in all six beautiful Elway bedrooms in Denver. Just before Super Bowl XXXIII, where he bettered the record to 2-3, he talked about what happened the first three times.

"We didn't put in the game plan until we got down here," Elway said.

"But Mike, having been with the 49ers, saw how they did it – they put it in the week before."

Following the 49ers' lead, Shanahan twice installed Bronco game plans quietly at home before leaving for the mandatory week of turbulence at Super Bowl sites, where Denver won both times.

"There are so many Super Bowl distractions," Elway said, "that it's nice to have an idea of what you're going to run before you get here. So when you do get here, you can just polish. As far as I'm concerned, it's one of the most important things you can do."

The defeats at his first three Super Bowls still rankle. But this is a player who has plenty to be proud of, too. One of only three NFL quarterbacks who have ever thrown three hundred touchdowns and only the second to pass for fifty thousand yards (putting him just behind Dan Marino), Elway became the most successful member of the celebrated quarterback class of 1983. Marino is the only survivor. Gone are Jim Kelly, Tony Eason, Ken O'Brien, Todd Blackledge, and now Elway

The coach of the New York Giants, Jim Fassell, thinks there are two reasons for the difference between Elway and the others in the class of '83. "I would say John Elway is the greatest quarterback of all time," said Fassell, who originally recruited him for Stanford. Second, the Giant coach said, "A big part of his success is with their running attack. It takes all the pressure off him."

So, once more: Davis and Elway. And Shanahan makes three.

"I would have loved to have been in this offense for the last sixteen years," said Elway, who might have become the biggest Super Bowl winner in history if, all that time, he'd had a coach like Shanahan and a running back like Davis.

Sixteen Davis-Elway years? Stop dreaming.

QUARTERBACKS:
Throwing and Thinking

1. Sammy Baugh on Calling the Plays
2. John Unitas: Confidence Man
3. Frank Ryan: Ph.D. Passer
4. Joe Namath Invents a National Holiday
5. George Blanda: How to Win Football Games at Forty-Seven
6. Jim Plunkett: The Sensitive Quarterback
7. Jim Kelly: How to Lose Four Super Bowls
With a Team That Wasn't That Good
8. Steve Young and the Passers of the Century

Probably no position in sports has evolved as drastically in the last ninety-nine years as football's quarterback position. In the early years of the century, the quarterback was nothing more than the player who handed the ball to other players. There have been times since then when he wasn't even that; during the long Single-Wing era, he was primarily a blocker. Then with the coming of the T Formation in the 1940s, as their sport became increasingly more sophisticated, quarterbacks moved from the bottom to the top.

On every NFL team, in a game increasingly given to big-play passing attacks, the mid-century quarterback was both passer and play-caller. As game-day commander, he was as important and influential as any coach. Among those who became, in truth, more influential were Sammy Baugh, Johnny Unitas, and Joe Namath.

Then in the 1970s, the quarterback fell back again, not all the way, but irrefutably, as the coaches invited themselves in, taking command. Following the lead of Paul Brown, calling all the plays themselves, the coaches turned the quarterback into a technician who in time, in an era of omnipresent passing, came to be evaluated almost exclusively as a passer. That is his state today. He is no longer in charge of anything, even his own passes. The quarterback has become a hired bazooka.

During earlier, big decades for quarterbacks when they served as their own play-callers, they all rated that as their most important responsibility, with passing a distant second. Even today, when earlier generations of coaches and players are discussing former quarterbacks – Namath, for example, or Baugh, Unitas, Terry Bradshaw or any of the others – they grade them on generalship first and *then* passing.

Thus, it can't accurately be said of any late-century player, even Joe Montana or Steve Young, that he is the best quarterback of all time, or even comparable with, say, Unitas or Namath.

Modern quarterbacks can be compared as passers – they can be judged, that is, on their physical ability – but historically, that had been only half the job, the easy half.

In 1950, as founder and leader of the Cleveland Browns, Brown settled in as the first NFL coach to call all the plays. Though other coaches were relatively slow to follow Brown's lead, by Bradshaw's time (1970-83), coach and quarterback were sharing the play-calling. As the Pittsburgh Steelers won their first two Super Bowls, Coach Chuck Noll called most of the plays. When they won their last two, Bradshaw called most of them. Subsequently in Oakland and Los Angeles, the Raider play-caller on two 1980s Super Bowl champions was also a quarterback, Jim Plunkett.

But Plunkett was the last of a breed, the last NFL player ever *awarded* that responsibility. By the mid-1980s, on every pro club, a coach was sending in all the plays. The only NFL player-play-caller since then has been Buffalo's Jim Kelly, who was not handed that responsibility. He seized it.

In Kelly's time the league's other quarterbacks were all, in leadership terms, robots, fundamentally, as they are today. But that is not to say they're irrelevant. In an NFL game, the quarterback still starts every offensive play, throwing or handing the ball off. On some teams more than others, he still changes plays with audible calls at the line of scrimmage. In a sense, therefore, he is still the leader on the field. And, to be sure, a great passer is still any team's greatest asset. The ability to throw a football accurately during moments of personal, violent attack is still much the hardest thing to do in this sport or possibly any sport.

But throwing *and* thinking was twice as hard.

1. Sammy Baugh: The First Great Passer

GOOD PASSING IS vital, but it was only half the job
when Slingin' Sammy was also the play-caller.

The man called Slingin' Sammy – that's Sammy Baugh – was the league's first dominant passer. It was as a Washington Redskins rookie in 1937 that Baugh began beating people up with his arm. Others, previously, had only done it running the ball.

Starting as a late-1930s passer, Baugh played halfback, or tailback. That was before the T-Formation revolution, and in Washington they had him throwing his bullets out of the Redskins' old Double Wing formation.

By 1946, having changed formations and positions, Baugh, now in the T, was the losing quarterback (to Bob Waterfield) in the first NFL game I covered, the Times Game in Los Angeles. A season-opening exhibition, it was the first of forty-nine years of Ram games in California.

Baugh also punted that night. The NFL's best punter for sixteen years, he finished as the greatest of all time. One season his punts *averaged* more than fifty yards (51.3 in 1940).

On defense, as a safetyman, he intercepted four passes one afternoon in Washington, setting a record that has been tied by fifteen other people but never surpassed by the specialists of the two-platoon generations.

In after life, Baugh was a rancher, a weather-beaten old Texas rancher who rose before sunup each morning to quarterback the thousand-odd mother cows with whom he shared twenty-seven thousand acres down there. But after years of punching the cows around, he still held eight major NFL records, as he still does. One season he completed 70.3 percent of his passes. One day he completed 85.7 percent.

In the Washington backfield from youth to middle age, Baugh led the league in passing six times. Only one other NFL performer, Steve Young of San Francisco, has ever matched that. On the first ballot for the NFL Hall of Fame in 1962, Baugh and Chicago Bears owner George Halas were the only unanimous choices.

In the winter of 1969, when Baugh returned to Los Angeles for a visit, it was still being said throughout the league, as it had been said for years, that there will never be another passer like Slingin' Sammy.

That February afternoon, however, Baugh remarked that he'd already found one: Joe Namath of New York. I found that fascinating. Namath was yet a youngster, with only four years experience, although one of his games was Super Bowl III, which he had just won in the football century's greatest upset.

I also found Namath's talent compelling, and since one rarely has the chance to ask, say, Bach about Beethoven, I pressed Baugh on his opinion. Answering, he turned a spotlight on both Namath and his position.

"In the next four or five years," Baugh said, "Namath can go down as the finest passer who ever played the game. Only two things could stop him, his knees."

If Namath has the talent of an All-Pro, Baugh was asked, how do you account for his occasional lapses from form?

"Very few people fully understand the value of experience for a quarterback," the old quarterback said. "Namath doesn't know his job yet. Neither did I when I was his age. Joe has had four years. I have always felt that my best year was my twelfth in pro ball. My best three were the tenth, eleventh and twelfth. Namath next year will still be making some terrible mistakes – some game-losing mistakes – that he will avoid instinctively when he's an old pro."

Provided he gets to be an old pro.

"I sincerely hope that his knees will allow it," said Baugh, who that year, along with the rest of us, lacked the knowledge that Namath's knees would ruin him prematurely. "A pro quarterback," Baugh continued, "can't be ranked with the great quarterbacks until he's played at least eight years. He has to prove he can handle himself over a distance of time. Playing ability alone doesn't mean that much. There have been a lot of flashes in the pan, a lot of great high school stars who didn't have the self-control to do a man's job over a stretch of time."

What is the quality that separates a great quarterback from a good one?

"The quick answer first: It's the ability to call the right play at the right time. That's all there is to quarterbacking. But wrapped up in that simple answer are so many thousands of things that nobody has ever mastered them all."

What's one thing, for example?

"You have to know every weakness of every player in the league – and the exact strength of each of your teammates in relation to all those defensive weaknesses. There's no sport in the world nearly so involved as football. Automatically, just by living, a quarterback gets better every year."

As a veteran whose sixteen NFL years are impressive, if not the longevity record, you must agree that most athletes retire prematurely.

"They used to. I think there's been a better understanding lately of the fact that an extra year of experience more than cancels out some loss of agility. The coach who took over the Rams (in 1966), George Allen, has grasped this point and convinced his players. I was disappointed that Otto Graham and Norm Van Brocklin both quit so early. As a football fan, I felt Van Brocklin deprived me of his best years."

Van Brocklin was a bomb thrower – which is a reminder that Sammy Baugh has been called a great short passer who couldn't throw long. How much does that disturb you?

"It hasn't bothered me at all because what it shows is a misunderstanding of football. The idea is to throw the ball where you have to throw it to complete a pass in the time you can rely on your protection to protect you. I was neither a long passer nor a short passer. I was a protection passer. And in the nature of things, that usually means a shorter pass. Van Brocklin threw too long too often when he started out in Los Angeles. He finally became a great passer in Philadelphia, at the end of his career, when he shortened down. The 1940 Redskins (Baugh's team) threw bombs about as often as the Eagles did in 1960, Van Brocklin's championship year. That was the year he convinced me that he'd arrived at the top."

Calling on your thirty-two seasons as NFL athlete and coach, what would you say is the best way for a player to develop his football ability?

"Only practice one way – the hard way. If you're a punter, always punt into the wind. If you're an end or halfback and the coach says to run it out fifty yards, run a hundred. If you're a passer, throw off balance in practice. Don't drop back into the pocket in dummy scrimmage. Don't see how accurately you can throw over the top. Throw it sidearm, or off your shoes, or left-handed. The coach knows you can throw accurately overhand with nobody rushing, or you wouldn't be in there. So practice the hard way. Then the games will come easier."

John Unitas told me one time that in practice, he aims to make things difficult for everyone else, too.

"Unitas is the example of what I mean. Nobody ever outworked him in practice. As a passer, Unitas has the best touch of all, and in this respect it will be a long time before Namath catches him."

How much does it distress you, thinking back to your wages as a pro quarterback, to read that Namath got $400,000?

"Not a bit. They'll make $4 million someday. What I say is, more power to Namath. He has the benefit of television – all their money – and also the pressure. All those viewers. I have to laugh when I think back to my rookie year in Washington. The three highest paid guys on the team got salaries of $2,750 – and we won the world championship. So one of them, Cliff Battles, asked for a $250 raise, and quit when the Redskins wouldn't pay him $3,000. Namath's taxes are higher than that – but pros don't play for money. They play for pride."

How do you define pride?

"There's something burning deep inside you that drives you to become the best man in the world at your job. I still have the same desire. As a cow-and-calf rancher, my goal now is to raise all five-hundred-pound calves in the six months before I sell them. When I get there, I'll shoot for five-fifty and then six hundred. The only other goal I have is, when I'm through, I hope to leave the countryside better than I found it."

2. John Unitas: Confidence Man

A COMMANDING PRESENCE rivaling that of
any coach made this quarterback a champion.

At quarterback for the old Baltimore Colts in the 1950s and '60s, John Unitas was a thin, crew-cut blond with watchful eyes, a long chin, long arms, long fingers, and, when things were going well, a bashful grin. In action, another quality distinguished Unitas: his boundless self-confidence. With that, he made up for certain limitations of ability, limitations he overcame to become the great quarterback of his time and, with Sammy Baugh and Joe Namath, one of the three greatest of all time.

Voted Hall of Fame Quarterback of the Decade for his achievements in the 1960s, Unitas played his two big games two years earlier, leading the Colts past the New York Giants in the two NFL title games of 1958-59. The first one, won in sudden-death overtime in New York, 23-17, is still referred to back East as the biggest football game ever played. Although pro football had already broken through in the Far West, with crowds in Los Angeles often over 100,000, Unitas' overtime win changed the nation's media hub, New York, from a baseball town to a football town after baseball's Giants and Dodgers had pulled out earlier that year for new homes in California.

Unitas as Baltimore's play-calling field commander that afternoon brought the Colts into easy field goal range in sudden death, then, in defiance of conventional wisdom, kept them going to the winning touchdown. In subsequent years, every other team that got into field-goal position in overtime kicked the ball, often on third or even second down. It was, apparently, Unitas' unique confidence that drove him onward that 1958 day in New York. As he said afterward, he had more faith in himself to produce six points than in his kicker to produce three.

"Unitas is the most confident man I've ever known," a contemporary All-Pro, Merlin Olsen, said one day in 1973, a year after Unitas retired. A massive (for his time) athlete who weighed 270 and stood six-five, Olsen during his brilliant career and afterward always deferred to Unitas, who was 170 and six-one.

"He was the greatest because he was a quarterback," Olsen said. "No position in football requires more ability. No position in any sport is even remotely as hard to play. NFL quarterbacks are the greatest athletes in America. And the bravest. John Unitas is the bravest man I've known in football."

Asked for an explanation or an example, Olsen said: "Out of the corner of his eye, when Unitas could see you coming, I swear he'd hold that ball a split second longer than he really needed to – just to let you know he wasn't afraid of any man. Then he threw it on the button."

Other athletes who played against Unitas a generation ago typically cited two other things. He won, they said, with passes and play-calling.

He had not been the league's most accurate passer when the NFL tried him out the first time in 1955; he was cut and driven back to Baltimore to play sandlot football for the year. But by working on his passing endlessly, he developed the competence he displayed when he came up the next time, in 1956, and as a result, two years later, he was playing for the NFL title and winning it.

Although he was accurate short and long with an arm of only middling power, it was the creativity of Unitas' passing that distinguished him. He and Colt receiver Raymond Berry, for example, invented the sideline pass that was really on the sideline, where Berry had to tip his toes in and lean out precipitously to snag a ball Unitas had seemingly thrown out of play. Unitas also invented a throw no other quarterback, then or since, has ever tried. With his tight end swirling out and down the field into an open spot in a zone defense, Unitas would feather a soft arcing ball just over the linebackers and just in front of the safeties. Caught by Hall of Fame tight end John Mackey at full stride, rather than stopped dead with back to the defense, this Unitas invention allowed Mackey to earn points toward the Hall by mashing little safeties flat.

His most conspicuous creation, however, is the pass now known as the "fade." In 1971, the first time Unitas played against the Oakland Raiders, he instantly concocted an antidote for the bump-and-run pass defense which the Raiders had created and with which they had torn apart many pass offenses. In action that day, Unitas seemed uncharacteristically inaccurate: Two of his long passes to wide receiver Willie Richardson fell yards short. Richardson apparently saved Unitas by slowing down, then leaping over his defensive back to make the plays that decided the game.

Braced in the locker room, however, Unitas said he put those balls right where he wanted them. "A bump-and-run corner has his back to me. He can't see the ball. I just put it up and let Willie jump for it." Today, from the twenty on in, we see this Unitas invention in virtually every game.

Nevertheless, the definitive Unitas quality, I thought in his first championship season, and I've felt ever since, was his shrewd generalship. In a close race, he's right there with former 49er Coach Bill Walsh for best signal caller of all time. In the locker room after winning, he was the first quarterback to explain big plays with a refrain that was to become a cliché: "I just took what the defense gave me."

His meaning: If the defensive team concentrated against the Baltimore fullback, Alan Ameche, Unitas threw the ball to wide receiver Berry. If the defense sagged linebackers off to double Berry, Unitas sent Ameche into the line. In the '58 title game, as the Giants feared yet another Unitas pass (he had just, astoundingly, thrown from the seven-yard-line for a first down on the two), it was Ameche who scored the overtime touchdown. On that play, moreover, as Giants stacked to the Colts' left, expecting a play that would position the ball for a field goal directly in front of the goal posts, Unitas sent Ameche off right tackle, instead, where he encountered no Giants at all.

A year later, I looked up Unitas in Baltimore, where he was fixing to win another championship, and questioned him on that classic set of calls. I asked him specifically why he was so confident that Ameche, or someone, would score that sudden-death touchdown.

In football, he said surprisingly, confidence can be made. The key, he added that November day in 1959, is that "I have learned how to concentrate. That's one thing I'm really thankful for."

But how does concentration build confidence?

"It doesn't exactly build confidence," Unitas said. "It keeps you from thinking about it. I am lucky enough to be able to concentrate so hard on the job to be done that I never think whether I can do it."

Suppose you throw an interception and your fans are screaming at you.

"I found a long time ago that nobody can do two things at once. It's impossible for a quarterback to hear a crowd of people *if* he's trying to hear himself think at the same time. Maybe I'd be better off to stop and listen to the fans. I'm sure they have some good ideas, but I just can't do it."

I was here the day you threw your first pass for the Colts, which was intercepted. That must have worried you a bit.

"No, I took it in stride. When we got the ball back, I raced into the game, called a running play, and we fumbled – and the Bears scored another easy touchdown. I learned right then it's six of one, half a dozen of the other. I have never worried about fumbles *or* interceptions again."

People say that's how you look – you never seem very emotional.

"The best way to play this game, in my opinion, is calm and collected. Keep cool, and keep thinking – that's the way to win."

Football coaches all talk about the value of enthusiasm or emotion, about being up instead of down, and so on. In your opinion, how vital are intangibles like enthusiasm?

"That depends on what you mean. You have to like football, you have to like anything to do it well. But as far as I'm concerned, this is a thinking man's game, not an emotional game."

Many coaches have said that football is sixty percent emotion.

"Nonsense."

What is it then?

"It's sixty percent preparation – physical and mental preparation. Myself, I work at it all week. I watch film and study and practice. That's my pep talk. I don't need a holler guy around."

But isn't a pre-game nap in the locker room going too far?

"Well, I've done that for many years. It's my theory that getting plenty of rest is beneficial, and that the holler guys and the worriers just burn themselves out. The way I look at it, the coaches should do the worrying, and the fans should do the hollering."

3. Frank Ryan: Ph.D. Quarterback

*A RICE INSTITUTE math professor
doubled as a champion NFL quarterback.*

After the Rams alternated two quarterbacks, Bob Waterfield and Norm Van Brocklin, to win the NFL championship for Los Angeles in 1951, they packed it in. They've never won since, either in California or Missouri;

and as a rule, they haven't even come close. There has in addition been one other constant. More often than not, they've blamed the quarterback.

The quarterback position is, in fact, one that is not widely or well understood, either in Los Angeles or the rest of America. In the whole of team sports, quarterbacks play the only position where great talent doesn't guarantee success. There are four other requirements, and no passer in a century of football has ever succeeded without them.

To win an NFL title, a talented passer must have the quarterback experience that Sammy Baugh was talking about a few moments ago; he must have the self-confidence that John Unitas talked about in the last essay; he must have talented support, both on offense and defense, and he must have, most crucially, good coaching.

In 1951, the Rams had all that when they won with Waterfield and co-starter Van Brocklin. But they changed coaches twice in the title-game years, the second time immediately after the one of three they won. Thereafter, the club failed repeatedly with Van Brocklin and his two successors who, after the Rams traded each of them away, demonstrated that blaming the quarterback is rarely useful: Astonishingly, the three ex-Ram passers quarterbacked three other teams to the championship. Chronologically, Van Brocklin was traded to Philadelphia, where he won the NFL title in 1960; Billy Wade was traded to Chicago, where he won the NFL title in 1963, and Frank Ryan was traded to Cleveland, where he won the NFL title in 1964.

Of those three, Frank Ryan may not have been the best quarterback, but he was incomparably the most interesting man. Playing a position that then required brains to accompany talent, Ryan, even so, was intellectually overqualified – as he proved when he won his championship the same year he earned a Ph.D. in math from bookish Rice Institute.

At Cleveland, in Ryan's first bid for the title, the quarterback he beat in one of the most surprising NFL championship games ever played was John Unitas. When I got up that morning in a Cleveland hotel, two days after Christmas, the wind was blowing a gale. And at game time it was still blowing hard. But when Unitas had the wind, for fifteen minutes in the first half and fifteen in the second, he unaccountably called un-Unitas-like, strangely conservative plays and failed, even once, to score. When the Browns had the wind, Ryan, the underdog, came out throwing to rout the Colts, 27-0.

As of that game, Ryan had been in Cleveland for three seasons after

172   FOOTBALL IN AMERICA

four seasons in Los Angeles, where, the day the Rams traded him, he told me they were premature. "It takes seven years to make a pro football quarterback," he said.

The next time I saw Ryan, it was forty-eight hours before the 1964 championship game. He was then twenty-eight years old, and, when he met me after football practice that cold, December week in Cleveland, he was just about on schedule. That was his seventh season in the NFL. And he was looking forward to his day with Unitas, brimming with the necessary confidence that seemed, nonetheless, unaccountable.

"I'll win," Ryan said flatly, making the same prediction that was to make Joe Namath famous when he guaranteed it four years later.

A trim, scholarly chess player who joined the Rice Institute faculty as a math professor four weeks after making good on his forecast, the former Ram passer had a fittingly logical set of reasons for his championship-quality confidence: "We have more offense than Baltimore has. Ours is a bit more conservative, which should be a better fit with this weather, and ours is a better-balanced offense than Unitas has this season in Baltimore."

What about the quarterbacks? I asked him that day as we stood on the practice field in a flurry of falling snow. Everyone, I reminded him, is saying that Baltimore has the edge with Unitas over Ryan.

"I haven't seen a Baltimore game this year," Ryan said, conveniently ignoring the fact that he's seen plenty of Baltimore movies. "But I do know that I'm a better quarterback than I used to be in Los Angeles. I've learned to make plays that I could never make out there. Did you see the Browns-Giants game on TV the other day?"

Yes.

"One of our big plays that day was the long pass to (rookie receiver) Paul Warfield, just before the half. It was sort of a broken-pattern operation. Paul was running what we call a double-out. He was supposed to go ten yards and out, then ten more and out again. But he broke it off after the first leg and kept going deep because he had his man beaten. It surprised me so much that if it had happened in my Los Angeles years, I'd have eaten the ball. But I've learned now that receivers can't always do what they're supposed to do. I stood in and threw. I must say that it wasn't a very good pass, but it got to Warfield, and he caught it."

In that same game, the play Ryan used the most was a quick pass to Warfield or sometimes (receiver) Gary Collins slanting in. It worked over and over against the Giants' (man-for-man) defense. How can you work it against the Colts' zone defense?

"I'm not prepared to answer that question yet. We'll talk after the game. In general, you fit the pass to the defense, of course. The Giants were giving us that pattern – a quick seven-yard slant-in. Warfield runs it like a veteran, and he's very fast, but the Colts may give us something else. With the coaching we have here, we think we can adjust to any defense. It's much better coaching than I had in Los Angeles."

Those were slow years with the Rams, no matter who the coach was. But what have they done with you in Cleveland that Ram coaching staffs couldn't accomplish?

"In Cleveland, they coach me. In Los Angeles, they assumed that I was a passer – and that if I didn't deliver, it was because I just wasn't good enough. One of the biggest fallacies in football is that passing can't be taught. They teach it here."

How do they do that?

"Coach (Blanton) Collier covers, in detail, everything there is to know about passing, as if this were the first place I'd ever seen a football. Then he breaks the job down to fundamentals, and criticizes me in detail when I'm the least bit off in execution. He talks about passing as a three-step procedure. First, you get set. Second, pick out a target. Third, drill the ball with authority. Several times a game, Coach Collier may have to remind me. He will say: 'You threw that one off balance, Ryan. Watch it.' Or: 'It looked to me like you just threw that in the general vicinity of Big Jim (Brown). Pick him out and drill him.' Or: 'You were pulling the string that time, Frank. Drill it.' That's coaching."

During the week, how much do you work with Collier on strategy?

"It works this way in the Collier system. (Offensive coach) Dub Jones and I do most of the planning. I take the movies home three times a week, so does Dub, then we get together. We weed out the plays from our basic offense that won't go against the defense we're playing, and maybe we'll make some additions."

It sounds like you have the same studious approach to football that you must use in math. But how much does the night work in football cut into the time you ought to be using for your Ph.D. dissertation?

"Very little, the writing is just about finished."

How much longer do you have to go?

"I'm set for the degree in June, and starting next month I'll be teaching a senior mathematics course at Rice. From now on, I'll spend the off-season on the faculty there."

What's the toughest part of the dissertation that you have left to do?

"Frankly, my hardest job right now is putting a definitive title on it. All I can tell you is the mathematics field it deals with."

Then tell me.

"It deals with asymptotic sets of functions holomorphic in the unit circle."

4. Joe Namath Invents a National Holiday

THE QUARTERBACK POSITION, in my view, reached its apogee with this passer. There have been great ones since Namath, but none better.

Broadway Joe Namath was football's nonesuch passer. During the decades since throwing a football began to be fashionable in the 1940s, I have never seen a quicker, more accurate, or more strategically aware passer. His Hall of Fame celebrity could rest on that alone. More than that, however, much more, Namath has been the key evolutionary figure in two of the most important breakthroughs of football's first century.

First, he made the Super Bowl a national phenomenon. That happened at the end of the 1968 season, when Namath's arm and leadership were decisive as the New York Jets upset an eighteen-point favorite, the Baltimore Colts, in Super Bowl III. Previously, the Super Bowl had been just another game. Since Namath, it has been the biggest of all football games, the biggest annual sports event in America. Each January, in truth, Super Bowl day is now in effect a national holiday.

Even more significantly, in terms of football's evolution as a sport, Namath was the inventor of the most efficient way to throw a football: the way many of the leading quarterbacks throw it today. Think of John Elway, or watch Dan Marino, Troy Aikman, or, for example, Chris Chandler. They deliver the ball as Namath did – with a quick and compact hip-and-shoulder turn that replaced the former fashion, which called for both a big windup and a lengthy pre-launch stride.

When Namath first joined the old American Football League in 1964, the classic throwing motion was Unitas' roundhouse, over-the-top, straight-ahead style, based on one (or two or three) forward steps. Unitas himself was quick and crisp in his maneuvers, but others who adopted his style were slowed down by a big windup and long strides.

When quarterbacking experts first saw Namath, by contrast, what he did happened so fast they couldn't see it clearly. In time, he and my son Bob wrote a book about it, with stop-action photos, called *A Matter of Style*, and his thoughts became a part of football's coaching culture.

In essence, what Namath did is replace a straight-line, forward motion with a hip-turning centrifugal motion. Setting up with his left side facing down the field and his left shoulder cocked under his chin, Namath would suddenly uncoil his hips and shoulders, with little or no forward step and no windup whatsoever. The ball would be gone in four-tenths of a second. As the stop-action pictures revealed, his motion was so perfectly refined that it matched in every detail, from foot placement through hip sway and shoulder swing, the turning motion of shot-put champions – whose motion is perfected by the heavy weight they must propel.

To the other quarterbacks of his generation and to every coach of that time, the Namath way seemed peculiar. But with it, he rose to national prominence as football's finest passer, a distinction that's still his.

In keeping with the great quarterbacks of his generation, moreover, Namath was also a masterful leader and a penetrating signal caller. No football player ever so thoroughly dominated an important game with his mind, with the pure power of consciousness, as Namath did Super Bowl III. His brash "I guarantee it" prediction, backed up by surgical play selection and solid passing, caused a melt-down in the Baltimore defense (by the third quarter two key Colt defenders were ignominiously benched).

At his best when spontaneous, Namath was certainly the best line-of-scrimmage play caller the game has seen. Often, he skipped a huddle selection altogether, telling his team simply, "Check with me." He reasoned, sensibly, that you could call plays better at the line, after seeing the defensive formation. And his calls struck fear into defensive players' hearts. Said All-Pro safety Dick Anderson of the great Don Shula-led Miami Dolphins teams, "You could hear it in his voice. You'd listen to him call an audible, and you just knew he had you."

Whether he called the plays at the line or in the huddle, Namath excelled at a rare skill – the ability to stay with a play that was working. Though this sounds absurdly easy – to keep calling a trap play, for instance, if the trap is gaining yards – in fact, for quarterbacks and coaches alike, it's one of the most difficult lessons to learn. Whether from the desire to fool the opponent, or to show off, or simply out of boredom, the urge to keep changing plays is all but overwhelming. For Namath, however, who could change up as well as anyone when the situation demanded, the ability to stay with a winner was deeply ingrained.

The most famous instance came in Super Bowl III, when Namath got fullback Matt Snell rolling on a weak side slant behind the blocking of left tackle Winston Hill and halfback Emerson Boozer and kept at it until he finally ran Colt defensive end Ordell Braase and outside linebacker Don Shinnick out of the game and onto the bench. Jets fans remember another time when, against the great Miami Dolphins team of the early 1970s which dropped linebackers into deep zones play after play, Namath drove to the winning score by throwing six consecutive swing passes to fullback Don Riggins.

For cult purists, however, the near-mythical example came in a 1971 regular-season matchup of Hall of Fame signal callers, Namath against John Unitas. In Super Bowl III, Unitas had been injured and, in relief, ineffective. But in this game, both were at full strength, and both played gloriously in a game that totaled nearly eighty points by both teams.

Halfway through the fourth quarter, Namath had a ten-point lead but Unitas had the ball. Orchestrating one of his seemingly inevitable master-pieces, Unitas called a little bit of this and just a taste of that, all of it exactly what the Jet defense wasn't looking for at the time, and drove the Colts sixty-seven yards to a touchdown.

Namath was down to a three-point lead. As he ran out on the field, he assumed that the Colts, who needed the ball back immediately, would blitz hard to stuff a run or disrupt a pass. This, he realized, would leave his speedy tight end Richard Caster one-on-one with a rookie safety leaning toward the line of scrimmage. Namath called a bomb to Caster, aired it out perfectly, and got his ten-point lead back in one eighty-yard strike.

Unitas then returned to the field and, inspired by his daring opponent, he reached into his bag of tricks to construct a Chinese puzzle of a drive, bamboozling the Jets play after play and moving to the touchdown that cut the Jet lead again to three.

Three minutes to go. One more kickoff through the end zone. One more time Namath faced the same situation, a desperate Colt defense that would come full force. And in a transcendent moment that will shine as long as football is loved, he called the same bomb to Caster, threw the same arcing pass, and watched as Caster raced away the eighty long yards to score.

Never in the evolving history of football as a strategic sport has genius so magnificently trumped genius.

For all his excellence, however, Namath in his own time was not universally admired. He was a 1960s person as well as a 1960s athlete. And to much of America, the freedom and forthrightness that came to be identified with 1960s guys added up to a gigantic mistake. Off the field

Namath appeared, for one thing, to be living a carefree life that every red-blooded, crew-cut citizen hated him for, a life prominently featuring bourbon and blondes. Worse, in public, he was at pains to nurse the image. For awhile as a football player he owned saloons in Florida and New York, until the NFL made him sell the New York place, Bachelors III.

Of those who in the 1960s resented Namath for his way of life, old football players and older sportswriters were particularly prominent. Until that era at least, most football people had been socially conservative, and they didn't mind criticizing any child of the 1960s, even Namath; or more exactly, especially Namath. Thus, in the September before Super Bowl III, an old Hall of Fame quarterback, Otto Graham, made a typical old-pro observation when he called Namath "a great passer who may never be a great quarterback because he doesn't have the respect of his teammates."

Continuing, Graham said: "The Jets have never named Namath their Most Valuable Player. They voted him fourth place once, but never higher. That's what his own team thinks of Broadway Joe."

During the 1968 week that Graham made that analysis, I was in Kansas City, as it happened, for an opening-day NFL game, the Jets at the Chiefs. Nobody knew then that that was to be Namath's big season. Nobody knew he'd be in the Super Bowl five months later. But I had concluded that as a football player, he was something special, and I'd determined to keep him in mind that year. So, on the day before his first game, I looked up Broadway Joe after practice.

After pleasantries and a couple of perfunctory questions, I asked him for a comment on Graham's complaints. His face darkened for an instant, then he smiled. Pulling his belt tight, Namath looked at his watch, looked up, and said, "I'll tell you what my own team thinks of me. They've just elected me captain. They voted me offensive captain of the Jets an hour and fifty-three minutes ago."

The players, it developed, had voted in a Kansas City locker room before morning practice, their final preseason practice of 1968. "It's the greatest honor of my life," Namath said. "The only thing close to it was the day they elected me captain at Alabama."

That morning in Kansas City, the Jets had flown in from New York. They had bused from the airport directly to the practice field for their short workout, then bused on to their hotel, where Namath had the only suite on the team floor. Suites were mandated in his contract, which, as negotiated by club owner Sonny Werbelin, made him football's first

$400,000 player at a time when most of the NFL's other good players were paid $25,000, or less.

On that afternoon thirty years ago, following an agreement we had made in the locker room, I knocked on the door of the Namath suite. When he opened up, he was wearing, all told, brown silk socks, a white towel, a new mustache, and the well-known Namath smile. The well-known, well-scarred Namath knees were also momentarily visible above the socks and below the towel before, with a trace of a limp, he turned back to the television set.

Offering me my choice of a beer or Coke, Broadway Joe kept an eye on the screen. He was rooting for the smaller of two boxers, Jimmy Ellis. "I've got a $5 bet with Milton Gross," he explained. Gross was a New York sportswriter.

As the host hunched over in his chair to keep up with the fighters, he looked as round-shouldered as Stan Musial. A hard, lean, 205-pounder, Namath led the league in sex appeal that year – women who hated football loved Broadway Joe – but it was clear that he would never be a West Point poster boy. In his prime, Namath and a football, in fact, resembled a bow and arrow – the bow was six feet two – and at practice that Saturday, the arrows, as usual, had been launched with impressive accuracy.

To watch him watch a televised fight, his feet resting on the coffee table, one knee terribly scarred, the other one worse, was to make a guess: Namath would go as far in this league as his knees would take him. The best forward passer some of us have ever seen was, at the same time, one of the most famous active cripples in sports, a survivor of three knee operations in four years. His guest wanted to talk to him about those knees, and so after the fight was history, and fresh, chilled draft beer was on the table, there was a question for Broadway Joe: Should the pro football establishment be taking more steps to guard and preserve its quarterbacks before it loses them all?

Namath tugged at his then-new mandarin mustache as he considered the question. "I've thought about that," he said at length. "This year I guess every quarterback is giving it some thought, but I have to hope they don't do anything. A drastic rules change would ruin the game. I'm not in favor of anything that would detract from the essence of the game."

What do you believe that is – the essence of football?

"The fight to get at the quarterback," Namath said. "The fight between the offensive line and the defensive line. As I was telling (Hall of Fame defensive end) Deacon Jones the other night, that's what pro football is today. And if the defense wins, you've got to give them their trophy."

The quarterback?

"Yep, me. Throwing a football is not that tough if you're just standing there throwing it. I know some girls who could do it, some very lovely girls. In pro football on practically every play, there's a receiver open. So when you talk about passing a football accurately, what you mean is the ability to find that receiver in that unbelievably crowded field, to see him, and throw the ball straight to him – or to where he's going to be – before angry seven-footers get to you. A few passers can do that, most can't."

It is being said more and more, however, that sports like auto racing and football – and even boxing – are too dangerous to continue in their present form.

"Speaking of my sport, I don't agree. I think there's a place for a contact sport like football, and I'll take it the way it is. Deacon Jones has a job, and I have a job. He likes his, and I like mine. Injury and risk of injury are a part of it, that's all. The only thing I fear is losing. I can't stand to lose a game."

In retrospect, what do you think today about the injuries you have had? (Raider lineman) Ben Davidson broke your cheekbone in Oakland last December, and got off with a fifteen-yard penalty. Did the punishment fit that crime?

"I suppose so, although I've been quoted as saying he took a cheap shot. That isn't quite what I said. I'm very much against anyone hitting me after I've thrown the ball, but my job is to throw it and get the hell out of the way."

They say you haven't spoken to Davidson since.

"I stay away from him. I always have. The first time I played Oakland as a rookie, he went for my knees. No one else ever did that. I'm not what you would call a Raider fan."

A week after breaking your cheekbone, you went down to San Diego and set the pro football record for yards in one season – 4,007. Didn't it bother you to have to play so soon with an injury that severe?

"A fracture only hurts for a couple of days, but I did add a bar to my face mask. I wear a double bar all the time now. If there was room, I'd wear a third one. A nose like mine is some target."

I noticed you limping today, a little. What have you hurt this time?

"I hurt my toe dancing."

Your toe?

The big one.

Where was the dance?

"Coach (Weeb) Ewbank gave the team an extra day off last week, and three of us went to town and got a suite. It was some weekend."

At this point in your career, would you say that the Namath lifestyle harms Namath the athlete?

"Maybe it's bad for me to say this, but I might be a better football player if I didn't like to stay up and see so many late movies. But I can't change the way I am. In the last ten years, right up to this minute, I've only changed one thing."

What was that?

"I gave up smoking on April 12, 1967."

What time?

"It was just after 3 a.m."

Where were you at such an hour?

"In Beverly Hills."

As a frequent California visitor since the year you signed that first $400,000 contract, have you had an opportunity to make a detailed comparison between California girls and New York's?

"They talk different in Los Angeles. That's a movie town, and in California the girls are all interested in that. But they're all pretty, very pretty."

Have you invited them to Broadway Joe's?

"My new restaurant? That's in Miami. We're going public this winter – a Wall Street company is handling the stock sale."

Can you wear that mustache on Wall Street?

"The mustache comes off when we win the Super Bowl. At least, that's what I told the lady last night."

Postscript: Showing Missouri

Twenty-four hours after our visit at his hotel, Namath had a game to play. The Chiefs, their next-day opponents, were among several in the American Football League rated ahead of the Jets at that time. And in the other conference, known then as the National Football League, at least a half dozen teams could beat the Chiefs or Jets, or any other AFC upstart. Or so everybody said. It was to be a storied season, one in which I covered Namath's first and last games. He won the first in Missouri, 20-19, beating the previous year's AFC Super Bowl entry, and the last in Super Bowl III, beating Baltimore, 16-7.

In both games Namath displayed the leadership and play-calling acumen which, combined with his quicksilver throwing motion, made him the great football player of his era.

To give the flavor of Namath in action, here are the first few paragraphs of the game story I sent back to the *Times* that day:

KANSAS CITY: Sept. 16, 1968 – New York Jets Captain Joe Namath, the most controversial quarterback in football, began his fourth season as a pro by upsetting a Super Bowl team here Sunday, 20-19, in a game he ended with an artistic ball-control drive. When the Kansas City Chiefs closed to the one-point margin of the final score, 5:56 remained, whereupon Namath took possession on his five-yard line and ran out the clock.

He held the ball for the game's last fifteen plays. "They were almost all audibles," the Jets' new offensive leader said later.

Before the largest sports crowd of all time in Kansas City, 48,871, Namath had opened a 17-3 halftime lead with two long passes to receiver Don Maynard, who was asked afterward if he can still run forty yards in 4.6. "It depends on who's chasing me," he said.

Kansas City won the second half by almost the same score, 16-3, because the Jets made one blunder after another, and because Jan Stenerud, the Chiefs' resolute kicker, made one field goal after another until he had a total of four.

It seemed likely that, before long, Stenerud would finish with a fifth field goal, the game-winner. For, when he kicked off after number four, a Jet halfback ineptly ran the ball out of bounds on his five-yard line. But this was to prove the final New York blunder. More than five minutes were left, and they all belonged to Namath.

"I was handicapped on some calls because I couldn't afford an interception at that stage," he said. "I had to pass safe – and that's something I never do if I can afford it."

During his last, long, 5:56 move, in a number of clutch predicaments:

• Namath could have escaped trouble on the drive's second play. From the New York four-yard line, although he reached Maynard slanting across the middle on second and eleven, the ball was dropped during a loud collision with the middle linebacker.

• Undaunted, Namath made his first clutch play on the next play. On third and eleven, he came back with the identical pass, which Maynard held this time for a net of sixteen yards. Asked why in such a grave emergency he would repeat a play that had failed, Namath said: "I was keying on the safeties, and they left Maynard for the middle guard

(linebacker). No middle guard can handle Maynard twice in a row."
- Namath survived three more third-down crises with straight throws that were caught each time for not much more than the required yardage.

As Namath marched, Stenerud, Kansas City Coach Hank Stram, and the big crowd died one play at a time. Namath kept going for fifty-six yards until there was nothing left on the clock but its motionless hands.

5. George Blanda: How to Win Football Games
(as an Age Forty-Seven Quarterback)

FOR QUARTERBACKS, THE key to longevity is to kick
the ball, meet the challenges, and ease up afterward.

The oldest NFL player yet was a quarterback, George Blanda, the only athlete who ever played big league pro football for a quarter century. Doubling as a kicker, Blanda lasted, in all, for twenty-six years, in which he scored 2,002 points, the NFL record. An Oakland Raider when he retired in 1975 at age forty-eight, he was older than many of his coaches. Many of his teammates were born after Blanda began his quarterback career with the Chicago Bears in 1949.

In his wildest game as a pro, Blanda threw seven touchdown passes for an NFL record he still shares. On football Sunday afternoons, no one was ever more active. But on weekdays at his home near Oakland, before leaving for football practice, Blanda was the certifiable embodiment of the lazy Californian on a long weekend. He had the godgiven ability to ease up, to cool it completely when away from the game, and he completely enjoyed that, as I learned in the December of his next to last season in football.

"The best part of the day," he told me that time, "is loafing around the house, reading the paper, maybe shooting a little pool, or just looking at the bay or the skyline of the city."

Blanda's apartment building edged the broad waters of San Francisco Bay on the Alameda side, and, as we visited there, he leaned back in his recliner, a big man in an old blue cardigan sweater, dark blue shirt, blue plaid plants and old loafers with a hole in one sole, like Adlai Stevenson's. Grinning, Blanda said: "You're wondering how an old man can keep up in a kid's game. I think the two keys are relaxation and challenge – in alternating cycles. I believe in long, regular periods of total relaxation to store up the energy needed to meet the challenge of football."

That made him laugh. "Or maybe," he said, " I'm just lazy."

But not always. It takes some energy to score 2,002 points, which is still three hundred points in front of the field. Explaining it, Blanda said: "I think of myself as a challenge-meeter more than a football player. Nothing excites me like a challenge. On the first tee of a golf course, I feel exactly the way I do kicking a field goal in the fourth quarter. At night, playing pool or giving a speech, I keep pushing myself to do better than last time. The day I threw seven touchdown passes I wanted to throw twelve. A challenge is all the motivation I need. I'm always up. Play the Star-Spangled Banner and I'm ready."

That was as true of Blanda in his forties as it had been in his thirties or twenties. Nor was there much erosion in his skills. His 236th NFL touchdown pass, thrown the week before I visited him, prompted the visit. For that pass beat a good team, the Dallas Cowboys, the team at that moment ranked first in the league.

Including high school and college, Blanda played quarterback, blocking back, tailback and linebacker for thirty-four of his first forty-eight years. He showed me the Christmas card honoring his long career that his wife Betty delivered to him personally the day before I was there. An art major when he met her at the University of Kentucky, she made the card herself. The picture was of Santa Claus visiting with Blanda. Said Santa: "You're the only little boy I gave a uniform to that's still using it."

The Blanda daughter, Leslie, then eighteen, was a freshman that year at San Diego State. George Jr., twenty-two, was an art major at Northern Illinois with ambitions to be a sculptor. As a kid, he never played football. "He's a senior, I think," Blanda said. "This is his fifth year. He'd better be a senior."

As a family, the Blandas, as they reconvened that December for Christmas and an Oakland Raiders weekend, were a comely group with, perhaps, one exception. At six-two and 224, George Sr., built like a linebacker, not only *was* forty-seven at the time, he looked it. He looked like the only player who ever lasted a quarter century in pro football. The hair was long and gray, the face lined and craggy. Like the rings on a tree, there was a crease in Blanda's face for every year he'd been in football.

Although his eyes were on the bay instead of a TV screen, Blanda, in appearance, was indistinguishable from the millions of other middle-aged Americans who used to sit in recliners like his and watch him kick field goals or throw winning passes. He had to be an inspiration to them and others, a symbol of everlasting youth to the middle-aged. If a Blanda nearing fifty could still play big-league football, there was hope for every man in the world in his late forties and fifties.

ii

Religiously, Blanda as a Raider rolled out of bed every morning at 10. He had eggs and bacon or sausage every morning, followed by a walk along the beach or a pool game before it was time to go to work. The Raiders practiced afternoons at a field five minutes from Blanda's apartment.

One day during a walk on the beach, he said, "As a quarterback, I never take a snap in practice any more, but I know everything they do and why. My greatest interest is offensive football."

Thus he studied the Raider offense with the care of a surgeon. Asked if he needed, or missed, practicing, he said:

"From a selfish standpoint, I'd very much like to run some plays during the week. But we have two other top quarterbacks (Daryle Lamonica and Ken Stabler) and there's no way a pro team can practice three quarterbacks. So the other two practice, and I watch."

Don't you even get in there for a series now and then?

"Yes, last week I got four plays," he said, "but the week before that, I didn't have any."

But wasn't that a week that you won the game?

"*We* won it."

You didn't even practice ball-exchange with your center (Jim Otto) that week?

"At one stretch this year, Jim and I went five weeks without exchanging the ball."

It's about time you lodged a complaint with the Oakland coaches.

"I can't do that because I think they're handling the situation right. Lamonica is number one and Stabler is a helluva quarterback, a great prospect. I have no complaints. During the fifteen-minute warmup period, I get to hand off to all our backs. And I throw the ball every day. And we're winning."

How can an NFL quarterback come in cold and win the game when he hasn't even been practicing the plays?

"One thing is more important than practicing, and that's play-selection. In football, play-calling makes a bigger difference than anything else in winning and losing. That's my opinion. At least I've given it more of my time than anything else in the last twenty-five or thirty years."

What do you mean by the term play-selection?

"When, where, and why you throw or run the ball and who gets to run it or catch it."

The four W's, as in journalism.

"I didn't study journalism, but there are a lot of throwers coming out of college these days who can throw the hell out of the ball. They can hit you anywhere on the field – except they don't. Today, nobody wins pro games with a passer who can throw straight. You win by hitting a receiver who is four yards open – and that's play-selection. Your sister can hit a target that's four yards open."

How do you get a receiver four yards open against a modern defense?

"The key is to keep the defense off balance. You have to bear in mind that any team in the league can stop anything it expects. The defense will stop you if they anticipate the play. You can only get a man open by surprising the defensive people."

And you can do all that without practicing?

"I have both the stamina and knowledge to run the offense the way (Oakland coach) John Madden wants it."

Madden is nearly a decade younger than you are. What did he tell you when he sent you in last week against Dallas?

"When John called me over, I asked him, 'What do you want me to call?' He said, 'Do whatever you want to do.' "

What did you do?

"I had been watching the Dallas defense and talking with (Raider receiver) Cliff Branch on the sideline. I'd been hoping I could go in. I told Cliff I'd call one of two plays on first down, if I went in, and to be ready. He was ready, and the one I called went for the touchdown."

iii

Back in the Blanda apartment after the bayside walk, the discussion turned to old man Blanda's football-playing longevity. What advice, I asked him, does he have for younger players to help *them* last a quarter century?

"I don't think there'll ever be another twenty-five-year man," Blanda said. "All my other records will be broken, but it takes a combination of unusual circumstances to last this long in this game. I'm fortunate to be a quarterback and kicker. No running back or defensive lineman could play twenty-five years, and I doubt if a kicking specialist or quarterback specialist could, either. The ability to do both helps you continue to do well at both. Second, I'm fortunate to have been free of injuries. Third, you have to love the game so much you won't give it up voluntarily for any reason. If I were looking for reasons to quit, I've had plenty. And fourth, you've got to be in the right organization. Most football teams start looking to replace you at thirty. Al Davis, who runs this team, thinks about it, too, of course – but he doesn't do it if you're still making a contribution. That's one reason the Raiders keep winning."

What will you miss most when you finally leave?

"The camaraderie. You can't believe how beautiful it is to be around the players and families of a winning football team. The Peter Principle is inoperative in football. Those promoted over their heads don't last twenty-four hours. So everybody has the same goal: winning. In other kinds of businesses, the petty jealousies are enough to drive you into the wall. Everybody wants to be the president of the company or sales manager, and to get there, they'll screw anybody they have to. In a company, the goal is to get to the top personally. On a football team, the goal is to get there together. When I'm out of the game, I'll miss that togetherness more than anything."

More than the money?

"Until 1970 (in Oakland) I never made more than $35,000 in any year. Money doesn't motivate. Don't tell Al Davis, but if he cuts my salary in half next year, I'll take it."

Looking back across your career, which year would you say was your best?

"This year. I reached my peak against Dallas. I'm throwing as well as ever now, and I never kicked better because I'm concentrating more. If you have the physical skills and the right attitude, you don't go downhill much over the years."

What have you gotten out of football?

"Everything I have. My family, a wealth of experiences, a wealth of memories and friendships, a good life and a little prosperity. A football player is looked on as a celebrity and meets the most interesting people. I mingle with U.S. presidents. I have also mingled with the lowest guys on the totem pole – the economy, I mean. Most football players are from the humblest of beginnings. They and their families have worked hard all their lives. My father was a coal miner. My first challenge was to get out of that."

When do you plan to retire from the game?

"When they tear off the uniform. Quitting is easy. Anybody can quit."

6. Jim Plunkett: The Sensitive Quarterback

THE STORY OF Jim Plunkett's resurrection as a powerful championship leader in his last years, with the Oakland and Los Angeles Raiders, is one of the more unusual in football's century.

Super Bowl XV, played in New Orleans in January, 1981, will be remembered as a dual rescue operation. That was the year that the Oakland Raiders brought quarterback Jim Plunkett back to life, after which he brought the Raiders back to life. Playing thereafter with guts and class, throwing short and long with uncommon accuracy, calling his own plays to great effect, Plunkett led Al Davis' Raiders to another Super Bowl win in 1984 (Game XVIII), and was still in charge of a playoff-calibre team on the day in 1986 that the managing general partner benched Marcus Allen for the rest of the decade.

But more than providing a pivotal win for a storied franchise, Super Bowl XV marked a triumph for a trait not usually associated with the sport of football. It was a triumph of simple human decency.

A nice guy named Tom Flores, the velvet-gloved coach of the boisterous Raiders, made the decisive contribution, recognizing the sensitive nature of another nice guy, Plunkett, and providing the only climate in which the former Stanford quarterback could flourish – warm and sunny. To use the language of that day, Flores in his relationship with Plunkett was continuously positive and supportive. And that is what it took.

For in the days before Davis picked Plunkett off the NFL ash heap, the Heismann Trophy quarterback had fallen as low as he could go. After a glorious career as a college winner at Stanford, Plunkett had been nothing but a professional loser until that first Super Bowl season. Indeed he had begun his NFL career with eight profoundly unhappy years.

Beginning at New England, playing for the team that had made him the first pick in the draft, Plunkett had been advised, in what seems certainly to have been the single worst coaching decision in the history of pro football, that he was a macho quarterback who could inspire an inept team by running the ball repeatedly on the college option play. Result: three shoulder operations in five years and a trade to the 49ers.

At San Francisco, he was asked to carry the franchise on his back. But a failed quarterback of Plunkett's psychological make-up can't be made to feel he must carry any football team, let alone a bad football team. Result: when the 49ers offered him around the league for a humiliating price, the $100 waiver fee, no team would pay it.

In time, Raider owner Davis decided to take a chance on Plunkett, and it is Davis who gets the initial credit for leading the rescue operation. Of the NFL's twenty-eight chief executives, he alone could see the possibilities in Plunkett. But day-to-day and season-to-season, the resurrection of Jim Plunkett was orchestrated by his coach, Tom Flores.

ii

The biggest man in the South that week of Super Bowl XV, speaking in a football context, was quarterback Plunkett. A tall, quiet, smiling flamethrower, Plunkett was the focus of attention because no one knew which of two hypotheses was true:

- It was possible, first, that a physically and emotionally battered Jim Plunkett, permanently damaged by a decade of pro football disgrace in which he lost his composure and failed conspicuously in both New England and San Francisco, would fold again in the pressure of the Super Bowl.
- The other possibility was that, astonishing the NFL, Jim Plunkett had made it all the way back – his damaged arm rebuilt, his shattered confidence restored – and that the prepossessing quarterback who led Stanford to a Rose Bowl victory in 1971 would dominate Philadelphia in Super Bowl XV an even decade later.

Not since Joe Namath in 1968, in those long ago days before Super Bowl III, had an NFL quarterback engendered such controversy and confusion.

Plunkett doubters were many and vocal, since no championship quarterback had ever emerged from such a compromised past. And yet there was a small group of sportsmen who felt that Plunkett, was, in fact, back, and that Jim Plunkett back was an awesome force. This group included his former coach at Stanford, John Ralston, his then current coach at Oakland, Flores, and several others in the Bay Area who, having followed his career for years, agreed to talk about him openly but privately. These were the old, old friends who knew him best. And their story – an intriguing, one-of-a-kind of sports story – amounted to a portrait of the controversial quarterback that differed greatly from his public image.

This is what was in their sight lines when these people looked at Plunkett:

They saw a veteran quarterback who at thirty-two was "incredibly shy and sensitive, almost neurotically sensitive." They saw a gifted athlete who, after leaving Palo Alto with the Heisman Trophy in 1971, was all but ruined at New England and San Francisco by "insensitive coaches and executives." At the same time, partially forgiving the Patriots and 49ers, they saw a "deeply insecure young man" with a kind of "split personality."

They said that Plunkett, on the one hand, carried a negative self-image so deeply ingrained that he had trouble functioning. On the other hand, they said, he was fueled by a titanic ambition to succeed. This continuous conflict between a tortured self-image and his driving ambition was a trauma that "has almost torn him apart."

They said that Plunkett, an undeniably able quarterback, needed a football team that above all understood him "and cares for him as a person." Surprisingly, they said, he seemed at last to be a member of such a club. And because the Raiders needed Plunkett as much as he needed someone like them, his friends saw a player and an organization that were meant for each other.

They saw a team that was on the brink of a big victory in Super Bowl XV. And they were right.

For Plunkett that year not only led the Raiders through three hard road victories from a wild-card entry to the playoffs, but dispensed, in the Super Bowl, a performance as close to flawless as a quarterback's can be. "He didn't throw a bad pass," Raider wide receiver Cliff Branch said after Oakland's 27-10 win over Philadelphia.

iii

If the person and the team were meant for each other, there was a ready explanation. To the Raiders, who even yet play football with a consistent long-ball philosophy, Plunkett brought the arm for the very long ball as well as the quick feet to stay out of trouble while Oakland's long pass patterns were developing. To Plunkett, the Raiders, and especially Flores, brought an attitude of patience and understanding, the off-field prerequisite for success for one of the nation's most complex and unconventional sports personalities.

The symbiosis lasted more than one game. After the team put Plunkett back together, he did the same for the team, leading the Raiders, after a two-year non-playoff skid, to one last six-year run at the top. He was the last winning quarterback the Raiders had in the twentieth century, and, in those six glory years, one of the best the game has seen.

The most baffling aspect of the strange Plunkett story to the NFL in general was that, despite all he had gone through physically and emotionally in so many disappointing NFL years, once reclaimed, he seemed to be the same great quarterback, artistically, that he had been at Stanford. Said his Stanford coach Ralston: "He was a great passer in college and he was a great passer for the Raiders. He had that same strong arm, he threw with the same accuracy, and he had the same great sense of timing."

Still, physical ability is only part of football. It is the psychological ability, the mental strength of a great quarterback, that is the possession of the few. And, said Ralston, "This is where Jim always walked a tightrope. He had what it took to be an NFL star, but his self-doubts were always a threat to bring him down. It was literally impossible for him to play for a coach who didn't understand him. He had taken so many blows from life that he just couldn't get hold of a normal view of the world."

iv

The blows that had all but crushed him began to strike in Plunkett's earliest childhood in San Jose, California. From the day his parents were married, after they had met in a school for the blind, they lived mostly on welfare. Said Ralston: "The first time I was in his home, they had a football game on the TV, and his father sat there with his face three inches from the screen. And he complained he couldn't see a thing. And this was the parent who could see. His wife was blind."

Slowly, however, Plunkett built around his feelings of inadequacy. At San Jose's James Lick High School, where he became student-body president, he "was voted most popular boy," a high school friend remembers. Moreover, as a successful senior quarterback in high school, Plunkett was invited to the North-South Shrine game in Los Angeles, where, his friend says, "the coaches took a half-hearted look at him and told him: 'You're a defensive end. We've got a quarterback who's better than you.'"

So Plunkett played all but two minutes – as a defensive end.

"Those coaches were right," Ralston said. "At the time, the other kid (Mike Holmgren, now coach of the Seattle Seahawks) was the better quarterback, but you can imagine what it did to the self-esteem of a fellow like Jim Plunkett. It ruined everything he had slowly built up about himself in high school. What he did next shows you the kind of man he is. He went out and made himself better than the other guy – and everyone else."

He did this at Stanford, where, "obsessed to be the best, Jim would throw the football until his arm fell off," Ralston said. And, gradually, under Ralston's coaching, the honors began to accumulate for Plunkett in college as they had in high school: All-Coast as a Stanford sophomore, All-American as a junior, the Heisman Trophy as a senior, then recognition as the number one football player in the country when the first team to draft in 1971, the New England Patriots, picked him first.

Arriving in New England at the top, Plunkett was asked to run through linebackers, and he spun again dizzily to the bottom. In 1976, the Patriots, disgusted with their handiwork, decided to trade him off. Astoundingly, when the deal was made, the 49ers gave New England three first draft choices and a second for Plunkett – plus a backup quarterback who played for the Patriots for years. The price they paid constituted the only evidence, through eight long years, of Plunkett's innate talent. "I don't guess any other NFL player ever brought four first-stringers and a second-team quarterback," a Palo Alto friend says, naming the NFL names that materialized from the numbers in that draft as a consequence of the Plunkett trade: wide receiver Stanley Morgan and defensive backs Tim Fox, Mike Haynes and Raymond Clayborn, each an All-Pro. If that helped Plunkett regain, in part, his sense of self-worth, it did not last for long. Then in their pre-Bill Walsh turmoil, the 49ers were in the midst of a coaching cavalcade, another one each new year, creating the type of inchoate atmosphere that would destabilize even a more tranquil sort than Plunkett. Within two years, the 49ers were to put Plunkett's name on the waiver list.

He was then only twenty-nine, but nobody picked him up. There were twenty-seven other clubs in the league, but nobody wanted a castoff quarterback who couldn't play for two of the worst teams in pro football. "I marvel that Jim kept his sanity," Ralston says.

But he did. In his first two years in Oakland, moreover, he regained his confidence on the practice field, then led the Raiders to a Super Bowl the first season he got to play. "Millionaire to bankrupt to millionaire to bankrupt to millionaire," Ralston said. "I don't think it's ever happened before in football."

v

During Plunkett's first season with the Raiders, in 1978, Tom Flores remembers they were at practice one day when he called across the field for his new backup quarterback – and the man didn't respond. So far as the eye could tell, Plunkett didn't realize he was being paged. "Maybe it was the way I asked for him," Flores says. "I called: 'Hey, rookie.'" Plunkett and Flores had agreed he would be handled as a rookie in Oakland – as if New England never happened, nor San Francisco, as if 1978 were his first in the NFL, as if the Raiders were the first to employ him.

"When he came to us, I could tell he'd had enough of pressure to last awhile," Flores says. "Everybody expected him to produce immediately at New England as a kid out of Stanford – and as a veteran in San Francisco – even though neither team had enough players to play NFL ball. It seemed to us that the best way to let him know the pressure was off was to treat him as a rookie. He learned our system at his own pace. We wanted him to be eager to play before he had to play."

That finally happened in his third year, in September of 1980. When Dan Pastorini got the first chance to succeed Kenny Stabler as the Raider passer, Plunkett went to Flores and asked to be traded. "I loved that," Flores says. "That was the signal that we had a quarterback."

A month later, Plunkett was in for Pastorini. At Raider practices, thereafter, Plunkett was the most conspicuous athlete in sight. All about him were teammates dressed in the Raiders' colors, the defense in black, the offense in silver, but the quarterbacks were in bright red shirts and pants – red meaning don't touch – and Big Jim Plunkett was the biggest of the men in red. He was six feet two and 205 pounds with massive arms, shoulders and head. He could have been the hero of a Zane Grey novel, black-haired, black-eyed, high cheekbones and all the rest. Although he was of German, Irish and Mexican descent, there wasn't much German and Irish in his appearance. Put him on a white pony and he could have played a Sioux chief.

He remained, nonetheless, a reluctant chief. Asked before his second Super Bowl if he was now the key player on his team, he said, "I hope not." After thinking that over, he said: "I doubt it. I'm one of the keys, along with the defense and our receivers." Then: "In my opinion, one of our receivers will be the key to the Super Bowl."

vi

That was the genuine Plunkett. And if his self-effacing approach to football was unusual in a quarterback – awkward, actually – it was consistent in him. In his habits and preferences, he was, in fact, consistency itself. At the peak of his Raider fame he still lived near his old friends in

Atherton, near his old school in Palo Alto, not far from where his mother lived with his sister in San Jose – an hour or so by car from the Raider practice field in Oakland. He referred to his roommate as Gerry. He had known her in New England. He had known everyone else in the Atherton area for a thousand years. He was only comfortable there. In his eight-year-old BMW, he would drive two hours a day to spend his free time among people he had known always. No sense making new friends when the old ones are perfectly good enough.

The trouble was, this denied the rest of the world access to a man worth knowing. Bright, warm, compassionate, Plunkett graduated as a political science major from Stanford, with an above-average grade-point average, and he maintained an interest in politics and books, mostly best sellers. He also ran several miles a day, in season and out, and sponsored an annual Fourth of July race known as Nuts to Zotts. Those were taverns owned by friends. In the Palo Alto area, it was then about seven miles from Nuts to Zotts. Some four hundred runners competed each year for Plunkett T-shirts (the first hundred competitors into Zotts) and gift certificates. As a rule, the gift certificates went to those who, understandably, were a little slow getting away from the taps at Nuts. This was Plunkett's idea of a ball. He knew them all, the swiftest runners and the slowest drinkers.

For many years when Plunkett did another kind of running – carrying the ball on the college option play for the New England Patriots – it kept him in touch with Stanford. He had to keep flying back and forth to the Stanford hospital for shoulder examinations and operations, three operations in all. This worried his Zotts friends, who thought he was killing himself. And he did have some tough moments. "I'm not the option type," he said later.

Why didn't he ask the Patriots to stop calling such a play? "My feeling," he said, "is that when they employ you, you should do what you're called on to do."

Analyzing himself, however, he thought he was a more physical package with the Raiders than in the days before he was injured. "Everything I've hurt has healed stronger than it used to be," he said. "You work so hard to strengthen an injured area, it's better than new."

If that betrays an unquenchable competitive zeal, it highlights half the reason that Jim Plunkett, in his final seasons with the Raiders, created a professional legacy that could yet earn him a spot in the Hall of Fame. The other half was supplied by the Raiders, Flores in the lead. Between

194

them they demonstrated, yet again, how even a masterful quarterback can be ruined by poor coaching, and, uniquely, how a shattered talent can be regenerated.

If it was a story of simple human decency on a team famous for renegades and brigands, it was, as well, the first pro football story based on a Chicano Connection. In all the years since the NFL began playing championship games, Flores was the first coach of Mexican descent to win one – or even compete in one – and Plunkett the first quarterback.

In their big run in the 1980s, they did themselves, and their families, friends and heritage, spectacularly proud.

7. Jim Kelly: How to Lose Four Super Bowls
(With a Team That Wasn't That Good)

*IN THE LAST two decades only one quarterback has
earned (or stolen) the right to call his own plays.*

Bucking long odds, Jim Kelly built himself into the most unusual quarterback of the 1990s – the only play-calling player of what was, and has ever since been, a coaches' era.

As an NFL player, what's more, Kelly had a most unusual coach, Marv Levy, the NFL's smartest, a Phi Beta Kappa academic. He and Kelly both reached Buffalo in 1986, when it was obvious that the Bills lacked the resources to compete for championships. By 1990, when they had improved some but not enough, Kelly decided to do something about it.

Using the hurry-up, no-huddle two-minute drill as an every-play offense, he took control of play-calling under the guise of speeding up the offensive tempo. Throwing the ball much more assertively than his sharp but conservative coach envisioned, Kelly (1986-96) advanced the Bills to four consecutive Super Bowls while leading average talent.

Those were years in which quarterbacks still called most of the plays in the two-minute drill, when there wasn't time for a coach to retain control with plays relayed from the sideline. By the late 1990s, the coaches had solved that problem by equipping their quarterbacks with helmet radios. But earlier in the decade, Kelly could, and did, seize control in Buffalo. He simply used the two-minute drill more or less continually, through much of the game.

Calling plays that the Bills, under Levy and offensive coordinator Ted Marchibroda, had practiced for Buffalo's two-minute or no-huddle offense – most of them pass plays – Kelly made the no-huddle famous, driving the Bills up and down the field to win game after game.

By contrast, with Levy and Marchibroda calling the plays, the Bills had been a slogging off-tackle team, running twice before throwing futilely. For two reasons, when he got the chance, Kelly frequently threw on first down. First, there aren't many running plays in a two-minute Shotgun offense, whose purpose is to move the team into scoring position swiftly, before the clock runs down on the half or the game. Second, like all modern quarterbacks who encounter sophisticated blitzing on second or third and long, Kelly preferred first-down throws anyway, when all defenses must first stop the run.

And for two other reasons, Kelly's no-huddle offense was a great favorite of Buffalo's sports fans. First, with all their passes, the Bills were livelier and more entertaining than the NFL's conventional, conservative teams. Second, they won.

Indeed, their 1990-93 teams reached the Super Bowl four years consecutively. Although the Bills lost all four times, their achievement in getting there to play in four successive Super Bowl games was among the most remarkable in NFL history – never achieved by any other team.

For the Bills never had the AFC's best talent in that era, when Kelly's generalship and passing were consistently beating better teams – the best of whom, in the AFC of the early '90s, were the Houston Oilers or Miami Dolphins or Denver Broncos or Kansas City Chiefs. To be exact, it was Kelly's calls, not his plays, that won four AFC titles consecutively. His passing, though often brilliant, was more erratic than that of any other winning quarterback of modern times.

What Kelly demonstrated, anew, was that hardly anything in football is more important than intelligent play-selection – meaning plays designed to surprise or confuse defensive players rather than run them down in their fixed defenses.

It took great mental strength and courage to do what Kelly did, and it also took a compassionate, clear-headed, low-ego coach, which describes Levy. Levy could see that Kelly's calls were moving the Bills better than Levy's had, and that the no-huddle offense as run by Kelly could hardly have been a greater contrast to Levy's own fullback-oriented approach. But Levy was more than intelligent. He was philosophical. He had the inner strength, and the breadth of awareness, to avoid taking the issue personally. Remarkably, he was able to give Kelly his freedom – without losing respect from, and authority over, the rest of the team.

No other quarterback since Kelly's time has had the savvy and boldness to emulate him. And, possibly, no other coach would allow it. As one example, when Joe Namath played his last season in Los Angeles, with a Ram team coached by Chuck Knox, the great quarterback could not keep himself from calling a more aggressive and sophisticated game than "Ground Chuck" wanted. As a result, Knox benched Namath at midseason and never let him play another down.

But Kelly and Levy were a remarkable team. And of the four Super Bowls they lost, the first should have been won. Levy let Kelly live, and Kelly put his team in position to win the game, whereupon his placekicker kicked it away. The late-game miss left the New York Giants victors, 20-19, in the Super Bowl game played in January, 1991.

None of the next three Super Bowls could have been won by any AFC team. In order, in 1992-93-94, Buffalo lost to the Washington Redskins, 37-24, and twice to the Dallas Cowboys, 52-17 and 30-13. It was the Bills' bad luck to reach the top in an NFC era. But it was a good-luck time for sports fans. In an age of faceless, stereotypical organizations – both in football and in society as a whole – the fans saw what a single individual could still accomplish if, as Kelly did, he has both courage and the correct conception.

8. Steve Young and the Passers of the Century

SAN FRANCISCO'S SIX-TIME passing champion leads
all fifteen of the century's other great quarterbacks.

During Steve Young's first four years in San Francisco, his annual salary was a million dollars, an NFL record for a non-playing backup quarterback. Some backups would have been happy with half that, or ten percent, but Young was displeased. He was also greatly disturbed. His 49er roommate, tackle Harris Barton, so discovered one day when, fresh out of sweat socks, he opened Young's sock drawer and picked up, instead, a 49er check made out to Young for $50,000 and change.

Thumbing dumfounded through the drawer, Barton finally found the socks he wanted, but only under a sloppy stack of other 49er paychecks, *twelve* other checks, each worth $50,000 – a game's salary, one-sixteenth of a million (less taxes). And change.

"I was too embarrassed to cash them," Young said later when confronted first by his roommate and then by 49er auditors. "Nobody should be paid that much for not playing."

Perhaps not. And, perhaps, nobody with Young's talent should have been forced to sit on a substitutes' bench for four years. But that was San Francisco in the Joe Montana era. And when the era ended, a funny thing happened. The 49ers not only went on winning with Steve Young, they threw the ball better than ever. Young set records that may never be broken *and* he started cashing paychecks.

In each of his first four seasons as Montana's replacement, Young led the NFL in passing – a record for consistency never exceeded or even matched in San Francisco or elsewhere in the league's first three quarters of a century. All told, Young has won the NFL passing championship six times, equaling Sammy Baugh's 1940s league record.

In 1995, Young had the best Super Bowl any quarterback ever had, throwing a record six touchdown passes. In the NFL's quarterback rating system, which counts touchdowns, interceptions, yards and other prime factors, Young has for years been ranked as the highest-rated (lately 97.6) passer of all time. And in average yards per pass attempt, Young is the only player ever over eight yards lifetime. His AYPPA is 8.03.

For these and other reasons, Young stands alone, I'd say, as passer of the century.

It is impractical, however, to classify him or anyone else as quarterback of the century. The evolutionary changes in the quarterback position over the years rule against such comparisons. In the pre-1980s NFL, Baugh, Namath and the others had to call the plays as well as pass. Thus, some NFL-watchers, citing the old guys' heavier workload, list Namath or Baugh or both ahead of Young or Montana or any other late-century player.

But that can be unfair, too.

Unfair to us, Young said.

"I don't see that calling your own signals is a sign of manhood," he said. "It would be fun to see if they could handle all the problems we have today. There weren't many specialists in their day. We have to deal with multiple substitutions all the time – on both sides of the ball. The (pre-1980s) game was far simpler. For us today, on almost every snap, the options are endless."

It follows that the relevant comparison isn't Young versus Namath – which can't be intelligently judged – but Young versus Montana, neither of whom, in the Bill Walsh system, ever left a huddle having called his own play. Although statistics and other facts suggest that Young is the leading modern passer, the material question may be this: Is he even the best passer the 49ers have had?

Those voting for Montana note, above all, that Montana won four Super Bowls, Young only one. And that is indeed a useful gauge. Some say it's the only gauge, but they're wrong about that.

In the Montana-Young comparison, Montana won more Super Bowls for these among other reasons:

- He was the first and for years the only quarterback in the pass-first West Coast Offense, which has since spread to the NFL's other good teams. This gave Montana two breaks: He played in the West Coast when it was new – before NFL defenses had adjusted to it – and his team didn't have to play *against* it.

- Young took over after most defensive teams had changed – both strategically and by using more agile, athletic players – the better to handle the West Coast. Whereas Montana was passing against stone-age defenses designed to blunt the running-play offenses that were universal when he joined the 49ers, Young is being judged as a passer against teams with steadily improving pass defenses.

- And whereas Montana competed for NFL titles on a team dedicated to pass offense against opponents dedicated to running-play offense, Young has been competing against teams with good passers directing good pass offenses, notably the Dallas Cowboys in the early '90s and the Green Bay Packers, among others, in the late '90s. When Troy Aikman three times led Dallas past San Francisco in 1992-93 and '95, the Cowboys, with an offense designed by pass-minded Norval Turner as Jimmy Johnson's offensive coordinator, used West Coast principles all the way – including first-down passes, closely timed short passes and a running game with a super counterpuncher, Emmitt Smith. As for Green Bay, the late-century Packers were built in the image of Walsh's 49ers. So Young, unlike Montana, faced the Cowboys at their peak and the Packers at *their* peak. In his most impressive Super Bowl game, Montana beat Don Shula and Dan Marino, but in his three other title-game wins he faced such typically mediocre AFC champions as Cincinnati and a Denver team that lost, altogether, three Super Bowls.

- Young's NFL coaches have been George Seifert and Steve Mariucci, who, though they seem clearly proficient, are obviously somewhat less qualified than Bill Walsh, the Hall of Famer who invented the West Coast Offense and who influenced an entire generation of his peers to throw the ball instead of running it. By contrast, Montana played his entire NFL career under Walsh until the day he landed in

Kansas City, where, as an aging star, his success was marginal.

The big argument in San Francisco when Montana and Walsh turned the NFL on its head, changing a running-play league into a run-pass league with a pass-play priority, was whether Montana was responsible for the 49ers' success or whether the radical new Walsh system did it. After Montana pitched the 49ers to their third and fourth Super Bowl wins – the fourth under Seifert with Walsh now gone – San Francisco sources said Montana was among the many who held that the credit for 49er success was largely his.

Thus in historical terms, Young's great philosophical contribution to football is that he validated the importance of the Walsh system over that of any individual technician, himself included. In successfully succeeding Montana on the 49er team, and equaling or surpassing him in all respects save numbers of Super Bowls won, Young demonstrated that the Walsh way was the decisive component.

ii

Now that Young has established himself as number one among modern quarterbacks, in the view of at least one voter, who are the other nominees?

And going back a quarter century or so, who were the ablest of the play-calling passers?

There has been so much talent in this position that the most helpful way to define the century's greatest is in groups of four. My nominations here are in both categories.

The Technocats

With the NFL's coaches now firmly in control on the mental level of football – sending in every play – modern quarterbacks can be compared only as technicians, primarily as passers. The four best of these all substituted, as a second skill, running ability for signal-calling:

STEVE YOUNG (1987- San Francisco 49ers) has been a widely underrated quarterback who in the course of leading the NFL in passing six times also carried the ball with the speed and skill of an NFL halfback, cutting by people when possible and running over them when necessary. At his peak, this gave Young a dimension that no other great passer has had.

JOHN ELWAY (1983-98 Denver Broncos) came to fame as a power passer, instinctive runner, and superb fourth-quarter player who could by now have won four or five Super Bowls if he had played all the way for passing coaches.

JOE MONTANA (1979-92 San Francisco 49ers) won four Super Bowls as the original passer in the pass-oriented West Coast Offense. His soft but marvelously accurate throws and Bambi-like grace distinguished a quarterback who is difficult to evaluate in 1990s terms because his was the only West Coast-style team in the 1980s.

OTTO GRAHAM (1947-56 Cleveland Browns) was a converted Single-Wing halfback who won league or conference titles every season for Paul Brown, the first and only play-calling coach in football across a period of several decades. For a technician, Graham called good audibles. As a strategist, Brown even won with Milt Plum.

The next four in this category are Green Bay's Brett Favre, Miami's Dan Marino, Dallas' Troy Aikman, and veteran Warren Moon, now of Kansas City, who, three of them at least, are close enough to move into the top four with another big year or two.

The Play-Callers

During the pre-1980s era when championships were typically won by thoughtful quarterbacks looked up to by teammates as take-charge leaders, the essential quarterback quality was productive play-calling. Of the great quarterbacks who played at that time, there were four standouts:

JOE NAMATH (1965-76 New York Jets) has to this day had only one rival, Dan Marino, for first place in passing accuracy and quickness of release, the two great technical requirements. All the same, the attributes that made Namath a champion – the winner of turning-point Super Bowl III as an eighteen-point underdog – were leadership skills and play-calling excellence.

JOHNNY UNITAS (1956-72 Baltimore Colts), a self-made passer, might not have made a 1990s pro club. But he was the toughest quarterback ever, and the NFL's all-time best play-caller except for a coach, Walsh. Moreover, Unitas was the most inventive of the accurate passers, the man who, for example, first envisioned the lobbed "fade" pass against bump-and-run coverage.

SAMMY BAUGH (1937-52 Washington Redskins), who could pass with unusual accuracy short and deep, made it a point to also work tirelessly on the tough off-balance throws so often necessary in successful quarterbacking. Even so, he once said the difference between good and great quarterbacks is "the ability to call the right play at the right time." Parlaying a great arm with the brain for consistently adroit calls, Baugh led the league in passing six times – an unapproachable record until Young tied it.

TERRY BRADSHAW (1970-83 Pittsburgh Steelers) played for coaches who sometimes called the plays. But when Bradshaw took charge, the Steelers were different and better – as was Buffalo in 1986-96 when Jim Kelly took charge. As play-callers, Bradshaw and Kelly both emphasized first-down attack passes, earning Kelly four Super Bowl appearances and Bradshaw four Super Bowl rings.

The next four in this category were super passers Norm Van Brocklin of Philadelphia and the Los Angeles Rams and Sonny Jurgensen of Philadelphia and Washington, two-time Super Bowl champion Jim Plunkett of the Oakland and Los Angeles Raiders, and Dan Fouts of San Diego.

iii

Of the century's sixteen leading quarterbacks as identified above, only two, Montana and Young, played back-to-back for the same team. That says a lot for the coach who developed both players – Walsh – and also for the 49er talent scout who brought both of them to San Francisco. That was Walsh, too. (For more on Montana, see Chapter VIII.)

As for the qualities that unite the two great San Francisco quarterbacks, one is boldness, which may have been in the genes of both. For Young, you can look back four generations. There you meet Brigham Young, who was Steve's great-great-great-granddad.

Looking back another generation, you meet Steve's great-great-great-great-granddad – Brigham's father John – who fought shoulder to shoulder with George Washington during the American Revolutionary War.

Starting in Missouri not too many decades thereafter, Brigham, a converted Mormon, led a group of persecuted Mormon pioneers from place to place to Utah, where he said, *"This* is the place." He was one of the few Americans to found their own state, which he populated with a hundred thousand others who shared his convictions. Preaching and practicing plural marriage, he had twenty-seven wives, sixteen of whom bore him fifty-six children.

Steve's lineage connects through one of the fifty-six directly to Brigham and Brigham's brother John. "I'm a matriarchic as well as patriarchic descendant of theirs," Steve said. "Both of them married within the family. In those days, people did that a lot."

Asked what he sees of himself in Brigham, Steve said: "I see the work ethic. He was a get-it-done guy as well as a creative visionary. A lot of creative persons don't back it up with drive. He did, and his legacy remains throughout the West." The records show that neither Brigham nor Steve's father, LeGrande, ever won a foot race. Yet footspeed is one of Steve's dominant athletic qualities. Where did that come from? "The other side of the family," Steve said.

From Brigham's side, Steve, who remains a bachelor today, traces his aversion to caffeine, tobacco and alcohol.

During Steve's boyhood, LeGrande, a corporate lawyer, led his own family from Utah, where Steve was born, back to Connecticut, where Steve lived until the day he replaced Montana, when he returned to Utah. The oldest of five children, Steve, for years, left Connecticut only to play football, first at Brigham Young University and then with the pros. At BYU, he developed the patience to wait complacently for Montana by first backing up Jim McMahon, the quarterback who was later to lead the Chicago Bears to their only Super Bowl win. Also at BYU, Steve, in time, studied law. Asked why a wealthy football player wanted to be a lawyer, he said: "Because medicine was too hard."

But such things can be serendipitous. Chances are that Steve's interest in medicine helped him judge the compound severity of the concussions that felled him three times in 1997. Finally deciding that he isn't one hit away from the end of his career, as some feared, he played through 1998 without incident, often running the ball as usual. "I don't see it as a high-risk situation," he said.

He agrees that Walsh made him what he is, rescuing him from Tampa Bay in 1987 when Montana was still at his peak. The strangest part of the Steve Young story is that Walsh saw something in him even when he was 3-16 as a Tampa Bay starter. The Buccaneers, always (until a recent ownership change) interested in cash money, accepted $1 million from the 49ers for Young along with two draft choices, a second and a fourth. Anyone else in the NFL who wanted a talented quarterback could have made that deal, but only Walsh, perhaps, could have turned him into a record-setting passer.

Throwing from the left side, Young was to become famous in San Francisco and throughout the NFL for his remarkable accuracy at every distance from four to forty yards although, in his boyhood, his father had tried to convert him to the right side. A onetime BYU player himself, a fullback, LeGrande told Steve: "I'm not going to have a left-handed son, especially a left-handed first son." Recalling those painful days, Steve said: "He tied my left hand behind my back for a couple of years. Then I think he realized he'd rather have a left-handed son than a right-handed spastic son." For awhile, left or right didn't much matter. Well into his career as a pro, Young was regarded as a skilled running back who was out of position at quarterback, both when he played for the 1984 Los Angeles Express in a short-lived league and with the Buccaneers.

Indeed, he continued to be so recognized in his early years with the 49ers, when he once won a big game with a forty-nine-yard touchdown run that few if any running backs that season could have made.

All this and his accompanying good luck have helped Young become the highest-income football player of all time with well over $100 million in total returns. His first Los Angeles contract made him the sport's first $40 million player — and according to sports attorney Leigh Steinberg, it really was $40 million, of which $37.5 million went into an annuity.

Young sent a bit of the rest home with a note specifying that it was to be used for an expensive convertible automobile that his father had always wanted but could never bring himself to buy. When his son's check arrived, he still couldn't. Instead, LeGrande used the dollars to fund college tuition payments for his other children. It's a family that has always had an extraordinary attitude toward money. There's also a family tradition that of Brigham Young's numerous descendants, great-great-great-grandson Steve is the only one who ever filed thirteen paychecks in a sock drawer.

CONTROL:
It's a Coach's Game Now

1. Amos Alonzo Stagg: The Old One
2. George Halas: Founder of the NFL
3. Paul Brown Systematizes Football
4. Clark Shaughnessy: Spiking the Shotgun
5. Vince Lombardi, Champion of the Century
6. Woody Hayes: Top Seven Tyrant
7. Bear Bryant: Football's Biggest Winner
8. Bobby Bowden: Best Active College Coach
9. John Madden: Football's Best Talker
10. Dan Reeves: Born to Win (in Georgia)
11. Mike Shanahan: The New Heavyweight Champion
12. O.A. (Bum) Phillips: Life Goes On

As shown throughout the century on American playing fields, football, the most complex of the team games, is most effectively played by people whose leaders are, first of all, wise and understanding.

In football's early years, when every team was coached or at least managed by one of its own players, the winning side on game day was the one led by the smartest athlete, as a rule, not necessarily the strongest, toughest or most talented.

In later decades, with adults in charge everywhere, football games and championships have almost always been won by teams with the most resourceful and discerning coaches – not necessarily the most talented players – even in eras when the dreary running game dominated.

Even in the flying-wedge era.

And especially today.

A winning football coach named Bum Phillips, talking about a bigger winner, Bear Bryant, summed it up briefly one day: "He can take his'n and beat your'n or take your'n and beat his'n."

Football is like that.

On every level, football coaches have more impact on their teams than leaders in any other sport. It's axiomatic: Great football coaches win, poor coaches lose, those in between win and lose. Football is a coach's game.

In a sport as complex as this, there can of course be no single best way to win. Football can be mastered by coaches who are as drastically different as Vince Lombardi, Paul Brown and Mike Shanahan. Of Lombardi, his players could say, with some truth, "He treats us all the same – like dogs."

In Dallas, though, Jimmy Johnson deliberately followed another course in the early 1990s when the Cowboys, with Troy Aikman as their passer, were winning back-to-back Super Bowl games. "I believe in a double standard," Johnson told his players one day early in his stewardship. "I'm going to treat you all differently. The harder you work, the better you play, the better you'll be treated."

Proving his point later, after two quarterbacks had fallen asleep at a team meeting, Johnson only cut one of them. Turning to the other, he said: "Wake up, Troy."

Over the years, it is their variations in attitudes – the differences in their approach to the game, one coach from another – that have caught my attention. The questions are ever the same: How do winners differ? What is there about their different ways that leads to success? What has each man learned, about himself and about his game, that allows him to excel?

And the answers are always different.

In my professional career, I have never met a group of men so various, so specific and quirky, and so endlessly fascinating as football's big-winning coaches.

1. Amos Alonzo Stagg: The Old One

A YALE DIVINITY student who couldn't make a sermon made good in football, where he coached for fifty-seven years, the intercollegiate record.

Of the thousands of football coaches who built their sport into the showiest of the century, the most distinctive was possibly Amos Alonzo Stagg. No one else ever coached football teams for fifty-seven years, which in Stagg's lifetime (1862-1965) was longer than most people lived. No other football coach lived to be 103. And to this day, only two others have won more career games than Stagg, who won 314. The leader with 323 is Bear Bryant, followed by Pop Warner, who won 319.

As of the turn of the millennium, what's more, in an era when a bad year or two is more likely to lead to unemployment than formerly, there's a chance that only two others ever will overtake Stagg. They are Joe Paterno of Penn State and Bobby Bowden of Florida State, both big winners and both still active after thirty-three years, each, in the game. No other active football coach is close.

Stagg in his 103 years spanned the whole of football's early history. When the automobile came in, he was already thirty years old. When the atomic age arrived, he was eighty. But he never had time for cars, bombs *or* statistics. By vocation, and avocation, Stagg was a football coach, and, first to last, he had but two other passions, plain food and clean living. "The greatest pleasure one has is keeping and feeling fit," he said one day.

He was ninety-nine when he said it.

As a pioneer coach, Stagg was characteristic of football's pioneers, inventing, for one thing, the tackling dummy. He thought of that in 1889, when he was a divinity student at Yale. It was the first of his many innovations in many sports, among them, reportedly, baseball's batting cage as well as the overflow troughs that line most swimming pools. Yet even though he swam like a fish, batted like a champion, and was known as the deadliest tackler of his generation, Stagg couldn't make a good sermon. So he left the field of religion in 1890 and took a job as a football coach, accepting an offer from the International YMCA School at Springfield, Massachusetts, known now as Springfield College.

Next, moving west, Stagg successfully coached football for forty-one years at the University of Chicago, winning six Big Ten championships before he was fired for being too old, seventy-one. Moving farther west, he coached University of the Pacific for fourteen years until fired again at eighty-five.

In his biggest year at Pacific, 1943, his team beat UCLA, 19-7, and Cal, 12-6, to finish in the nation's top ten as Stagg made Associated Press Coach of the Year. He was then eighty-one.

His extended career was an advertisement for the clean living he valued and for which he pitched. He never smoked anything and, except for water, never drank, not even coffee, never gambled, and never cussed. His angriest epithet was jackass. He called himself a stoic. And according to *Miami Herald* sports editor Edwin Pope, Stagg celebrated his eighty-ninth birthday anniversary with a dinner of pea soup, two ears of corn, peaches, and milk. "I never ate a hot dog in my life," he once said.

Those who didn't like him too much called him stuffy. They recalled that at the University of Chicago, he once refused an assistant's suggestion to send in a substitute with a play that his staff thought would win the game. "The rules committee," the old man said disdainfully, "deprecates the use of a substitute to convey information." Chicago lost that day, 21-18.

In the same spirit, Stagg, in 1898, produced football's first clean-shaven team, using his own razor on the last man himself.

Stagg was Eastern-bred. During the second year of the American Civil War, he had been born in poverty in a neighborhood of Irish laborers at West Orange, New Jersey, where his father began his career as a shoemaker's apprentice at age seven. As it happened, young Alonzo was a good athlete, and even then, in the 1870s, that got him to Phillips Exeter Academy and eventually Yale. Though a stocky 150-pounder who would fatten up to 166, Stagg was a Walter Camp All-American end who in the spring months doubled as a pitcher, leading Yale to five national baseball championships.

At 101, looking back, he said he was proudest of his football inventions, not only the tackling dummy but also the reverse play, the huddle, lateral pass, cross blocking, wind sprints, knit football pants, the numbering of plays and players, and, among other things, the awarding of letters or monograms. But he never changed personally. To the year he was 103, Stagg never had a hot dog.

2. George Halas: Founder of the NFL

IN THE BEGINNING, times were so tough for the NFL and the Chicago Bears that their founder fired himself four times.

When at eighty-one George Halas kicked himself upstairs to chairman of the board of the Chicago Bears, he was asked one day about the birth of pro football. He recalled that in 1921, he and a group of his friends were trying to strengthen an obscure, wobbly league they had first put together a year earlier under a ponderous name, American Professional Football Conference. A lifelong newspaper reader, Halas realized instinctively that an organization called, for short, the APFC would never make him famous. As he sat around the house one morning, Halas, a Cub fan, reached perfunctorily for the paper to check the National

League baseball standings when a new name came to him: National Football League.

"If I'd been a White Sox fan," he said, "I guess it would have been the American Football League all these years."

So Halas was there when pro football began. And as owner and director of the Bears for the next sixty-three years, he set a world record. No one else in any sport has ever run a team that long, although Connie Mack was up there for awhile, starting fifty years with the Philadelphia A's in 1901. Asked to account for his long career, Halas said, "I've heard you can live forever if you work six days a week and ride a bicycle six miles a day. That's what I do."

Chicago-born, George S. Halas was a college football star in 1915, graduated from Illinois in 1918, played in the Rose Bowl a year later for Great Lakes Navy, organized an Illinois pro club in 1920, and moved it from Decatur to Chicago in 1921. At twenty-six, he was the team's head coach and left end when it won the 1921 championship for Chicago in the league's first year under the NFL banner. In 1920, representing Decatur, Halas' team had finished second in the only year of the APFC, which had been laced together, loosely, by a group of club owners from Midwestern town teams, including, most prominently, Halas himself.

Early-day pro football was a time of uncertainty and rejection. Extensive public interest in college football made the pros seem almost irrelevant. As Halas and the other early owners groped through their first years with not much income, some teams increased their cash flow by passing the hat at halftime. The only cash investment Halas ever made in the Bears, he said, was $38,000, which he used to buy out his only partner in 1932. The money was borrowed from a Chicago bank and, he said, repaid out of profits.

Halas and his family were to run the $38,000 into $38 million, and, before the end of the century, $380 million. As the big town in the nation's heartland, Chicago has for years exceeded any other U.S. city in profit potential in any sport.

Yet in the beginning, for the Chicago Bears, it was a hard, slow go. The only fun they had was playing the games, or, in Halas' case, playing and coaching.

Altogether, he coached the Bears for forty years in four separate ten-year tours, winning at least one NFL championship each time. In football, however, championships aren't enough to save a man's job even when he owns the club. As the only NFL owner who ever fired himself, Halas threw Halas out four times.

Overall, he was to coach the Bears to 326 wins, an impressive football statistic. The goal in the pro business is 100 wins, which Vince Lombardi, for one, never reached.

Halas' record as one of the NFL's biggest winners qualified him, perhaps, to express opinions on the state of late-century U.S. sports. In interviews he focused on two points:

- Competition is the key to excellence and success. "You don't improve much if you aren't competing," Halas used to say. "In addition to talent, you only need three things to play football well: size, speed, and desire. Modern athletes are bigger and faster than we were, but they don't have any more desire."
- Competitive balance is, by extension, the key to the continued success of sports leagues. Articulating a lesson baseball has yet to learn, Halas said "The NFL will last as long as there is a balance of power between teams. The point of the draft is simply to spread the talent around."

Halas in his last decade as a coach won his last game at age seventy-one. "I'll never forget the day," he said. "In the locker room afterward, I was crying a bit when I got the boys together and said, 'Gentlemen, this was my last game. From now on, you're on your own.' Then I went across the hall and told the officials the same thing."

ii

How much did Halas enjoy retirement?

"Hell, I'll never retire," he said at his Chicago apartment one morning in his eighty-first year. "I'm at the office every day, and working at home many a night."

And loving it all.

The hair was thinner and grayer as he sprinted into his eighties, but he closely approximated the Halas dimensions of the day he was voted Player of the Game in the 1919 Rose Bowl. He was still a bit under five-eleven and over 182. The face was still square and beaming, the eyes thoughtful and probing. Think of actor Barry Fitzgerald playing an old man on a bicycle and you have Halas as he aged.

In the exercise room of his Chicago apartment, the owner of the Bears rode the bike morning and night, pumping the equivalent of three miles each time. After warming up with a set of heavy barbells, he set the bicycle's stress levers for a half mile on the flat, then two and a half uphill. "You aren't exercising," he said, "if it doesn't fatigue you."

Regardless of when he got home in those days, Halas without fail swung the barbells nightly, and rode the three miles. His philosophy was that of an awesome competitor: "Never go to bed a loser."

iii

During Halas' years as chairman of the board, those calling on him at his office on the twelfth floor of a new Chicago building were often asked to match him lifting weights. The prescribed weight was a table-top statue of Halas in a business suit and snap-brim hat, crouching on a sideline in a fist-waving pose familiar to millions. He smiled indulgently when a California visitor couldn't budge the heavy little statue, then leaned over and, taking hold carefully, raised it waist high. Still smiling, he set it down gently.

That was in the days before the Bears moved to the suburbs, setting up shop in the woods of Lake Forest. Halas always preferred the big city. He was in love with the city. And from his elegant corner office, the largest in what was then the Bears' new suite of offices, there was a wide-angle view of Chicago's two historic landmarks, the lake and the loop. As Halas glanced outside, water-skiing youngsters were speeding in the summer sunlight on Lake Michigan at the same time that taxpayers with briefcases were hurrying through the shadows of the old elevated railroad that loops around the city's downtown area, giving it its name.

A block away in full view was Michigan Avenue, which on its way north becomes Lake Shore Drive, Chicago's gold-coast roadway fronting Lake Michigan. Halas lived eight miles up that road in a lakeside apartment. He moved into it the year the Bears beat the Washington Redskins, 73-0, for the NFL's 1940 championship.

All this was Halas country. It's true that Abraham Lincoln was nominated in Chicago in 1860 and that, sometime thereafter, an icon named Michael Jordan seemed to be in charge. But in Halas' time, Chicago was Papa Bear's place. It was his base when he got the NFL going, and, more than a half century later, he was still there, still going strong, still surprising and impressing a new group of Bear rookies each summer. Running into George Halas in Chicago, they used to say, was like finding George Washington alive and well at Mount Vernon.

A self-made multimillionaire, Halas lived like it. He could see and thrill to wind-driven winter blizzards and summer thundershowers – the elements that make Chicago what it is – without ever having to feel either, game day excepted. Mornings, he took the elevator down eighteen floors from his air-conditioned apartment – a big one that had massive lake and city views in three directions – to a weather-tight garage. There he stepped into his air-conditioned blue Continental and drove it out the door and through the gale into another air-conditioned garage under his air-conditioned office downtown. In a Chicago storm lasting a week, he was never outdoors.

"I live a little differently now than I did growing up," Halas said one time. "But there is one tie. I have always been an apartment man. Never lived anywhere else. We called them flats in the neighborhood where I was born, an immigrant neighborhood on the west side of Chicago. My dad had come over from Pilsen, Bohemia. That's Czechoslovakia now. He was a tailor, and very early he invested in real estate. He bought a triple three-story flat not far from Wrigley Field, and we lived on the second floor. It seemed all right at the time, but today it seems like a long time ago."

iv

The athletic ability that lifted George Halas out of obscurity took him first to Illinois where he played end both ways for an early football legend, Bob Zuppke, and then in 1919 to the New York Yankees. There, he played the outfield and hit a triple one day off a baseball legend, Rube Marquard, in an exhibition game. Sliding into third that time, Halas hurt his leg, and the Yankees, discouraged, made an offseason trade, replacing him with a man from Boston, a portly left-hander named Babe Ruth.

Returning to his home town, Halas became not only the first coach of the Bears but also their first trainer, first film editor, and first public relations director. Those were difficult times for the pros. The twin kings were college football and, renewing itself every spring like Easter, big league baseball. Chicago had, as it still has, two baseball clubs. In time, Halas stirred up some interest in the Bears by keeping things simple and, for a time, as much like college football as possible. For instance, selecting a color scheme for the Bears, he borrowed the school colors he had loved at Illinois, blue and orange. He named the team Bears because they played in Wrigley Field, home of the Chicago Cubs. "Football players are bigger," he liked to say. "If baseball players are cubs, football players must be bears."

He often said there was not much to tell about the founding of the NFL in the early 1920s except for the widespread desire for uniform rules. That was an era when town teams representing nearly every little Midwestern town – from Green Bay and Canton to Akron, Muncie and Tonawanda – challenged other town teams each fall, when rule differences made a serious and continuing problem. The NFL was basically formed to codify the rules for the teams that played pro or semi-pro football in the teen years and early '20s. "There were so many teams and rules," Halas recalled, "that you might say that the NFL, or something like the NFL, was inevitable."

In the only job Halas ever had after leaving the Yankees and organizing the Bears, he served briefly as a basketball writer on the old *Chicago Journal*. He had struck up a friendship with the *Journal's* editors when dropping by with Bear handouts.

"Did you write this?" an editor asked him one day toward the end of the season.

"Sure did," said Halas.

"We need a basketball writer next week," the editor said. "Interested?"

Halas was. But only for awhile. His destiny, he was certain, was pro football.

In later years, his newspaper background was to make him wary of picking an all-Halas football team, but he said, "The backfield is easy." He proved it isn't by naming two fullbacks, Bronko Nagurski and Bill Osmanski, and three halfbacks, Red Grange, Gale Sayers and George McAfee, along with one quarterback, Sid Luckman. He also named two centers, George Trafton and Bulldog Turner, two guards, Dr. Danny Fortmann and George Musso, three tackles, Joe Stydahar, Link Lyman and George Connor, and two ends. One is Harlon Hill. The other, he said shamelessly, is George Halas.

As a coach, Halas was ahead of his time for awhile, keeping the Bears in the T Formation twenty and thirty years before it became the thing to do elsewhere. Not often noted as an innovator, he experimented with the Single- and Double-Wing formations, among others, he said, but threw them out in the 1920s. "We kept good records on all the formations we used," he recalled. "And the T was the most productive."

Not until the 1950s did the last of the Single-Wing holdouts make that discovery.

His greatest contribution to football was, in Halas' opinion, something else. "The thing I'm proudest of," he said, "is a rule recommendation. I introduced the rule forbidding a pro team to take a college player until his class has graduated."

Even though the courts in time struck it down – deciding that such a rule discriminates against young athletes who are talented enough to succeed in pro sports – Halas insisted that the NFL was "obviously" right.

"We made that pledge away back in 1926," he said. "It saved college football – and ours, too."

Teen-agers aren't as a general rule mature enough for professional sports, Halas believed, making a judgment that the courts wouldn't buy, unhappily. At a time when only the NFL had the four-year restriction, he said: "Professional baseball and basketball would both be stronger if they had our rule and let their players mature for four years after high school before turning pro. I hate to think of the number of kids whose lives have been ruined by playing pro ball before they were ready for it. The exceptions who make good are the only ones you hear about."

As for the future of the NFL, Halas predicted throughout his lifetime that its continuing success would depend on two things, the first of which is good high school coaching. "That's a big plus for us now," he told me one time a quarter century ago during an interview at the Los Angeles Coliseum. "The preps have made this a big league by giving young prospects the right start. It wasn't like that in my day. Red Grange told me his high school football coach was his manual arts training instructor. Mine was at least a gym teacher. But it takes football coaches to make football players, and that's what we've got now in the high schools all over the country – good football coaches almost every-where."

The NFL's other need, as Halas observed prophetically in that interview twenty-five years ago, is a continuing interest in new rules. "Our rule changes have made football what it is," he said. "One of the big ones in the 1930s legalized passing from anywhere behind the line of scrimmage. That was the beginning of offensive football as we know it today. Football is the kind of game that can't stand still. The changes we've made in the last fifty or fifty-five years are the reason football has grown faster than any other game. (For confirmation, see Chapters II and III.) And I predict it will be bigger than ever fifty years from now."

The NFL is, clearly, a product of the brilliant rules it has created and introduced since the 1920s. And for sixty-three years, Halas was a constant force for that. It stands as his great legacy. Founding the NFL was easy –"inevitable," to use Halas' word. The hard part, the important part, was changing the NFL into what it is.

3. Paul Brown Systematizes Football

TRYING FOR total control over his football players, this coach came up with the most workable gimmick yet: calling all the plays.

As a position, if quarterback has changed more outrageously than any other during football's long evolutionary course, the inventor who changed it the most was Paul Brown. In 1950, as the first coach of the old Cleveland Browns, Brown became the first NFL coach to lobotomize his quarterback – by calling every play in every game. Before mid-century, all quarterbacks were known as signal-callers; now they are all signal-hearers.

Brown's move came years – decades – before everyone else did it. But the fact that everyone else *did* commit to coach-called plays, eventually, underscores the significance of Brown's thinking and his contribution.

His opponents were at first so reluctant to follow his lead that in the buildup for the NFL playoffs in 1970 – twenty years after his signal-calling debut – a Cincinnati-Baltimore game was hailed as a matchup of football's two most famous play-callers: coach Paul Brown versus quarterback John Unitas.

By then, Brown was an owner-coach of the Cincinnati Bengals. He had been fired in 1963 by the new Cleveland owner, Art Modell, after twelve distinguished years with the Browns – the team that was named for him in 1946 when he organized it as a charter member of the old All-America Football Conference.

Brown's pre-Cincinnati run had been impressive. To begin with, calling every play, he had coached the Browns to four championships in the four years of the AAFC (1946-49). Then in the next eight years, after the NFL admitted Cleveland, Brown took the Browns to seven more league title games and won three NFL championships. He had won, year in and out, about four of every five games. His record for fifteen years with high school, Ohio State, and World War II service teams was 130-21-6. His record for fifteen years with the old Cleveland Browns in two leagues was 152-42-6. During his first thirty years as a football coach he was thus about an eighty percent winner. From then on, in Cincinnati, where he headed an expansion team competing against teams that had learned many of his lessons, he and his successors were to prosper everywhere but in the won-lost columns.

From Brown's Ohio State days through the big Cleveland days and into his final days in Cincinnati, I covered his football activities more closely than those of any other out-of-state coach, filing, altogether, two dozen Paul Brown interviews. One of these was arranged in his third year at Cincinnati, when he had somehow pushed the Bengals into the playoffs – one of the earliest arrivals ever by an expansion team.

He was then in his sixties, and time had rounded off the sharp Brown features, although in bearing and outlook he remained the thin, urbane intellectual of his big winning days at Massillon (Ohio) High School. That was before Ohio State, before Cleveland, long before Cincinnati, at the start of a career that began during Herbert Hoover's presidency, the year before Knute Rockne died.

Part legend, part humanist, part genius, Brown was football's first organization man – the first to arrange matters scientifically under a full-time staff with systematic concentration on movies, playbooks, play-calling, game plans, closely-timed practices, tactics and strategy – particularly pass offense and pass defense tactics and strategy.

His obvious goal – to gain control as completely as possible over a game of challenging complexity – had with some rivals earned him the reputation of an autocrat. And no area of his operation opened itself to that interpretation more easily than his theories of player relations. "The principles haven't changed for forty years," he told me that day in Cincinnati, "and the first principle is that you've got to enjoy yourself. That means you have to surround yourself with nice people. Good football can only be played by good people – by those who are nice people inside."

How, I asked him, do you define nice people?

"I don't know how to define it," Brown said, "but when you meet them, you know them. A clinker can win a game now and then, but they don't win consistently. The players you can win with are the ones who are quick and fast and love to play football. They are the players who agree with me that life is a bowl of cherries. In Cleveland, we didn't bother to change individuals, and we don't bother now. We try to draft or trade for the sort we want, and we only keep that kind. We don't draft guys that sleep on the beach."

Those who coached with Brown often said that the way he handled his players led to his success. Starting in the Massillon days, when Brown became the most celebrated high school coach in the land, he had worked out a detailed way to proceed, a way that in time helped him immensely in relationships with players as difficult as the greatly gifted Jim Brown.

"Never keep a secret from your players," Paul Brown said, going down the list of essentials. "Never tell any athlete to do anything unless you are prepared to tell him just why you want him to do it. And never lie. The smartest coach in football couldn't fool the dumbest player."

On the other hand, Brown conceded that he could be fooled, for awhile, by a player who might be skilled and intelligent but troubled.

"Drinkers and rounders can play good football for a few years because of the wonderful resiliency of youth," he said. "But they represent nothing of what we value in football, so we don't keep them around after we find them out. Like a husband with an errant wife, we learn about it later than others, but we always find them out."

Brown's attitude and his penchant for casting away great athletes who failed as human beings – in the opinion of nobody but the head coach – led to the complaints that he was a dictator. Of all the coaches of the comparatively free and easy 1940s and '50s, Brown was most frequently subject to criticism for his off-the-field actions. How much, he was asked, do you mind that?

"I never do anything about it, if that's what you mean," Brown said. "Vince Lombardi telephoned one day and said it bothered him to be referred to as 'Mussolini' by newspapermen and by some of his former players. He asked me what I did about things like that. I said I ignored them. You have to, because the problem is built into the situation. The two basics that make winning possible are understanding and authority. The players must always understand exactly what you mean. And the authority must be in one person 100 percent of the time. There can be only one place for a player to go for an answer. I doubt if any football team can succeed very long unless the coach has the final word on everything from the draft and trades to all the responsibilities of a general manager."

Lombardi agreed with him on that. So did Bill Walsh, who as a 1980s autocrat was to build the San Francisco 49ers into a power that exceeded even Brown's in longevity. By the 1990s, of the big winners who had full charge of football operations in their franchises, the most conspicuous three were Bill Parcells of the New York Jets and both 1999 Super Bowl coaches, Mike Shanahan of Denver and Dan Reeves of Atlanta.

"Whether the coach is right or wrong on a given issue isn't as important as establishing the right to *be* right or wrong," said Brown, who probably would have backed Parcells when he left the New England Patriots in 1997 after a draft dispute. The fact that the Patriot personnel people were right and Parcells wrong was irrelevant, Brown would have said.

Absolute authority can lead, of course, to absolute embarrassment for the dictator who has to cut diligent young players after training camp each summer, depriving so many of a livelihood. Brown had worked out an answer to that, too.

"I put it in the form of a question," he said. "In what other business can a man discover in two months whether he's good enough to make it? Let's say another boy wants to be a lawyer. He invests four years in college, three years in law school, and maybe two years in law practice, only to discover, after all that time, that he can't cut it as a lawyer. The break is just as painful in football, but quicker."

The players he cut were invariably told precisely that.

The most celebrated example of Brown's passion for total control was his insistence on calling the plays himself, an idea that turned his quarterbacks into robots – even Hall of Famer Otto Graham. The system Brown used was different from today's. At gametime, after Cleveland's offensive plays, he simply alternated guards. Standing on the sideline in his familiar brown hat and brown business suit, Brown told the guard what to tell Graham, who, after the guard trotted into the huddle, finally learned whether he would next have to pass, run or hand off.

In the late 1960s and '70s, when other NFL coaches finally began to pick up on Brown's philosophy, some worked out a way to wig-wag the signals to the quarterback – meaning they could keep their two best guards on the premises for every play – and in time, when the technology improved, the league approved helmet radios for all NFL quarterbacks.

The losers, then, were football fans. For most coaches are more cautious than their quarterbacks. No one will ever know whether that was even true of Brown and Graham. But the question for Brown was an obvious one: Why did you take the play-calling responsibility away from your quarterback?

"Let me ask *you* one," he replied. "What's the first thing the quarterback does after he takes the ball from center? He turns his back on the defense. Coaches, in other words, have a better view of the defense than quarterbacks. Second, if we've sent in the play, we know where to look when the ball starts to move. On a given pass, if all three receivers are covered, we can see the kind of defense they're in, and what to do about it next time."

As Brown spoke, the polaroid camera was in its infancy. He lacked the technology that during NFL games has provided today's coaching staffs with instant still pictures of every play from the first quarter on. In the 1950s, Brown basically relied on the two eyes under his brown hat, prompting me to remark that football coaches of that time had poorer views of the game than any spectator – as they often said.

218   FOOTBALL IN AMERICA

"The press box has a better view, and that's why we have a telephone to our assistants there," Brown said. "But the quarterback's view is the worst of all. I played that position, and I know. A quarterback has his hands full. He calls the offensive blocking. He calls the defenses. He manipulates the ball. Then he turns his back to pass. His wife sees more of the game than he does."

The title of an Otto Graham magazine article after he retired was a Graham quotation: "Why the Quarterback Should Call the Plays." His coach was asked for a reaction.

"That wasn't the way he felt when he played for us," Brown said. "He never questioned the idea of our calling the plays although he was fully capable of doing it himself – as he proved in Chicago a few months ago at the College All-Star Game. The first chance Otto got to coach a football team, he sent in the plays just the way his old coach used to do it in Cleveland."

These days, defenses are stunting more than ever. As a play-caller stuck on the sideline, how do you cope with that?

"Here's what some people don't realize: Our quarterbacks have always been flexible at the line of scrimmage. Otto won a lot of games by changing my calls. (Cincinnati starter) Ken Anderson checks off as much as a third of the time."

You're winning with the plays he changes. Some players would say that Anderson has earned the right to be the first-string play-caller.

"Try looking at it like this. If something goes wrong on the field, I'd rather have people blame me than my quarterback. Quarterbacks improve faster and play better when they aren't criticized for everything that goes wrong."

Another factor, I imagine, is that you enjoy play-calling.

"Yes, I can't hide that. I like to be involved. I get more kick out of it than anything else I do, in or out of football."

In still another way, Brown was out of step with most coaches of his or any other time. Most are workaholics. Of the teams that make the playoffs each winter, most have coaches who virtually work around the clock. Nobody ever accused Paul Brown of doing that.

"Personally, I fold up every night about 10," he said. "I get sleepy, and when Brown gets sleepy it's all over. So, for us, football is mainly a daytime industry. When people call me a man with a fiendishly one-track football mind, I don't mind it at all – as long as I get nine hours sleep a night. And winter vacations in Florida."

Do Cincinnati's assistant coaches take the winter off, too?

"No, for the coaching staff, there are a million things to do between seasons, including thousands of feet of film to study. I fly up and talk to them once in a while."

What do you do the rest of the time?

"Sit. We own a home in Coral Gables, and I try to swim a little one day, and golf a little the next, and maybe fish once a week. But the thing I like best is the beach chair."

How often do you review Bengal movies down there?

"Never. All I do in a football way is think about it. I think football in that beach chair all winter."

Year-round, (former Notre Dame coach) Frank Leahy used to set aside an hour every day to meditate offense and defense. What does football meditation do for you?

"I would say the best ideas I have had about football have come along while I was relaxing in Florida. The leisure to think is the most productive thing about vacations or days off from any job, I imagine. It would be hard for me to keep up in this fast-moving business without an opportunity for relaxed, easy-going thinking."

You've been through everything: building expansion teams, climbing, winning championships in college and pro ball. What's hardest?

"Staying up there once you've got there. In Cleveland, we were in that last big game at the end of the season eleven times in thirteen years – and each one was harder than the one before."

Speaking of Cleveland, when you left the Browns your endowment was $80,000 a year in severance pay. Why did you give that up – in your sixties – to run a new team in Cincinnati?

"I can't think of any two or three other things I'd be satisfied with indefinitely, even if two of them are golf and spending money. I went back to football because it's my life. Call it chess in hip pads. Or call it miniature warfare, it's exciting, it grabs you, it's a man's life. And I like to call the plays."

4. Clark Shaughnessy: Spiking the Shotgun

*WHEN A RADICAL new offense terrorized the
NFL in 1961, Clark Shaughnessy stopped it.*

More than a third of a century ago, the San Francisco 49ers, with Howard (Red) Hickey coaching, startled the NFL with a new offense they called the Shotgun Formation. With ordinary talent – except for the three alternating 49er quarterbacks, John Brodie, Bobby Waters and rookie Billy Kilmer – Hickey showed what coaching creativity can accomplish: On successive Sundays, his team routed two title contenders, the Detroit Lions, 49-0, and Los Angeles Rams, 35-0, in the first month of the 1961 season.

The NFL's capacity for surprise hadn't yet, however, been tested.

The bomb fell two weeks later when the 49ers, off to a 4-1 start on the season with their electrifying new offense, went into Chicago and failed to score a point against a Bear defense coached by Clark Shaughnessy. Final score, Bears 31, 49ers 0.

It was hard to tell immediately which was the greater or stranger achievement: San Francisco's impersonation of a flying machine that year or the way Shaughnessy grounded it – temporarily. But looking back, it can be said, first, that Hickey started something – his visionary formation is still very much alive in a league that continues to play Shotgun football every week, if intermittently – and, second, that Shaughnessy in one afternoon damaged it irretrievably as a full-time system.

As used today, the Shotgun is a specialty formation most often seen on third and long. Teams use the Shotgun to insure that the passer, who stands far behind center, gets a longer look at the defensive alignment and at the defensive rush, particular the blitz.

In its first incarnation, however, the Shotgun was not a passing novelty but an offensive way of life. With four or five receivers spread from sideline to sideline, Hickey rotated in a new quarterback for every new play, stationed him back of center like a Single-Wing tailback, and ran all three quarterbacks – against the spread-out defenses that scampered to contain them – as often as they passed.

For defensive players accustomed to more conservative offenses, the spectacle of a fresh new quarterback sprinting in between plays to throw a big pass, possibly, or scramble far and wide, was unnerving.

In the fall of 1961, when I talked with various 49ers and Bears about the new Shotgun football and ways to stop it, Kilmer and Shaughnessy were clearly the most articulate. Kilmer at the time was between UCLA – where as an All-American Single-Wing halfback he led the nation in total offense the year before – and the Washington Redskins, whom he led into the 1973 Super Bowl. Shaughnessy, after giving the world the T Formation twenty years earlier, was again revolutionizing football as the Bears' defensive coach.

ii

As a tailback, Kilmer was the first since Sammy Baugh to rise from the campus to instant stardom in pro football, where, as the rookie member of Hickey's quarterback triumvirate, he led the NFL's quarterbacks in ground gaining. "I wouldn't be up there in rushing or anything else," he told me that fall, "if I had to call the signals like other pro quarterbacks. Our coach, Red Hickey, does that. All I have to think about is running or passing, and that's a full-time job for a rookie."

Explaining a 49er quarterback's game-time relationship with the coach, he said, "We huddle with Red after each play. But that's a lot different from taking the play-calling responsibility yourself. I don't see how any rookie could keep his mind on strategy and execution at the same time. A lot of veteran quarterbacks have trouble. I'll tell you how tough this pro game is. I've learned more about football just since July than I learned in the rest of my career put together."

On the sideline in those days, when one of San Francisco's three quarterbacks was at work on the field, the other two used to stand next to the coach, one on each side.

"We concentrate on how the defense reacts to the play that was called," Kilmer said. "Five of us know what play was sent in: the quarterbacks, Hickey, and the spotter upstairs. We get a picture of the play right now. It's like a movie. Red makes the decisions, but he takes suggestions all the time."

Hickey's critics sometimes noted that with three quarterbacks rotating in and out, none was in action more than one-third of the time, causing all three to, possibly, lose the feel of the game.

"That would be true, I'm sure, if the quarterbacks were calling the plays," Kilmer said. "But when one mind is responsible for continuity, I'm just the passer or ballcarrier. In this system, I run as often as if I were playing sixty minutes – and I throw the ball a lot more than an orthodox T quarterback runs. The defense has to be ready for both."

Are you more vulnerable to injury than an orthodox T quarterback?

"I think those guys are in more danger of getting hurt," Kilmer said. "T-Formation quarterbacks get blindsided. Nothing is worse. I like to size up the man who is hitting me, and on 49er running plays I can."

iii

A couple of weeks later, Kilmer and Hickey, still running, ran into the

Bears in Chicago, where Shaughnessy was revising the way to play defense. In one spirited afternoon, he gave the San Francisco Shotgun people a preview on how defensive football was shortly going to be played everywhere by NFL coaches borrowing the two Shaughnessy virtues, motion and deception.

He talked about the 1961 Bear-49er game later that week. Never easy to find, Shaughnessy sat still long enough to report that his team had killed the Shotgun with a possum.

"But first," he said, "I want to tell you that you have to be lucky to shut down the Shotgun. It's different, and in football, anything that's different is tough to handle, anything at all. And that's the most original offense in the last quarter century – since George Halas opened up the T."

An unassuming sort, Shaughnessy, the inventor of the modern T, used to follow the Bears' party line in T Formation discussions, giving the credit to the team for the invention instead of taking it himself. He didn't really care, and Halas *did* care.

"We were lucky to beat the Shotgun," Shaughnessy continued, "because our linemen executed their possum assignments perfectly. We faked out the offense instead of letting the offense fake us. Our middle linebacker, Bill George, was a perfect possum in that game. He lined up head-on the snapper, playing possum, but just before the snap he jumped one yard to the left, or one yard to the right. The blocker assigned to George couldn't find him."

Warming easily to his subject, Shaughnessy spilled detail after detail: "We were in what appeared to be a six-man line. They all played possum until just before the snap. Sometimes they jumped away at the moment of the snap. You can do that against the Shotgun because a Shotgun play never starts as fast as a T play. That's the weakness of the Shotgun. The reason the 49ers couldn't block us was, they couldn't find us."

To confuse the 49er quarterbacks, Kilmer, Brodie and Waters, the Bears also blitzed on a prearranged program of fixed percentages – antedating the fifteen-play scripts that most modern offensive coaches favor.

"George blew in one-third of the time," Shaughnessy said. "On the average, he possumed twice and blew once. We always rushed at least two men, almost always three or four, often five, and occasionally all six. Our basic defensive alignment was a six-five. Against the (conventional) T, a four-man secondary is usually enough, but you need at least five against the Shotgun. They have five speedy receivers coming down the field at you, spread out from sideline to sideline. That's the strength of the Shotgun. We moved a linebacker, Larry Morris or sometimes Joe Fortunato, into the secondary as our fifth defensive back."

The essential Shaughnessy difference that day, and the essence of his seminal approach to defense, can be summed up in two points: (1) most defenses react to what the offense does, whereas (2) Shaughnessy's defensive players did what *they* wanted.

As he said, "Most football defenses are based on keys. A defensive tackle might key on an offensive guard, for example. If the guard goes one way, the tackle reacts. At Chicago, in our dictionary, there's no if. We have no keys. We substitute responsibility for keys. In each of our defensive alignments, every man has one responsibility, either an opponent or a zone. Regardless of what the offense does, he's responsible for that one opponent, or that one zone. He plays possum as long as he can – pretending to be reading keys – and then rushes to his assigned man or zone. It's a simple system."

But it's a rigid system, obviously, Shaughnessy was reminded. And any structured system has a weakness.

"Certainly," he agreed. "That is the nature of defense. Every defensive team in the league exposes a weakness when it lines up. We expose a glaring weakness on every play. You gamble that they won't find it."

It is the most inexplicable fact of twentieth century football that Clark Shaughnessy is not yet in the Hall of Fame. He started the T and stopped the Shotgun, while recreating the game from first principles. Perhaps his lack was ego. To the end of his career, for example, Shaughnessy remained respectful of the Shotgun he had spiked. He was asked at the time to list the advantages of that original Shotgun:

"There are those five ends (five receivers) – that's the main thing," he said. "And the three quarterbacks are conferring constantly with the head coach, talking over every play personally. That's a tremendous advantage. You'll see a lot of Shotgun football in this league from now on, not on every down, maybe – but there are a lot of downs when it will be the best offense." All those years ago, Shaughnessy was right about that, too.

5. Vince Lombardi: Champion of the Century

*THE NFL'S ONLY five-time champion turned football into
a game of simple plays and exact execution.*

When Vince Lombardi was an assistant coach with the New York

Giants in 1958, his best friend was the man who owned the club, Wellington Mara. I used to see them, dinner-bound, leaving the locker room together after practices or games. So if anyone could have foreseen that Lombardi would shortly become the NFL's biggest winner, it was Mara. But he didn't. And, a few months later, Lombardi said goodbye to his old friend in New York and left the biggest city in the league for the smallest, Green Bay.

In retrospect, after Lombardi's teams had played in six NFL championship games in his nine years in Green Bay, people said it was inconceivable that Mara could have let him get away. But that is a view that misses the mark. The lesson is not that Mara erred but that nobody knows about any head coach until he's a head coach.

There have been other individuals like Lombardi who after years as assistant coaches moved on and up successfully. But there have been those who, after brilliant apprenticeships, failed. And there have been many who muddled along, winning some, losing some.

Indeed, a first-time football coach is entering what may be the world's only job wherein it is wholly impossible to predict whether he will flourish or fail. Character, background, brains, charisma, dedication – none of these can give the answer in advance. The job is so complex and multi-faceted that, until you fill the bill, no one knows you can.

The incredibly swift rise of Lombardi in Green Bay stands as a twentieth-century example of that.

Older than most rookie head coaches, Lombardi was forty-six when he got his chance in Green Bay. And since midway in his Packer run, he has been widely if not quite universally called the greatest coach of all time. Certainly, no one before Lombardi and no one since could win five NFL championships in seven years (1961-67). After winning two, he lost to Chicago and Baltimore in 1963-64, then won three in a row. In his last two years as an NFL champion, the unified AFL-NFL people played the first two Super Bowls, enabling Lombardi to double twice as a Super Bowl champion, in consecutive seasons, after which he quit.

In 1959, to begin his unprecedented run in Green Bay, he had hit the ground running and yelling, and he never let up. An eager, snarling, screaming winner, he provided the American century's classic case of the dominating, domineering football coach, the coach of all the movie scripts and the cartoons and legends. But he was no cartoon character. As an NFL winner, he was like no other:

- Before Lombardi won seven of twelve games in 1959 to turn Green Bay around, the Packers had experienced twenty awful years under six losing coaches, among them Hall of Famer Curly Lambeau, who in his last eleven years at Green Bay never had a winning season.
- After Lombardi slipped on his second Super Bowl ring in 1968 and retired, the Packers resumed losing and stayed at it this time even longer – for a quarter century – under five more unsuccessful coaches – before a new general manager, Ron Wolf, brought in Coach Mike Holmgren to restore order in the 1990s.

Football is a coach's sport.

ii

Withdrawn, even embarrassed in one-on-one situations, Lombardi wasn't easy to know. I had run into him several times during his many years in New York, where he had begun as an All-American center at Fordham, and we met again as casual acquaintances in Green Bay during his rookie year as a head coach. But I could never see that he was going anywhere. Then during the 1960 exhibition season, ahead of his second season with the Packers, after his opponents had exchanged the 1959 Packer movies, I discovered that Lombardi was already the most frequently and extensively discussed individual in the league as well as the NFL's most widely respected leader, Paul Brown excepted.

Considering Lombardi's inexperience as a head coach and his unremarkable 7-5 won-lost record in 1959, that came as a shock. Clearly, I had missed something. So I scheduled a side trip or two to Green Bay that summer whenever I was in the area.

There I saw one source of my oversight. He was friendly enough in person, but projected little warmth. He appeared, in fact, to have two personas. Strangely reticent, seemingly shy, from one moment to the next in private settings, Lombardi became suddenly outgoing, assertive, even combative in football settings – even in exhibition football games.

Hoping to reconcile the differences, I reached him again by telephone in September of that 1960 season, during the NFL's second regular-season week, after the Packers had lost their home opener to the Chicago Bears, 17-14. He was preoccupied at the time with his strongest division opponent – the Detroit Lions were to finish second to Green Bay three years running – but even so, he agreed to make time for an interview. He asked only that I fly to Wisconsin to see him in person. It was in that conversation, as his first championship season was just beginning, that I began to understand his unique approach to the game that was his life.

I started with a comment about his next opponent. The Detroit defense is one of the NFL's highest rated, I said. What's the best thing to do against a team like that?

"We'll hit them at their strongest point," Lombardi said. "We'll keep it uncomplicated and attack their strength."

I suggested that other pro clubs attack weaknesses and asked: Why try to beat a team like Detroit where it's strongest?

"I learned most of my football from Red Blaik when I coached under him at West Point," he said, "and Blaik believed in giving battle to the best players on the other side. My offhand recollection is that you're right – our opponents do seem to hit us where they think we're weak – but we want to do it the other way. We want to break their morale. If you can beat down their very best men, it's all over."

Suppose you were up against a defense with six or eight All-Pro types. That might be the place for Shotgun plays or some other variation on your usual plan.

"No, we believe in keeping the offense simple. We know that souped-up new offenses may beat us once in a while. All fancy offenses are troublesome, but you can't win with them over a twelve-game season. Mistakes decide most football games, and the team with the simplest offense and defense makes the fewest mistakes."

Surely there's a time for rollouts or reverses, or *something* livelier.

"I'm not against these things, but to do them you've got to have two offenses. And it's hard enough coaching one offense, let alone two. You must first have an offense that's good all over the field. You've got to be sound on your five-yard line, for instance – and theirs. And you want to be sound in the fourth quarter of a close game. Of course there are times when you'd like to get fancier – but there isn't enough practice time to put in a sound offense and a fancy offense too."

How many hours do the Packers practice each day, on the average?

"You can't practice a football team more than an hour and a half. On Fridays, it's an hour, and next to nothing on Saturdays and Mondays. Time is so limited that we have to spend it all on the few things we do best. If we don't get those nailed down, we're out of business."

Suppose you had been stuck with really inferior personnel at Green Bay. I've heard people say that that's the time to try things that are more imaginative.

"The poorer the personnel, the simpler I'd keep the offense. Let's do what we can do right."

Some people complain that this style hurts pro football as a spectacle for the fans.

"Well, I doubt that. And anyhow, I don't look on football as a spectacle. Fans who go to a pro game to see a show are going to the wrong place."

What should pro football fans expect to see?

"A pro football game."

I think it can be documented that some of the touchdown explosions in the other league this year have been appreciated by AFL fans.

"The pro football fans I know would rather see pro football than basketball."

What specifically attracts them to football?

"First, I think they like to see a well-coached team that makes good plays. They also appreciate individual effort, and they like to watch good defenses. The main reason football is popular with sports fans is the skill and violence they see. If it weren't violent, it wouldn't draw."

One more thing. A number of Green Bay's good players have to spend most of their time on the bench. How do you keep all of them happy?

"I don't worry about that. They better keep me happy."

Might any of them play this week?

"They better be ready."

How can they impress you enough to start? What quality do you most prefer in a football player?

"It's all w-a-n-t in this business. The boy who wants to play is the one I'm looking for. The day I don't want to coach, that's the day I'll quit."

iii

With nine big years in Green Bay behind him, Lombardi took a year off from coaching, then took over the Washington Redskins for his tenth and last season as a head coach. Before his health failed, he turned around another loser, compiling a 7-5 record that matched his first-year 7-5 at Green Bay.

He had left Green Bay because, as he told me in 1969, he couldn't think of another new way to motivate a team that had been continuously successful. And for him, that was an understandable reason. When the stress is on muscular rather than mental agility, when it's on running plays instead of passes, the troops must somehow be inspired, over and over, to play hard, to put out. And though Lombardi was the most emotional coach of his time, there aren't an infinite number of ways to inspire an offensive guard to beat up on a defensive tackle. When the Packers had heard every line he had, he quit.

He resettled in Washington where the Redskins hadn't had a winning season in fourteen years. What was it like for football's finest and most famous coach to change bases in mid-stream?

"The most difficult part of a new job," he told me one day at his new headquarters, "is analyzing and understanding the personality of each player. This got most of my attention in the early days at Green Bay, and it's the top-priority thing on this team. You can't begin to coach a forty-man team until you understand each of the forty men."

Why is that important?

"The problem is that you can't coach without criticizing – and it's essential to understand how to criticize each man individually. Some can take constructive criticism in front of a group, and some can't. Some will take it privately, but others can only take it indirectly. Football is a pressure business, and on my teams I put on most of the pressure. The point is that (in an era before the player limit was raised to fifty-three) I've got to learn forty ways to pressure forty new men."

Of the various procedures and policies that worked ten years ago in Green Bay, I wanted to know, which ones was Lombardi applying to the Redskin problem? What were the high-priority missions?

"Broadly speaking, the two main things on a new job are personality analysis and talent analysis," he said. "The idea is to make sure that every player is in his best position."

What has the talent analysis shown so far?

"The veterans here are better than they have played to date."

You said the same thing at Green Bay in the spring of 1959.

"Did I? Maybe I'm an incurable optimist."

Overall, what do the 1968 Redskin movies reveal about your new players?

"They show only what the players have done – not what they're capable of doing – and that is the trouble with relying too heavily on pictures of a new team. I'm really not sure yet what I have in Washington. The pictures don't tell you the big thing – the potential of each player. Football is a game played with emotion, not just muscle, and if a man is merely playing satisfied, that doesn't come through in the pictures. What can he do under stress and duress? What is he capable of if I push him to the limit? What *is* his limit? Those are the things I have to know, and I can only approximate the answers by grading the Redskins in last year's games."

What other priorities do you have on a new team?

"Just analyzing the opposing defenses and offenses, and discussing techniques with a new coaching staff."

Hiring a new staff was easy for you, I'd guess. As an NFL coach, you have won with seemingly all kinds of assistant coaches.

"The point to be made here is that there are no bad coaches in this league. All the coaches are good ones, the head coaches and the assistants. If you have played in this league – or if you have just been deeply interested in what we do, and if you deeply want to coach – you can be a coach, and you can coach for me or anybody."

It seems likely that many assistants have a deep interest because they hope to be head coaches some day. Why does it take so long for some of them to get there?

"The dividing line is on the question of direction. There are assistants who are great at taking direction – but can't give it. Most people need direction. And most fans don't realize that comprehensive football knowledge is not the most important thing in coaching. What I ask of an assistant is that he be a good technique man."

Is that all?

"No, I also demand loyalty – loyalty to the Redskins and loyalty to me. I have worked with many kinds of assistants – but this they've all had. I won't tolerate anything less than complete loyalty. Contrary to what you may have heard, I *will* tolerate practically everything else – if the man can coach techniques."

It has been said that even on techniques, you are something of a dictator in relationships with your staff.

"That isn't true at all. This spring in Washington, I suppose my coaches and I are devoting most of our man hours to a study of techniques. And I'm not dictating anything. At our staff meetings, I might say that on a given play I'd like to have it blocked this way. Then I ask, what do you think? If any coach – offensive or defensive – has a better way, I change. Most definitely, I value assistants with creative ability."

On most clubs, offensive and defensive coaches work apart. Why do you ask them to sit together?

"It's the only way to do it in the spring. First, I want all my coaches to be thoroughly familiar with both our offensive and defensive concepts. Second, I want a defensive coach, for instance, to be familiar with other NFL defenses. And third, when a trained defensive coach puts his mind to offense – or vice versa – he can often help the rest of us find a solution."

Provided he has accepted the overall Lombardi philosophy.

"Well, there are many ways to play football, and it's not too important what you decide on – as long as everybody is in agreement. You call me a dictator. The fact is that I'm reluctant to take any step that doesn't have the wholehearted support of my whole staff."

iv

A man as successful as Lombardi is rare in any field. Thus, every chance I got, I talked him over with such former associates as Tom Fears, one of the Los Angeles Rams' all-time receivers, who was an assistant coach at Green Bay in Lombardi's first season. A Hall of Famer, Fears noted that one argument between and among the football men of the time centered on Lombardi and Paul Brown. Which, they asked, was the greater coach?

Fears said, "You have to remember that Brown had two years to build his team before he ever played a game in 1946. At Green Bay (in 1959), Lombardi found himself in the most mixed-up situation in the league. He walked into a hornets' nest, and got them all making honey."

How good, Fears was asked in 1960, are Lombardi's players?

"They're just fair," he said. "His best back, Paul Hornung, isn't any better than Frank Gifford (whom Lombardi coached as offensive coordinator of the New York Giants)."

Is that bad?

"Gifford is an average runner and ordinary passer. Every back and end we have on the (1960) Rams, except Tom Wilson, is a better receiver than Gifford – and Wilson is a better runner."

How does Gifford make All-Pro every year?

"When Lombardi was the Giant backfield coach, he built Gifford into an All-Pro. Vince put in an offense in which the fundamental play was the halfback option, run or pass. He and Gifford worked on it until that one play was the biggest threat in the Eastern Division. It made Gifford an All-Pro halfback – that and the fact that Gifford is a terrific competitor. In Green Bay, Lombardi deliberately set out to make Hornung into another Gifford, and he got the same results with a back who is just as ordinary."

Otherwise last year, Green Bay's assistants got a chance to test the theory that strict, stern coaches are not always beloved. How did the players react to Lombardi?

"An unusual thing happened after our opening game. Hornung and the other Packers felt so good about the way things were going that they put Lombardi on their shoulders, and carried him off the field."

What was unusual about that?

"The Packers had lost the game."

v

Former Green Bay safety Willie Wood, the Hall of Famer who played eight seasons for Lombardi, was asked about him after he (Wood) retired and joined the San Diego Chargers as an assistant coach. "Lombardi's secret was getting along with the players," he said. "He wasn't a dictator at all, contrary to public opinion. He was a conciliator. The thing that made him strong was his ability to solve the personal problems of the players."

What, Wood was asked, do you mean by personal problems?

"Something wrong at home, financial problems, things like that," he said. "Vince was a beautiful father confessor, a man you could really confide in."

He appeared to be the last person anyone would go to with an embarrassing personal problem.

"Ah, you didn't go to him. He went to you."

How did he know you had a problem?

"That's the thing that really explains Lombardi," Wood said. "In the first place, he had so much confidence in his judgment that when he picked a man for a job, he knew he had the right man. Therefore, if the man's performance tailed off, Vince knew it had to be something personal. And instead of letting the problem fester, as a lot of coaches would, Vince went right to the player, and had it out with him."

That's amazing. How about an example of the kind of personal thing he solved?

"If it was personal, how could I know what it was?"

Then how did you know he solved anything?

"Sometimes after a man had been playing badly, he would play well, and I'd congratulate him. He'd say, 'Vince helped me with a little personal thing.' Problems are usually small. There aren't many big problems. When you talk them over with somebody who is sincerely interested in you, they suddenly don't seem so serious. Most people who think they have problems just want to touch base with someone who cares. Vince cared about his players. That's how he kept forty of them playing at their peak, and that's why we won."

If you were lecturing at a coaching clinic, what other attributes of Lombardi's would you bring up?

"I'd mention first that he was honest with his players. Nothing is more important than being scrupulously honest in all matters at all times. Secondly, he demanded our best at all times. Your second best gets you second place. And third, he had a sincere relationship with his players. That's hardest of all. You can't feign sincerity indefinitely. Vince really was sincerely interested in the welfare of the kind of guy who would go out and die for the Green Bay Packers."

Do you suppose Lombardi agonized over players he fired?

"I know he did. He gave this subject more attention than almost anything else, especially in the last days of training camp, when you have to cut the last two or three men. I saw the way he handled it. It was hard on him, but he did it like a man. I don't think one guy left Green Bay bitter in all the years Vince was there."

If true, that's a unique record.

"I think it's true. He would cut or trade a player in such a way that the guy could see it wasn't personal. A traded player is inclined to think the coach has it in for him. You think the coach doesn't like you. Vince made them see otherwise."

How?

"He sat down and showed them the whole picture. If he intended to trade for a receiver, for example, he said so, then he explained how trades work. If you're short on receivers and long on linebackers, you may have to trade a linebacker to get what you need. Vince said this so persuasively that the guy sometimes walked out of camp thinking he had personally delivered us our next championship."

Put it all together and you have the coach of the century.

6. Woody Hayes: Top-Seven Tyrant

MOVING IN SYNCH with Lombardi, tough conservatives like this Ohio State coach dominated football all the way up to the 1980s.

One of the most stimulating college football coaches of the century, one of the most tyrannical, possibly the most colorful, among the ablest, was Woody Hayes of Ohio State, a brawler who brawled with everyone, it often seemed, except those who agreed with him. He particularly enjoyed squabbling with sportswriters. And his end as a football coach came the day he walked onto the playing field after a play that displeased him and punched out one of his players.

By then, Hayes had outlived his time, which was the 1950s-'70s, when a belligerent winning coach could get by with almost anything. The concept of political correctness was coming into use the year he hit the player, a young man put in his charge, and his action was plainly politically incorrect. Ohio State fired him.

On the evidence, it can be argued that Hayes had a character flaw, but in all-time wins he is in college football's top seven behind only Bryant, Warner, Stagg, Paterno, Bowden and Osborne. And as Ohio State's top dog, he spent a lot of New Year's Days at the Rose Bowl, getting there with an old-fashioned, Lombardi-like, fullback-oriented offense that disrupted every Big Ten football program except, occasionally, Michigan's. So at the height of his career I called on him one day at his office in Columbus, Ohio, resolved not to fight with the man but to hear him out.

At sixty, Hayes was a driver who had become in appearance the sort of man he most admired: an army commander, erect but heavily built, obviously well fed, obviously in charge. At the start of a somewhat different kind of Woody Hayes interview, he was asked to explain why he wins all the time.

" 'You Win with People,'" he said. He was then the author of a new book with that name. "In college football, success attracts the better athlete," he continued. "The mediocre man won't try it with us. In this respect, college and pro ball could hardly be more different. The pros today are more like the rest of the world."

What is there about college football that is out of step?

"College winners aren't penalized," Hayes said. "In the NFL, they are. Bottom pro teams get the best choices in the draft. The pros, in other words, reward you for losing – like most other things in our society today. The income tax is another example. So are the rules of football, as a matter of fact: The team that's scored on gets the ball in either college or pro football. But except for that, college football is the exception to the way things are going in this country. Success leads to success in college football."

In a successful coach, what quality is most important?

"I would say total dedication. There are some similarities between football and war, as you have doubtless heard many times, and this is one of them. Winners are men who have dedicated their whole lives to winning. The fact that really explains General Patton is that in World War

II, he fought his battles where he had spent his honeymoon years earlier. He anticipated."

Football, of course, is less brutal than war.

"The goals are different. It's the strategy that's similar. For example, at Ohio State, we consider ourselves the cleanest team in football. Clean teams play better football, in our opinion. They concentrate better on their assignments. They feel they get more leverage."

As entertainment vehicles, how do you compare college and pro ball?

"College ball is more versatile. That's because we run three or four backs, including the quarterback. The pros run only one or two. Secondly, I have to think the pros have hurt their game with all their good field-goal kickers. Every time I've had a good placekicker here, our goal-line offense has suffered. It's some kind of mental reaction to the fact that it's so easy to get three points."

In the NFL, a running quarterback is soon an injured quarterback.

"It's been our experience that the only way to toughen up a quarterback is to run him. You certainly don't get tough throwing. A quarterback who runs some does a better job against a tough rush than a passer who just drops back and fires all the time."

If the road to success is paved with tough running backs, why isn't Ohio State in the I Formation or the Wishbone?

"In the I Formation, the fullback is third in the pecking order to the tail-back and quarterback, and we decided we didn't want to do that. We'd never relegate the fullback to a blocker. In fact, we'd rather run the fullback than anybody. It tends to make everybody else on the team tough and team-oriented. As for the Wishbone, the year we used it in the Rose Bowl, it only got us seventeen points. We think we can be more versatile in other for-mations, get more receivers out quicker. The other thing is that you don't do as good a job with the fullback in the Wishbone. It's hard to get a Wishbone fullback off tackle, for one thing – and as a coach, that has troubled me."

As a coach, if you were to list your assets, what would you list first?

"I run it."

You're in charge, you mean. You make the decisions.

"Yes, I'm in charge, but no, I don't decide everything. I'd guess that at Ohio State, the assistants and even the players make more decisions than they do almost anywhere else. What I mean is, I don't depend on other people. I'm the first guy to work in the morning. There's no job too small for me. In football, the little things are really the big things. On this team, I make the hospital runs myself."

What hospital runs?

"It's a tough business. We're having two operations tomorrow morning, for instance, and when an Ohio State football player wakes up in the hospital, the first guy I want him to see is me. There's no way you can delegate that – and I have the best staff of assistants in the nation."

I notice that most of your assistants have just come aboard.

"They keep leaving me – always vertically into better jobs, never laterally. That's because everybody knows Ohio State's success is due to my coaches. Recruiting assistant coaches is more important than recruiting players because the assistants recruit the players."

When there's a vacancy on your staff, how do you fill it?

"The nominations come from my coaches. For two reasons. They know the candidates, and they know me. They make a list of about ten guys who have the requirements. Then we sit down and discuss who'll do this better and who that. Finally, we interview about three of them. That's where I come in, and because I know all three are well qualified, I only want to know one thing."

Yes?

"I want to know why he wants to come with me. If his answer isn't satisfactory, we don't hire him."

What's a satisfactory answer?

"If he says he wants to be a head coach someday, and this is as good a place as any to learn it, I'll take him. I know I'm dealing with an honest man."

Did you say your staff recruits Ohio State's players now, too?

"The way we work it is, my coaches only come to me if they have a difference of opinion on whether to take a boy. In that case, I usually decide we don't want him. So they bring me fewer and fewer things to decide. One of our starters now dips snuff, for instance. I'd have decided against him if I'd had the chance, but he's a good tough player, and I'd have made a mistake. So I've learned that some good people dip snuff, and you win with people."

7. Bear Bryant: Football's Biggest Winner

THE ALL-TIME champion was a self-created character,
the real stuff behind a broad and even bizarre front.

Paul (Bear) Bryant, the Alabaman who won 323 games in the twentieth century – more than any other coach in the college football big time – was in California recruiting new players one offseason when asked to say a few words at a high school coaches' banquet. As he rose slowly to his feet, Bryant, using his usual speaking voice, mumbled: "I want to talk to you gentlemen tonight about your real good football players. If there are any 'A' students among 'em, I'd like for you to send 'em to Stanford – the Hahvahd of the West. Your 'B' students, I'd recommend Southern Cal or UCLA. Yes, suh, I'd send my own kin theah. Your 'C' students – put them in the other great schools of this great state. But let me also say this to y'all. If there are any gin-drinkin', hell-raisin', meaner-than-hell 'D' students on your team, please send 'em down to the old Bear."

Nobody else in his generation could compare with the old Bear. The most unusual university leader of his time (1950s, '60s, '70s), he was also the century's biggest winner. A college football coach for thirty-eight years, Bryant won Game 323 in 1982, overtaking Pop Warner (319) and Amos Alonzo Stagg (314). As a rule, a longevity record isn't as meaningful as a one-day or one-year statistic or achievement, but Bryant's is. Whereas Warner, Stagg and other early-century coaches operated in relatively stress-free days, Bryant lived and worked in a high-pressure era. By the final years of the century, few Division I-A coaches were fighting off the alumni and sportswriters long enough to win a hundred games. To win three times as many was obviously something special.

Joe Paterno of Penn State also did it, and Bobby Bowden of Florida State was doing it; but both spent most of the century looking up at Bryant, who made his record run in 1981-82 after reaching 307 impressively in the first game of 1981. That first night at Baton Rouge, Louisiana, Bryant led Alabama past LSU, 24-7, to tell the world that, yes, he had team enough to shortly set the all-time record.

Still, it's who he was rather than what his teams did that most interested the other coaches of his generation.

Said former Arkansas Coach Frank Broyles: "Bryant was so dignified that I was always expecting him to say, 'Let us pray.' But there was another side to him. When he was at Kentucky, he was the only coach in the country who found out that a good young high school player in Texas was a Catholic. The prospect had about decided on Notre Dame when Bryant got him by dressing up one of his assistant coaches as a priest – black suit, white collar and all. The boy was overwhelmed when Bear's assistant dropped by and told him: 'Young man, the Pope wants you to go to Kentucky.'"

LSU Athletic Director Paul Dietzel, who coached on Bryant's staff for a number of years, remembered, "Even at parties, Bear would do anything to win." One night after a night game, Dietzel said, when the coaches were playing charades with their wives, Bryant's team won although he had never, until then, heard of the game. "Bear beat us when nobody could guess the name of a book he called a real book," Dietzel said. "He told us it was 'Fordyce on the Cotton Belt.' Who's going to act out Fordyce on the Cotton Belt? I found out later that's where he's from – but not in time to call my boss a liar at 3:30 in the morning"

Fordyce, Arkansas (population 3,206), is indeed where Bryant went to grade school and high school. He was actually from a suburb of Fordyce called Moro Bottom (population 37). He was born on a farm there. They were already calling him Bear in high school, where he played tackle for the Fordyce Redbugs. He became Bear after a wrestling match.

"A promoter with a real live bear came to the Lyric one year," said former Redbug quarterback Ike Murray. "The guy offered $1 a minute to anyone wrestling the bear, and Paul volunteered." Murray couldn't remember who won, Bryant or the bear. But, he said, "I do remember who cheered. Half of that crowd was pulling for the bear."

To earn his way through high school, Bryant drove a grocery truck after school and lived in an unfinished room on the top floor of the Kilgore Hotel, where Murray, later attorney general of Arkansas, was the night clerk. "If I'd been writing the class prophecy for our senior class at Fordyce," Murray said, "I'd have written this about Bear Bryant: 'He'll be lucky to stay out of the penitentiary.'"

ii

The all-time winning record that Bryant went for in 1981 appeared to be held by Stagg, who had won 314 games in his fifty-seven seasons ending in 1946. As far as Bryant or anyone else knew in the early 1980s, Warner had only won 313 games in his forty-four-year career, which ended in 1938. When, subsequently, the statisticians discovered that Warner had actually won 319 games, it didn't ultimately matter to Bryant or his friends because, by then, Bryant had raised the bar to 323.

All the drama of Bryant's race to be winningest was packed into the 1981 season, when the statisticians announced that he was chasing Stagg and when I was assigned to two Alabama games – the first as the Crimson Tide rolled over LSU on opening night and the last when Bryant rolled past Stagg. For the LSU opener, Bryant flew his team over from Tuscaloosa in two planes. He also brought along his wife, Mary Harmon, leaving two children at home, a boy and girl. I asked him if he and his wife, thinking of the children, were always careful to fly in separate planes. "I'm always careful to fly with the starters," he said.

He was in a seersucker suit with white shirt, blue tie and one of his four hundred plaid houndstooth hats. A closet businessman, a millionaire, he owned part of the New York firm that made those hats. The familiar sun-baked face seemed more deeply etched than ever. It was the face of a heavy cigarette smoker and drinker who had defied the odds and lived to be sixty-eight. A half year earlier, doing his weekly television show, Bryant had reached for an ashtray one night, missed, and squashed a cigarette in the upholstery of a nearby chair. As he droned on, smoke and then flames were visible on almost every TV screen in Alabama. Just in time, the producer rushed in with a bottle of cola, said, "Excuse me, coach," and put out the fire.

On either television or in person, Bryant, six feet two, 206, could have been the aging grandfather of the Marlboro man. But age didn't dull his flair. During a short walk on the Louisiana campus on the day of the LSU game, he exchanged smiles and a few casual words with a young woman student, who afterward told me, "Mr. Bryant knows how to talk to a lady, and how to look at a woman."

She also said he seemed shy, which may account for the rumbling, growling, low-volume monotone of Bryant's normal speaking voice. "Half the time we can't understand him," one of his players said. But they always knew what he meant.

Two hours before that Alabama-LSU game, driving up to the stadium behind two wailing police cars, Bryant and his players got out of the bus and slowly walked around the field from end zone to end zone. It was a ritual they used to follow regularly at road games, testing the turf, and acclimating themselves to the taunts of the enemy.

In this case, thousands of LSU students hooted them all the way around. Though the college boys and girls were mostly in short shorts on an eighty-two-degree night, Bryant and his players were all carefully groomed in jackets and ties. In an Alabama-red jacket, Bryant led the parade, and to Boston sportswriter John Powers he was just "a tired old man, shufflin' along, trying to stay out of the hospital." But New York writer B.J. Phillips said: "The message is clear: Alabama is checking things out. Alabama will be ready."

And Alabama was.

To succeed as a football coach, Paul Bryant worked out a unique formula for himself, one that separated him from other coaches. His plan: "Accept the responsibility, every time, for everything that goes wrong." To listen to him after any game, to read his quotes, was always to tune in on a set formula piece in which Bryant blamed himself for any and all Alabama problems, and credited others for any successes.

A former Bryant assistant and NFL coach, Bum Phillips, said: "Here's how Bear ran a players' meeting. He started talking about all the good things everybody did, individually – each guy's blocking, tackling, whatever they did good. Pretty soon he got all the players nodding and agreeing. Then, gently, he brought up a few wrong things. A guy sitting there would tell himself: 'The old man's been bragging on me, and I know he's right about that. Maybe he's right about this, too.' "

At coaches' meetings, the formula was similar. "He blamed himself for so much," Phillips said, "that pretty soon he had the other coaches saying to themselves, 'Hey, wait a minute, maybe I could have done something better myself.' It's only human to resist when somebody is bawling you out, so Bear did just the opposite, and got everybody leaning with him."

It was clear to his staff that before any big game, Bryant ran the strangest coaches' meetings in the history of football. "He would sit around for an hour or more offering little bits of ideas," Phillips said. "Eventually, one of his assistants would catch the drift and make a suggestion. Then Bear would slap the table and say: 'Damn, why didn't I think of that? We'll do it.' Next thing, he was bragging on the guy in the newspapers. Everybody who knew him well was surprised out of their head every time Bear lost."

But what kept the old coach going?

Bear said it was fear. "The thing that's moved me all my life," he said, "is the fear of going back to driving mules in Arkansas for fifty cents a day."

That could explain how he managed to avoid the worst hazard to longevity in coaching, fear of changing football styles and routines. Most of the great ones, back to Bernie Bierman, Bob Neyland and beyond, mastered one way of playing the game, and retired prematurely when they couldn't or wouldn't adjust to new and better ways.

Bryant almost alone of all the big-league coaches won and won big with all the offensive variations: the Single Wing, Notre Dame Box, T Formation, Split T, Pro Set, and Wishbone. And in his most challenging years, typically, he made the rigid Wishbone into a formation of infinite flexibility.

What's more, Bryant throughout his career closely studied and won with crew-cut kids, bearded kids, white kids, black kids, the sons of a disciplined generation, the sons of a permissive generation, with those who couldn't think for themselves, with those who questioned all authority, with those who weren't allowed a water break all afternoon, and with those who when Bear learned better – he was always learning – got a water break every ten minutes.

A guy like that is apt to win more games than Amos Stagg.

iv

It was in the final game of his 1981 run at Stagg that Bryant overtook the former record-holder. Against Alabama that time, Auburn put up a fight but couldn't match the high morale of Bryant's players on a night when he and they came from behind in the fourth quarter to beat Auburn, 28 to 17, and Stagg, 315 to 314.

Even in his hour of triumph, the old coach was thinking of next year. "I liked coming from behind," Bryant said a few minutes after the game. "Give me my druthers, we'll do that every time. It proved to our players that they have class and character, and it showed them what can be done in the future."

To win number 315, Bear's team sustained two up-hill, beautifully coached touchdown drives in the last ten minutes after Auburn – which outplayed Alabama much of the time – had opened a 17-14 lead at the top of the final period.

"This was one of the greatest games ever played," Bryant enthused shamelessly, standing bareheaded, for a change, after someone had pilfered his familiar houndstooth hat in the instant the game ended. "I feel like I ought to go back and check the scoreboard," he said, "to make sure we won."

Staying in character, Bryant praised Auburn and thanked everyone he had ever been associated with in football: his players everywhere he'd coached, his assistant coaches, even two "deceased coaches who coached me as a boy." Asked if it was a relief to finally overhaul Stagg and extend Alabama's 1981 record to 9-1-1, Bryant said: "I think so. It's been a hard year. I haven't been strong enough, or bright enough, not until the last few days."

On the night that Bryant reached 315, his new intrastate adversary, Coach Pat Dye of Auburn, was reaching for 60. And in a tense Wishbone duel, they fought to 7-7 in the first thirty minutes. Even after the first fifty minutes, it seemed possible, maybe probable, that the new record would elude Bryant until New Year's Day, if not later. For Auburn seemed slightly the better team.

But Bryant's players wanted the record more than Auburn wanted the game. As one of the old coach's young players, Berry Perrin, said afterward, "Every time we lined up in the fourth quarter, we would say in the huddle: 'We can't give up. This is for 315.' "

Accordingly, after compiling but ten first downs in the first three quarters, Alabama reached back to win the game with its last two possessions. Backs to the wall, ten minutes remaining, thinking about the old Bear, Alabama was unstoppable on the moves that altered the score from 17-14 Auburn to, at the end, 28-17 Alabama. Reflecting on the tension, tight end Jesse Bendross, an Alabama star with two touchdowns, said: "It got to the point at one time (in the second half) when we were very nervous. But Coach Bryant tells us to keep the faith and not give up. If you don't think you can get beat, you won't."

Bryant's skills as a leader, developed through more than a third of the twentieth century, shone through all four Alabama touchdowns. No other major college or pro coach, for one thing, has ever routinely and deliberately used as many players every week as Bryant did, for he was forever getting ready for next year, and the next. Even though this was his last regular-season shot at 315 that year, he had all three Alabama quarterbacks on the field as usual, and each of them had a hand in at least one touchdown:

- After Alan Gray's unusual sixty-three yard quarterback sweep to the Auburn 21-yard line, Alabama powered it over on six runs, the last a one-yard Gray keeper – thus showing Auburn its strength first.
- Bryant next showed the Tigers some finesse. At the Auburn 26, ending a fifty-five yard drive, his number-two quarterback, Ken Coley, shoveled a little pass on second and fifteen to split end Bendross. Circling back to catch the ball at the line of scrimmage, Bendross broke for the end zone, and got there just ahead of the Tigers.
- In the fourth quarter, down 17-14 with ten minutes of 1981 left, Alabama came with a first-down play-action pass to score the go-ahead touchdown easily on number-three quarterback Walter Lewis' throw to Bendross from the Auburn 38-yard line. To their dismay, and sorrow, the Tigers went for a running back's fake.
- For Alabama's final touchdown, Bryant called on his best runner,

Linnie Patrick, whom for some reason he didn't call on often. During a forty-nine-yard drive, Patrick carried the ball twice, first taking Gray's handoff and breaking four tackles on a first-down thirty-two-yard run. Then, speeding up as Auburn's spirits fell, he swept the final fifteen yards around end.

The last half of the last game of the year was thus Bryant's biggest and best, leaving only one question unanswered. Do you suppose he planned it that way?

8. Bobby Bowden: Best Active College Coach

IN THE YEARS when most college teams ran the ball, Florida State threw it to win with a coach who's still throwing and winning.

Among America's active college football coaches, the most impressive, I have believed for years, is Bobby Bowden of Florida State. The other great late-1990s veteran of thirty-three years in the big time, Joe Paterno of Penn State, has totaled a few more wins, but he's done it with more traditional, more conservative ways.

At Florida State, Bowden's teams have thrown the ball much of the time since 1976, thus contributing in important ways to the football trend of the century: away from runs and toward the pass.

Further, if postseason success counts, Bowden counts. His won-lost bowl-game percentage is the highest in history among those coaching in eleven or more games. It is more than a hundred points higher than Paterno's and more than two hundred above Bear Bryant's. Bowden once won a record eleven consecutive bowl games.

I wear it as a badge of pride that I called on both Paterno and Bowden very early in their days at Penn State and Florida State, respectively, meeting with Bowden just as he was turning around one of the worst football programs in the South. Not yet a big winner in a community where a winning football team of any kind was a novelty, he was even then being called the most eminent citizen of Tallahassee, the state capital. "The governor is a poor second," enraptured alumni kept telling me.

Still, for several years, Bowden proceeded warily. He remembered that he had been similarly celebrated, for a while, at his last stop, West Virginia. There after four consecutive winning seasons, he finished under .500 for the only time in six years at Morgantown, whereupon the townspeople hanged him in effigy.

For Bowden that year, losing was a learning experience, primarily. "I learned I'd better not do it again," he told me one morning in his Tallahassee office, laughing about it, sort of – laughing through remembered tears.

Jovial, high-spirited, outgoing, Bowden seems entirely the wrong sort to hang in effigy, anytime, even if he were losing every game. But it's made an impression. "You never forget it when they run you up a tree," he said, still smiling. "My children could hardly stand it. They'd come home at night and say, 'Daddy is still up there in that old tree.' Finally, one of my assistant coaches went out and cut it down, and I'm here to tell you, I've kept hiring that man every year since. He has a job for life."

On the Florida State team, no doubt.

For at Tallahassee, shaken by his West Virginia experience, Bowden began by making the most sensible contractual agreement in football. Every morning when he got up, he had a new five-year contract with the Seminoles. They contracted to pay him for five full seasons if they ever fired him. The hitch was that if Bowden ever left for a better job, *he* had to pay Florida State more than a half million – more than any 1980s college coach could have come up with out of pocket, least of all Bowden. As indulgent as most extroverts, he has always provided the best for his family.

His first contract, since replaced by a more conventional agreement, was for several years exceedingly helpful in three ways. For one thing, it freed Bowden of personal financial worries. Second, it discouraged, among others, at least one university that went after him, LSU, along with at least one pro club, the Jacksonville franchise of the once-promising but now defunct United States Football League. But most beneficial of all, the revolving five-year contract encouraged Bowden to develop one of the most entertaining offensive teams in college football without worrying about interceptions and the other calculated risks of a lively passing game.

ii

A sign in Bowden's office reads: "I firmly believe that man's finest hour, his greatest fulfillment to all he holds dear, is that moment when he has worked his heart out in a good cause and lies exhausted on the field of battle . . . victorious." That is the spirit that unites him to other winners. But unlike running-play ball-control winners, Bowden wants to do it in style.

His objective is to put a team on the field that can advance the ball every which way – running every kind of offensive play and throwing every pass.

"We'll throw it wherever it is," he said when asked to sum up his offensive strategy. "They have to defend every corner of the field."

Unlike the overwhelming majority of 1980s coaches, who were conservative philosophically, Bowden started most plays by dropping his quarterback straight back. "Our goal is to score every time," he said. "I don't want to punt – I hate to punt – I want the ball. And to move it, you have to throw it. We're as likely to throw on our goal line as theirs – more likely. From our goal line we have 109 yards to pass in. From theirs, only eleven. It's much harder to throw down there. We work more on our first-and-goal pass offense than any thing else we do."

iii

Now nearing seventy, Bobby Bowden remains a younger, pudgier, more puckish Bum Phillips without the hat and boots – as friendly as Phillips was in his day as an NFL coach, as popular with the media, but bubblier. Everyone who knows the Florida State leader calls him a joy to be around. Like many old football players, Bowden, who stands, at most, five feet ten, has always fought the battle of the bulge, and always joked about it. "I go up and down like a balloon, losing twenty pounds, gaining twenty," he said.

His vice is food. "I've got no prejudices," he said. "I'll eat anything."

He no longer smokes, but for years his favorite toys were the long unlit cigars he bit into from time to time morning, noon and night. Sitting at his desk in a day's growth of whiskers, saggy-eyed, usually smiling, looking up at a visitor through half-glasses, he appears to be a 1990s Benjamin Franklin.

There are days when Bowden is at work at 4 a.m. "I don't set an alarm clock but I start to work whenever I wake up," he said. "Some nights I go home and just can't wait for sleep to be over. Just so I can go out and begin the next day." A lifelong Baptist and still a lay preacher whose sermons have been heard in many churches in the South, Bowden once told a Tallahassee sports editor, Bill McGrotha, "When I was young, people used to tell me I ought to be a minister. But I never felt like I was called. It was more like I was called to coaching."

It happened in Birmingham, where, son of a realtor, Bowden was born next to a football field. "From our front door," he said, "you could kick the ball through the goal posts." That was at Woodlawn High School, which he attended before making Little All-American as a quarterback at Birmingham's Howard University, now Samford. Actually, like any Alabama prep sensation, Bowden had gone to Alabama first. But he had left a girl back in Birmingham and couldn't stand to be without her. Asked why he didn't marry the girl, a five-foot-two brunette cheerleader, and take her to Tuscaloosa with him, Bowden said: "She was still in high school. When I did marry her, Ann was only sixteen. I was nineteen."

They have four sons, two daughters. "My sister also has six children," he said. "Every time we had one, they had one – within a month of us every time. Then we both had operations and that's all that's kept me from starving. For fifty years I've been head over heels in love."

His sons all played football on Bowden teams and three of them later coached on his staff, where Jeff is still an assistant. Tommy coaches Clemson. Terry, formerly at Auburn, is now between jobs. One daughter married a football coach and the other a football player.

"I remember the Saturday all six of us got beat," Bowden said. "My wife cried all day, then wiped her tears and called them all up. 'Don't let this get you down, dear,' she said, over and over. 'Remember, it happened to Daddy, too.' Oh, that was a morbid scene, I tell you. Morbid."

Looking suddenly serious, Bowden remembers that his oldest son is a college professor with a Ph.D. in religion. "The black sheep," he said.

iv

The Bowdens live on a Tallahassee golf course in a big house that's a mob scene at family reunions with children, grandchildren, cousins, second cousins and others.

They all like to come back to Tallahassee, a pleasant upper Florida town with Spanish moss dripping from the many oak and pecan trees. There are only two industries in Tallahassee, education and government, and the population is around a hundred thousand when the university and legislature are both in session, much less than half that in the hot summers.

Florida State, which began as a women's school but has been a football-playing university since 1947, spreads around on the hills of the only rolling countryside of an otherwise depressingly flat state. In one of the American Indian languages, Tallahassee means seven hills. The campus has a traditional, somewhat sleepy, Deep South look. At Gainesville, by contrast, the University of Florida is faster paced and more modern with a brick-and-glass look.

Nobody at Florida seems to like Florida State, and nobody at Florida State likes anyone at Florida, which is about a hundred miles east and fifty miles south. A traveler asking directions to Gainesville is told to "go east until you smell it and south until you step in it." Later when a Florida professor was advised of this message and asked for a comment, he said, heatedly, "That's our line. They stole it like they steal everything else."

Bowden appears to be somewhat removed from all the acrimony. When he isn't coaching, he plays golf, his only other passion. "Golf has helped my football," he said. "It's taught me patience and that you're never out of it. I've seen the pressure you can put on somebody by playing golf well, and that works in football, too."

v

On his first day at Tallahassee, Bowden took charge of a Florida State team that had gone 4-29 in its most recent three years. The Seminoles in Bowden's twenty-three seasons, counting the rebuilding seasons, went 219-53-4 (.801) – making everybody proud of him in Tallahassee, the more so because of his success on the road.

Despite rigorous out-of-town schedules, Bowden, as a Florida State coach, started 1-1 at Nebraska, 2-0 at Ohio State, 1-0 at Notre Dame, and 4-1 at LSU.

An early 1970s Florida State athletic director, Clay Stapleton, gave Bowden that opportunity, dreaming up difficult out-of-town schedules to make some money for the university's athletic department, which was then nearly bankrupt. Though Stapleton held the job only a year or so, he lined up seventy-two games with teams in the nation's top ten "on their terms, and in their towns," as he once said.

Thus, in his fifth season at Tallahassee, Bowden found himself scheduled against five powers on consecutive Saturdays, on their terms, and in their towns: Lincoln, Nebraska; Columbus, Ohio; South Bend, Indiana; Pittsburgh, Pennsylvania, and Baton Rouge, Louisiana. "I'd have quit before the season," he said, "if I hadn't had that danged contract."

Astonishingly, he won three of the five, and since then he has never looked back, proceeding to compile a Florida State road record of 103-37-2. And any way you look at it, that's better than a hanging.

9. John Madden: Football's Best Talker

THE MOST ARTICULATE football coach of the game's first hundred years went from the NFL to TV, from the luxury of Amtrak to a bus.

Before John Madden started riding the expressways of America in a bus, he led a more civilized life in an Amtrak Pullman car. And before that, he was an NFL coach who after ten seasons as a winner retired in 1979, at forty-two, to become a respected television analyst.

Not everyone gets to coach a Super Bowl champion, as Madden did the year he led Oakland past Minnesota in Game XI; not everyone gets a prominent second-career chance as television's dominant football commentator; not everyone gets to live half the year in one of Amtrak's luxury bedrooms while dining well, three times a day, in a gently rocking dining car that's like a good restaurant with picture windows.

So Madden is unique.

Of all the coaches who have delivered impassioned halftime addresses, Madden has become, in the final decades of the millennium, the most fluent and articulate – some would say loquacious – football coach of the century. And after riding to games on trains or buses, he has done more than any other coach to explain football to America.

During his time at the top in two careers, he seemed most content and relaxed, I thought, in the Amtrak years, when I joined him one time on the Dallas-bound Sunset Limited out of Los Angeles. As the cars rolled along, there was talk about trains, television and football with other club-car idlers, in the midst of which there was a question for Madden about his aptitude for a career in broadcasting after so many years in athletics.

"For twenty-five years or more," he said, "what I've tried to do – what I've learned to do – is look at anything on a train or at home or in an office building, anywhere, and say a few words about it."

"Anything?" he was asked.

"Anything or anybody," he said. "I practice all the time."

"Say something about this," a fellow traveler suggested, pointing to one of the swivel chairs facing the club-car window.

"It was made by someone who wasn't an American," Madden said smoothly, starting a commentary of about fifteen seconds. "When they designed this car, comfort wasn't a consideration. . . There are seats for two people in a space that's about right for one. . . The ash trays are inaccessible. . . They should have just copied the old club-car chairs."

No one but a chronically nosy individual – or one with a profound interest in the world about him – would think that deeply about a chair. An individual in the latter group, Thomas Jefferson, once said: "Not a blade of grass shoots up that is not of interest to me." Confirming his own catholic tastes, Madden said he wasn't aiming for TV or any other line of work in the early years when his curiosity drove him into his novel hobby. He just liked to think and talk, briefly, about this and that.

Madden's job as a football analyst is thus an exercise in serendipity requiring nothing more than ten- to fifteen-second commentaries about "anything that pops up on the screen," or so he told his fellow loungers over the faint soprano notes of the train's whistle. In his judgment, his job was comparable to that of a photo caption writer on a newspaper. "All I really do is talk about pictures," he said. "There are a hundred people down there (on the sidelines and the field), but the camera only closes on a handful at any one time, and it could close anywhere."

It could even close on the moon, and one night it did. Madden's director, television veteran Sandy Grossman, was choosing from a half dozen mostly football scenes in a stadium somewhere when he abruptly filled the screen with a live picture of the moon. "I wonder if they'll ever play football up there," Madden remarked, off the cuff and, as so often, on the mark.

Revealing another secret, Madden told his club-car listeners: "I have always been a people watcher. I can't remember when I didn't look at a man or a woman – everybody – and make up short little stories about them in my mind."

On TV these days the difference is that he just relays what he's heard or knows in short bursts, fifteen seconds ideally, to a million listeners.

In conversations with Madden during and after his Amtrak days, I learned that his strange mastery of a strange art form did two things for him. It made him possibly the most popular conversationalist on the railroads of America, which he rode to every game, traveling more than a hundred thousand miles a year as Amtrak's number-one customer. And it made him television's top football analyst or color man – and even, some believe, the best of all sports announcers. In his first year, he became the first color man to win the industry's prestigious Golden Mike award. And subsequently, each year for nearly two decades, he has been widely acclaimed as TV's best football analyst or sports analyst or both.

It can truthfully be said of Madden – as of most radio and TV announcers – that he talks too much. Still, no other football man on radio or TV so well combines the informative or technical aspects of this difficult work with the entertaining. And he is deliberately technical.

"That's what people want," he said. "I mean they want technical information if it's understandable. The guy who did the most to prove that was the doctor (Dennis O'Leary) who came on television some years ago when Ronald Reagan was shot. His subject was complex surgery, but he used drawings and descriptive terms to make the whole thing clear. I told my wife if a doctor can explain surgery, a football coach should be able to explain a game." And soon thereafter, frankly imitating Dr. O'Leary, Madden was using drawings himself, scribbling Xs and Os directly on his instant-replay slate.

The quality that makes him able to do this rapidly and accurately is the extraordinary vision he developed in his football days. Whereas most football spectators watch only the man with the ball, Madden seems to watch almost everybody. "When a play starts after the center's snap," he said, "I can sit in the press box and tell you what all twenty-two players are doing." That seems impossible. All? "I may miss somebody now and then," he said, "but not often."

How does he do it? "The key is knowing which specialists are on the field," he said, "and being aware of each player's strengths and weaknesses. First, as the play starts, I look at the offensive formation and place the offensive players in my mind with a coach's code words – east or west, left or right, I or slot, and so on. Then I look at the defense to see where the offense is heading – where the hole should be if they run, or where the quarterback should throw the ball if the defense is giving them something."

What Madden means is that as a TV commentator, he's still anticipating with a coach's mentality. As the center puts the ball in the quarterback's hands, the movement of every player is briefly etched in Madden's head, helping him follow the play, as it develops, the way he once followed each play as a coach. "If it's an important play," he says, "I think the fans want to know why it worked or why it didn't."

So he tells them, speaking unaffectedly, using up another fourteen or fifteen seconds, as if he were sitting around an Amtrak club car.

ii

It has never been easy to walk down the aisle of a passenger car on a moving train, and, lord knows, it isn't easy on today's roadbeds. To maintain one's balance, one must walk rapidly, legs wide apart, hands raised like an offensive lineman's to grab anything or anybody if the train lurches. And Madden, arms up, was always ready.

Rolling left and right with the sway of the train, bound for the dining car, he always took big, fast steps, legs apart, hands moving. A massive but stooped figure, he came on like an ax murderer.

By 1970s football fans, he is remembered as a bulging, arm-flapping redhead. Striding about the field aggressively, he was larger than most football players – and at six feet four and 270, he still is. And the dark red hair is still unruly, as if combed with his ax.

By 1980s railroad fans, he is remembered as a big guy who dressed for the road in jeans, old tennis shoes and, sometimes, a T-shirt with blue horizontal stripes accentuating the obvious, namely, that this is one immense man. On his left hand, fittingly, he wore an immense present from his wife – a ring that shouted "100" in flashing diamonds. This identified Madden as the only coach who ever led an NFL team to a hundred wins in ten years. The day he coached a Super Bowl champion was recalled in another mass of diamonds on a right-hand finger.

Three years after navigating the 1976 Raiders past the Minnesota Vikings in the eleventh Super Bowl, Madden lost his enthusiasm for coaching. He retired for that reason. And within three years after retiring, he had become the nation's most dedicated train freak. A claustrophobic disposition put Madden on the rails. The world's largest airplanes are too small for him, too confined. He could put up with air travel as a football coach (it was coaching he tired of, not flying) because one can move around on charter jets visiting with one's friends. "But in a commercial plane," he said, "there's no place to go except the bathroom. And how many times can you go to the bathroom?"

He never found out. On a commercial flight shortly after his departure from the Raiders, he panicked before the plane even left the ground. Sweating, eyes glazed, he struggled to his feet and shouted, "Let me out of here." They did, and he never went back.

Like other victims of claustrophobia, Madden also panics slightly in small cars, elevators and TV booths. His problems on one trip to Dallas were typical. Arriving at the game, he and partner Pat Summerall walked together into Texas Stadium, where the press elevator and an escalator are on opposite sides of the main lobby. There they parted, Summerall taking the elevator, Madden even objecting to the escalator. Asking them to please stop it, he walked up the escalator steps.

Together again in the press box, Summerall and Madden soon parted again, Summerall walking down to the field, where, like most announcers, he likes to mingle with the coaches and club owners while their teams warm up.

In the CBS booth, Madden paced around like a caged lion. He'd resign if he had to fight his way down through the crowd just to see a football coach. Just being in the ballpark was bad enough. He was glad to get back to the train.

He said he likes everything about trains: the motion of the cars, the clatter of the wheels, the furnished bedrooms, the big windows and the changing landscape, the changing cast of characters, the lifestyle. In those days, he relaxed totally on a train, blending into the scene, sleeping until noon or later, working (on his files and charts) when the spirit moved him, talking the night away in the club car as, on some trips, a bright moon crossed slowly from port windows to starboard.

As an Amtrak patron, he traveled like a circus travels. After a game in Atlanta he entrained for New York, where he worked a day or two, then took another train to Detroit. Returning to New York, his headquarters during the football season, he soon boarded a train for Minneapolis. Logistically, the difference between him and other football announcers was that they spent an hour or two getting to an assignment and he spent a day or two.

On a train, he took a geography student's interest in the countryside. When the conductor or somebody announced Lordsburg, New Mexico, Madden looked out the window and beamed. "How many people," he asked, "know what New Mexico looks like?" Recalling his first trip to Denver, he asked: "How many people have sat all day and watched Wyoming?"

His life on trains wasn't the healthiest, nor, I'm sure, is his bus life now. As a bus traveler in recent years, Madden has traded in the glamour of the train for the convenience of a wheeled vehicle that can roll right up to the press box elevator. But on either train or bus, it's hard to exercise on the road. There isn't much to do but sit and read or talk and smoke cigarettes, and that's how Madden puts in half the year, usually pulling on a diet cola, even at dinner. Nutritionally, Amtrak is an Indianapolis coffee shop with tablecloths and canned vegetables, but if you like it, it *is* a great life.

iii

At 1:30 in the afternoon, as the Sunset Limited raced through a little Texas town, Madden's bedroom door was still closed. He had turned in at 3 a.m. after discussing new surgical techniques and the effects of cortisone on the scapula joints with an M.D. from Glendale. His friends of the night before, finishing lunch, doubtless figured he was still in the sack, but he was studying. During the football season, Madden spends much of the midweek reading up on the teams he'll be talking about Sunday. And for doing that, he ranked the Amtrak environment as unmatched.

"You can do it anywhere, but a train is ideal," he said. "There's no mail, no interruptions. It's just you and the track. You close the door, and close out the world. I come aboard with suitcases full of every scrap of information I can find on the teams coming up. And when I get off, the best stuff is all in my head."

He takes no written notes to games because he has "total recall of the things I'd like to recall."

He learns some of that at home, where he studies football in the off-season. Home is in Pleasanton, California, which isn't far from Daly City, where he spent his boyhood. Son of an Irish auto mechanic, he was the baby in a house with two older sisters. According to Madden's wife Virginia, he's a man of few interests. "His hobbies," she said, "are poker, people and working with the mentally handicapped." Pausing to think about that, she continued: "He is a very compassionate person."

iv

In the 1970s, property investments with various owners of the Raiders left Madden, if not actually rich, comfortable enough to contemplate retiring from coaching at forty. He stuck it out for two more years for strictly statistical reasons. The most meaningful coaching records are based on a minimum of ten years as a head coach, and, as an admirer of former Green Bay Coach Vince Lombardi, he wanted to top Lombardi in games won. He went on to finish 103-32-7 (.763) to Lombardi's 96-34-6 (.738). The Madden percentage is the NFL's highest, all time.

Thus it was hardly a surprise when, talking about sports announcers recently, a rival network executive said: "John Madden is the most knowledgeable expert on the air."

And he doesn't just know football. He also seems to know more about TV than many TV veterans. Those watching the network put together the Summerall-Madden broadcasts have noted that Madden often appears to be in charge of the whole production. Some testimony:
  • During the 1980s NFL fight over free agency, when the players walked out from the sidelines for their pro-union solidarity handshakes before

a San Francisco kickoff, Madden turned to a cameraman and said, "We've got to be getting this."

- At a Dallas game when the coaches and other staff members walked onto the field, Madden told a director: "Tom Landry has a new hat. We can get close (closeup) on that."
- At a Detroit game, after one member of his television team had erred on a minor matter, Madden made a short speech to the crew reminiscent of his coaching days when the Raiders were behind at halftime. "I'd like to coin a phrase right here," he said mildly. "When you start to accept mediocrity, the best you will ever be is mediocre."

This was, most likely, a rebuke to a professional who was a television regular when Madden was still on the sideline. The explanation is the ambition and competitiveness that drove Madden to the top in football. He wants national-championship recognition every year both for himself and his network team.

"And not just the recognition," he said. "I mean to be the best actually, every time out, preseason, regular season, postseason, whenever."

On the air, Madden's play-by-play colleague, Summerall, a one-time Russian history major at Arkansas, is more professional than Madden – indeed he is the most professional of the ex-athletes – whereas Madden sounds like a player or coach. And this, Madden said, is the way he wants it. "I think you can get by in radio and TV if you remember to be yourself," he said. "The key to the whole thing is to be natural. When we're on, I talk and act as if I were talking with my quarterback or my wife."

His passion for naturalness and openness takes him in several directions. For one thing, he never uses the ubiquitous phrase, "off the record," and doesn't like to hear it. Coaches who think they're speaking privately with Madden wind up speaking to the nation. Nor does he talk about "skill positions," a phrase that has become an unpleasant cliché. "What do the other guys play?" he asked. "Unskilled positions?" At home, studying, what's more, Madden never listens to a Madden tape. "I wouldn't like myself, and I'd want to make some changes," he said. "How many snapshots do you like of yourself? Doing things like changing the pitch of your voice makes you a phony."

Finally, on the road, he never calls room service, preferring to sit with the crowds in hotel coffee shops and dining rooms. "Room service," he said, "makes you a recluse."

And Madden is anything but a recluse. He is out there, on the road, living large.

10. Dan Reeves: Born to Win (in Georgia)

FRIENDS OF THE Atlanta Falcons coach say he'd ask to
think it over if the choices were win and die or lose and live.

Long before Dan Reeves began coaching Super Bowl teams, including the Atlanta Falcons against the two-time champion Denver Broncos in the 1999 renewal, he was playing golf in Texas one day when, as he tells it, a cold rain drove him into the clubhouse.

Georgia-born, Reeves was then a young Dallas Cowboys halfback doing golf in the offseason. And the lesson he got from the golf pro that day, as rain rattled the clubhouse roof, was one he can't forget. Bouncing a golf ball on a table, the pro caught it on the back of his hand and said: "Bet you $5 you can't do that."

Reeves, an inconceivably intense competitor, replied: "Give me five practice shots and you're on."

An hour later, frustrated and still failing, having lost more than he wanted to lose, Reeves packed up and grumped home. "The rain had stopped, but the temperature was under thirty," he remembers. "I put the car in the barn, and went straight out to the patio with a bag of golf balls. It was so cold I almost froze to death, but before midnight I could catch that little old ball on the back of my hand every time I bounced it. And the next day, I went back to the golf club and got my money back."

That's Dan Reeves. A friend from his Cowboy days, Cornell Green, the former All-Pro cornerback, said: "Danny wasn't much of a running back, no speed, no size, but he outhustled everybody for nine years, and he memorized every assignment of every player on every play. He knew exactly where every player was going to be, and that gave him his edge running the ball. Made him look good. He even led the league in touchdowns one season."

It has been clear for a long time, in other words, that Reeves is a football-wise competitor – clear, that is, to those who knew him as a Super Bowl warrior at Denver, and before that as a player-coach at Dallas, and before that as a college quarterback at South Carolina, and even earlier on the farm in Georgia. The Falcons confirmed it again on January 20, 1997, when they put him in charge of the home-state team despite the disaster of his 32-34 record in four years with the New York Giants. And at Atlanta, Reeves has already twice confirmed the Falcons' judgment, first elevating the team insistently from the ashes of 3-13 in

1996 to 14-2 in 1998, and then rising gamely from midseason quadruple-bypass heart surgery to direct another conference champion, his fourth, from a Super Bowl sideline.

It is also in the record that Reeves' teams have lost all four Super Bowls, but the reasons for that have little to do with the thoroughness and intensity of his approach and much to do with his old-fashioned strategic philosophy. Simply put, Reeves, despite his long internship with Dallas' Hall of Fame passing coach Tom Landry, still distrusts the forward pass. In a passing era.

It is a great irony. At fifty-five, Reeves is one of the great football coaches of his time, having repeatedly driven NFL teams into the playoffs. But as a Super Bowl strategist, he keeps losing with champion passers – three times with John Elway and most recently with Chris Chandler, who in the 1998 regular season outperformed Elway in every vital passing category and criterion.

The difference between two 14-2 teams in the decisive first half of Super Bowl XXXIII, as the Denver Broncos won at Miami, 34-19, was that Reeves grounded passer Chandler and ran running back Jamal Anderson, running him unsuccessfully against a defense that was set for Anderson every time on third and one, and even fourth and one, as well as first and ten. In similar circumstances, Elway simply threw the ball, once on first and ten for an eighty-yard touchdown, to win easily.

Two weeks earlier, Reeves had authorized the Atlanta quarterback to throw it, too, on the day that Chandler's passing upset the Minnesota Vikings, but in a Super Bowl setting Reeves has always played conservatively.

That's a sad thing for his fans because in other respects he plays it about right. When Reeves has full control of football operations – as he has in Atlanta but didn't have in New York – he is competitive every-where but on Super Bowl fields.

He can't even go to a party without trying to win.

"When time starts to drag," a former Dallas associate, Steve Perkins, once said, "Danny will pull out a dime and bet you $5 you can't blow it into a glass of water. Funniest thing I ever saw – Danny leaning over and blowing a dime off the table into a cup or a glass."

Reeves estimates he has paid a tuition of several hundred dollars to learn such stunts from various other competitors. "One of the tough tricks," he said, "is moving an egg from one shot glass to another without touching it – and without cracking the eggshell. You have to *blow* it across. I'll bet you five bucks you can't do it."

As in many other Southern towns, football is a religion in Columbia, South Carolina, home of the University of South Carolina, where Reeves was a 1960s quarterback. They'll never forget the play that made him famous. "We had the ball on our own one-yard line," Marty Rosen, one of Reeves' teammates, recalled. "I don't think Danny even looked at the defense when he went back to pass." Just as he threw, an opponent stepped forward and tackled the receiver in the end zone. "It's still in the book as the only forward pass ever completed for a safety," Rosen said. "We're all very proud of Danny."

In school, Reeves had the first of eight knee operations – as a result of which, he said, he "can't stand completely up" and "I don't walk right" – but he ignores the problem. And Rosen's Carolina friends are hardly the only people who are proud of him. For he has spent most of his days as a winner. As a head coach, Reeves started 10-6 in 1981, his first Denver season, when he'd had no pro football training other than in Dallas. And all these years later, he stands eighth in lifetime NFL wins, just behind Paul Brown. As player or coach, Reeves has been in forty-eight NFL playoff games, eighteen as a head coach, and he was a participant in nine of the first thirty-three Super Bowls. He ended the 1998 season as the pro league's winningest active regular-season coach with 162 wins.

So it wasn't surprising that fellow Georgian Jimmy Carter showed up as Commissioner Paul Tagliabue's guest at Super Bowl XXXIII to cheer Reeves on. The ties between Reeves and his kinfolk and the former President and *his* kin go back a long way. The large Reeves family settled in Georgia near the town of Americus early in the century when the large Carter family was digging in around Plains. The first game young Dan ever played in, a grammar school basketball game against a team of other seven-year-olds, was at Plains, and as usual there were Carters on the other side. "We beat them 65 to 2," the Falcon coach remembers proudly.

A native of north Georgia, Reeves was six weeks old when the family moved to the farm where he lived until age eighteen. When I dropped by one year during Reeves' Denver tenure, his father, C.E. (Edd) Reeves, who owned 275 acres of Georgia, said: "As a kid, Dan could plow a mule. He didn't like it much, especially night plowing, but he could do it."

Said Dan: "I didn't even like night plowing with a tractor. It was too scary. I was always afraid I'd meet an escaped convict (from Andersonville). When very young, I learned to turn the tractor around so fast I set a county record for plowing peanuts." The old record, he thinks, was held by a Carter.

Some of Dan's friends believe his passion for the active life is a reaction to a sickly childhood. "He was in bed most of the time until he was six years old," his mother Ann said. "I remember getting down on my knees and praying he'd live. It was an unusual fever of some kind, and they finally got it with a new antibiotic."

Dan also remembers a scene or two from those difficult times. "They put me in the hospital to get a needle every four hours, day and night," he said. "Every shot, the nurse gave me a new car for the plastic train I got for my birthday, and eventually that little old train ran around my bed three times. It wasn't easy, but I set another county record. Most needles in the rear end."

Almost as soon as he could walk, Dan was out playing football, basketball and baseball, and from the start he played to win. Recalling the competitive spirit that drove him even then, his sister JoAnn said: "That came natural. His daddy didn't want any good losers in the family." Dan's unreal dedication to sports awed his mother. "I felt for him so," Ann Reeves said. "When he was in high school, football practice went on for half the year, it seemed, and Dan wanted to do so well so badly he was always a mass of bruises when he came home. I'd put hot pads on the bruises every night, and soak him in a hot tub, just like a trainer, so he could go back and get bruised up again tomorrow."

During his senior year in high school, when he was a three-sport star, Dan pitched Americus to the Georgia state baseball championship. "As a pitcher, Dan was very fast and very wild," said his cousin Jerry, later an Americus banker. "It was pretty funny, the headline they put in the paper one day: 'D. Reeves Pitches No-Hitter as Americus Wins, 15-13.'"

Early on, Dan developed the time and energy to also date Americus High School girls. "He was a cute boy," remembers one of them, Pamela White, who was to become Pam Reeves, mother of his children. "When he was a junior athlete, I was a freshman cheerleader, and one night he asked me out." On their first date, when they went to a sock hop, Dan didn't add too much to the evening. "He said he'd really rather be hunting," Pam said.

Assuming that football was Reeves' best game, it wasn't immediately apparent. As a high school senior, he wasn't even in the family's top ten. On the football team, that was the year that cousin Jerry was the Americus MVP, so when South Carolina offered Dan a scholarship, he snapped it up.

A week later, quarterbacking the winning team at Atlanta in the annual state high school all-star game, Dan had a big night and was voted MVP. In a wink, he was a sensation far beyond the peanut country. "Talent scouts came to our farm from universities all over the South," his mother said. "Dan had always wanted the state university, and now they and everyone else wanted him."

His father remembered that one night after finishing his chores, Dan, troubled, wanted to talk it over. "Like to see you playing football here at Georgia," said Edd Reeves.

"I'd like for that, too, daddy," said Dan.

"By the way," his father asked, "wasn't Carolina the only school that came after you last month?"

"Well, yes, daddy, that's sure enough true."

"And didn't you give your word to those folks?"

"Yes, daddy, I surely did."

"Well, then, son, where you reckon you're a-going?"

"I'm going to South Carolina, daddy."

The rest is historic.

iii

Some of his old associates are of the opinion that the strangest Reeves move, all time, was made in 1973 when he quit coaching flat. One year he was a content, ambitious Dallas assistant coach, or so it seemed, and the next year he was selling real estate.

"Probably the best thing I ever did," he said one day. "Coaching is a hard life, but real estate is harder. Try it sometime. A big reason I quit football was to spend more time at home and make my family happy. What I learned was that I can't make anyone happy unless I'm happy."

With real estate no longer an option during the years when his children were growing up, Reeves figured out a compromise lifestyle that was probably unique in the NFL. Arising early, he hung around the house until the kids left for school, whereupon he raced to work. After spending all day at the office or on the practice field, he rushed home every night for dinner with the family, then worked all evening in his den with a movie projector. Even Minnesota's Bud Grant spent more hours at the office. Asked about all that, Reeves said: "I doubt if many coaches outwork me. A projector is a projector anywhere."

But children only grow up once.

"Dan stayed in there with that projector of his until all hours," his wife Pam said. "He often wasn't with us mentally, but the important thing was that he was always available. If one of the children had a math problem, he'd come out and help."

Pam Reeves' game is tennis, and in Dan's offseason she has sometimes tried to get him out for mixed doubles. The trouble is that "tennis is a social game," she said. "You compliment your opponent for a well-hit ball."

That poses a very big problem for Dan Reeves. "He has never had much fun playing tennis," Pam said, "because it hurts him so much to say; 'Good shot.' He'd rather bet you $5 that he can bounce a tennis ball over the clubhouse."

11. Mike Shanahan: The New Heavyweight Champion

IF GAME-CHANGING coaches come along every twenty years, we're due, and Mike Shanahan might be the man.

Mike Shanahan, the combative offensive scholar who coached the Denver Broncos to the top of the mountain in 1998 and once more in 1999, remembers that he was home from college one summer day a quarter century ago when he decided to ride his motorcycle into downtown Chicago.

At the time, Shanahan lived in a Chicago suburb, Oak Park, where a college friend asked to go along and do the driving.

A cheerful risk-taker, Shanahan agreed. And that saved his life. When their speeding bike shortly collided head-on with a speeding motorist making an illegal left turn, Shanahan was thrown a hundred feet through the air. His friend was killed.

Today, at age forty-seven, Shanahan says, "It wasn't my time."

And proving that it still isn't, he still speeds around the Denver area on his motorcycle. A new motorcycle, to be sure.

Risk-takers are the only people who are truly alive, some psychologists believe, referring to skiers, surfers, race drivers, bungee jumpers and the like. These people aren't hamstrung by their fears, say those who think about such things, and their exploits cause their bodies to pump out the neurochemicals that reward them with alertness and exhilaration.

They are the type who, while coaching in a Super Bowl game, might follow an opponent's botched field goal attempt with a first-down, eighty-yard bomb. This Mike Shanahan did in January 1999, in the last Super

Bowl of the millennium, with execution by John Elway. Before that roll of the dice, his Broncos were in a close game with the Atlanta Falcons. Afterwards, it was all over.

Although Shanahan says he isn't, really, a risk-taker, especially on the football field, it's clear to everyone who knows him that, as an offensive coach and signal-caller, he swings from the heels.

His offense today is the most aggressive, the most combative in football, and the big bomb he dropped on Atlanta was a typical Shanahan call. He is always in an attack mode. His goal is domination. His wish is obliteration.

"Our players believe in dominating everyone we play," he said recently, putting the blame on them for thinking his thoughts. "Our players believe they can put people away. They're always looking to score forty points."

Tight End Sterling Sharpe, Denver's most important receiver, agrees. "Yep, that's our approach," Sharpe said. "Anything less than total domination is not acceptable."

Son of an electrician and a graduate of Eastern Illinois, Shanahan also went to school at the San Francisco 49er academy founded by Bill Walsh. But from the millennial perspective, it may be that he's taking Walsh one step beyond.

Where Walsh led with the pass, usually short and quick, nibbling his opponents to death, Shanahan looks for big, killing plays – runs or passes – plays that exude the intimidation factor.

With a regularity unmatched by any previous NFL or college coach, Shanahan, during his four seasons in Denver, has found ways to set up big plays alternately from his quarterback of those years, Elway, and his running back, Terrell Davis. The explanation is old – "take what the defense gives you" – but the means are new. Thus, Shanahan's wide receivers are chosen not for their ability to catch passes, as you might expect, but for their will and skill as blockers.

"To attack an NFL team properly, you need big plays, so our players keep looking for the big play," he said. "And on running plays, that means every receiver has to block for Terrell."

You can get helpful short runs, Shanahan noted, with wide receivers out in their usual passing patterns. That's where they hang in Bill Walsh's West Coast Offense. But whereas the West Coast seeks short plays for ball control – which keeps the other team's offense idling on the bench – Shanahan wants the long plays, which are more demoralizing.

"Pass receivers don't mind blocking when they see Terrell run," tight end Sharpe said. "Early in my career, my job was to go out there and catch seventy-five, eighty balls. Mike comes in and asks me to play a smaller role in the receiving game but more of a role in the running game because you don't get to the Super Bowl if you don't have a vaunted running attack. And I'll tell you something. Blocking is not difficult at all. It's just want to."

ii

During his short term in Colorado, an interval that began on January 31, 1995, Shanahan, the world's most successful active football coach, has put up some nonpareil numbers with his high-scoring Broncos.

Denver is:

- 54-18 (.750) in Shanahan's four years ('95-'98).
- The first NFL team ever to win 33 games in a two-year span ('97-'98).
- The first to win 46 in three years ('96-'98).
- The only '98 NFL team to close out the season with a 22-2 record in its most recent 24 games.
- The AFC team that ended the NFC's thirteen-year Super Bowl winning streak, 31-24 over 1997 Green Bay, in a game that was at once one of the biggest big-day upsets and one of the best-ever Super Bowl games.

Shanahan, moreover, is:

- The first to win two Super Bowls in only his first four years as the team's coach.
- The NFL's winningest active playoff-game coach (7-1).
- One of five coaches with back-to-back Super Bowl wins (joining Vince Lombardi, Don Shula, Chuck Noll and Jimmy Johnson).
- One of two coaches with four wins in a single NFL postseason (joining Tom Flores, the other wild-card champion).

Asked recently to explain all that, Shanahan said, "You need three things: injury luck, the right players, and a club owner who gives you every chance."

The right players have been Elway, Davis, Sharpe and the people in Denver's blocking line and defense.

Their injury luck has held for two years.

The Denver owner is Pat Bowlen, who has been Shanahan's strongest supporter, allowing him a free hand and, when first offered and accepted, the NFL's largest salary, $2 million annually. Bowlen is on friendlier terms with his coach than other owners seem to be with other coaches. The Bowlen and Shanahan families often vacation together. In the

Bowlen era since 1984, the Broncos have won seven division titles (to three for their closest AFC West pursuers) and have played in seven conference title games (to at most one for any other division rival).

The total control Shanahan sought and got from Bowlen – which both say was necessary to their success – was a reaction to the lack of control he'd had earlier in his brief tenure as coach of the Al Davis-dominated Los Angeles Raiders (8-12 in 1988-89). In press conferences before the 1999 Super Bowl, without mentioning the Raiders by name, Shanahan said: "I've seen situations where the coach and management are working against each other. I've seen times when management wants a draft choice to become a player because he was their pick even though it might have been a mistake."

There are no such feuds today in Denver, where, on top of good luck, good players, and a good owner, the Broncos, in the opinion of some Shanahan-watchers, have an exceptionally good coach.

"I think Mike might be the best coach I've ever been around," veteran San Francisco line coach Bobb McKittrick told *Denver Post* writer Adam Schefter. "He's an in-depth coach in more areas than anybody else I've ever seen."

A veteran of twenty years on the 49er staff under every coach since Walsh's first year, McKittrick told Schefter that Shanahan understands "line play better than anybody else and attacks weaknesses in a defense better than any coach I've ever been around. He can figure out what defenses are doing quicker and more accurately than any other coach I've ever seen."

Although Shanahan appears to most who know him to be an uncommon combination of single-minded dedication, on one hand, and considerate gentlemanliness on another, he has one soap-opera controversy in his past. In an earlier stop with the Broncos, as offensive coordinator for then head coach Dan Reeves, Shanahan was cast by Reeves as Iago to John Elway's Othello. Shanahan, Reeves said, was poisoning Elway's mind against Reeves. Although the friction between the run-minded Reeves and the pass-minded Elway both pre- and postdated Shanahan's tenure, Reeves blamed Shanahan and fired him.

The truth of Reeves' allegations can only be accurately assessed by Elway and Shanahan, but close observers of Shanahan have deduced his character from his current connection with the Bronco team. "He isn't really a players' coach," Bronco cornerback Ray Crockett has said. "What he does is make it as comfortable as he can for you to come to work. He wants you to feel comfortable and good about yourself."

Instead of being broken down by their coach, that is, Shanahan's players seem to feel lifted up. The pattern is not usual.

For years on other teams, most winning football coaches have seemed to be respected but feared by their players. That was Lombardi's status with the Packers, Walsh's with the 49ers. Today's best example is Bill Parcells, now with the New York Jets. But on the Denver team, Shanahan appears to be respected *and* liked. For a big winner, this is something new. And it hardly typecasts him as Iago, literature's most villainous villain.

iii

Risk-taking is so beneficial to modern mankind that every U.S. community should subsidize ski trips, horseback-riding weekends and the like for its citizens. That is the view of a preventive-medicine professor at Illinois, Sol Roy Rosenthal, who continued:

"Risk exercise is essential because it's in the inheritance. During most of the years of his evolution, man has engaged in physical activities associated with risks. He has risked himself to procure food, to protect his territorial rights, to protect his family. Long ago he became attracted to dangers, if not addicted. He was happiest under their influence. If they're absent today, he's left with a void, he operates on low voltage, the lights grow dim."

Or as Charles A. Lindbergh said on May 20, 1927, when he left New York for Paris in a single-engine airplane: "Life without risk is not worth living."

Of those who seem to know all that instinctively, Shanahan is on the cutting edge. "I enjoy things like cliff-jumping and fast cars," he told me one day, remembering vacation jumps that took him over sixty-foot cliffs in the Caribbean as well as vacation joyrides in NASCAR racing machines, which, it's said, he has driven 160 miles an hour.

On one of his favorite rides, he once spent forty-five minutes hang-gliding three hundred feet above the waves during a vacation in Mexico. And in Cancun one summer he went bungee jumping with son Kyle and daughter Krystal but not wife Peggy.

"I think it's crazy," Peggy told Denver writers consulting her on Mike's penchant for risk exercise. "But that's the real Mike. He isn't the controlled person you see on the sideline."

So his new Harley is here to stay.

As a career, though, neither motorcycle nor automobile racing has ever for him been an option. He said he'd be in sales now if for some reason coaching hadn't worked out. And those who know him agree that Shanahan is a born salesman. Among other things, he sold Al Davis on taking a non-Raider coach for the first time in Raider history. And in Denver today, despite salary-cap and other problems, Shanahan's sales procedures have brought in, and retained, almost every player and coach he wants. He's almost the only NFL coach who can say that. Nearly everywhere else every year, the coaches moan, mourning free-agent losses.

"One thing I like about both coaching and sales," Shanahan said, "is that you get to spend so much of your time influencing other people."

iv

Few NFL coaches have been more widely educated in the many basics of football (including defense) than Shanahan, whose advanced degrees were earned in two sciences, domination and perfection – the two that drive the Broncos.

As coach of the Raiders in 1988 and until fired in 1989, he strengthened a natural bent for domination, which from the first was Al Davis' stated goal in the good old winning years of the Raiders. As the 49ers' offensive coach during their most recent Super Bowl run, Shanahan strengthened his perfectionist bent – an essential Walsh legacy.

Shanahan brought that perspective to Denver, where linebacker Bill Romanowski, talking about Bronco attitudes one day, said: "Everyone on this team strives for perfection on every play."

Wide receiver Rod Smith agrees. "We try to do everything perfect," Smith said. "We have never had a perfect practice, but that's the focus. Every practice – I don't care if we're going through walkthroughs. If it's a meeting, we try to have perfect meetings. If you have that mindset that you want everything perfect, knowing that ninety-nine percent of the time it's not going to happen, but you just approach it that way, you're going to get a lot more things accomplished."

Confirming that he preaches that in Denver, Shanahan said, "How you practice is how you play. It's hard to get perfection on game day if you don't get it in practice."

As a theory, that is pure Walsh. Although Shanahan never coached or worked with Walsh, he landed in San Francisco at a time when Walsh's philosophy, players and coaches were mostly still in place. And as the club's youngest assistant, Shanahan, the self-tutor, began by closely studying the films and tapes of every Walsh game and practice.

By 1994, his third and final year in San Francisco before moving into his present billet at Denver, he was second only to Walsh as an expert on the West Coast Offense. Proving it in the Super Bowl game that ended the 1994 season, Shanahan called every play on the day that the West Coast reached its peak – the day quarterback Steve Young threw a record six touchdown passes.

In Denver these days, Shanahan is in no respect a Walsh clone. Yet he continues to lean on him in the following among other respects:

- The Broncos share the same willingness and fearlessness to pass on first down. That is probably the starting point for any late-century NFL team that aims to win.
- Balancing runs with passes, Shanahan, as Walsh did, shoots for a fifty-fifty first-down ratio. By contrast, in the dull and strongly conservative 1960s and '70s before the Walsh revolution, the NFL ratio was roughly nine runs to one pass throughout any game that was still on the line – still there to be won or lost.
- As well organized as Walsh, Shanahan scripts the first fifteen or twenty game plays each week as well as every practice play – and every practice move.
- Like Walsh, he also scripts every training-camp move. Heading for summer practice last July, Shanahan told reporters: "Oh, yeah, I've got my first eight speeches for training camp." A Bronco player said: "Mike even scripts his family's vacations."
- Since the early days in Denver, Shanahan has modified the West Coast because of differing personnel – Elway, for example, always preferred to throw downfield rather than short – but the Broncos still feature such Walsh staples as five receivers out, a quick quarterback drop, and a spread field.
- Like Branch Rickey in baseball as well as Walsh in football, Shanahan prefers to trade or cut good old veterans a year early rather than a year late. In San Francisco, the 49ers let All-Pro safety Ronnie Lott go when he still had considerable Pro Bowl football left. In Denver, Shanahan cut All-Pro safety Steve Atwater, age thirty-two, shortly after he had played well not only in the 1999 Super Bowl but also in the 1999 Pro Bowl. The Broncos said they deliberately cut Atwater early in the offseason to give him a shot at a significant salary that might not be available later in the year on most teams, which all have salary-cap problems. And indeed, the New York Jets did snap him up. But after

ten years, Atwater's heart was still in Denver. The world of winners is a cold world.

- In San Francisco during Walsh's big winning years, he focused on second-line players, signing, among others, two complete platoons of backups, offensive and defensive. Shanahan has likewise made sure that the Broncos have signed everyone he wants – every valued starter and every serviceable backup. Instructively, as his first major personnel move during his first season in Denver, Shanahan signed, for seven years, a kicker, Jason Elam, who has kicked successfully ever since. The free-agent drain that affects other NFL teams hasn't yet hurt the Broncos.
- In his own personal contracts with Denver, Shanahan, like Walsh, Lombardi and other big winners, has insisted on the right to make every football decision – in trades, the draft and all other personnel areas. Day to day, Shanahan usually defers to Bronco personnel expert Neal Dahlen and other Bronco leaders, who have proved so far that they can get him most of what he wants. And, usually, Dahlen does the actual contract-signing after Shanahan has determined the financial parameters. But in any instance, after ownership sets the overall budget, Shanahan can overrule anyone in the organization.

It has been widely demonstrated that a good coach isn't necessarily a good talent scout and vice versa. To a great extent, these are mutually exclusive skills. But Shanahan, like Walsh, has so far obviously judged well as a scout, packing the Denver roster with overachievers. Throwing a light on the coach's attitude toward the NFL's annual, mistake-laden college-player draft, where the Broncos seem to have found a way to make fewer mistakes than most teams, Shanahan said: "I think the hardest area to know about a player is how good he wants to be."

Ten of the 1998 Broncos were other teams' cuts, including defensive tackle Maa Tanuvasa, a Ram cut who became a sack leader in Denver. Said Tanuvasa: "Mike does a great job of finding players." Said Elway: "Mike gets not only good football players but quality people." In any case, such procedures can be more helpful than spending a fortune on a free agent. Coaches who have the ability to accurately evaluate low-round draft choices and other people's cuts can invest their salary-cap funds in *several* players.

v

To achieve these and his other goals, Shanahan regularly works a hundred-hour week throughout the seven-month football season. He's at it about seventeen hours a day except on weekends.

He drills the team nearly three hours a day, or about twice as long as the Packers practiced under Lombardi in the 1960s when they were winning five NFL titles. The game is now that much more complex. On the Bronco team, the workday starts with a forty-five-minute walkthrough and thirty minutes of special-team practice. It ends with an hour and a half of game-speed drills. "No pads," Shanahan said. "The tempo is the key."

From September through the playoffs, the offensive game plan gets Shanahan's early-week attention. He hands it down in three stages over the first three days of the practice week.

On Day One, the Broncos work on nothing but one down: first and ten. Since first is the most important down in the Shanahan book, the players, returning to the practice field after any game, are required to focus exclusively on the passes and runs they'll use on first down next Sunday. "The objective is to gain at least a yard or two on first down even if we're in the wrong offense for the defense they come out in," tight end Sharpe said. "*Never* let it be second and twelve or thirteen. If there's some positive yardage, Mike can stay on his game-plan page."

On Day Two, the Broncos focus on three game-time situations: second and long, third down, and short-yardage or goal-line plays.

On Day Three, it's red-zone plays (those run inside the opponent's twenty-yard line) and the two-minute drill. The Broncos then review the first two game-plan parts and begin work on the scripted plays, the fifteen or twenty they'll use at the start against the next opponent.

"By Wednesday," Shanahan said, "the players know the game plan."

So an off-the-cliff risk-taker is also a fine-point detail man. The combination of domineering aggression and in-depth intelligence has put Shanahan at the top of his profession at the end of the millennium. Whether he is the next Rockne or Walsh is yet to be told, of course, as we enter a century which will never see John Elway throw the long ball again. But if Shanahan wins the Super Bowl for an unprecedented third straight time, with such as Bubby Brister at quarterback, backed up by Brian Griese and Chris Miller, he will certainly have a strong case.

Shanahan partisans point out that Brister, Griese and Miller are all talented quarterbacks that nobody else wanted. Brister and Miller, in fact, were both out of football when Shanahan called, old pros who had earlier played well in those few instances where their coaches had been even reasonably competent. Only Shanahan, perhaps, is so thorough in his scouting that he checks the retirement communities.

Short Elway, therefore, he nonetheless has three talented quarterbacks, counting the youngster Griese, plus a powerful emotional advantage. His players will be highly motivated to prove that they can win the big one without their Paul Bunyan quarterback of the last sixteen years.

And if Shanahan does win that first Super Bowl of the new century, he will have not only assured himself of a Hall of Fame slot in just five years. He will have also put himself in the class of the Fab Five, of Camp and Rockne, of Shaughnessy and Lombardi and Walsh.

There's arguably a chance, remote but conceivable, that the next few years will come to be known as the age of Shanahan.

12. O.A. (Bum) Phillips: Life Goes On

WHAT DOES A winning football coach do at retirement? If you're a rancher at heart, you might pound an oat bin into place.

On a November Sunday in 1986, thirty-one miles straight south of the Houston Astrodome, O.A. (Bum) Phillips, who used to work in the Astrodome, was building an oat bin. He had been building it since sunup with the help of three neighbors, who agreed unanimously that they'd have things nicely pounded into place before suppertime.

"Man cain't build an oat bin in a day, he should find some other way to make a livin'," Phillips said.

A rancher in Rosharon, Texas, Phillips once coached football teams. He was a coach for thirty-seven years, most famously in Houston and New Orleans, where he led the Oilers and then the Saints. He was the only winner the Oilers had in their last quarter century in Houston. He was also one of the media's darlings, a down-home humorist who said what he meant while you laughed.

But there's a time and place for a man to retire, even a winning football coach; and in retirement, Phillips didn't make time for football.

"It ain't that I hate football," he said. "It ain't that at all. I love football more than anythin' else in this world except horses and my wife. But I'm too busy nowadays for football. Maybe there's times I see the second half of the Monday night game; but since I got this place, I been workin' seven, eight, nine days a week, and lovin' it all."

This place is the two-thousand-acre Oak Tree Ranch, which Phillips leased from an oil-rich friend. About halfway between Houston and the Gulf of Mexico, the ranch steams and shimmers in the humidity of some of the hottest, flattest land south of North Dakota. The week I visited the place (in order to follow a football coach into retirement), there were five hundred Phillips cows, a dozen horses, and thousands of low-growing oak trees on the property, plus three little ranch houses and ten or twelve barns, sheds and other buildings. The help lived on the ranch, but Phillips lived with his wife nineteen miles up the Houston road in a fine and spreading home in Dewalt, an old Houston suburb.

"Ranchin' is one of the only two things I ever wanted to do," said the man called Bum, the name he's had since the 1920s, when a baby sister couldn't pronounce brother. "Ranchin' and coachin' football. No fishin' for me. No golfin'. Just horses and football. And when I let up a bit, dominoes."

ii

During his life as a rancher, Phillips, who was seventy-six as the century ended, remembered with pleasure his life in football. "The day I took over the New Orleans Saints (in 1981) was one of the most excitin' days of my life," he said. "They had fifteen hundred people at a booster luncheon, and every last one of them wanted to be my friend."

One of the fifteen hundred was the priest who delivered the invocation that is an invariable component of football in the South, at games, luncheons, whatever. "It was a powerful prayer," Phillips remembers. "The priest said: 'Oh, lord, when Israel was in trouble, you sent them three wise men from the East. I hope you know what you're doing now, dear lord, sending us one bum from the West.'"

Recalling that moment, the happy rancher grinned a little, but instead of the dais on which he once sat as the toast of New Orleans, Bum Phillips was sitting on a tractor in a desolate Texas field. Otherwise, he looked much as he did in the days when the 1970s Oilers played Pittsburgh one tough game after the next. The big face was a little fuller and older, and there was a bit more to the stomach than there used to be. But the big Texas Stetson could have been the one he used to wear on the sidelines at Three Rivers Stadium. The jeans could also be the same. And the old cowboy boots doubtless *were* the same.

One thing was new, the white shirt with the modest inscription on one sleeve, "New Orleans Saints." He wouldn't have worn that during the old heart-stopping Pittsburgh-Houston games, when, as he remarked one day in an apt phrase that has taken root in the language, "The road to the Super Bowl runs through Pittsburgh."

The Oilers and Steelers played in the same division, and it was Phillips' misfortune to come up with his best teams in the years when the Steelers were a shade better and going to the Super Bowl all the time. Phillips had Hall of Fame running back Earl Campbell at his peak during the peak years of Pittsburgh's Hall of Fame quarterback, Terry Bradshaw, and each fall, for four straight years, they split their two-game series. In the playoffs and in title matches, though, the great passer always beats the great runner. For Phillips, the road to the Super Bowl always stopped in Pittsburgh.

"You got to remember that a lot of fellers never get that far," he said, with a touch of pride.

The pride was well founded. Phillips was well thought of in the NFL, and rewarded accordingly. At New Orleans, he was working for $600,000 a year, a salary on the high side for its time, when, with four games left, he abruptly stepped down in 1985. Had he stayed around to collect on a long-term contract, he would have improved his net worth nicely, for every dollar was guaranteed. "I walked out on all of it," Phillips said. "I walked away from a million three – actually a million, three-hundred fifty thousand. When I told (club owner) Tom Benson that I was leavin', I told him he didn't owe me a penny. I don't think Tom would've fired me, ever, but even if he had, I wouldn't've let him pay me. Way I see it, a man don't earn it, it don't belong to him."

Earlier, Phillips said, he had told Houston owner Bud Adams the same thing. "When he hired me, I said: 'Someday you'll fire me, Mr. Adams, but don't worry about it, you won't owe me a damn penny.'" An even six years after that pledge, Adams frivolously got out the ax, and wielded it, although Phillips had led the Oilers to consecutive 11-5 seasons following a 10-6 season.

Without Phillips, the Oilers slumped instantly, and in no time were down to 2-14 and 3-13.

"I only said one thing when Bud Adams fired me," Phillips recalled. "I thanked him for six good years and told him, 'We're even.' I've always said there's only two kinds of coaches – them that's been fired, and them that's goin' to get fired."

Phillips' final NFL season in 1985 was a painful one. He departed with a 4-8 record. His son Wade, who took over, finished 1-3.

"I'd decided (before the season) to make that my last year in football," said Bum, who was a college lineman at Stephen F. Austin a half century ago. "When it got to where I couldn't get to .500, I thought somebody else should take a shot. Sure, I could've used the million dollars, but I wasn't desperate. This is a league that has a great retirement plan for coaches. When you coach as long as I did (fifteen years in the NFL) and if you make as much as I did in your last five years, you earn the maximum, and the maximum ain't bad. Under their retirement plan, they'll be payin' me $90,000 a year for the rest of my life. Man cain't make it on $90,000, his livin' expenses are too high."

iii

The difference between Phillips' town and some of the other little towns on the flatlands along the gulf was that Rosharon had a stop-and-go light, reportedly the envy of Sandy Point, and even Guy, Texas. Although no other vehicle was anywhere in sight, Phillips stopped and waited patiently for the green light before turning left and heading north. He was driving a late-model red pickup truck that boasted many of the comforts of civilization, things like power windows and a cassette player. Carrying his music with him, Phillips put on a country tape. He never listens to the radio. "I don't need the news," he remarked idly, turning the volume down a bit. "If they have a war, I figure someone will tell me."

The music reminded him of his early days in Beaumont, Texas, where his father, an auto mechanic, ran a dairy on the side. "Ain't much fun milkin' cows 367 days a year, twice a day," he said. "Way it is now, my calves nurse 'em."

In childhood, Phillips, an inconspicuous member of a large family, had two role models, his grandfathers, who both lived baronialy on giant Texas ranches. Well over a century ago, one grandfather was a cattle driver on the old Chisholm Trail, which ran from San Antonio to the railhead in Abilene, Kansas. "Them were the days," Phillips said.

Nineteen minutes up the road from the Oak Tree Ranch, Phillips turned into the driveway of his Dewalt residence, which he put up on a ten-acre lakeside plot when he was still coaching the Oilers. He first showed a visitor the little private lake. "I built it and stocked it (with fish) before I built the house," he said.

The dedicated angler in the Phillips family was Bum's wife, Helen. Because it was a twelve- or fifteen-minute walk around their lake, she used a motorized golf cart equipped with a bait tank. "She fishes from the cart all the time, but she's no good at untangling lines," said Bum. "So I go along with her when I can, and watch her fish. I like that, 'cause she's a fine-looking woman. 'Course, I wouldn't've married any other kind."

All told, there were seven women in Phillips' life, including five married daughters. A small bumper sticker on Bum's pickup truck disclosed the whereabouts of the other daughter, who was twenty that year. The sticker read, "I am a TAM Dad." TAM is Texas A&M.

Inside his spreading ranch-type house there was a pleasing view of Lake Phillips from a living room about the size of the main dining room in a luxury hotel. A long, curving bar seated twenty-six, including, sometimes, all seven grandchildren. A domino table had a place of honor in front of a picture window. "This is the first year I ever had time to play in the Texas state domino tournament," Phillips said. "But I ain't goin' to enter that again. They won't let you talk in them tournaments. You cain't say a word, and bee-essin' is half the fun of dominoes."

Phillips' big-screen TV was connected to a big satellite dish outside. "My wife sees all the Philadelphia games," he said. Their son Wade, now coaching the Buffalo Bills, was then the defensive coordinator for Philadelphia Coach Buddy Ryan.

Monitoring his wife instead of the screen, Bum said he was beginning to suspect that she preferred football to horses and the other baggage of ranch life. "I heard her on the phone one night," he said. "She was talkin' about the old days in New Orleans, an' she was sayin', 'The only place I ever went was a football game. And now he don't even take me there.'"

Helen Phillips' car in those days was a Mercedes. It was parked next to Bum's truck when he walked back outside to inspect the orchard that shaded their house – the pear, peach, plum, fig and pecan trees he planted even before he moved in. "A squirrel got all the pecans again this year," he said sadly. "Feller told me he'd loan me a gun to shoot the squirrel with, but after thinkin' it over, I said, 'No, thanks.' I told him that I'd go to the store and buy my pecans. That way I'll have some pecans and the squirrel, both."

iv

The one restaurant in Rosharon that year was more like a small coffee shop, with a few old wooden tables set out here and there. After ordering a hamburger, Phillips leaned back as a young stranger carrying a camera walked up. "Recognized you the minute you come in," the young man drawled. "I'd sure love to have your picture. Mind if this guy takes you and I together?" Phillips replied cheerfully: "My pleasure."

He is still a favorite of Southern sports fans and reporters, and also football players, particularly an old Hall of Famer named Earl Campbell, who retired from football a very rich man. Campbell boarded his horse at Phillips' ranch.

"Last year, Earl asked me if he could keep it here two days," Phillips said. "Well, that ol' horse is still here. My barn, my feed. There's no one I like any better than Earl, but confidentially, he's a little close with his loose change. I never worried about Earl on drugs. You have to buy it, and he ain't goin' to buy it.' "

The economics of ranching are such that Campbell's money wouldn't help much even if he paid his way at Oak Tree. "This ain't a big-money business," Phillips said. "Everybody goes broke ranchin', eventually. The good thing about it is that if you play your dominoes right, it does take a long time. It takes longer to go broke on a ranch than almost anywheres else in America."

He leases, instead of buying, in order to stretch his cash reserves. "There's just no way to come out even these days raisin' cattle on land you own yourself," he said. "You cain't make the interest payments and come out."

If there's no money in it, why do it? Phillips thought about this for an instant, then said: "I like to fool with horses, and watch things grow. On a ranch, you can see what you're accomplishin'. It's like coachin' football. Everythin' sets right out there in front of you. For fun I like to ride cuttin' horses. I raise 'em and train 'em and ride 'em, and you cain't do that in town."

And what are cutting horses? "You and your horse cut a calf out of a herd," Phillips said. "In a cuttin' horse contest, you got two and a half minutes to do your thing – make your horse behave just right while he's goin' after the calf. It's a great sport."

In this weather?

"This is beautiful weather," Phillips said. "I cain't stand snow and sleet and ice. They remind me of Pittsburgh."

In Texas, it's the neighbors who make life a joy in the ranch country, Phillips said. Neighbors are, among other things, the south Texas labor force. They come from miles around to help one another build, say, a new barn. "Man here cain't afford to hire much help," he said. "So we scratch each other's back. Take this here oat bin. Three neighbors and me put it up in ten hours. 'Course, only two of us were doin' much work. Two of us were laughin' an' tellin' jokes and drinkin' a hell of a lot of beer."

274

EXEMPLAR:
Team of the Century

1. San Francisco 49ers: A Record Eighteen Years on Top
2. Joe Montana: Four-Time Champion
3. Eddie DeBartolo: Model Club Owner
4. Bill Walsh on West Coast Football

1. San Francisco 49ers: A Record Eighteen Years on Top

THE 49ERS made pass offense doable first, then mandatory,
to climax football's evolution with its longest success story.

Football's metamorphosis is still happening. The hundred-year pattern of persistent change that has made this game increasingly distinctive is still visible. And, lately, it has been most visible in the offensive performance of the San Francisco 49ers and their emulators: their numerous rivals who have come to believe in the 49er way, which, though called West Coast football, is really Bill Walsh football.

It was Walsh who, taking his sport a step beyond, originated the fast-tempo pass offense that the 49ers and their followers have used to win the last seven Super Bowls and nine of the eleven since 1989.

This has climaxed a century of progress in football. The Ivy League's pioneers, wresting a new game out of older pastimes in the 1880s and 1890s, established a tradition of constant innovation and improvement – a tradition that was still alive and vibrant when in the 1980s and 1990s the 49ers reached a new aesthetic, athletic, and competitive peak. Transforming the game with their new offensive approach, the 49ers earned Super Bowl titles a record five times in fourteen seasons (1982-95).

If their breakthrough shook up the league, the end is not yet. During a stretch of eighteen years in all, through 1998, the 49ers:

- Have held on as a big winner for a longer period of time than any NFL peer or predecessor.
- Have been winning with a creative flair based on willful passing, thus achieving a final transition from football's static nineteenth-century soccer days to the dynamism of our day.

Those two specifics, the consistency of their success and their stylish approach to football, have made the 49ers the team of the century. No other NFL team has, in an eighteen-year run, been comparably influential or effective.

To the witnesses who recall the universal power-running tedium of just a few seasons ago, the change in the way the 49ers and their imitators now play football is dramatic. For, these days, Super Bowl games are only won by people who lead with the pass – who on early downs, instead of running repeatedly, are ready to throw well-rehearsed, well-timed passes. That is the Walsh way. That's how the 49ers, with Joe Montana and Steve Young throwing, won the championship five times. That's how Dallas, with Troy Aikman throwing, won it three times. And that's how Green Bay and Denver, with Brett Favre and John Elway throwing, won the last three.

In the last couple of years, as defenses have reacted to the Walshification of football by stocking up with small pass defense specialists in the backfield – and with acrobatic but less bulky pass rush experts up front – quite suddenly long game-breaking running plays have returned to the game after disappearing in the 1950s. But even the big-play running renaissance (as in the case of Denver's Terrell Davis) is due to the passing emphasis: Pass defense specialists haven't the heft or the focus to counteract a well-executed running game when they have to watch for the pass on every play.

Walsh, Montana, Aikman, Young and, now, Favre and Elway have made it a spectator-friendly game in a league that, for too many long years, favored the run over the pass, and got neither.

It was in 1981, suddenly and astonishingly, that Walsh, early in his first tour as a head coach, came on to make it a different game.

For the first time, an NFL team – the novel 1981 49er team – showed itself to be endlessly unafraid to throw the ball. For the first time, a sound and thoughtful NFL coach had his players ready each Sunday not to run first but to pass first, and frequently, and effectively.

That season was Walsh's third with the 49ers. And the consequence of his new offensive attitude and approach was exceptional. Memorably, conspicuously, the 49ers started winning Super Bowl games and regular-season games in bunches. And as improbable as it must seem to football fans in Chicago and St. Louis and Philadelphia – not to mention Cincinnati and Oakland and Houston and Indianapolis and New Orleans – the 49ers, still in Walsh's system, still throwing the ball deftly with ever-changing personnel, were still winning eighteen years later.

During the eighteen-year period beginning in 1981, the 49ers reached the playoffs sixteen times, won eleven of every fifteen of the regular-season games they played, won ten or more regular-season games in each of fifteen seasons, and won the Super Bowl an average of once every three and a half years.

That set an all-time NFL record for sustained excellence.

And as Walsh says in an accompanying interview, the meticulously timed short pass – which in his system replaces the simple-minded off-tackle run as football's basic offensive play – made the elemental difference.

At the same time, it made San Francisco the team that entertains as it wins. Most significantly, it made San Francisco the most important team of its century.

ii

The two coaching giants in this half of the century, it's clear now, have been Walsh and the 1960s leader of the Green Bay Packers, Vince Lombardi. In the evolution of their sport, the defining difference between them is that after Lombardi brought to perfection the standard power-running game that traced its lineage back through the Single Wing to the flying wedge, the more creative Walsh launched a new and improved way to play offense.

In most other respects, Walsh's approach to football is surprisingly similar to Lombardi's. Their highest priorities appear to be identical: first, sound defense; second, skilled, comprehensively drilled players, and third, thoughtfully designed offense. They have differed, however, in results:

At Green Bay, the winning era with Lombardi ended after only eight years.

At San Francisco, winning has now gone on more than twice as long, reflecting, for one thing, the difference between the emotional nature of running and the intellectual, skill-oriented nature of passing.

When Lombardi resigned at Green Bay after the 1967 season, he acknowledged that a powerful running game demands highly motivated blockers to root out fierce and aggressive defenders. And he confessed that he had run out of ways to motivate the same old blockers and runners every year – as dedicated and talented as they plainly were.

By contrast, Walsh, with a new kind of offense led by quarterbacks he had personally and extensively trained, has shown that a carefully schooled quick-rhythm passing team can work its way successfully through emotional ups and downs, week after week, year after year. What the 49ers have proved is that in the long term, a good passing team – relying on mental acuity and intensively practiced eye-hand coordination rather than emotional, man-to-man battling – is a more certain winner than a good running team.

Until Walsh came along to change the complexion and rhetoric of football, losing coaches used to say of winning teams: "They were up and we were down." And in the days when pluck came first, that was often the most important won-lost explanation.

By no means the least of Walsh's accomplishments is that his way diminishes much of football's old emotional urgency.

iii

At San Francisco, during the years when Walsh was constructing a new kind of football team, he worked with a club owner who, on his record, is the ablest franchise holder football has had. That is Eddie DeBartolo, the only NFL owner to win the Super Bowl five times. Fact is, DeBartolo provided the supportive and imaginative front-office leadership that made it all come together for the 49ers.

What's more, during their extended winning streak, Walsh and his successors have had the services of two remarkable quarterbacks, Joe Montana and Steve Young, the passers who rank as the NFL's all-time top two – Young first, Montana second. In the history of pro football, these two are the only quarterbacks who have scored a career 90 or more in the NFL's rating charts for passers, Young with 97.6, Montana with 92.3.

So Walsh didn't do it alone.

The greatness of 49er quarterbacking throughout an unprecedented eighteen NFL seasons – Montana won four Super Bowls, Young won the record fifth – has, however, obscured the truth that both passers were premeditated Walsh creations. The question indeed is whether either would even have been heard from if supervised by any other head coach.

In the supercharged NFL world:

- It's no cinch that a third-round draft choice with a high-school arm would have received – anywhere else – the extensive opportunity and the remarkably thorough coaching Montana got at San Francisco.
- It is even more questionable, perhaps, whether Young, who was known in his pre-49er career as the league's best white running back but out of position at quarterback, would have made it anywhere else after failing at his first two pro stops.

Walsh in the early 1980s was a coach with a full-blown, fresh, extraordinary football system that would work with any decent quarterback who was willing to listen to the best quarterback coach of the century. Flexible, farseeing, Walsh simply adapted portions of his system to a noticeably unusual kind, Montana, who was the best he could find.

Then as Montana aged, the 49ers worked Young into the same system.

In the years when it all began at San Francisco, it was not, in fact, their passing arms, or previous successes, that first recommended Montana and Young to Walsh. The one quality they needed and shared was escapability. For, even when designed by Hall of Famers, pass plays don't all succeed. And a team that means to live by the pass needs a quarterback who can escape the rush when the pass breaks down.

One of Montana's prime assets was instinctive mobility – and Young is faster. A quarterback with halfback moves, Young has a fullback mentality.

But though both brought fast feet to the 49ers, the record shows that on arrival in San Francisco, neither Montana nor Young was, in terms of NFL needs, much of a passer. It was on the 49er practice field – where the Walsh ethic of perfection was like no other in NFL history – that each *became* a passer. For in 49er drills, no Walsh quarterback was ever allowed to throw other than a perfect pass.

In truth, the coach's demand for practice-field infallibility is the bottom-line reason for the success of Montana and Young – and their teams.

iv

In dynastic terms, the unique strength of Walsh's system is that it works so well with new parts. The 49ers since 1981 have had to replace everyone on the club, including, for years, Walsh himself, yet they keep steaming to the playoffs year after year. Wondrously, in the seasons after winning their fifth Super Bowl in fourteen winters, the 49ers remained in NFL title contention as usual, gaining the playoffs again and again in 1995, '96, '97, and '98. In big-league football, that kind of consistency had been unheard of. For three quarters of a century, all other NFL champions – most recently the early '90s Dallas Cowboys – have nosedived after a few winning years.

With Walsh's revolutionary pass-first offense, the 49ers, uniquely, have continued as a playoff team under three head coaches, Walsh, George Seifert, and Steve Mariucci.

They actually reached their peak in Walsh's offense after Walsh was gone. That was in 1994, the 49ers' fifth Super Bowl season. Montana was gone that year, too, when a new coach, Seifert, and the new quarterback, Young, showed the NFL that incredibly, the West Coast Offense can, on its own, win big – without help from either a particularly good defense or professional-level special teams.

During an eight-year head-coaching career as Walsh's successor, Seifert made the biggest impression on football men by simply hanging on and winning as the replacement for a legend. In pro football, that doesn't happen often. His 1994 defensive team was, however, ordinary, and his kicking team worse.

In a sport where prevailing wisdom had long held that championships are won with defense and special teams – not offense – the 49ers that season had *naught* but offense.

But it was offense at a level never seen before.

Through a 13-3 season, after the new signal-caller, offensive coach Mike Shanahan, learned Walsh's system, Young passed the 49ers effortlessly up and down the field to run up 42, 38, or 50 points, or 37, 41, 42 or 44. They finished with over five hundred points that symphonic year – averaging, each Sunday, four touchdowns and a field goal – as Young threw thirty-five touchdowns, only ten interceptions, and set the NFL record for passing efficiency with a rating of 112.8.

That winter at Miami, against the San Diego Chargers in Super Bowl XXIX, the self-sufficient San Francisco offense climbed to the top of Mount Walsh. On a day when the 49er defense surrendered 26 points, the Chargers were never in the game. Young threw a record six touchdowns as San Francisco overwhelmed San Diego with offense alone, 49-26.

Spectacular passing had invalidated the seemingly eternal verities of smash-mouth football. The 49ers had brought to the summit the new game they invented.

v

Improbable as it seems, the 49ers could have won – almost certainly would have won – seven Super Bowl games in fourteen seasons (1981-94) but for the Jimmy Johnson-Jerry Jones team in Dallas. During his brief tour as coach of the Cowboys in 1989-93, Johnson, a modern legend, overlapped not the legendary Walsh but Walsh's players and legacy. And in the 49er-Cowboy games of the early 1990s, it can be said that Walsh – though gone in those days to coach Stanford University – clearly dominated. For Johnson and Seifert both played West Coast football as implemented by two aggressive offensive coordinators, Shanahan and the Dallas strategist, Norval Turner.

Under Johnson, the Cowboys were customarily identified as a power-running team – even though, on Sunday after Sunday, Turner called Dallas' plays in the pure 49er style while constantly using, as Walsh has always taught, the same five assault weapons in a set lineup (the same two backs and two receivers and tight end) with the quarterback always under center. As led by the Walsh and Johnson staffs and their successors at San Francisco and, for awhile, Dallas, the 49ers and Cowboys never used Shotgun plays.

Thus in what were termed the real Super Bowls of 1993 and 1994, the Cowboys beat the 49ers at their own game

As Turner called continuously imaginative plays for Dallas, halfback Emmitt Smith ran for miles on passing downs while quarterback Troy Aikman continuously passed effectively on first and other running downs, taking his place as one of the league's great quarterbacks.

The Cowboys then, in walkovers, still operating Turner's 49er-type offense, twice routed AFC teams in the nominal Super Bowls on Aikman's first-down touchdown passing. In the first of the Cowboys' Super Bowl wins, as one instance, Aikman dispatched four touchdown passes, each on first down.

In the late '90s, parenthetically, after losing Turner to the Washington Redskins, Johnson was much less successful in Miami. As coach of the Dolphins, he reverted to an old-fashioned run-first offense – and that cost him. Evidently he actually believed, as most commentators at the time had said, that his Cowboys had been a power-running team featuring

Smith off tackle. The confusion amused offensive coordinator Turner, who once told me, "Emmitt Smith would get 135 yards one week and I'd have guys around the league calling to congratulate me on sticking it to that team. What they didn't notice was that Aikman had 195 yards passing in the first half while we built up our lead." That was pure Walsh football – pass for the lead in the first half, then run to protect it in the second (when the defensive linemen are fatigued and dispirited). Nothing more clearly indicates the mindset of most coaches, even today, even when only the passing teams win, than Johnson's inability to see what was happening in Dallas on his own team.

Meanwhile, in the years since, the Cowboys and 49ers have split two more Super Bowls. But for both teams – and for Denver and Green Bay as well – the late-century years have been clouded by one undecipherable mystery: Can any winner keep its dynasty going in the age of free agents and salary caps?

The precise question is whether free agency will have the same ruinous effect on the leaders of dynastic football teams that it had twenty years ago on Charlie O. Finley, the 1970s owner of the Oakland A's. Under baseball's old rules, Finley, on a long roll, built a record five consecutive division champions and three consecutive World Series champions before a set of radical new rules (the rules establishing arbitration and free agency) took him down.

The possibility is real that new rules will inevitably take down the 49ers, too. Who knows?

But something else is out there now for everyone to see, something more significant: The 49ers have already had their revolution.

In pro football, passing has become the thing to do. The game of the future will doubtless be dominated by teams that move easily through the air. It will be Bill Walsh's game. It seems plain that good passing teams like the ones Walsh has bred can only be beaten by those who can also throw with distinction: the Cowboys with Johnson, Turner and Aikman; the Packers with Mike Holmgren and Brett Favre; the Broncos with Mike Shanahan and John Elway. If the running game, finally freed from the NFL's defensive focus, now adds its share of big plays to the offensive excitement, even then it is passing that makes it possible.

And so, personally, there are satisfactions. The offense Walsh created and that others are now emulating has made football what for most of the century I thought it could be.

As the better teams keep throwing the ball, I like what I'm seeing.

Passing can dominate. Brains and beauty can beat brawn. More than that, in the context of a tough and physical sport, the Walsh or West Coast Offense amounts to a triumph of qualities that are distinctly human. It's a triumph not of overweening power to the exclusion of all else but of creativity and intelligence and refined skill.

Maybe Vince Lombardi would call this basketball.

I call it brilliant.

2. Joe Montana: Four-Time Champion

THE QUARTERBACK when the 49ers started winning was a born athlete who hung around to win four Super Bowls.

During the various games of his first ten years on football teams – in high school, at college and with the pros – Joe Montana spent less time playing than watching. His coaches continually, if rather privately, questioned Montana's ability to throw the ball. What they really wanted was another Joe Namath. Or Terry Bradshaw. Or even Steve DeBerg – the quarterback who was the San Francisco 49ers' starter for awhile in the years they consigned Montana to the bench. The 49ers, in fact, remained reluctant to bet their jobs on Montana until the final big weeks of his third season in the NFL.

Through all the early years, however, his teammates at every stop, prep, college or pro, were Montana fans.

This was most strikingly demonstrated one day during his junior year in college, when, as Notre Dame's third-string quarterback, Montana finally showed up late in the third game of the season – a game the Fighting Irish were losing at Purdue. As he ran out for his first play that afternoon, the Notre Dame players, who were huddling in the center of the field, caught sight of him and, incredibly, raised a cheer. "Some of them were so pleased they jumped up and down," a witness remembered. "It was the most amazing sight I'd seen in thirty years of watching college football."

The witness was Roger O. Valdiserri, who, recalling his days as a Notre Dame executive, said: "The team thought Joe would pull it out. And, of course, he did."

By 1981, thousands of California fans knew just how that Notre Dame team felt. Coming from nowhere, the 49ers won their first ever conference championship that season – Montana's first as a first-string NFL quarterback, and only his third as a pro athlete – and not surprisingly, they won it in the last quarter of their last game, when he brought them from behind to knock Dallas out and send San Francisco into Super Bowl XVI.

That was a watershed moment in the first century of football. Montana and his coach, Bill Walsh, were about to change everything. Because of the admiration and loyalty the young quarterback inspired in his teammates and because of his professional attitude and characteristics as a competitor – certainly not because of his always second-rate arm – Montana was to give Walsh the player he needed to turn the NFL upside down.

At the moment that Montana moved in, it was the AFC that was up. NFC teams, in a storied losing streak, had blown eleven of the most recent thirteen Super Bowls. And nobody could have predicted that in the most famous of all Super Bowl losing streaks, AFC teams were about to blow fifteen of the next sixteen – including thirteen straight until the day that the Denver Broncos upset the Green Bay Packers in Super XXXII.

For that transposition, Montana was the catalyst. In the changeover from an AFC world to an NFC world, it was Montana who won the turnaround Super Bowl, the first one the 49ers played, Game XVI. Then he won three more.

On a passing team, how could any quarterback do that with a passing arm that Jeff George would have thrown back? Obviously, San Francisco was introducing a decidedly different kind of quarterback. At twenty-five, Montana was the youngest star in pro football when he won that first Super Bowl and the most unusual. His was the harum-scarum style of the born athlete who just dropped in to see if it's as tough to play quarterback as people said.

In time he smoothed it out. In time he was to become the most polished performer of his age. And he was always all but unbeatable in a clutch crisis – having proved it at Purdue long ago as a relief pitcher for Notre Dame and as he was still proving against Dallas in the game that put the 49ers in their first Super Bowl.

Most NFL quarterbacks are specialty passers who can only run enough to stay out of trouble. By contrast, Montana specialized in athletics. If you were grading him when he came up, he'd have rated a B minus, if that, as a passer. But you'd have given him an A plus for escapability – for, that is, the ability to lure defensive enemies into frustrating, fruitless wild-goose chases – as well as an A plus for quickness, which is probably the definitive trait of the superstars. The great ones from Babe Ruth to Jim Brown to O.J. Simpson to Michael Jordan and Barry Sanders have come in different sizes, with differing strengths, and they've dominated different sports, but the quality they've all shared is quickness, or what has been called ethereally innate agility. And Montana was in that mold.

As Valdiserri said: "Let me tell you how quick he was: During a telecast at Notre Dame one time, the camera stayed on Montana after he'd thrown a touchdown pass. He has such a quick release that the cameraman didn't see him pull the trigger."

Watching him on film later, Montana's college coach, Dan Devine, said: "Montana even thinks quick."

In San Francisco, however, in the beginning, the new young quarterback was something of a disappointment precisely because, on the practice field, he wasn't a quick study. Nor had it yet been verified that his coach, Walsh, was the century's best quarterback judge. Of the known facts, the most notorious was the fact that Walsh had felt no need to draft Montana before the third round. It was also known that at first, Walsh couldn't seem to work Montana into his singular new offensive scheme: the one eventually called the West Coast Offense – the one that eventually ended the thirteen-year age of the AFC and opened the sixteen-year NFC era. Considering Montana's later success, it was all very strange.

Here after all these years is what California sports fans didn't know in those evolutionary early days: They didn't know that Walsh had to severely curtail his radical new offense to accommodate Montana. Subsequently, the West Coast proved to be a five-read offense – five reads for the passer in two seconds or less, when one of his five targets was bound to come open.

But with Montana as his only plausible quarterback candidate as the 1980s came to San Francisco, Walsh, to get things perking, made it a two-read offense.

In all, Montana was given three options: hot receiver, secondary receiver, run.

And the revised plan worked – almost instantly. It worked, first, because Walsh rather desperately, and, he hoped, temporarily, had stripped away three-fifths of his full-blown new offense, leaving only the short-pass stuff – all of which was well within Montana's range and all of which he executed with world-class accuracy – and it worked, second, because Montana as a scrambler never ran to run. He ran to pass.

He scrambled until he located a target – which was often – thus restoring some of the action in the lost three parts of Walsh's five-part offense.

In other words, in the beginning, Montana's great running skills made Walsh a great passing coach.

It might all have been ordained. For, in Montana's hometown, it has been suggested for some time that he spent most of his first twenty-five years getting ready to play quarterback for the 49ers. Though neither he nor the 49ers suspected that until it happened, the truth is that the father, Joseph Clifford Montana Sr., raised his boy to be a champion.

Joe Sr., a remarkable co-conspirator with Joe Jr., was forty-six the year the young man signed with Walsh. And the first day I saw him, the first thing the old man said was that when his son was growing up in Monongahela, Pennsylvania, he never wanted him to hold any kind of job. "Working is for adults," said Joe Sr., who spent most of his working years as a Western Electric equipment installer. "A kid should be a kid."

Over the years, Joe Sr. and Theresa, the quarterback's mother, were usually seen at Joe's big games, where they usually arranged to stay at or near the team hotel, and they loved to talk about him.

"Joe had Joey throwing footballs when he was four years old," Theresa said one day. "The earliest memory I have of Joey is toddling around the house with a ball in his hand – a baseball in summer, then a football, then a big basketball in the winter. When my husband wasn't home, Joey was always pestering somebody to throw him the ball."

One summer when Joey, by then in junior high, was lounging around the house playing with his baseballs, his conscience got the better of him, provoking a hitch-hiking trip to the country club outside town. There, hiring on as a caddie, he scrupulously reported early for work each day. His father disapproved of the whole thing, but decided, reluctantly, to hold his tongue until the Wednesday night that Joey was scheduled to pitch the 6 p.m. game for an insignificant kids' baseball team. "When Joey wasn't there at 5:45, Joe went after him," Theresa Montana said. "He picked up Joey's baseball uniform at home, drove out to the country club, took him off the golf course, had him change clothes in the car, and got him to the ballpark in time for the first pitch."

That was the last day Joe Montana ever worked, unless, as some believe, playing football and announcing TV games are work. He was to spend several years as a TV and radio commentator after finishing his NFL career in 1994 at Kansas City.

Theresa thinks Joe's course as an All-Pro winner was set the night he came home with his father from the golf course after detouring to the kids' game.

"Joey's father had a few words with him that night," she said. "He told him: 'We'll have no more of this, son. If you need money, I'll give it to you. If I can't afford it, you'll go without. You came close to letting your team down tonight. You almost let down your teammates, their parents, your parents, your coach, and most of all yourself.' "

It is a measure of Joe Jr. that he listened to the old man and obeyed. "His humility is the most appealing thing about him," said a former coach, Jeff Petrucci.

Polite, quiet, well brought up, Montana in his pro football years impressed almost every interviewer with his straightforward, uncontrived, soft-voiced approach to his position on the team and to everyday life. "Poised and graceful, that sums him up as a football player," a 49er associate said.

Think of any smart-aleck you've known and you have the opposite in Montana the football player. Early on he was called a blond Joe Namath, and his smile is as engaging as Namath's, but the image he has always called up is very different. Reminded at a round-table press conference one Super Bowl week that Namath once predicted and guaranteed the outcome of the game, Montana smiled broadly and said softly, "I'm not going to do that."

That day, answering questions from newspaper reporters from everywhere, he turned and looked directly into the face of each of his questioners, always meeting their eyes. His, everybody noticed, are bright blue. The full head of hair was as dark as you can get and still qualify as a blond. In a sky-blue jogger suit, he looked thinner but no taller than his 192 and six-two. With a surfboard under his arm, he would have been a California beach boy. Asked about the hype of Super Week, he said, quietly, "I enjoy it."

He always did.

Montana still wears a tiny scar just above the mouth on the left side, all that's left of a bloody wound that once required a dozen stitches, and at the round-table discussion that week I asked him if there's a story about that. "There is," he said. "I was bitten by a dog." Laughter. "I really was," he said. "It was when I was about eight years old. He was my aunt's dog. He wanted to quit playing, and I didn't."

Joe Montana never does.

iii

The first sound the San Francisco quarterback remembers from his babyhood wasn't his mother's voice. It was the sound of a Notre Dame football game. Every Saturday during the season, his father had every radio in the house tuned loudly to Notre Dame. "Joe never had a chance to go to Pittsburgh (only thirty miles away) or any other university," Joe Sr. said. "He was brainwashed."

As tall and wiry as his son and for years as white-haired as 49er Coach Bill Walsh, Joe Sr., who played a little football in the Navy, has been a rabid sports fan forever. But he only began to live when Joe weighed in as his only child. At that time, Joe Sr. became one of the hundreds, let's say hundreds of thousands, of American fathers who have envisioned a son playing quarterback for Notre Dame. He seems only a little surprised that the fantasy came true. Asked to list his hobbies, he said:

"Watching my son."

Although he and Theresa flew to California for most of Joe's 49er games, they had all the TV tapes, too, and their idea of a big night in Monongahela in those years was putting on a tape and watching their boy pull out another game. Joe Sr., mentioning the team's owner, Eddie DeBartolo, who lived not far from them in Youngstown, Ohio, said: "Mr. DeBartolo used to send us his tapes. Then we made our copies and sent his back."

A couple of generations ago, the Montanas were all still in northern Italy. "The name was either Montagna or Monteni, something like that," Joe Jr. has always said when asked. "I think there was a 'g' in there some place. My mother is a full-blooded Sicilian."

His parents still lived in Joe's boyhood house when Joe was playing in San Francisco. "His room is just the way he left it the day he left," Joe Sr. said after one game, "except it's kind of a trophy room now. We have all his trophies and the newspaper clippings there – more than ten thousand clippings before he ever played in a Super Bowl."

Adding a family footnote, Joe Sr. said he's hired an out-of-work former high school teammate of Joe Jr.'s to paste the clippings into scrapbooks. Of the teammate, who had been only recently laid off, Joe Sr. said: "He was a helluva kid and a good athlete himself. There isn't that much difference between the National Football League and standing in an unemployment line."

iv

When Joe Jr. was a year old, his father left home. Wanting more for his family than he could get in a workingman's town near Pittsburgh, Joe Sr. left the boy and his mother in Monongahela and found a job in Los

Angeles at Northrop Aircraft. "The first week I was out there, I went into a restaurant and ordered steak and onions," Joe Sr. said. "The waitress told me the onions would be twenty-five cents extra and I said: 'Back where I come from, you get twenty-five pounds of onions for twenty-five cents.' She said: 'This here's a desert, mister. It's harder to grow things here.' I told her: 'Skip the onions.' And I told myself: 'The hell with this. I'm going back where there's some green grass.' "

From the start, he liked to say, he had been a Monongahela fan. "My roots, my friends, have always been in Money-go-to-hell," he would say, meaning the town that is also known as Mon City. "You do what you want to do there. You do things together. We all went to Joe's games in midget football, and of course to all his high school games."

Theresa interrupted at that point to correct the record. "I went to every game but one," she said. "We'd had a week of bad weather, and the question was whether to take two cars out of town or one. I told them one car is safer, I'll stay home." She was to regret that decision. "Joey came home with a hole in the forehead of his helmet," Theresa said. "I was so frightened I said never again, I'll never miss another game. We went out the next morning and bought him a new helmet, one of those one-size-fits-all water-and-air helmets. He wore it through midget football and junior high football and all the way through high school football. I don't know if it helped him, but it sure helped me. I felt a lot better."

The big, expensive helmet helped give rise to one of the few tales or truths or rumors or myths about Montana the football player. "We used to think that Joe didn't like to get hit," said a next-door neighbor, Stan Robin, who played midget football with Montana.

At one Super Bowl game when the subject veered around to baseball, Montana said he used to beg off as a baseball catcher because "I don't care for foul tips." Asked if he gets a thrill out of running the football downfield, he said, frowning, "Oh, no. You're live bait. That's why you see those quarterback slides."

Montana's high school coach, Joe Bramski, said: "Joe isn't as strong as he ought to be, and never has been. He'd be a better quarterback by thirty percent if he'd concentrate on building up his body. He just didn't want to go into the iron house (weight room), and his father didn't want him to hurt his arm lifting weights – but it's the only way to go these days."

Bramski's wife, Theresa, said: "I used to hear the men say: Joe Namath played with pain, will Joe Montana? If he's not hurt, they said, he'll surpass every quarterback who ever lived. Joe never played defense in high school. Defense makes you tougher, and Coach Bramski made everyone else play defense, but Joe's dad didn't want him to."

Asked about all this, a veteran football coach said: "Montana is every bit as tough as any quarterback in the league. They don't any of them like to get hit." An NFL scout said: "I'll tell you what this comes down to: Montana is a great athlete, and great athletes don't have to play guard in football or catcher in baseball. They don't even have to run the ball – if they can play quarterback. They can scramble and throw it away. A great athlete can pick and choose when they're going to get hit. And Montana is just that smart."

v

When his friends talk about the qualities that drove the unique old San Francisco quarterback to all those championships, the two things they mention first are his passion for sports and his competitiveness. There isn't a game Montana doesn't like, apparently, and he plays them all to win. "Except skiing," his first wife Cass once said. "That isn't as competitive as some sports. The reason I like to ski with Joe is that he doesn't say, 'Last one down does the dishes.' When you play golf with Joe – that's something else. That's one of his favorite games – and he doesn't like you to win a hole."

In the July of their third year in San Francisco, Cass and sports fan Montana got up one morning and played eighteen holes of golf. Then they went home and got married. "Joe wanted an afternoon wedding," she said, "and didn't see any reason to waste the morning."

They have since divorced, and Montana has remarried, but his old Notre Dame friends still talk about the day that Joe met Cass. She was a flight attendant. It was a sad day for Notre Dame because the plane was taking the team home from Montana's last college game.

Like many other people whose jobs enable them to live anywhere, Cass was living in California at the time, in a Manhattan Beach apartment, and Eastern-born Joe could see the advantages of that. At the conclusion of his college days, to the consternation of his family and friends in Pennsylvania, he moved to Manhattan Beach and became what he appeared to be anyway, a beach boy.

He stayed in shape for the NFL's 1979 draft by running in the sands of Manhattan Beach and trying out for the Rams, who rejected him for the usual reason. "Nice guy, no arm," they said.

Montana's first San Francisco home was on an acre of a hill thirty miles south of the city. It was a little old three-bedroom ranch house, where, from one side, there was a splendid ocean view. From the other, there's San Francisco. It is horse country. Joe and his first wife each had their own horses there, even though, during the late summer and fall, Joe always got the short stick. "He doesn't ride during the football season," Cass said at the time, "but we're still equals in the barn. He does his share of feeding and grooming the horses and shoveling the, ahem. . ."

Said Joe: "Not from choice."

An animal fan, he still likes dogs despite his experience long ago with his aunt's fierce face-biter. But possibly because of that experience, Joe's own two dogs, when he could first afford purebreds, were runts – miniature dachshunds named Broadway for Namath and Bosley for a TV character.

At the ranch in his first San Francisco winters, using pine cones and tennis balls, Montana practiced his passing with Bosley, who practiced catching. They both got pretty good.

3. Eddie DeBartolo, Model Club Owner

*THE OWNER OF the 49ers through most of two
historic decades has been Edward J. DeBartolo Jr.*

There has been a strange dividing line all these years between Eddie DeBartolo Jr., the San Francisco winner, and the club owners who have used the NFL (as more than one of them says) to "maximize our financial potential." DeBartolo's goal is to maximize his Super Bowl potential.

So when there was a fight over former Los Angeles Raiders line-backer Matt Millen in 1990 between the 49ers and Los Angeles Rams, it only lasted about thirty-five seconds. The Rams dropped out of the Millen bidding as soon as DeBartolo made his first offer.

This was consistent with what has been a mountain-sized change in the San Francisco club since its origin in 1946:

- In three depressing decades BDB (Before DeBartolo), the 49ers – as steady losers in two leagues (the old All-America Conference and then the NFL) – had never won the championship of anything.
- In their many years since turnaround 1981, as stoked by creative coaching and DeBartolo's determined ownership, they could hardly lose for winning.

Their future is, nonetheless, unreadable. As this book is written, DeBartolo has run afoul of standard business practices among the politicians of Louisiana, where he has been named in a hotel-casino investigation. Pending the denouement, he first stepped down temporarily as leader of the 49ers, and then, in the midst of a bitter family argument, stepped away, ceding control to his sister, Denise York. One of York's advisers is her husband, John.

Down South, where the cops have been using the builder of the 49ers to get to an ex-governor accused of selling favors, the facts are still in dispute. But DeBartolo pled guilty to an investigation-related charge, paid a fine, and plans, in time, to come back to his ballclub provided that's agreeable to his family – which isn't making any promises. More than one newspaper, more than one bakery, more than one factory has been built up so beautifully by the most resourceful party involved that it became almighty desirable to everybody.

And under new leadership, the 49ers could collapse overnight.

So there are doubts now about where the 49ers are going. And doubts about the direction that DeBartolo will take. But there are no doubts about the DeBartolo legacy. In truth, as the biggest winner in NFL history – as the only club owner who has ever worn five Super Bowl championship rings – DeBartolo has done more for San Francisco in the 1980s and '90s than any other sports figure has done for that city or, probably, any other city.

During what has been an era of ups and downs in the won-lost columns for fellow executives in most sports leagues, DeBartolo's teams have won three-quarters of the time for eighteen years, setting an NFL record for accomplishment and consistency.

A knockout puncher who is feistier than most other owners, but also friendlier and more candid, DeBartolo is a fighting man who knows what he wants. And there's never been much question about what he wants from football. As he has said at every 49er Super Bowl, "It isn't much fun if you don't win. The only reason you're in football is to win."

That's who he's been.

ii

In addition to this daunting competitiveness, three things about Edward J. DeBartolo Jr., careful critics point out, have always distinguished him from the many club owners he has bettered repeatedly:
  • He has hired coaches and front office people who make good player decisions – good decisions, that is, on how to spend his money.

- He has created a harmonious, winning atmosphere on the ballclub by treating his players as valuable human beings.
- He has proved to be an expert in an owner's most important job – how to choose a winning coach.

But it didn't happen instantly.

At age thirty, DeBartolo got off to a slow start in the 1970s at San Francisco. Following standard operating procedures for new NFL club owners, he started as a loser. While learning football, he went through five coaches in his first four years with the 49ers (counting the incumbent when he arrived). He hired and fired coaches faster than any owner in memory – a new one every year – denying each the customary three-to-five year shot. He lost every year. But he was beginning to get comfortable in his new arena. For his 1979 coach, he imported Bill Walsh – and although Walsh lost, too, for two years, it was DeBartolo's great contribution to know what he had. The frantic coaching scramble was over.

And the results have been historic: Of the three head coaches DeBartolo has had in the last twenty years, the first two, Walsh and George Siefert, won three and two Super Bowl games, respectively, and the newest hire, Steve Mariucci, is 13-3 and 12-4 in his first two seasons, extending an old 49er custom: His were the fourteenth and fifteenth seasons in which the 49ers have won ten or more games since 1982, when a destructive strike-lockout led to one of the league's most ruinous years.

On some NFL clubs, the logic behind DeBartolo's long run is not really understood. There has been grumbling that all he's done is use a fortune to buy Super Bowl championships. One of the league's most widely shared perceptions is that teams owned by some of the NFL's poorer millionaires "don't have a shot against a billionaire," as one of the former has said.

It's true that DeBartolo does have money, and does spend it, at times, for folks who turn out to be very good football players. He's the son of a rich man. The late E.J. DeBartolo, Sr., his father, boosted the family's net worth above $1 billion as a builder of shopping malls. What's more, when Eddie wanted to go into football, E.J. helped him raise the $17 million to buy the 49er team twenty-three years ago, when a man would have been hard put to use $17 million to better purpose. Any old NFL team is worth $200 million today and some are worth more than $600 million – with few sellers.

But it was Eddie's decision, nobody else's, to make that extraordinary investment all those years ago. And, since then, it has been his decision to forgo large profits most of the time in favor of a continuously representative ballclub. In 1989, for example, he was a big player in the convoluted free-agency market known as Plan B.

Welcoming Plan B as if it were for the 49ers exclusively, DeBartolo began by paying more than $2 million to a group of five NFL castoffs, a very large sum, at that time, for that purpose. Then he entered the bidding for two useful, available veterans, nose tackle Jim Burt, who played for the New York Giants in the 1987 Super Bowl, and former Raider Millen, one of the league's smartest linebackers. To win both players, the 49ers easily outbid their peers and soon won another championship.

A few years later when the NFL embraced an even more pandemic free-agency policy and coupled it with a supposedly hard salary cap, the 49ers were the first to raise salaries with guaranteed signing bonuses, which didn't count under the cap, only in Eddie's checkbook.

So that's the question: Is he taking advantage of the NFL with his wealth? "If you'll think it through," DeBartolo said when asked about it, "I think you will agree with me that the other clubs can compete this way, too, if the desire is there."

In a free country, in other words, every multimillionaire is free to make more millions, if he can, or – on the other hand, if he's in football – to make more champions.

It all depends on desire.

DeBartolo argues persuasively that pro football's really astronomical expenses in a share-the-wealth league are the ones that are more or less fixed – the basic payroll, for instance. In almost every city, these costs are similar. "The free agents and the other extras we get don't add that much," DeBartolo said. "It's like buying insurance. But I'll tell you this. If it weren't for Millen and the other depth we had one season, there's no way we're in the Super Bowl. We'd lost some really great defensive starters to injury that season."

In trading cash for second stringers, as DeBartolo did then and for many other years as the 49ers won year after year, he was executing a policy formulated by Walsh in his final seasons as 49er coach, when San Francisco began stockpiling gifted backups. "We don't have the NFL's highest paid starters," John McVay, one of the club's 1980s general managers, said at the time. "(Free safety) Ronnie Lott is the only guy we have who leads the league in salary at his position. But we have the league's highest paid backups."

If that helps explain how and why the 49ers could hold on at or close to the top through the 1980s and '90s – defying the maxim that such a thing can't be done in pro football – two examples of the way they did it are named Steve Young and Terry Tausch.

As the do-nothing backup to quarterback Joe Montana for four years, Young sat around collecting $1 million a year.

Terry Tausch was a talented offensive lineman who came to San Francisco one fall at the conclusion of a bidding war involving, altogether, six teams. Talking about it afterward, Tausch, a guard who played a few games as a 49er regular, said: "The 49ers called and said to go and see the five other teams and then see DeBartolo at the end."

At the end, DeBartolo topped them all with a $1-million offer, including $350,000 in first-season salary and signing bonus. That's where DeBartolo's money goes. Said Millen that year: "In the short time I've been with the 49ers, the thing that's struck me is the way they go out and get anything they need."

But as the cliché sums up, winning takes more than money. Pennants are hard to buy – a truism the old Boston Red Sox learned during years of trying. Indeed, the 1997 Florida Marlins are probably the only champions ever purchased and paid for in any one season, in any league. And the Marlins cost the owners so much that year – in a city that wasn't ready for championship baseball – that they immediately sold off as many of them as they could.

Former NFL Coach Sid Gillman, a Hall of Famer, has the definitive judgment on the 49ers' way – which makes for steadier success: "They waste less money on bad decisions than other teams."

iii

During most of his years in pro football, DeBartolo has maintained a dual residency in the San Francisco area and in Youngstown, Ohio. Why Youngstown? He was born there, went to grade school and high school there, married a high school girlfriend there, and has usually lived there. "It's home," he said not long ago. "Youngstown, Ohio, is a small mid-western city, a good place for raising children, a place where you can appreciate the change of the seasons. My oldest friends are my neighbors. The best guys I know I went to school with in Youngstown. Some of them still live on my street. They say you can't go back, and I guess you can't, but you can stay."

It was in high school that DeBartolo began dating Candy Papalia, who was to become his wife and the mother of his daughters. A half century ago, Candy's father ran a grocery store in a Youngstown suburb. A century or so ago, DeBartolo's grandfather was a paving contractor who put in many of the streets and curbs of Youngstown. In time, DeBartolo's father branched out, first into the construction of duplexes and houses, and then after World War II into shopping malls. "My father got into malls at just the right time, just when America was ready for such an evolutionary development," DeBartolo said.

Over the years, the family corporation, which was recently merged with another, has built more than one hundred million square feet of retail shopping space in malls from coast to coast.

A booster of higher education, DeBartolo's father preceded him to Notre Dame, and in his last years contributed $30 million to his alma mater.

Eddie entered the family business when he was in grade school and began at the bottom, shoveling snow and mowing lawns at a Youngstown mall. He joined up full time after college.

iv

San Francisco in the twentieth century has had two famous earthquakes, one starting a big fire, the other interrupting a World Series. And it's in the DeBartolo family record that when the earth began shaking at Candlestick Park the second time, Lisa DeBartolo, the proud possessor of a book of World Series tickets, had just pulled into the parking lot. The oldest of the 49er owner's three daughters, Lisa had driven across from her Oakland apartment less than fifteen minutes before the Bay Bridge collapsed.

It was two and a half hours before she could telephone her family that she was safe and well. "Let me tell you," Eddie DeBartolo said, "there are easier ways to spend two and a half hours."

He was so relieved he bought her a new car.

He is known as a family man who reasons that nothing is too good for Eddie's daughters. Everyone around him says that. And, apparently, nothing has been too good for what he calls his other family, the 49ers. Everybody says that, too. Montana, identifying one of DeBartolo's most welcome winning traits, said: "With Eddie you go first class all the way."

That means that wherever the 49ers stayed on the road during their long winning streak, each veteran got his own room in a fine hotel.

(Other clubs schedule two players to a room, sometimes in a Holiday Inn.) And aloft, the 49ers moved about only in wide-body jets, with two or three seats for each player. (Other clubs, saving first class for the boss's friends, sometimes jam the players in coach.) At mealtime, moreover, for as long as DeBartolo paid the bills, all 49ers got first-class dinners.

Such treatment is thought of as extreme in other NFL cities, where management not infrequently expresses open disdain for its players. On such teams, the players are viewed, and treated, not as partners, but as competitors and enemies. By comparison, DeBartolo pays well, distributes perks lavishly and talks with players as friends. If he comes across as a genuinely kind person, DeBartolo is also sophisticated enough to realize that players well treated fight harder.

This is not to say that the 49er environment was persistently sunny and trouble-free during the decades when DeBartolo was putting together all those winners. You can be sure that ego and envy, the forces widely believed to have destroyed the Jimmy Jones-Jimmy Johnson partnership in Dallas, are not unknown in San Francisco. In Walsh's heady days as a winning coach, he was a prima-donna type, often prickly in dealings with people who didn't, or didn't want to, understand him, including newspaper reporters. Star 49er athletes like Jerry Rice, Ricky Watters, Montana and others have also displayed on occasion the self-centered arrogance that greatness can breed. (If you could catch like Rice, would you be unfailingly humble?) Let it be said that the distractions that are endemic where athletic greatness is the norm ruffled the owner, too. Through all the annoyances, however, DeBartolo, working on his self-control, managed to stay above the stuff and nonsense – and away from the hot air that keeps blowing in from the town's 49er critics – to create an atmosphere in which his temperamental athletes could thrive.

Or as Montana said: "Eddie was here before Bill Walsh or any of us were here. He had some tough years at first – but he learned how to win."

4. Bill Walsh on West Coast Football

THE COACH WHO led the 49ers and the NFL into the age
of air is still football's foremost authority on offense.

This is another Bill Walsh year. In this era of football, every year is. The 1980s coach of the 49ers – back by the end of the century as their general manager – is the man who vitalized passing. Though he has retired from active coaching, he is still being represented in the NFL by his greatest invention, the game-changing West Coast Offense.

Among football men, there has been a lot of talk about that offense for years because Walsh, they know, is a Hall of Fame coach with a rare mind (he is both creative and systematic) and because it's clear now that it took both qualities to remake the game.

Nationwide, the West Coast has also broadened spectator interest in football.

But as an offense, what is it?

The best source is Walsh himself. And in a conversation with the man who got it going, you hear that West Coast football is a system based on three principles in particular, of which the first and most important is "a willingness to pass on first down."

Second, Walsh says, "You have to complete a bigger percentage of your passes in this offense than most football teams can. You're trying to keep possession throwing the ball – you're trying to move down the field – and the best way to do that is with closely timed short-to-medium-range passes."

Third, says Walsh, "You want the other team to keep using most of its base defensive people instead of situation specialists. So you attack them with a base set that threatens everything, everywhere, on every down. That means a possession receiver, a speed receiver, a good receiving tight end who is also a very good blocker, and two running backs who are also good receivers. In the pure (West Coast system), there are very few plays with four wide receivers or even three."

Isn't it true that the West Coast objective is to establish the pass in the same sense that most coaches try to establish the run?

"No, our objective is to establish the offense," Walsh says. "On first down, we want to establish that we can move the ball either passing or running. And that means being ready, able and willing to do either. The big thing on first down isn't throwing – it's a willingness to throw."

Football players since boyhood have tried to grind it out on first down. How do you make them willing to pass?

"You need a pass offense that they can count on," Walsh says. "What it takes is a sound way to throw the ball that will make the assistant coaches as well as the players feel confident that they can do it."

Why is it so important to throw on first down?

"Because that's one time when the defense can't gear up against passes. On first down, they always have to be ready for the run, too."

So there's less blitzing on first down?

"Usually much less. And the linebackers aren't cheating back into pass coverage either."

Critics say the West Coast Offense is just a bunch of short passes and long runs after the catch. Why do they think of it that way?

"Because that's what they see."

But that isn't what it is?

"Not quite. We call as many long passes as any other team. We might call a particular deep pass five times and not throw it once. What we do in every game is go to the outlet receiver quicker than other teams. If the deep pass isn't open right now, we go immediately to the tight end or a back."

What is the basis for your assumption that ball-control passes are more efficient than a ball-control running game?

"We've learned that it's too difficult to go head to head against today's defensive linemen and linebackers on a running play that they anticipate. They're too quick and mobile. When was the last time you saw a good offensive line block seven guys to the ground? A well-designed pass offense is more reliable for ball-control."

Even when your passer is attacked by aggressive pass rushers?

"If you're ready to throw a short pass quickly, you can throw over them."

What theory are you advancing here?

"Offensive football is like this: If a team is trying to establish the run, charged-up defensive players will climb through good blockers to get your ballcarrier. And there goes your rushing game. But pass offense is skill, not muscle. An effective pass offense neutralizes emotion. That's one of the great things about it."

Moving along to your third aim or principle in West Coast football – the need to perfect a base offense – why is it more productive to stick with the starting lineup on every play than, on occasion, to insert specialist groups of, say, four wide receivers?

"When you leave your base offense on the field – with the quarterback under center – the defense has to account for every run and pass you have on every down (power plays, traps, sweeps, draws, quick passes, deep passes). We're not against formations with four or five wide receivers provided you're using them for either of two reasons: to see if the defense makes a poor adjustment or gives you a major mismatch. But we think it's counterproductive to bring in three or four wide receivers just to confuse the defense by giving them a different look."

Why counterproductive?

"Timing is critical to pass offense. And the more people you have milling about, the harder it is to get your timing down. I think all cosmetic things hurt offense more than they help. Perfecting your own timing is more important than trying to confuse the other team with motion plays, Shotgun Formations, situation specialists, or any other gimmick."

In West Coast football, how do you perfect a base offense: an offense with two backs all the time, two wide receivers, the same tight end?

"What we recommend is going into training camp knowing every play that's going to be called in the first six regular-season games. We simulate game-time conditions for every play we practice – everything we do – both in training camp and in a regular-season practice week. We isolate every possible game-time contingency – first and goal, third and fifteen, the four-minute offense, the two-minute offense, and so on – and we practice every play we have in one of those situations."

How many such situations are there altogether?

"We isolate four kinds – time on the clock, position on the field, down and distance, and field conditions – and no offensive or defensive play is ever practiced except in one of those contingencies."

Is one contingency more important than another?

"We think the four-minute offense is the most underrated and overlooked part of the game. The NFL is so competitive that most games are won and lost in the last four minutes of the half or the game – when too much or too little time is too often taken off the clock."

What's most important in down-and-distance planning?

"We have distinct plays for, say, third and five, or six, or seven, or eight. The most difficult down is third and three."

Why?

"That's a long way to pound the ball on a running play, and the defense knows it."

Do you always expect to win?

"We approach every practice as if we're a one-point underdog. To a winner, complacency and overconfidence can be destructive. To losers, desperation and despondency are just as harmful. So on the practice field, we're always slight underdogs with a chance to win."

What does this sort of planning accomplish?

"People concentrate better in practice when they're in a game situation mentally. If you visualize the game all the time you're working out, you're better prepared."

Do pass plays or running plays get most of the practice time?

"During every regular-season game, there are occasions when you absolutely have to be able to run – you're in short yardage, you're ahead in the fourth quarter, you're on the opponent's goal line, times like that. So you work on it. But in the NFL today, it's very difficult to line up and run early in the game, or relatively early, when both teams are fresh and inspired, and thinking clearly, and determined to win. The only thing you can rely on to circumvent the strength of today's defensive teams is the timed short-to-medium pass. We allot more practice time for that."

How do you define a timing pass?

"You drop back, say, three steps and throw to a man who will be there when the ball arrives."

The 49ers have had an eighteen-year run at the top of the NFL, winning it all every third year or so. No other team ever did that. Is the way you time the short-to-medium pass a principal explanation?

"It's the elemental difference in what we do. But I'd say the explanation for why the whole thing works is our attention to organization and detail. We have a format to do everything, a role for everyone, a plan for scripting every moment of practice as well as the opening (fifteen or twenty) plays on Sundays after the opening kickoff."

What's the theory behind scripting early plays?

"We want to show the defense a lot of formations and read their adjustments; we want to get in our basic runs to set up play action for later; it takes the pressure off the coaches to make critical early decisions; it helps the players to know ahead of time what plays are coming."

Other teams are also scripting the first fifteen or twenty plays these days as the West Coast Offense spreads around the league.

"Yes, there are things about this offense that can be and are being used now by many coaches. It's an offense that is a little different everywhere. Everybody including me revises it every year. The aim is constant improvement. The emphasis is on developing the skills of the athletes and giving them a platform to play on."

But why is it called the West Coast Offense? Why not the Bill Walsh offense?

"Some of the people who used to play for the Cincinnati Bengals wonder about that. When I was Paul Brown's offensive coordinator there (in the 1970s), we were doing pretty much what the 49ers do now. This is an offense that originated in Cincinnati – which doesn't even have a suburb on the West Coast."

APPENDIX

ON FURTHER REVIEW

A. *The NFL Evolution*
B. *Super Bowl: Winter Holiday*
C. *The Baseball Difference*
D. *The Five Hall Of Famers*
E. *All-Century Team*

A. The NFL Evolution

Collge football came first to America – the pros were a distant second – but the National Football League has been either gaining on or ahead of the campus establishment ever since Walter Camp died in 1925. A prime reason is that the league has usually been served by farseeing commissioners, among them Pete Rozelle and now Paul Tagliabue. Of America's many pro and college sports, the NFL has also been first in communications under Vice President Joe Browne.

During the last three quarters of the century, here in summary are a few of the NFL's achievements:

1926: College players ruled ineligible for the pros until their class graduates. This rule stabilized both pro and college ball into the present lawsuit era, which has brought many immature free agents into not only the NFL but all other professional leagues.

1933: Small (Eastern and Western) NFL divisions authorized and a national championship game established. The colleges have yet to agree to an NFL-type postseason program even though a short tournament of some kind, bypassing the bowls and climaxing with a title game on the Sunday before the Super Bowl, would mean limitless revenue possibilities for each of the top-division schools without disrupting the academic programs of most. Instead, at present, the colleges aim each year to play their national championship game in a New Year's bowl, a naive plan that debases the other bowl games while raising little new money. As for the NFL's small divisions, their competitive and public-relations values are still insufficiently understood in other sports.

1933: The NFL, in a milestone year, legalized passing from anywhere behind the scrimmage line. This, the landmark passing rule, gave the pros an opportunity to open up the game, and Clark Shaughnessy soon showed them how.

1934: Chicago's first College All-Star Game. Matching the NFL champions of the preceding year against the best of the new season's NFL rookies – most of them All-Americans – was the making of the pro league at a time when college football still seemed dominant. A preseason game, it endured into the 1970s.

1936: The first annual NFL draft of college players, with teams selecting in inverse order of where they finished a year earlier. Plainly illegal as collusion and restraint of trade but unchallenged for many years, the draft has given each NFL club a chance each spring to hire some talented college seniors. Before 1936, new players went to the high bidders, usually the wealthiest teams.

1946: Transfer of the Rams from Cleveland to Los Angeles. This move, a Hall of Fame feat proposed by Ram owner Daniel F. Reeves, established the NFL as the first national league in any sport. Baseball was to remain a sectional sport in the U.S. East for another decade until 1958, when the Dodgers and Giants left Brooklyn and New York for California.

1952: Equal split of TV revenue mandated for all NFL franchises. Combined with the draft, this socialistic rule (and another one awarding forty percent of all gate receipts to visiting teams) spread the wealth and the competition in ways that have built and sustained the economic foundation of pro football. Today, baseball still lags as a competitive pastime in large part because its richest club owners have declined to authorize similar socialism.

1953: NFL home-game TV banned; full road-schedule television mandated. This was an imaginative response to baseball's financially harmful home-game TV policy in Eastern cities, a policy which, in the early years of television, nicked baseball's ticket sales. The NFL's road-game TV plan became the major factor in building a national public following for pro football.

1967: First Super Bowl (on January 15).

1970: First Monday Night Football game (as at first visualized only by NFL Commissioner Rozelle.)

1978: Bump-and-run defensive play limited to the first five yards downfield. This was the landmark modern rule change opening up the passing game.

1982: 49ers win the Super Bowl. As the first pro club dedicated to the pass – a key refinement that had eluded prior NFL teams – the 1980s 49ers changed the nature of the game. Replacing power football with a scheme based on passing, they ran the ball off the threat of the pass to win a record five Super Bowls.

1993: Free agency for veteran NFL players sanctioned, guaranteeing labor peace long into the twenty-first century.

B. Super Bowl: Winter Holiday

Pro football's extensive role in the continuing invention of the nation's most compelling sport continues.

And one gauge of its success is the unprecedented national acceptance of the Super Bowl game each year.

During the first half of the twentieth century, no annual event anywhere was remotely as popular as the Super Bowl series is today. That's a fact that leads to a question: How did this event, which since 1967 has brought together the NFL's two conference champions, get so big so fast? What makes Super Bowl day like another winter holiday now in America?

There are some ancillary factors. For example:

- It's a one-game event. By contrast, baseball has a long World Series and basketball has a late-winter sequence of championship series and tournaments.

 - The Super Bowl is the championship game of a contact sport. A twenty-game winner pitching to a .300 hitter can be absorbing on a certain level. Watching a Super Bowl blitzer go after quarterback Brett Favre is something else. Will he get him? Will Favre get up?

- The Super Bowl is played the same day of the same January week every year. A heavyweight championship fight can be bigger than the Super Bowl – but it might happen in June or November, and a big one might not happen at all for years. There's a curious, stimulating rhythm to the annual Super Bowl hype that is lacking for big fights or other activities.

Most significantly, however, the Super Bowl game each year is simply the climax event of six months of regular-season pro football. Due to seventy-five years of creative NFL moves, the sport keeps an unparalleled, timeless hold on the American audience. All fall, NFL games are annually followed closely not only in NFL markets but elsewhere in the fifty states.

Pro football's in-season national attention is missing in the other sports. There is no longer even a network game of the week in baseball.

In a sports-minded country, in-person spectators for most sports these days are, it's true, substantial. Baseball, basketball and hockey games regularly attract sizable regular-season crowds in most U.S. cities, indicating considerable local interest. But in these sports, in every sport, in fact, but football, the nation as a whole snaps to attention only for the playoffs.

The difference in pro football is that, week in and out during the regular season, there is a national focus on NFL results and on the various races leading toward the Super Bowl. TV ratings are high for routine NFL Sunday games and even higher Monday nights.

"The Super Bowl is like the last chapter of a hair-raising mystery," former Commissioner Pete Rozelle once said.

In the event's first fifteen iterations, while the Lombardi influence lingered, the last chapter was often a letdown. Now that teams have to throw passes to gain entrance, the Super Bowl can live up to its hype. There's never been anything like it.

C. The Baseball Difference

With pro football's steady improvement through the years in both style and substance, I have sometimes argued that it's an art form like, for example, jazz music. Conceivably, in fact, jazz and football are the *only* U.S. art forms.

All that seems to bother George Will and other baseball fans. Writing often in anger, they insist that, along with football players and jazz musicians, a third group, baseball players, should be included among "the most distinctively American artists."

The question is, if jazz players and football players are artists, aren't baseball players?

My answer is, not quite. Probably the key word in a definition of art is *creativity.* The key word in a definition of science is *knowledge* – and essentially, baseball is applied knowledge.

Most decisions by baseball managers are rooted not in creative urges but in a study of percentages. They choose between taking and rejecting the percentage. Hitting and pitching are obviously sciences. Fielding brings to baseball its closest brush with art, although rarely, in the more spectacular plays of a Gold Glove outfielder.

Football today, on the other hand, is the product of years of creativity. Imaginative coaches have made and remade their sport as surely as Count Basie and Ray Charles have revised and upgraded the quality of music. Their strengths are that music and football are both showcases for individual talent exercised on the spot, right here, right now.

Thus in the violence of a pro football game, the knowledge of what to do is transcended in every clutch instance by the art of getting it done somehow. Improvisation is as necessary and exciting in football as in jazz – as revealed variously in the alternately swirling and herky-jerky style of Detroit running back Barry Sanders, the daring "shall I run, shall I pass" forays of San Francisco quarterback Steve Young, the elegant, last-second flick-aways by Dallas defensive back Deion Sanders.

It has been accurately reported that a majority of the cultural expressions of this country were imported from abroad – but not jazz, and not football. These two were made in America. These, it seems to me, are the U.S. art forms.

Baseball, by comparison, plainly fails to go anywhere. Through this century of continuous progress in football, the sport that was formerly America's national pastime has remained basically static.

The two games couldn't, in respect to change, be more different. Baseball's most important new rule of the century, an unfortunate rule that allows designated hitters for pitchers, is still being opposed by one of the two major leagues.

Otherwise, since increasing the pitching distance long ago from fifty to sixty and one-half feet, baseball has put on a show almost every summer day that has looked nearly identical to such diverse enthusiasts as the trolley Dodgers of nineteenth-century Brooklyn and the freeway Dodgers of twentieth-century Los Angeles.

If it seems strange that I enjoy both pastimes – if it seems unusual that the sports fans and entrepreneurs of the same country should have two entirely different attitudes toward change in two of their favorite games – it is.

Apparently, few of us mind that after both pastimes descended from English games, the one has been standing still in America and the other, fantastically, can't stop growing.

Asked for a comment one day, a baseball spokesman, Joe Reichler, the former assistant to a former commissioner, said: "These are games in which different things are important to sports fans. In baseball, it's tradition. In football, it's excitement. The baseball fan wants to relate to everything grandpa told him at his first game twenty years ago, forty years ago, sixty years ago. Baseball sells nostalgia. Football sells spectacle. It means a lot to the baseball fan to compare Pete Rose as a hitter to every great hitter of the last hundred years. That can only be done with statistics that mean approximately what they used to mean. The football fan doesn't have time for statistics. He's only interested in what's happening now. He doesn't oppose *any* change that makes football more exciting."

A football spokesman, former president Tex Schramm of the Dallas Cowboys, said: "Baseball is a game of precision, with a rigid number of strikes, balls, outs, bases, infielders, outfielders. There is nothing rigid about football. A baseball play can only start one way, with a pitcher throwing a ball. In football, plays start many ways, with short passes, long passes, end runs, line bucks, kickoffs, punts. In football, an offensive coach can deploy his eleven men any way he wants to, sideline to sideline, as long as he keeps seven men on the line of scrimmage The defense doesn't even have that restriction. In baseball, there are rigid places for all nine players to line up. Football lends itself to change, baseball doesn't. To keep their game in balance, all baseball has to do is keep the right amount of rabbit in their ball."

All football has to do is change a rule.

D. The Five Hall of Famers

One way to look at the history of a sport is to collate and evaluate its best players. Anybody can do it. As the last remaining member of the original Pro Football Hall of Fame Selection Committee, I have been doing it since 1962.

In that first year, I endorsed only four players and a coach for the first Hall of Fame class, which, in the upshot, numbered seventeen.

Reviewing what was at that time the entire forty-two-year life of the NFL, I found that I could support only the five pioneers who, to me, stand out from all the others who have played or worked in the NFL.

They are Sammy Baugh, Washington's model passer; Don Hutson, Green Bay's model receiver, and three Chicago Bears, coach-player-owner George Halas, tackle-fullback Bronko Nagurski, and halfback Red Grange.

The twelve others elected at the same time in 1962 should have been named in a later year, in my view then and now, to emphasize the difference between the transcendent five and everyone else who has ever been in football. The reasoning:

Baugh (1937-52), the last surviving member of the Hall of Fame's charter class, might have been the favorite to win the starting position at quarterback on any NFL team that has played since then, including Joe Namath's and Johnny Unitas'.

Hutson (1935-45) has lasted for most of the century as the NFL's number-one receiver and has to this day had only a single challenger, Jerry Rice (1985-98) of San Francisco, who in his prime did not dominate his era as certainly as Hutson did his.

NFL founder Halas (1920-83), the only player-coach-owner who was in the league throughout its first sixty-two years, won at least one championship in his every decade as a coach, four in all, and, first to last, doubled as one of the most farseeing of the rule-changers.

Nagurski (1930-43), a fullback who outweighed the biggest linemen, was the most feared of the running backs before Jim Brown (1957-65). In the NFL's first two title games (1932-33), Nagurski made the winning plays as a passer.

Grange (1925-34) was in a sense the Michael Jordan of his day. An Illinois All-American halfback who turned pro during his senior season to save the NFL, the spectacularly elusive Grange attracted the large crowds that had eluded pro football in its first discouraging seasons, and set the league on its way.

During my participation each year as a voter on two national Hall of Fame committees, pro football's and baseball's, I have regularly encountered two opposing factions in each sport: those who annually lobby for either large or small classes. The large-class argument is that there are a lot of great players. The opposing argument is that there are only a few Hall of Fame players.

As a small-class advocate, I think of prestige as a Hall of Fame's main asset, perhaps its only important asset. It would seem a given that outsized numbers of those elected harm any hall's prestige. The essential, the only, criterion is Hall-of-Fame quality.

What, you ask, is that?

Think of Red Grange, Joe Namath, Pete Rozelle, Lamar Hunt, Terry Bradshaw, Vince Lombardi, George Blanda, Jerry Rice. A distinguished player, Grange *made* the NFL; Namath made the Super Bowl; Rozelle made, among other things, Monday Night Football; Hunt made the AFL (the only one of the NFL's many competitors to survive); minus Bradshaw, Pittsburgh doesn't win four 1970s Super Bowls in six years; minus Lombardi, Green Bay doesn't win five 1960s NFL titles in seven years; Blanda, a quarterback and kicker, was the only pro football player who ever lasted a quarter century, who ever played 340 pro games, who ever scored two thousand career points; Rice is the only receiver ever mentioned in the same sentence with Hutson.

At the Pro Football Hall of Fame selection meetings across more than a third of the century, I have voted for other champions, too, some of whom haven't been elected yet. One of those still improbably on the outside is Clark Shaughnessy, the intellectual who made Hall of Fame contributions on each side of the line of scrimmage. He is the only coach who ever did.

In Hall of Fame voting, I measure every new candidate against Grange, Namath, and Rice. And Shaughnessy.

E. All-Century Team

Who were the best players of them all? To make the question tougher, you can limit yourself to just the best eleven, as they did in the days of single-platoon football. The question then is, position by position, who were the best eleven football players? Here's a subjective answer.

The first great football player I saw was Bronko Nagurski, the 1920s tackle and fullback for the University of Minnesota. Of the three best I ever saw, two played at times for Los Angeles teams, David (Deacon) Jones, a Ram defensive end, and USC halfback O.J. Simpson. The third is Dick Butkus, a linebacker for the Chicago Bears, who in a long career doubled in the offensive line, as a center. It's still true that the game's most famous guard was Pudge Heffelfinger, an 1890s Yale player, but he got there running the ball in the flying wedge. The leading ends/receivers of my time were Don Hutson of the Green Bay Packers and Jerry Rice of the San Francisco 49ers, although on this kind of team there is room for only one receiving specialist.

Ernie Nevers of Stanford's 1920s teams was the most famous of the fullbacks before Jim Brown. Conceivably I've erred in overlooking the two great Californians, Rice and Nevers. I have also ignored legends such as Jim Thorpe, whose greatness is now hard to verify. A 1990s defensive halfback, Deion Sanders, was, as he has repeatedly announced, number one in his field. More than that, Sanders was a finalist (with Butkus and Deacon Jones) for best defensive player. My pick is Jones.

The only quarterbacks considered were football's classic field generals, those who, in addition to throwing advantageous passes, called most of their own plays: Namath, Unitas, Baugh and Bradshaw. Of the great quarterbacks, Namath was the boldest (on and off the field) and most often injured. His audacity has been compared to that of boxing champion Muhammad Ali. Thus, Namath was the target for more physical abuse than the others, and, handicapped by knee injuries in his every season as a pro, he had the shortest career. But Namath might have been the best natural athlete who ever played his position. And like Ali, he was possibly the most vigilant student of his sport. In his best year Namath was, as he indicated himself after Super Bowl III, number one. You'd take Baugh, possibly, or Unitas, if they were the same age as and on the same team with Namath, but I'll take Namath.

In the following all-time lineup, the football players selected were the eleven best at their positions, I'd say, irrespective of whether they played offense, defense, both ways, college, pro, two years, or twelve.

> End Deacon Jones, Rams, South Carolina State (1960s).
> End Don Hutson, Packers, Alabama (1930s).
> Tackle Bronko Nagurski, Bears, Minnesota (1920s).
> Tackle Jim Parker, Colts, Ohio State (1950s).
> Guard Danny Fortmann, Bears, Colgate (1930s).
> Guard John Hannah, Patriots, Alabama (1980s).
> Center Dick Butkus, Bears, Illinois (1960s).
> Quarterback Joe Namath, Jets, Alabama (1960s).
> Halfback O.J. Simpson, Bills, USC (1970s).
> Halfback Deion Sanders, Cowboys, Florida State (1990s).
> Fullback Jim Brown, Browns, Syracuse (1950s).

AFTERWORD
A WRITER'S LIFE

There is singularly nothing that makes a difference . . .
except that each generation
has something different at which they are all looking. . . .
By this I mean that otherwise they are all alike.

— Gertrude Stein

The most outrageous newspaper scandal California has known shocked the West one day in the 1930s when a state legislator, naming eleven Los Angeles sportswriters, said they took race-track money. Three sports editors and eight others, the man disclosed, were all on the payroll of the most prosperous sporting enterprise in the vicinity, a race track in Tijuana, Mexico.

Of the double-dippers, one was the sports editor of the evening *Herald-Express*. One, sports editor of the *Evening News*, also represented the old *Daily News*. Three were *Los Angeles Times* sportswriters, illustrating the comparative prominence of that paper. And six, including the sports editor, were *Los Angeles Examiner* sportswriters.

In the turbulence of the Great Depression, after the conspirators confessed, newspaper jobs suddenly opened for ten young aspirants who had been living, until then, on odd-job income ranging up to $3 or $4 a week. The eleventh opening was lost when the *Evening News* stubbornly declined to fire a man who, the publisher said, was just trying to better himself.

The Examiner, in the Los Angeles of that day, was obviously the consummate site. Though at the time I was disturbingly underemployed, I didn't even consider the *Times*. But when I got to the *Examiner* office that April morning, four of the six positions had already been taken, and another candidate, Gus Vignolle, hat in hand, was talking to the new sports editor. The prize was $25 a week, the Newspaper Guild's entry-level wage in the 1930s. And Vignolle won his a few minutes before I won mine.

In an era when newspaper assignments were dictated largely by seniority, Vignolle was offered his choice of the last two available sports beats, pro football and bowling. And after thinking it over carefully, he chose bowling.

So it was that pro football chose me.

In the 1930s that meant, in Southern California, the minor-league Los Angeles Bulldogs and Hollywood Bears. Super Bowl I, which in the 1990s seems so far in the past, was then far in the future. But I was on my way.

As a newspaper reporter for the last sixty years, I remain troubled by one story I can't investigate. It is frustrating to realize that I can never learn how in former centuries, my grandparents and their forefathers put in their time from year to year and day to day – at work and at play. What I most want to know about all persons, from athletes to ancestors to authors, is, simply, how they live or lived their lives.

Unhappily, it looks now as if I won't be able to talk with my great-great-grandparents about that. Nor can I ask any of my favorite writers of other years, from Shakespeare to Abraham Lincoln, about *their* lives and times. But I do have this one chance to tell the select few I'd most like to know in future centuries, my great-great-grandchildren, about my own life as a writer – about a guy who would and did spend most of *his* century writing about the supreme spectator sport of his time.

Speaking as a present-tense person, I agree that the relevance of yesterday and tomorrow is never easy to determine. Composer Paul Bowles has said, "There's no such thing as the future. . . I remember the past as one remembers a landscape, an unchanging landscape. . . I live in the present."

In sports, clearly, today's title contenders matter most – not yesterday's champions – at least to me. Nor is nostalgia useful. But history is.

They tell me that starting about age three, I hustled out to get the morning paper on the front lawn every day, rain or shine. That was in Aberdeen, South Dakota, where my earliest recollection is sitting on the front steps at dawn one summer day inspecting the front-page pictures and headlines in a fresh new copy of the *Aberdeen Morning American*. I wasn't yet in kindergarten.

My father subscribed to four newspapers, the *Morning American*, *Aberdeen Evening News*, *Minneapolis Journal* and *New York Times*. And by the time I was in Simmons Junior High, I was reading them all.

One day I hurried home from school, sat down with the newspapers, and began copying front-page stories word for word with an old black pencil — asking myself after each paragraph why the reporter wrote the story the way he did. My industry surprised my mother, who at all times showed a compassionate interest in her four sons. I was the oldest. And watching me scribble that afternoon, she asked what I was up to.

I said: "I'm practicing to be a reporter for the *Times*."

She said: "Writers these days have to write on a typewriter."

So she invested in a second-hand Underwood and asked my father to bring home an instruction book. Every morning after breakfast, my mother read up on that day's lesson, always staying one lesson ahead of me. And she taught me to operate a typewriter in a short burst of intensive afternoon classes, although, to the end of her life, she couldn't type herself.

Many years later, after five years of college and five on a metropolitan newspaper, I was classified by the U.S. Army not as a historian or public relations specialist but as a typist. My mother would have loved that.

Even though I have spent my life writing sports, mostly football, my primary interest has always been not sports but newspapers. There are, as I have learned, a lot of fascinating ways to pass the time on a newspaper. I neither aimed for nor ruled out the sports section, either as a young adult in California or as a boy in South Dakota, where I opened with seventeen years in Aberdeen and finished with four years at Yankton College. But I've never avoided sports. My games as a schoolboy were football and tennis, each indifferently played. My high school tennis partner was a classmate named Wally Hay, and one year the most talked about headline in the *Morning American*, where I worked summers, was: "Hay and Oates Win State Title."

Aberdeen was a railroad town. The second largest city in the state, home to eighteen thousand of us, it was served by four railroad lines. And I still recall with sorrow the morning I stood across the way from the Great Northern depot and learned that I'd never have the throwing accuracy to be a quarterback, or even a pitcher.

That day I'd been invited out by a group of older boys to participate in a popular local sport, throwing rocks at the hoboes who often rode trains through town. When I got there, a slow-moving coal train was rumbling by, and dozens of migratory hoboes were running along the tops of the cars, dodging rocks, and aiming handsful of coal at my friends. Angrily, I fired back, but couldn't hit the broad side of a railroad car. Only later did I learn that the leaders of the rock throwers were just out there to stimulate a shower of coal, which they carefully loaded up and carried home.

In that crowd of Aberdeen kids, three were sons of the Lutheran minister, a St. Olaf College alumnus who named his boys Matthew, Mark and Luke. The congregation waited impatiently to hear if the minister's fourth child would also be a boy. It was, and he named him Olaf.

Northeastern South Dakota in my time was a flat godforsaken wind-swept prairie, but Aberdeen itself was recognized for miles around as an oasis of pleasant parks, tall trees, attractive residences, and friendly residents. And it still is. The weather is South Dakota's only problem – monotonously fierce summer heat; long, freezing winters – but the people there rise above it somehow, managing to be both upbeat and public-spirited. In the last years of the nineteenth century, not far removed from the pioneer era, they taxed themselves heavily to distribute colleges throughout a state that is still thinly populated.

In all, those old South Dakotans built seven tax-supported colleges and universities, and the one they placed in Aberdeen, known now as Northern State University, employed my father for a quarter century as financial vice president. My father was a neat, stocky, self-educated Iowan – born William Maclay Oates – who in his first Aberdeen years met and married a college student named Idah Armstrong, a pretty farmer's daughter from Illinois. In earlier generations, their families had lived in Wales and England, respectively, although, among her forebears, my mother counted Scotch-Irish and Spanish people, too.

My father, an amateur singer, was also the best public speaker in Aberdeen. The crowd for his annual sermon at the First Methodist Episcopal Church was always one of the two largest of the year, matched only by the Easter Sunday turnout. The crowds for his annual high school speech were so large that students and alumni stood three and four deep in back and along the sides of a big assembly hall. Though my father

316

always had a message, they came, I'm sure, to hear his funny lines and jokes. He told us one day about the time when, at a party, he sang "Carry Me Back to Old Virginia." Noticing afterward that a young woman was in tears, he asked her, tenderly, "Are you a Virginian?" Looking up at him, she sobbed, "No, I'm a musician."

When I was in high school, my father made $300 a month, a not-bad Depression salary. He and the president were the school's two highest-paid employees. To this day, my father's portrait hangs in his old office along with pictures of the six others who have succeeded him.

I'd like to see some pictures of *his* father, Henry Oates, but they don't exist. Reportedly named for nineteenth-century Senator Henry Clay, my grandfather was a small-town Wisconsin hardware merchant who came home for dinner one noon and, as my father told the story, advised the family that the city council had voted wet that morning. That meant beer, wine and liquor were legal again after a ten-year prohibition. My grandmother, who had helped found the Women's Christian Temperance Union, said: "We're moving, Henry."

Said grandfather: "I'm selling the store this afternoon."

And he did, buying another hardware store in a dry township close by. And when that town voted wet, he moved again. All told, my father used to say, his family lived in nine little towns in Wisconsin and Iowa before he was fourteen years old, when Henry settled down for good in an Iowa River town that is *still* dry, Iowa Falls.

That's all I know about my grandparents except that they obviously pushed their points of view effectively. For, at all times, my father warmly embraced their morals and conservative attitudes, and, arriving in South Dakota, began a lifelong fight against tobacco and alcohol. He only had two vices himself, reading newspapers and driving new cars.

MINNEAPOLIS

The best football in my neighborhood during the years when I was growing up was played by the Big Ten team at Minnesota, whose stadium stood exactly 312 miles due east of the big old barn my family had in Aberdeen behind our big old house on South Jay Street.

I measured the road myself one October Friday.

My father always parked the family automobile in that barn. He was an indefatigable motoring buff who, after trading in a horse for his first car, took a joy ride around town every night of every year for the rest of his life. And that dark Friday morning, looking forward to the long drive to Minneapolis, he backed the car out of the barn at 4:15 for a twelve-hour trip – on the dusty, pockmarked gravel roads of those days – to see the glamorous Golden Gophers.

Before or since, I have seldom known a more magical weekend. To begin with, my father left my brother William and me on our own for the first time that Friday night at the Minneapolis YMCA, a cheerful new building, while he and my mother moved on to the staid old Curtis Hotel. The next morning, we drove to the stadium hours early, my father bravely steering through the heavy streetcar and motorcar traffic of a football Saturday in Minneapolis. After parking at the stadium, still moving with enthusiasm, he even got out the lunch. He was, possibly, the first tailgater.

That was an era when the Minnesota team always seemed to be getting better and better – Bernie Bierman was shortly to coach the Golden Gophers to four national championships – and for a pre-teen boy, it was breathtaking that sunny Saturday afternoon to experience, for the first time, the show that is college football. The star was a huge Minnesota fullback who also played tackle, Bronko Nagurski.

Piling it on, my parents treated us that night to a double feature in Minneapolis' newest movie palace, which, between films, turned a spotlight first on a mighty pipe organ and then on a stage show with a name band led by Duke Ellington. Though it would make us late arriving home, we spent Sunday morning at my father's favorite church, Hennepin Avenue Methodist, the most magnificent in the Midwest. For Sunday dinner, we were in my father's favorite dining room, the YMCA cafeteria.

Afterward, as he headed the car home, I was all but overcome by a fit of sadness. It was so painful leaving Minneapolis behind, after watching Minnesota beat Iowa as the centerpiece of a storied weekend in the first big city I'd seen, that I made a silent promise to myself: I'll never do this again. The excitement of the trip wasn't worth the agony of withdrawal.

It was a promise I couldn't keep – my father carried us along on one fabulous Minneapolis football excursion after another through high school. But the memory of that painful first departure is still vivid – along with the memory of the first game: that enchanting introduction to big league football. One unbreakable thread of my life was in place.

And I remain grateful that my father was so fond of football that he would go far out of his way to keep up with the nearest big-time team at a time when, in a small, remote, provincial town, nobody else seemed to care.

SOUTH DAKOTA

For two disparate reasons, the 1930s Depression, as I experienced it during those early years in South Dakota, wasn't the trial to me personally that it was to many others. First, my father invested in a new car every year, without exception. Second, Aberdeen and Yankton were both large enough for good daily papers.

Starting not long after the invention of the horseless carriage, my father began picking up a new two-door Chevrolet sedan each spring, trading the old one in for the next model at a yearly cost of about $250, or nearly a month's salary.

And every night an hour or so after dinner, he lifted his heavy gold watch out of its resting place in his vest, clicked it open, looked at it and said: "Let's go, boys." As we raced for the car, we were only thinking about two things, popcorn and ice cream. For each evening, during our forty-five minute ride about Aberdeen, we each had to choose between a five-cent sack of popcorn and a five-cent ice cream cone. After mashed potatoes, those are my two favorite dishes, and having to choose between them – when my father stopped at the store on Main Street – was the toughest decision I had to make every day of my life in Aberdeen.

One spring night as my father put the car back in the barn, he said I could have it Friday for the junior prom. And that opened still another window on the world. I discovered that girls love new cars, too.

For a school kid, it doesn't get much better than a new car every year.

In those days I also found that my early interest in journalism was still growing. One year I published my own newspaper, *The Boy Scout Times*. A print-shop fan at Aberdeen's Central High, I got *The Times* out once a month, printing each issue on a small hand press. I also set the type myself. Dipping into the print shop's large wooden cases of loose metal letters, I set every stick by hand, piece by piece, the way Gutenberg did it. In the idiom of the country editors of a distant day, most of my material was actually written *at the case*.

During the summer after my sophomore year in high school, advancing my newspaper career, I stepped in as a vacation pinch hitter for reporters at the *Morning American* and *Evening News*. In retrospect, the first day was routine, but I walked the beat proudly, calling at the mayor's office, railroad stations, courthouse, and, at noon, the Lions Club. The trip yielded one priceless item: Sinclair Lewis, who wrote "Main Street," would be passing through town a day later, and might be glimpsed when the Milwaukee train stopped at the Main Street station. For that time and place, front-page stuff.

In the *American-News* editorial department, the workday began at 7 a.m. But no one I knew left a wake-up call in those years in Aberdeen, where the railroad lines angled out in all directions. At dawn, your alarm clock was the distant whistling of the switch engines. That was the age of steam; and in any little Midwestern town you could tell the temperature each morning, without getting out of bed, by the pitch of the steam-engine whistles. On a summer morning in South Dakota, the train's high notes made 100 or above seem likely, but on winter days the pitch fell drastically. The deeper the whistle, the colder it was outside. On winter mornings, you knew by the hoarseness of the sound whether you'd need to gird for the half-mile walk to work or school with three pair of long johns, or just two.

Every year, though, soon enough, it was much too hot in South Dakota for long underwear, or even short. On summer days, it cooled off only at Enemy Swim Lake, sixty miles northeast of Aberdeen, where I spent an idyllic two or three weeks annually in Boy Scout camp. One summer, my patrol won the state knot-tying championship, largely due, as I've often said, to the clever way I could throw a clove hitch. The next year, on hikes in the shade of the nature trail, I learned to identify twenty-three kinds of birds. That qualified me for the coveted prize known as the bird-study merit badge – and for an essay prize that fall in an English class.

I liked everything about high school – the teachers, the parties, the lake, the birds, the newspaper office, the football trips, my dad's new cars. High school in South Dakota was for me a three-year run of good times.

> *Like painted kites the days and nights went flying by.*
> — Johnny Mercer

College was even better.

A southeastern South Dakota private school with an enrollment of four hundred, the Yankton College I knew in the 1930s was a handsome collection of old brick buildings and residence halls in a park on an eminence named Observatory Hill.

From the front steps of the observatory itself – which had a seven-inch refracting telescope, the Dakotas' largest – you could see nearly all of the city of Yankton as it spread out and down to the Missouri River two miles away. A tree-crowned community of seven thousand, Yankton, named for an Indian tribe, was once the capital of Dakota Territory. It was the state's leading river town, having begun as a steamboat stop.

In time, I was to catch on downtown as a reporter for the *Yankton Daily Press* & *Dakotan*. But on the hill, there was also a good college paper; and as a campus editor one year, having fun with a tabloid-size weekly, I learned about the impact that big pictures make on newspaper readers.

On that occasion I scheduled a photo of the homecoming queen for the front page – for the entire page, that is, except for the headlines above and a column of news to one side. When the printer downtown balked, demanding $13 extra for such a large engraving, I telephoned the queen's father in Spearfish, South Dakota, and asked if the project would be worth $13 to him. He sounded thrilled. I got a lot of comment on the page. And the next day, I got his check for $13.

Although Yankton won that homecoming game, the football team was usually a disappointment at a school that registered top of the line in three other ways, academically, socially and culturally.

Academically, before our class got there, Yankton College was already known for its Rhodes Scholars, seven of them, more than the combined total produced by the nineteen other state and private colleges and universities of the two Dakotas.

Socially, one Yankton attraction was the Saturday-night dance. And for me, the first dance, in my first week away at college, remains the most memorable. The best dancer there that night was a slim beautiful freshman, a state debate champion, age sixteen. Her name, I soon learned, was Marjory Collins, whom her family called Marnie. I learned by asking her. I also asked her to marry me, and eight years later she did. Still the most important person in my life, Marnie was the first winner I was to know well. Golden-natured, unpretentious, and greatly gifted, she won the national extemporaneous speaking championship for Yankton College the spring that students from Stanford and Alabama finished second and third. In our senior year, long before females were politically acceptable in most precincts, Marnie was elected student-body president

– the first woman at our college to hold that office. To this moment, she's the only woman I've met who has everything.

Culturally, there were two very good things about Yankton College. One was my date. Marnie liked the things I did. The other was the variety. One night, the school even brought in the Imperial Russian Symphony Orchestra, which was a hit right up until it surprised everyone with its final number, "Hail Yankton College." As we all jumped to our feet, the musicians missed a bar or two. We didn't learn until later that our music school, commissioned long ago to produce a college anthem, had instead freshened up an old marching song, the Russian national anthem.

Culturally, also, Yankton College was distinguished by an outdoor theater, the Garden Terrace, which had been built without seats on a large tree-shaded lawn sloping gradually down to a stage with a permanent roofed balcony for "Romeo and Juliet." On spring nights when the theater was dark, that balcony, as seen dimly in the moonlight, has proved inspirational over the years to generations of Yankton College women. A classmate, Lawrence Brewster, counted forty-one couples there one warm evening, with room for many more. One boy always brought his radio, connected it to a socket on stage, and tuned in the name bands — Benny Goodman, Earl (Father) Hines, the Dorsey brothers – playing marvelously from hotels and ballrooms throughout the nation. It was almost as much fun when it snowed.

One year at the Garden Terrace Theater, I had a speaking part in a Shakespeare play, "The Tempest." Marnie was proud of me, I noticed, even though it was just a one-word part. With the passage of the years, unhappily, I have drawn a blank. For the life of me, I can't remember that word.

I do remember that nearly every evening after rehearsals, a group of us, as few as four and as many as nine, gathered in Dave Bates' room at Look Hall to play cards. Our game was no-limit poker, the only card game worth a man's time besides contract bridge. In the 1930s, the ante was a penny or two, and seven cents was a good-sized bet, but you could make them pay two or three times that, or more, to see your cards, if that's the way you felt about it.

By that year, I was also on the staff of the *Press & Dakotan*, a six-day daily. Holding my first full-time newspaper job while also attending college, I earned $10 a week as city editor on a four-man news staff. It was an active period for me – daytime job, afternoon classes, play rehearsals, and poker games long into the night – but never dull. The two-mile hike up and down the hill to the P&D office was a bother only when the wind blew hard, which was almost every day, so my father advanced me the money to buy my first car, a 1928 Whippet. In that depressed year, it was one of only two cars privately owned by Yankton College students.

One night when the weather was unseasonably warm for November, I decided to leave it out overnight in front of my home away from home, a campus rooming house known as the House of Warren; and I still recall with dismay that the next morning, from my upstairs window, I couldn't find the old Whippet. In an all-white landscape, it was completely buried in the snow that had started falling after midnight.

That, nonetheless, was only the beginning of a wonderful winter, if you like South Dakota winters, and I usually did. The weather was so cold in one stretch that the college closed down classes for a week, meaning that the revolving poker game that time lasted seven days and seven nights.

Count me among those who as a rule enjoyed the change of seasons in South Dakota. The summers, though everlastingly hot, were just right for the long hitch-hiking trips I sometimes made in high school and later as a college student before joining the P&D full-time. On such trips, every twenty-four hours, one needs a place to sleep – and in summer weather, my choice was usually the back seat of a parked car. At 10 p.m. or so, walking down a dark street, if I deduced that someone's car might remain there overnight, I crawled in and went to bed. As a hitchhiker, the only time I ever slept in a real bed was at a world's fair in Chicago, where, at the model House of Tomorrow, I slipped into a closet one night while they closed up, then stretched out for eight hours in the master bedroom.

I think of that period of time – roughly the interval between the two world wars – as a relatively crime-free window in U.S. history, perhaps the only one. Climbing into a stranger's car today could get you shot. And it was often that dangerous in the old Wild West. But in the America of the '20s, '30s and into the 1940s, crime seemed to be out of style, leading many citizens to leave the doors of their cars and houses continuously unlocked. Most people lived in small towns then – in a United States with half the population of the overcrowded 1990s – and hardly anyone ever confronted any criminal except a bootlegger.

In such an environment, on my most extended hitch-hiking tour, I was on the road for two months the summer after my freshman year at

Yankton. Heading first for Niagara Falls, New York, and Atlantic City, New Jersey, I doubled back all the way to California and invaded both Canada and Mexico on an excursion that carried me into more than half of the American states. And the drivers who stopped to pick me up seemed no more afraid of me than I was of them. On the first day alone, two of my chauffeurs were women, one a seventeen-year-old high school student who, before turning off for her home up near Duluth, left me standing on the highway. There a friendly woman in her seventies, driving a new car, stopped and carried me on for another hundred miles.

That night as usual, I walked into a restaurant – this one was in Blue Earth, Minnesota – and volunteered to spend an hour or two as a dishwasher in exchange for dinner. Few restaurateurs that summer turned me down. On the entire see-America trip, after starting out with $10 cash, I spent but $9.49. Breakfast was frequently a five-cent quart of milk.

There was law trouble only in Pittsburgh, where I was captured by the police one morning and jailed for most of the day. I was on the roof of a tall building that time, one of Pittsburgh's tallest; and following my usual practice in big cities, I was examining the downtown area when the police closed in, guns drawn. There had been a robbery a week earlier, and the thief had been last seen on my roof.

Sitting in a jail cell that afternoon, I had nothing to read but my girlfriend's letters, which, at my urging, she had been sending general delivery from time to time. Opening one of them again, I suddenly realized that I had picked that letter up in a Washington, D.C., post office on the very day of the great Pittsburgh robbery. I was innocent! I could prove it! And after banging on the jail cell bars, I did. Marnie had saved me again.

Not until the late summer ahead of my senior year at Yankton College – long after the end of my career as a hitchhiker – did I face another serious personal crisis. A P&D old-timer by then but still the newspaper's junior employee, I was required to start work at 7 a.m. for the most important assignment of the entire day in South Dakota journalism: turning on the Associated Press receivers. The AP began ticking out the news at that hour, creating a major conflict with life at a small school. The Yankton College subjects I needed to graduate on schedule, in history, economics and political science, were only offered in 7:40 or 8:40 classes — the critical working hours on any afternoon paper.

The dilemma – work or graduate – has confronted many others, but that didn't make it easier for me. Nor did it help much that I had a campus job offer: editor of the school paper. The money was comparable – by then I was making $18 a week as both city editor and sports editor on what had shrunk to become a three-man P&D staff. But the college paper was only a weekly, and I was already a daily newspaperman.

One night in the last week before classwork resumed, I spent the entire night on my feet, pacing and thinking the problem through, and making pro and con lists. As an editor-reporter on a daily paper, I now had what I'd always wanted. But since first grade, my parents had been pushing me toward college. A day never went by without a reminder of some kind from my father that the only civilized people were college graduates. And shortly after dawn, I decided to give the P&D a week's notice. Two weeks would have been more civilized, but I only saw that later.

My departure in those circumstances foreclosed a return to the *Press & Dakotan* after graduation. I had been replaced on a small staff, the new guy was proving out, and there was no place for me.

In that crisis, happily, I had an option. My coast-to-coast hitch-hiking expedition had left me with the certain knowledge that as a place to live and work, Los Angeles was incomparably far ahead of whatever was second in America.

More to the point, that's where Marnie was headed. Her home until then had been in Tyndall, South Dakota, where she grew up in the care of her grandparents. When her father, a Los Angeles dentist named Cecil Hickman Collins, urged her to go west – and drove back to Yankton with his new wife to retrieve her – she made the heart-rending decision to leave her childhood home. Had she stayed, I'd have stayed, and we might still be running the Tyndall paper, then and now a weekly.

For the California migration, I was ready with an improved vehicle. Flush with newspaper and poker earnings, I had traded in the 1928 Whippet for a 1927 Ford roadster, which, in the middle-1930s, was still one of the two sportiest cars in Yankton. The other was the banker's Duesenberg. The 1927 models were the first Model A Fords, and mine had both a rumble seat and a radio, one of the few car radios in the county at that time if not the state.

All the way to Los Angeles, the crowd of three in the front seat included two large Yankton College football players, Pete Hurtig and Maurice Rundell. Our luggage was in the rumble seat, and my mother's priceless Underwood typewriter was on the floor. In California, Pete and I became charter members of the Yankton College Contract Bridge Club of Los Angeles, which after sixty years is still in business.

CALIFORNIA

Before television changed the country, five Los Angeles newspapers, competing energetically for 1930s circulation, brought out numbers of new editions every day. In sports at that time, the majors were all still eastern leagues; but in both football and baseball, the Pacific Coast had the nation's fastest minors. And on game days, as a result, the newspapers printed even more editions than usual.

It seemed clear enough that, for the first game I covered as a Los Angeles football writer, I would need a spotter to help get me through all the deadlines on time. The *Examiner* had hired me on the strength of my South Dakota experience as a reporter and sports editor – but this wasn't Yankton versus Spearfish. The spotter I had in mind was the national speaking champion from Yankton College – if she would accept my invitation. She would. And as the game began in old Gilmore Stadium, home of the Pacific Coast League's champion Hollywood Bears, I sat down between Marnie and a Morse code expert.

On one side, Marnie kept telling me what was going on. And on the other side, the Western Union's Morse code operator, reading over my shoulder, and never waiting for me to finish any sentence on the old Underwood, kept telling the *Examiner* office what I was writing. He was using a telegraph key like the ones you see at railroad stations in old Western movies. And the whole game passed through me to him from Marnie without, I swear, my knowing anything about it.

Even so, the finished product was pretty well written, I thought, looking over the game story at breakfast the next day. Thus I wasn't surprised when the sports editor hurried up to me as I walked into the office.

"Hi," I said nonchalantly.

"Congratulations," he said, beaming. "You didn't miss a deadline."

At my request, Marnie stayed around. She was still helping me at the Coliseum from time to time after the Cleveland Rams became the Los Angeles Rams in 1946 as the first pro club to move West.

Otherwise at the *Examiner*, in those first California years, I was trying to bridge the gap between papers with circulations of four thousand in Yankton and four hundred thousand in Los Angeles, and I was finding a few differences. There were never any newsroom signs or banners, for instance, at the Yankton P&D. The first day I saw the inside of the *Examiner* office, a huge sign crossed the newsroom, wall to wall, carrying three questions in large red type on a white background. To the left, the first read: "Is It Accurate?" In the middle, the next question, in much larger type, asked: "Is It Clear?" The final question, in really large words, demanded: "Is It Interesting?"

The bottom line was: "William Randolph Hearst." And those were his priorities, although, if you made it interesting enough, he tended to ignore the first two.

Working for him the last dozen years of his life, I could see that the *Examiner* was his favorite of the twenty-six Hearst papers in what was then by far the largest U.S. newspaper chain. His love for Los Angeles was built into the stylish *Examiner* building, which is still a national landmark at Eleventh and Broadway, and which he topped with a third-floor penthouse for himself. Along the east side of the building at street level, large plate glass windows faced Broadway for a half block. And behind those windows, Hearst placed the massive *Examiner* presses, which, printing Sunday supplements for half of the country's Hearst papers, rolled magnificently for most of every day. Those presses were the best show in town. One morning, the streetcars could hardly get through the cars and buses dropping off schoolchildren to see a real newspaper.

Hearst's interest in sports news was, however, minimal. So ours was the most cramped department on the editorial floor. The three youngest sportswriters all shared one desk, where my personal allotment was two small drawers. One day I was searching for a pencil there when I got a memo from the managing editor with a printed notation: "From the desk of Raymond T. Van Ettisch." And that gave me an idea for my own stationery. My printed notation read: "From the drawers of Bob Oates."

During my first year at the *Examiner*, I worked the first 325 days consecutively. After they paid me for a five-day week, I went back on days off to learn about metropolitan newspapers. By the mid-1940s, from the day the Rams set up shop in Los Angeles, I was both the Ram beat writer, writing stories and columns from every town in the National Football League, and assistant sports director. For obscure reasons, we then had, instead of a sports editor, a sports director, Ben Woolbert. Sitting in for him on his days off, I decided to specialize as a photo editor for two reasons: Since experimenting with oversized photos in college, pictures have always been my second interest, professionally, and they were W.R. Hearst's *only* sports interest.

On the afternoon of my first USC-Notre Dame game at the Coliseum, I had eight staff cameramen out there, strange as that was, at the time, in sports journalism. After hurrying back to the *Examiner* office in the fourth quarter, I first selected a one-per-second sequence of photos of the day's big play – photos taken from high in the stands with a long-lens *magic eye* camera. Then I threw out all but the four best of the day's big action pictures – leaving at least three photographers entirely unrepresented. One picture consumed half the front page. The others consumed page three. The big-picture concept was a newspaper rarity a half century ago, and I heard one day that the first time W.R. saw that edition, he reacted with a smile.

In recent years, sequence pictures and picture pages have fallen out of favor with newspaper editors, who reason that they can't compete on that level with TV – but I don't think they're right about that. TV pictures are transitory. Newspaper pictures are *there*. They helped W.R. Hearst build an empire.

I was in direct communication with him only once. On one of my early days at the *Examiner*, after a late-afternoon deadline, I happened to be almost alone on the editorial floor, probably examining my drawers, when the editorial telephone operator rang me to say she had Mr. Hearst on the line from San Simeon.

I said: "Yes, Mr. Hearst."

He said: "I want you to look up something for me, young man. What's the name of the third stomach of a cow?"

I had a quick mental picture of Hearst at his desk writing another stern anti-Roosevelt farm-policy editorial, but all I said was something like, excuse me? He repeated the request, and I promised to get back to him, very, very soon.

First, though, I walked over and asked the operator: "Who was that man?"

She looked at me for a moment, then said: "Who do you think? Get moving."

So I rushed to the encyclopedias, found the word, double-checked the spelling in several places, and within ten minutes, proudly, I placed the call.

I said: "About that word, Mr. Hearst."

And I spelled it out carefully.

There was nothing but silence on the other end. The line seemed to have gone dead. Finally, I asked: "Are you still there, sir?"

He said: "Yes, I'm here. But it doesn't fit."

Nervously, I asked: "Doesn't fit what, sir?"

That prompted him to tell me that he was working a crossword puzzle – and not just any crossword puzzle. He confessed that he had been stumped – this man with twenty-six newspapers and a bunch of national magazines – by a puzzle in a rival paper, the *L.A. Times*.

As a circulation-builder, the *Times*, I knew, was then having a crossword-puzzle contest, with a first prize of $10,000. I'd also heard that Hearst's own newspapers were in trouble financially – that W.R. might not ride out the Depression. He *needed* that $10,000, and I'd let him down.

I promised to try harder.

That evening I braced nearly every *Examiner* employee who was a known crossword-puzzle addict. And at last one of our cartoonists told me that his father had it, had a lock on the $10,000. In the name of the *Examiner*, and the financial well-being of the Hearst empire, not to mention my financial future, and his, I begged the young artist to call home and get the word. Eventually, reluctantly, he did.

"I think we've got it," I told Hearst.

He wrote it down and said, "Thank you, young man," and hung up.

I never learned if he won. All I heard was that when our people sent in his entry, they used a false name.

The *Examiner*, a morning paper, survived Hearst (who lived into the 1950s) by only ten years. His children shortsightedly abandoned the morning market in 1962 and merged us into an afternoon paper called the *Herald-Examiner*, although, as the highest newsroom executives at the *Times* conceded privately then and later, the *Examiner* was still the best paper in town. Simultaneously, the owners of the *Times*, living up to their end of the deal, closed their afternoon paper, realizing, before others did, that televised evening news was already replacing afternoon papers.

Doubling as Ram beat writer and assistant sports editor of the *Herald-Examiner* in what was, abruptly, a two-newspaper town, I got up every morning asking myself the same question: "What can I do to beat the *Times* today?" I had been comparing daily journalism tactics and procedures since the year in South Dakota when, not yet old enough for school, I began reading my father's four newspapers. And now, with de facto editorial control of the sports section, I was able to express my sometimes revolutionary ideas of what good journalism is.

Ignoring speculation that the *Herald-Examiner* was doomed, I concentrated as an editor on three things: colorfully made-up pages, large action pictures, and the day's biggest news stories – to the exclusion of other stories. We started by stressing horizontally laid-out pages, building on a design scheme with which I was familiar. As a junior editor, I had invented horizontal makeup. At least, I had never seen it anywhere in our large supply of exchange papers until, one day in the 1930s, the *Examiner* advanced me to a low-priority job as sports editor of the Sunday *bulldog* edition – the one printed the Friday before. That was when I discarded the vertical-makeup system and began presenting most stories in packages three to ten inches deep and three to eight columns wide under multiple-column headlines. The drill elsewhere in the world then and for years afterward was a mix of vertical stories, dribbling down the page in single columns, as, on its front page, the *Wall Street Journal* does it to this day.

By the middle 1960s, our front-page goal in every *Herald-Examiner* sports section was two big stories with two banner headlines above the fold – much as *USA Today* does it now. The reasoning: Give the reader an immediate choice of two special stories by suggesting, with bold horizontal makeup, that they're special. In the rest of our sports section, most other stories were also placed under multiple-column headlines, a practice that is now common; but in those days we felt the excitement of pioneers.

Despite limited space at the *Herald-Examiner*, we also displayed our action pictures prominently on the first two or three pages much as *Sports Illustrated*, with a great deal more space, has done it in recent years.

Our third scheme was to confine our coverage basically to major news and daily features on all the major beats, particularly football and baseball. Rather than throw away space on minor sports and neighborhood news, we catered to the interests of the largest sports constituency in Los Angeles, big league fans. We reasoned that the second interest of a Dodger fan isn't high school baseball, or hunting and fishing, but rather the San Francisco Giants or other major league ballclubs. High school fans, we knew, could read their neighborhood papers, of which Southern California has scores. As for hunters, they'd rather hunt than read.

The big league sports fan could turn only to us for focused, in-depth big-story coverage.

This plan proved doable largely because of the cooperation of the Page One sports columnist, Melvin Durslag, and the sports editor, Bud Furillo. As a great columnist, Durslag contributed humor, apt commentaries and timeliness. Furillo, the most creative of Hearst sports editors, also provided, as a writer, sound angles and good coverage on big stories.

In content and presentation, those mid-1960s *Herald-Examiner* sports pages were, I still believe, the best in sixty years of U.S. sports. They helped keep us comparable with the *Times* in total circulation (some seven hundred thousand apiece) in an era when the morning-paper advantage was everywhere and everyday getting more pronounced.

And so at the *Herald-Examiner* I achieved editorially what in all my years as a newspaper student, going back to the Aberdeen days, I had hoped and wanted to do. Ending a quarter century-plus on Hearst papers, my career as an editor-reporter climaxed in those last years before a strike-lockout shot the *Herald-Examiner* down.

But I've been lucky: There was to be another and even more satisfying climax at the *Los Angeles Times*, where in a new and distinctly different role – as a national-assignment news-and-feature sportswriter – I've spent another rewarding quarter century-plus.

In the late 1960s, the *Times* sent for me when the *Herald-Examiner* crumbled. I was grateful but waited six months in the vain hope that Hearst's children would call off the strike-lockout. Finally, not wanting to miss a football season, I moved along.

I began at the *Times* as I had begun at the *Examiner*: working every day. For 159 consecutive mornings that first year my pro football stories were in the *Times*.

Though by now the biggest paper in the West, it had never been highly thought of by Los Angeles journalists – even those at the *Times* – except as a business institution. It had always made money. But with Otis Chandler in full charge as publisher, and with Bill Thomas heading the newsroom as one of the nation's great editors, the *Times* not only overcame its dreary past but quickly shot to first in America in excellence as well as net income.

The editorial budget rose proportionately; and though I continued to cover the Rams, the editors sent me out on more and more national stories.

During the decade that arrived in 1970, no newspaper in the world made room for longer pieces on a greater variety of subjects than those in the *Times*.

And as my job description grew to encompass more sports and more states, my assignments were increasingly surprising and stimulating.

Coincidentally, the 1970s were the heyday of competitive sports. The Pittsburgh Steelers, whose players were the most physically talented in football history, fielded their four Super Bowl champions in the 1970s, when the best modern baseball team, the Oakland A's, won three consecutive World Series titles. The Los Angeles Lakers won their unprecedented thirty-three consecutive NBA games in that decade and the UCLA basketball team astonishingly won a record eighty-eight consecutive college games. Also in Los Angeles, college football's all-time best team, the 1979 Southern California Trojans, sent no fewer than twelve first-round draft choices to the NFL.

Individually, Muhammad Ali became the world's greatest-ever fighter in the 1970s, when Reggie Jackson once hit four World Series home runs with four consecutive swings.

It all climaxed scant weeks into the decade of the '80s with what has been called the biggest sports event yet, the Winter Olympics triumph of America over a seemingly unbeatable Soviet hockey team.

Those were years when, from one month to the next, traveling for the *Times* was making my job continuously engrossing. Life on the road was like a party. There was, for example, the afternoon of a Los Angeles-bound flight from New York – a 1970s jet trip that was in most ways typical of all the others in that decade – when cocktails and hors d'oeuvres were, as usual, brought out at 5 p.m. Two flight attendants were always in the first-class section in those days – along with three or four passengers, rarely more – and this time three other travelers and I were up there to get the front-cabin treatment: five-course dinners served on white tablecloths with distinctive dishware, silverware, and glassware and, for each course, appropriate wines.

But the thing I remember most about that flight was none of that. The most memorable thing was the personal tribute I got from the other passengers when we were about two hours out of New York. I had spent those hours typing a *Times* story steadily on a noisy old portable typewriter; and when the cocktail hour began, as I leaned over to set the typewriter on the floor, the three others in first class all stood and applauded.

By contrast, one of those Eastern assignments – in an early year of the computer revolution – led to the most devastating trauma I've had at the *Times*. On a Tuesday morning, they called me in, handed over a small gray box – which turned out to be a word processor – and said I'd have to use it from then on, starting Sunday at the football game in Philadelphia.

Sports columnist Charles Maher, who also got his first computer that day, talked back. "*Anything* that makes writing harder is a bad idea," Maher said; and though I didn't protest, I agreed.

So that week I took two tools to Philadelphia – my old portable typewriter and my new computer – and because on out-of-town assignments I am always a sightseer, I had both with me that Sunday morning when I toured Independence Hall. I think of the Declaration of Independence, which was signed there in 1776, as man's greatest single literary production. A framed copy of the Declaration hangs on one of my living-room walls, as it has for forty-five years; and I never miss a chance to revisit the place where Jefferson submitted the original. It was inconvenient – absurd, really – to walk among the inkwells of two hundred years ago carrying a typewriter and a computer, plus a briefcase; but on the morning of a football game, it's my practice never to let my tools out of my sight.

And that afternoon, covering the New York Giants versus the Philadelphia Eagles, I wrote the game story on the portable typewriter as usual. Then, laboriously, I typed the whole thing into my computer, and, miraculously pushing the right modem buttons, managed to fire it off to Los Angeles on a telephone wire. I felt sorry for the Western Union operator who was in the row just ahead of me. A skilled, accurate craftsman, she had for years dispatched most of my copy from Philadelphia. Now as she sat there with nothing to do, I thought I saw a tear in her eye. I know there was one in mine.

By the 1990s, distressingly, the festiveness had gone out of travel. Airline deregulation had led to overcrowded airports, overcrowded airplanes, fewer flight attendants, fewer flights, and, in the abominable hub-city era, the obligation to stop in Dallas, and perhaps St. Louis, in order to move from Los Angeles to Cleveland. The *Times* since the early 1980s, moreover, provoked like all newspapers by financial worries, has put its employees in the economy section of every airplane, forsaking Otis Chandler's standing instructions, which were: Regardless of destination (Sacramento? New York? London?), *Times* writers always go first class.

The change, however, has never affected either the *Times* as a product or me as a contributor. In late years, as my work base shifted again, I settled in as the go-to writer whenever the editors asked for in-depth stories on any subject. Though continuing as a football analyst, I have specialized for most of every year in magazine-length material. In the 1940s, '50s and '60s, I had often averaged seven stories a week. By the 1990s I was averaging – except in the football season – one story a month. My friends, assuming that I had twenty-nine days a month off, envisioned me at my computer on the thirtieth, working like hell around the clock. And sometimes, I did.

BALDWIN HILLS

In a country with fifteen hundred daily newspapers, eight sportswriters have been there to cover each of the first thirty-three Super Bowl games. As one of the eight, I most distinctly remember an early Super Bowl day in New Orleans. The game site in those years, before the rise of the Louisiana Superdome, was Tulane Stadium, and I've always enjoyed the walk to Tulane through the Garden District. That day, however, the weather was wintry for New Orleans, close to freezing, so I rode the St. Charles Avenue streetcar instead, climbing in out of the biting cold.

Somehow, in an open press box, we all lived through the game. Then, heading back to the press hotel near the French Quarter, I hitched a ride with a New York writer who habitually travels in rental cars. Thus in an accounting era when the hotel bill went directly to the newspaper's auditors, my only out-of-pocket expense all day was the streetcar. And when I got back to Los Angeles, I sent in the smallest one-day expense-account total in *Times* history, as I learned later: fifteen cents.

If that turns a spotlight on the cost of living in New Orleans, at least in the 1970s, it also says something about my personal lifestyle inclinations. And lifestyle, whether the individual is famous, unfamous, or infamous, is a particular interest of mine.

Were I to have a conversation with my forebears, what I'd most like to know is not only how they spent their years but also their days and hours. Were I to converse with my descendants, they'd inquire into all that, too, I'm sure, if they're anything like me. They'd want to know about my lifestyle philosophy, my house, my cars, the way I live, the things I do; and here I am to talk to them.

When on the move, I prefer to walk rather than ride anything (except sailboats). I'll take streetcars or cable cars over taxis or limousines or rentals, and I never fly if there's time for an overnight train. One of the great things about covering the Rams in the early days was the ride to San Francisco in a night-train berth on Southern Pacific's luxurious old Lark.

In general, as those preferences may indicate, the philosophy I endorse is as simple as it is unoriginal: You're only here once. Every day is Christmas. It's great to be alive. Live the life you love. And the best things in life are free.

For me, the three most enjoyable days of every year have always been Christmas, the first day of vacation, and the first day of football practice, but I have never particularly looked forward to any of them or to anything else, even weekends or holidays or parties. There's no such thing as the future. I'll take today.

I'd have retired long ago, I know, if alarm clocks had played any role in my life. I still feel the damage that, on college mornings, wake-up calls did to my nervous system. But since then, I haven't had to set an alarm. At home in the Baldwin Hills area of Los Angeles, my daily routine has for decades begun the same way. It starts whenever I wake up, which is usually when the birds start calling outside.

And because a simple routine helps a writer, I get to work right away, following the lead of novelist James Michener, who told me one time that because he could happily fritter away the morning hours, he had the morning paper delivered at noon.

I simply decline to look at the *Times* until Marnie gets up at 8 or 9 and sets it out with breakfast. For fifty years, every other morning, we've had bacon and eggs and waffles with the morning paper. The rest are cereal days. Back at the computer after some upper-body exercise sweeping the patio, I work until lunch at 2. The afternoon is for research-related activities. I prefer not to write after lunch except in a press box.

In the late afternoon of nearly every day, we hike for thirty minutes or so, walking nearby through tree and meadow in what for us is the most attractive residential park in Los Angeles, the Baldwin Hills Village Green. During most of my years at the old *Examiner*, where I worked at the office four days a week, I did my hiking downtown, pacing the surrounding streets; but in subsequent decades, I have visited the downtown office an average of but once a week.

In the late, late afternoon, continuing the simple life, I manufacture a couple of dry martinis (his and hers). On workdays as well as days off, the best two hours of every day are the breakfast and cocktail hours with my wife. For cocktail-time entertainment, I put on big-band phonograph records, of which I have hundreds, and listen to the only form of popular music that has ever combined great musical skill with harmonious richness of sound.

There is also a fire in the fireplace nearly every night we're home from October to late June. Though incompetent in most handcraft situations, I have with some effort learned to do three difficult things with style: build a fire, program the video cassette recorder, and, on big-breakfast days, open the tomato juice.

My dinner-hour preference is a VCR movie, one I've previously taped. The multiply talented five-star chef I married sets out dinner on small tray tables in the living room, after which we finish the movie – or a taped installment of, say, "NYPD Blue" – before I resume my lifelong second career as a dishwasher about 9 p.m. Then I turn in with a book. I am one of those who read two books at the same time, in my case usually fiction and history.

For variety, two or three times a week, we head out in the late afternoon for live jazz by the musicians playing in one Southern California venue or another. Monday is dinner-dance night at the Alpine Village Inn twenty-five minutes down the freeway. The orchestra there is directed by Tracy Wells, who leads one of the last of the active big swing bands: five trumpets, four trombones, five reeds, four rhythm. The Wells sound is an updated reprise of the best there was a half century ago in the Peacock Court at my favorite San Francisco hotel, the Mark Hopkins, or in the Madhattan Room of the Hotel Pennsylvania in New York. My notion of the finest in entertainment is still, after all these years, a dinner-dance. Or, but only at home, a movie.

All this, I'm sure, doesn't sound like heaven on earth to everyone. I'm confident that many others could wish for something more than four trombones or a walk in the park or a computer screen that stares back six or seven hours a day. But for me, I have to say, somebody laid it out right.

Home base for this simple life (as my great-great-grandchildren will doubtless ask about) is the house we've lived in for an even fifty years. As Jefferson said, let the world roll on. Ours is a three-bedroom cottage that I found when, during my 1940s days at the *Los Angeles Examiner*, it was under construction. I picked it out for its functional design and Westside location. The salesman said the Baldwin Hills area is twenty minutes from everywhere; but in the freeway era, it has proved to be less than that to Los Angeles International Airport, to the Hollywood Bowl, to the *Times* office downtown, and to the beach or Marina del Rey.

I deliberately chose a house without a breakfast nook or kitchen table. I don't much like either. Instead, daytimes, we headquarter in our small dining room, where my wife's desk is the dining-room table. In her primary role for many years, she has been a private investor, a nearly full-time position. Financially, the soundest instruction I've had came from the 1930s football coach of the Hollywood Bears, a multimillionaire who said anyone can be a multimillionaire. "Budget and invest," he said. From her desk chair, my wife's view through sliding glass doors is of our brick-floored patio, where, exercising a prejudice against concrete surfaces, I laid the patio bricks myself forty-nine years ago.

Close by, two of our bedrooms are furnished as compact libraries. And on workdays in the smaller of these rooms, I unpack a portable word processor – which succeeded generations of earlier models and portable typewriters – set it up on the rolling library table I designed three decades ago, and create an instant newspaper office that looks out on a Baldwin Hills forest.

In our living room, Marnie's grand piano stands in one corner. Against an opposite wall we've placed our classic 1960s Packard-Bell entertainment center – seven feet broad, three feet high, solid walnut – with a sliding panel across the television screen. It's been with us for thirty years. Our old phonograph records, as they revolve at some thirty-three revolutions per minute, still sound as if the big bands are in the room with us. The Packard Bell also plays my new compact discs and cassette tapes.

Behind our house, our back yard, a hundred feet deep, seventy feet wide, is ringed by shrubs and trees, including a massive avocado tree. Our sons, Bob and Steve, played football there. Our grandsons, Christopher and Andrew, play soccer. The playing field is private: A concrete wall fourteen feet high, more than a half mile in length, edges our property in back. In front, our street ends in a traffic-free cul-de-sac. In a flinty, great city, it's a suburban-like retreat.

From a jet landing on the north runway of the Los Angeles airport, you can see the Baldwin Hills, which are just to your right. From a jet taking off from the same runway, you can see, also off to the right, our sailboat at Marina del Rey. It's a thirty-four-foot Hunter sloop that we own with Steve and his wife, Susanne, and two friends of ours, Kirk and Beverly Busby.

I chose that particular boat because it has three cabins that close off, aft, main and fore. I frequently go aboard to run the word processor but can't sail the boat myself. We use it mostly as a beach house. Steve and Kirk are the seamen; and once in awhile, they take us to Catalina Island. Otherwise, the *Delfin* is a very quiet place to write. Every day is Christmas.

The area that includes our neighborhood and our marina has our kind of weather: cool mornings and sunny afternoons. The California climate is widely misunderstood, even by Californians. If you live more than a half dozen miles from the ocean, you might as well be spending the summer months in South Dakota or Texas. By contrast, mornings are often chilly and overcast in the Baldwin Hills, conducive to work, and the prevailing early-afternoon west wind off the ocean pushes the smog east each day. Air-conditioning is unnecessary. When in previous decades the air-conditioning went out in our cars, we didn't bother to get the units repaired.

You do need cars in Southern California. And we've had ours so long they're now both classics. Marnie drives a carefully maintained black 1961 Thunderbird convertible, the one that looks like a twin-engine rocket ship. Mine is a light green 1967 Mustang convertible. I like the cars I like, but I didn't inherit my father's new-car passion. I also have a problem with the appearance of the 1990s models, which seem to be burrowing their noses into the road. We don't drive much anyway.

About the only place my wife goes is to the tennis courts at Marina del Rey. She plays at the California Yacht Club, where her game, paddle tennis, is something like tennis on a half-size court. It was my game also for thirty years until I went down not long ago with a rotator-cuff tear. Not that we ever excelled as athletes. Once a year, on the average, Marnie can beat one of the women's champions, Joan Swanson or Jackie Leebody. And I distinctly remember the day that I beat the men's champion, Dick Dulgarian, whose backhand is internationally renowned.

On vacation, Marnie and I, joined by Bob and Steve when they were younger, have taken motor trips in new rented automobiles at least once in each of the last fifty years, although, in all that time, we've only owned five cars. For awhile, we drove similar his and hers 1950 Pontiacs, a rust-colored hardtop coupe and a black convertible. The coupe was the motor industry's first hardtop and, when we bought it new in 1950, the most beautiful car on the road. Our first purchase, an eternity ago, was a battleship gray 1939 Chevrolet four-door that had everything but a tape deck, which, in the '30s and '40s, you didn't need. Radio stations in those days all played big-band jazz.

A privilege of life in the late twentieth century is being able to move around, by land, sea or air, with one's own cassette or disc music. On city streets, there's nothing like the big-band sound to drown out the rock or rap in the next car.

THE PRESS

On an early morning in a 1930s South Dakota newspaper office, looking up from my typewriter, I noticed that one of the older reporters was absent. "Where's Charles today?" I asked.

"He had to take the day off," the editor said. "Alice called in sick."

Alice must be Charles' wife, I thought at first. Then I remembered: Alice was one of the linotype operators in our back shop. She was an indispensable employee, the only operator in the building who could read Charles' handwriting. On her day off, he had to take a day off.

"I wish Charles would learn to run a typewriter," the editor grumbled.

But he never did. A good reporter when sober, he was one of the last of a now-extinct species: the tramp newspapermen who moved from city to city in the early years of the century, carrying their own quills or pens and pencils, and occasionally their own ink, from one newspaper office to the next.

So I've seen it all: quills, pencils, typewriters, and computers. And through it all, the press has been, for me, an important avocation as well as vocation. My lifestyle can be simple because my principal focus, my occupation, has also been an inexhaustible source of stimulation and entertainment.

I am interested in anything and everything about newspapers, or about writing for newspapers, or about writing in general. And like most other newspapermen, I have some opinions. Among them:
  • I value day-in day-out reliability and consistency of excellence above all other newspaper qualities. In a publication issued 365 mornings a

year, the everyday reader is not well served by journalists who chase the numerous one-day prizes of their craft. The journalistic challenge is to show up every day with your best work.

• I have never had a friend on any sports team or in any sports organization. In fraternization, I feel sure, conflicts of interest are unavoidable.

• When confident that a news source is not telling the truth, I never quote him directly. If that hurts my stories sometimes, I have at least denied one forum to a liar.

• When asked, I recommend journalism school to all media candidates. At the urging of Bob Lochner, then executive sports editor of the *San Francisco Chronicle*, I took a master's degree in journalism at UCLA. And later I taught that subject for two years in the UCLA English Department.

• Even so, it's my view that the surest road to newspaper employment is simply to volunteer, as an unsalaried intern, to answer copy-desk telephones. I didn't learn that in time to profit by it, and today it might not apply everywhere, but one thing is still true of all newspaper people: They hate to answer the telephone – even, sometimes, their own.

• Several years ago in his final newspaper report, columnist Eric Sevareid, describing what he'd been up to all his life, identified himself as an elucidator. For a sports reporter or any other communicator, an attempt to analyze or elucidate seems a reasonable aspiration. I feel sure that most readers are receptive when, on topics that interest them, the critical points are made plain.

• The optimal way to write anything is with a light touch – thus acknowledging that almost everyone out there in a despairing world yearns to laugh. But it is equally correct to say that all comedians have a conspicuously low batting average – even those with a great natural gift for the comic. And so, early on, I set a different goal for myself: to be as clear and specific as possible in every sentence while using a minimum of clichés. That isn't easy, either. There's no easy way.

But for sixty years I've loved the trying.

As Gertrude Stein said, every generation looks at something different. When my great great grandkids ask what I was doing with my time when I wasn't listening to the big bands or walking in the park, tell them I spent it watching words take shape.

OATES

NAMES MAKE HISTORY

Abdul-Jabbar, Kareem, 128
Adams, Bud, 271
Aikman, Troy, 154, 199, 201, 206, 276, 281, 282
Ali, Muhammad, 311, 332
Albert, Frankie, 57, 90
Allen, Doug, 146, 147-148
Allen, George, 47, 167
Allen, Marcus, 141-145, 158, 188
Ameche, Alan, 170
Anderson, Dick, 176
Anderson, Jamal, 256
Anderson, Ken, 219
Arens, William, 12
Atwater, Steve, 266-267
Barton, Harris, 197
Batchelor, E.A., 105
Battles, Cliff, 168
Baugh, Sammy, 55, 57, 107, 163, 164, 165-168, 198, 201, 222, 309, 311
Bendross, Jesse, 242
Benson, Tom, 271
Berry, Raymond, 116-117, 169
Berthelsen, Richard, 146, 147, 150, 151
Berwanger, Jay, 137
Bierman, Bernie, 47, 240, 318
Bimson, Howard, 87
Blaik, Red, 32, 47, 227

Blanda, George, 183-188, 310
Blood, Johnny (McNally), 108-109
Bowden, Bobby, 207, 234, 237, 243-247
Bowden, Jeff, 246
Bowden, Terry, 246
Bowden, Tommy, 246
Bowlen, Pat, 262-263
Bowles, Paul, 314
Bradshaw, Terry, 133, 164, 202, 271, 310, 311
Bramski, Joe, 289
Bramski, Theresa, 289
Branch, Cliff, 186, 190
Bray, Ray, 114
Brewster, Lawrence, 322
Briggs, Dean, 43
Brill, Marty, 28
Brister, Bubby, 268
Brodie, John, 90, 221-223
Brondfield, Jerry, 19
Brown, Jim, 127, 129, 153, 284-285, 309, 311
Brown, Larry, 129
Brown, Paul, 163, 164, 201, 215-220, 231, 301
Browne, Joe, 303
Broyles, Frank, 237

Bruckner, D.J.R., 88
Brundage, Avery, 102
Bryant, Paul "Bear", 206, 207, 234, 236-243
Burt, Jim, 294
Busby, Beverly, 338
Busby, Kirk, 338
Butkus, Dick, 133, 310, 311
Camp, Walter, 12, 27, 36-39, 41-43, 44-45, 48, 51, 53, 62, 303
Campbell, Earl, 153, 271, 274
Carter, Jimmy, 257
Chandler, Chris, 160, 256
Chandler, Otis, 13, 331, 333-334
Clay, Henry, 138
Coley, Ken, 242
Collier, Blanton, 174
Collins, Cecil, 325
Conner, George, 115, 213
Cozza, Carmen, 82
Crockett, Ray, 263-264
Crowley, Jim, 29-34
Culver, Peder II, 76
Cunningham, Gunther, 154
Cunningham, Randall, 143
Dahlen, Neal, 267
Daley, Charley, 26-27
Daugherty, Dick, 113-115
Davidson, Ben, 180
Davis, Al, 142-145, 187, 188-189, 265
Davis, Glenn, 32
Davis, Parke H., 39, 52
Davis, Terrell, 152-161, 261, 262
Davis, Willie, 87
DeBartolo, E.J., Sr., 293
DeBartolo, Eddie, Jr., 278, 288, 291-297
DeBartolo, Lisa, 296
DeBerg, Steve, 283
Devine, Dan, 285
Dickerson, Eric, 153
Dietzel, Paul, 238
Dorais, Gus, 26
Dornbusch, Sanford, 90

Doubleday, Abner, 42
Douds, Forrest "Jap", 113
Dryer, Fred, 130-134
Dulgarian, Dick, 338
Durer, Albrecht, 33
Durslag, Melvin, 331
Dye, Pat, 241
Eisenhower, Dwight, 79
Elam, Jason, 267
Ellis, William Webb, 40
Elway, Jack, 160
Elway, Jan, 160
Elway, John, 90, 154, 155, 158-161, 200, 261, 262, 263, 267, 276, 282
Elway, Lee Anne, 160
Favre, Brett, 154, 201, 276, 282
Fassell, Jim, 161
Fears, Tom, 48, 115, 231-232
Feltes, Robert, 85
Ferguson, Joe, 127
Finley, Charlie O., 282
Flores, Tom, 188-189, 190, 192-193, 195, 262
Ford, Henry, 44
Fortmann, Danny, 108-109, 130, 213, 311
Four Horseman, 29-34
Fouts, Dan, 202
Furillo, Bud, 331
Gallico, Paul, 20, 21
George, Bill, 141, 223
Gifford, Frank, 118, 231
Gibbs, Alex, 157-158
Gillman, Sid, 59, 113-115, 295
Gipp, George, 27-29
Gleason, Bill, 21
Graham, Otto, 60, 178, 201, 218, 219
Grange, Harold "Red", 31, 99, 100-106, 107, 109, 112, 213, 214, 309, 310
Gray, Alan, 242
Green, Cornell, 255
Griese, Brian, 268
Griese, Bob, 61

Griffith, Howard, 155, 158
Grossman, Sandy, 249
Halas, George, 56, 57, 99, 100, 101,
    110, 165, 208-214, 309
Hannah, John, 311
Hargadon, Fred E., 90
Harper, Jesse, 26
Hayes, Woody, 47, 233-236
Hearst, Garrison, 156
Hearst, William Randolph, 327, 328-329
Heffelfinger, W.W. "Pudge", 53, 153,
    310
Hein, Mel, 108-109, 113
Heisman, John, 42
Hickey, Howard "Red", 58, 220-224
Hill, Harlon, 213
Hinkle, Clark, 108-109
Hirsch, Elroy, 48
Holmgren, Mike, 62, 191, 226, 282
Holt, Milt, 82
Hornung, Angela, 139, 140
Hornung, Loretta, 139-140
Hornung, Paul, 136-141, 142, 231-232
Hubbard, John, 93-96
Hunt, Lamar, 310
Hunt, Mary Jane, 76
Hurtig, Pete, 325-326
Hutchins, Robert M., 84, 85-87, 88
Hutson, Don, 108-109, 309, 310, 311
Ibanez, Vicente Blasco, 33
Jackson, Reggie, 332
Jefferson, Thomas, 249, 264, 333, 336
Johnson, Jimmy, 199, 206, 262, 281-282
Jones, David "Deacon", 123, 310, 311
Jones, Dub, 174
Jones, Frank, 83
Jones, Jerry, 281
Jordon, Michael, 284-285
Joyce, Reverend Edmund P., 25
Jurgensen, Sonny, 202
Keers, Pete, 88
Kelly, Jim, 164, 195-197, 202
Kilmer, Billy, 221-223
Knox, Chuck, 133, 197

Kramer, Jerry, 141
Krause, Edward W. "Moose", 21
Lambeau, Curly, 226
Lamonica, Daryle, 185
Landry, Tom, 61
Layden, Elmer, 29-34
Leahy, Frank, 220
Leebody, Jackie, 338
Lekrone, Mike, 76, 78
Levens, Dorsey, 154
Levy, Marv, 195-197
Lewis, Walter, 242
Lieber, Jill, 160
Lindbergh, Charles A., 264
Lipscomb, "Big Daddy", 118
Lochner, Bob, 340
Lombardi, Vince, 47, 48, 51, 60-61, 62,
    121, 137, 138, 141, 206, 217, 224-233,
    253, 262, 264, 268, 277, 310
Long, Howie, 143
Lott, Ronnie, 134-136, 266, 294
Luckman, Sid, 213
Luisetti, Hank, 90
Lyman, Link, 213
Lynch, Mary Ann, 86
Mack, Connie, 209
Mack, Tom, 119-121
Mackey, John, 169
Madden, John, 186, 248-254
Mader, Dr. Robert, 68
Maher, Charles, 333
Manning, Archie, 133
Marchibroda, Ted, 195, 196
Marino, Dan, 161, 199, 201
Mariucci, Steve, 199, 280, 293
Marquard, Rube, 212
Mason, Leslie, 86
Matson, Ollie, 118
Maynard, Don, 182
McAfee, George, 213
McCaffrey, Ed, 158-159
McDonald, Tommy, 138
McElhenny, Hugh, 117-119, 153
McGee, Max, 139

McKay, John, 47, 95
McKenzie, Reggie, 125, 126
McKittrick, Bobb, 263
McMahon, Jim, 203
McNeil, Freeman, 149
McVay, John, 294
Mercer, Johnny, 320
Michener, James, 335
Millen, Matt, 291, 294
Miller, Chris, 268
Miller, Don, 29-34
Miller, Rip, 23
Modell, Art, 215
Montana, Cass, 290-291
Montana, Joe, 153, 164, 198-203, 276, 278-279, 280, 283-291, 296, 297
Montana, Joseph Clifford, Sr., 286-287, 288-289
Montana, Theresa, 286-287
Moon, Warren, 201
Murray, Ike, 238
Musso, George, 213
Nagurski, Bronko, 57, 107-113, 153, 213, 309, 310, 311, 318
Nagurski, Eileen (Kane), 107-108, 109
Nalen, Tom, 158
Namath, Joe, 60, 128, 163, 164, 165-166, 167, 175-183, 189, 197, 201, 287, 310, 311
Nevers, Ernie, 31, 32, 311
Neyland, Bob, 240
Noll, Chuck, 47, 164, 262
Oates, Andrew, 337
Oates, Bob, Sr., 313-340
Oates, Bob, Jr., 337, 338
Oates, Christopher, 337
Oates, Henry, 317
Oates, Idah (Armstrong), 315-317
Oates, Marjory "Marnie" (Collins), 321-322, 325, 326, 337, 338
Oates, Steve, 337, 338
Oates, William Maclay, 315-319
O'Leary, Dennis, 250
Olsen, Merlin, 121-124, 133, 169

Osmanski, Bill, 213
Otto, Jim, 185
Page, Mike, 81
Paige, Woody, 154
Parcells, Bill, 217, 264
Parker, Buddy, 47
Parker, Jim, 311
Parks, Dan, 78
Pastorini, Dan, 193
Paterno, Joe, 207, 234, 237, 243
Patrick, Linnie, 243
Patton, General George, 234-235
Payton, Walter, 111
Perkins, Steve, 256
Perrin, Berry, 242
Perry, Joe, 118
Peters, Seaver, 81
Petrucci, Jeff, 287
Phillips, B.J., 239
Phillips, Helen, 272-273
Phillips, O.A. "Bum", 206, 240, 269-274
Phillips, Wade, 271, 273
Plunkett, Jim, 90, 143, 164, 188-195, 202
Pope, Edwin, 207-208
Powel, Harford, 38
Powers, John, 239
Pricer, Billy, 117
Prothro, Tommy, 132-133
Prusmack, A. John, 37, 39
Ralston, John, 189, 191, 192
Rashad, Ahmad, 126
Reagan, Ronald, 28
Reeves, Ann, 258
Reeves, C.E. "Edd", 257, 259
Reeves, Dan, 159-160, 217, 255-260, 263
Reeves, Daniel F., 102, 304
Reeves, Jerry, 258
Reeves, Jo Ann, 258
Reeves, Pam, 258, 260
Reichler, Joe, 308
Rentzel, Lance, 132

Restic, Joe, 82, 83
Reynolds, Bruce, 43
Rice, Grantland, 20, 30, 33-34
Rice, Jerry, 297, 309, 310, 311
Richardson, Willie, 170
Rickey, Branch, 266
Robertson, Bill, 148, 149
Robin, Stan, 289
Robinson, John, 95-96
Rockne, Kenneth "Knute", 12, 17-34, 35, 51
Rockne, Lars, 23
Rodgers, Pepper, 71
Rogers, Will, 19
Romanowski, Bill, 265
Roosevelt, Theodore, 53
Rosen, Marty, 257
Rosenthal, Sol Roy, 264
Rozelle, Pete, 148, 149, 303, 305, 306, 310
Ruetz, Joseph H., 89-92
Rundell, Maurice, 325
Ruth, Babe, 212, 284-285
Ryan, Frank, 171-175
Sample, Steven, 93
Sanders, Barry, 153, 155, 284-285, 307
Sanders, Deion, 307, 311
Sayers, Gale, 111, 127, 130, 133, 153, 213
Schefter, Adam, 157, 263
Schramm, Tex, 308
Seifert, George, 199, 280, 281, 293
Sevareid, Eric, 340
Shanahan, Krystal, 264
Shanahan, Kyle, 264
Shanahan, Mike, 52, 62, 144-145, 155, 158, 160-161, 217, 260-269, 280, 281, 282
Shanahan, Peggy, 264
Shaughnessy, Clark, 12, 50-52, 56-59, 90, 220-224, 304, 310
Sharpe, Sterling, 261, 262
Shell, Art, 147

Sherrod, Blackie, 75
Shula, Don, 199, 262
Siegel, Dave, 108
Simpson, Marguerite, 125, 126
Simpson, O.J., 32, 124-130, 136, 153, 154, 284-285, 310, 311
Skorupan, John, 130
Smith, Emmitt, 154, 158, 199, 281-282
Smith, Larry, 133
Smith, Rod, 265
Spears, Doc, 110
Stabler, Ken, 185, 193
Stagg, Amos Alonzo, 20, 84, 85, 105, 206-208, 234, 237, 238
Stapleton, Clay, 247
Steger, Herb, 104
Stein, Gertrude, 313, 340
Steinberg, Leigh, 204
Stenerud, Jan, 182
Stuhldreher, Harry, 29-34
Stydahar, Joe "Jumbo", 115, 213
Summerall, Pat, 251
Sutherland, Jock, 47
Swanson, Joan, 338
Swayne, Harry, 158
Switzer, Barry, 69
Tagliabue, Paul, 148, 303
Tanuvasa, Maa, 267
Tarkenton, Fran, 108
Tausch, Terry, 295
Thomas, Bill, 13, 331
Thomas, Bob, 28
Thorpe, Jim, 311
Topping, Norman, 93
Towler, Dan, 115
Trafton, George, 213
Trantalis, Jeff, 86
Turner, "Bulldog", 213
Turner, Norval, 199, 281-282
Unitas, Johnny, 60, 116-117, 123, 163, 164, 167, 168-171, 172, 173, 175, 177, 201, 215, 311
Upshaw, Gene, 145-152

Valdiserri, Roger O., 283, 285
Valentino, Rudolph, 33
VanBrocklin, Norm, 48, 60, 62, 121, 153, 154, 167, 171, 172, 202
Vice, James, 87, 88
Vignolle, Gus, 314
Wade, Billy, 172
Walsh, Bill, 12, 51, 61-62, 170, 199-200, 201, 202, 203, 217, 264, 265-267, 275-283, 284, 285, 293, 294, 297-301
Warfield, Paul, 173, 174
Warner, Pop, 20, 207, 234, 237, 238
Waterfield, Bob, 48, 58, 60, 62, 115, 171, 172
Waters, Bobby, 221-223
Watters, Ricky, 154, 297
Wells, Tracy, 336

Werbelin, Sonny, 178
Wilkinson, Bud, 47
Will, George, 306
Wilson, Tom, 231
Wimmer, Ferdinand, 65-66
Wolf, Ron, 226
Wood, Willie, 232-233
Woolbert, Ben, 327
York, Denise, 292
York, John, 292
Yost, Fielding H. "Hurry Up", 47, 104
Young, Brigham, 202
Young, John, 202
Young, LeGrande, 203
Young, Steve, 154, 164, 165, 197-204, 266, 276, 278-279, 280, 295, 307
Youngblood, Jack, 133
Zuppke, Bob, 102, 104, 212

Quality Sports Publications

24 Buysse Drive
Coal Valley, IL 61240
(800) 464-1116
(309) 234-5016
FAX (309) 234-5019

Dear Sports Fan:

Thank you for purchasing *Game of the Century.* I hope you enjoyed it. We have numerous titles, all on sports. No novels, mysteries or sci-fi, only hard-hitting, slam-dunking, hole-in-one books with the true sports fan in mind.

Quality Sports has many titles in stock and we add new ones each year. For information on all of our books please call toll-free 1-800-464-1116 and we will send you information on all of our terrific sports books. You can also check out our web site at www.qualitysportsbooks.com.

Quality Sports takes pride in the production of all our sports books. But, if for any reason you are unhappy with the books you purchase from us, please call us and we will kindly and quickly refund your purchase price.

Thank you,

Duane Brown
Publisher

Please call
1-800-464-1116
toll-free for a free brochure or visit our web site at
www.qualitysportsbooks.com